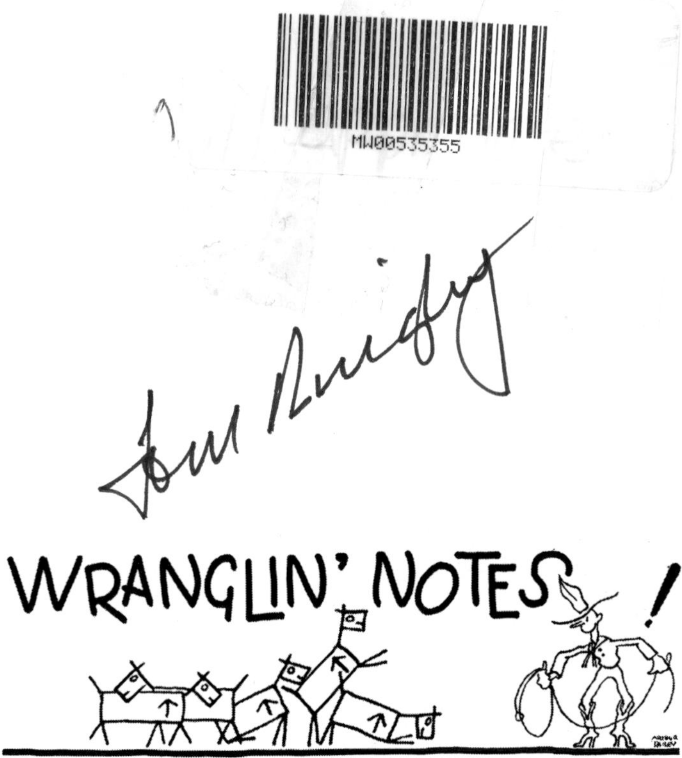

A Chronicle of Eatons' Ranch

1879-2010

TOM RINGLEY

ISBN# 978-1-932636-67-3 Trade Paper

Library of Congress Control Number: 2010935282

Drawings by Joe DeYong courtesy of Eatons' Ranch
Cover Design: Antelope Design
Front Cover Photo: Courtesy of Eatons' Ranch
Back Cover Photo by Douglas Barker, Courtesy of Eatons' Ranch

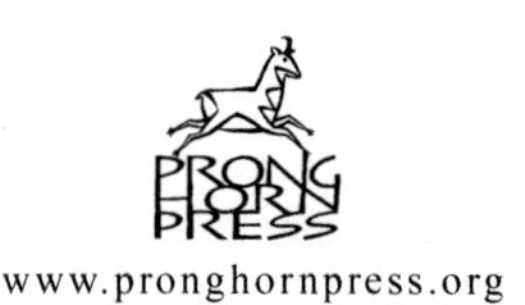

www.pronghornpress.org

For the four Eaton brothers—
Howard, Willis, Alden and Charles.
Could they have imagined their legacy?

CONTENTS

CHAPTER 3
Family, Dudes and Change

PART TWO
Wolf

CHAPTER 4
Eatons at Wolf 1904-1920

CHAPTER 5
The Twenties

CHAPTER 6
The Thirties

CHAPTER 7
The Forties

CHAPTER 8
The Fifties

CHAPTER 9
The Sixties

CHAPTER 10
Eatons' Forty Years Later (2010)

FOREWORD

There is an allure to Eatons' Ranch that is difficult to explain. Not only has this land provided a home for our family for over one hundred years, but it has cast a spell on many others during that time, as well. Guests come for one vacation and end up returning for generations. Employees plan to spend a summer here and wind up marrying another employee or even a family member. Families come here to reconnect, couples come here to get married and start their lives together, and more than a few have chosen to have their ashes spread on this ground. People do more than spend their vacations here; they seem to leave a bit of their hearts behind when they go.

Tom Ringley has written wonderfully detailed histories of ranches, events and individuals in Sheridan County. We were honored when, after some prodding from Karen Ferguson, Tom said he wanted to write a book about Eatons' Ranch. Until now, much of the history of Eatons' Ranch and the three Eaton brothers has been an oral history passed from generation to generation. I remember sitting on my great-grandmother Patty Eaton's knee when I was young, asking her to tell me stories about the Ranch, Big Bill—whatever she could remember. How I wish I had recorded those conversations, but I will never forget the time I spent with her. Esther McWilliams made the first attempt to chronicle the Ranch and our family on paper; for our 125th anniversary in 2004, my wife Jennie edited and updated Esther's work.

These brief accounts served as a good beginning for Tom, but he came up with so much more during his research. He spent months going through old files that included corporate minutes, correspondence and old *Wranglin' Notes*, which ended up being his greatest resource. When Tom realized the amount of historical information available to him, he went right to work putting everything down on paper. Anyone who has a connection to Eatons' Ranch or is interested in western history will enjoy reading this account of one family's journey west and the legacy that was started so long ago. Tom has provided an amazingly detailed record of our family, a family whose history is inextricably linked with those of our guests.

I wonder if the Eaton brothers ever imagined that 131 years later, the ranching business they started in North Dakota and later moved to Wolf, Wyoming, would still be owned and operated by their descendents. Eatons' Ranch has always been a family business, and as a member of the fifth generation, I am fortunate to have the opportunity to be a part of the Ranch and to carry on the family tradition of dude and cattle ranching. We, as a family, are so fortunate that those who came before us not only picked the most magnificent spot at the foot of the Bighorns, but that they always intended to keep it a family business. My three-year-old son Garrett often asks, "Daddy, why did the Eaton brothers choose Wolf, Wyoming, as the place for our family to live?" I tell him that I'm not exactly sure why, but we are all very glad that they did.

Jeff Way
General Manager
Eatons' Ranch

ACKNOWLEDGMENTS

I am glad that Karen Ferguson encouraged me to write the story of Eatons' Ranch in Wolf, Wyoming. My research of one of the oldest dude ranches in America and an important part of western history proved to be a most compelling odyssey. The experience transported me through a 131 year period accompanied by a wide ranging cast of interesting characters and members of the Eaton family, dudes and Ranch employees. I hope this book will provide the same pleasant experience for the reader. So, thank you Karen for your encouragement and your valuable perspective.

Eatons' Ranch has been the subject of numerous articles in magazines, journals, periodicals and newspapers, but the real story, from beginning to end, has never been told in its entirety. I am grateful I was given the opportunity to add the whole story to the body of Western literature.

This book would not have been possible without the treasure trove of information available from Eatons' Ranch: corporate records, staff correspondence, personal family letters and various written historical reflections from some family members. The most notable source was *Wranglin' Notes*. The Ranch's remarkable periodic publication from 1924 to the present provided a feast of details about life at Eatons' Ranch. Indeed, my challenge was how to deal with such an overabundance of information. I hope my decisions on what to include were the right ones.

I am indebted to Frank Eaton, President of Eaton Brothers, Inc. for his total cooperation. He willingly opened the doors to the basement below the office where all the old Ranch records are stored and told me to "have at it." Frank is also an endless source of "stories" about Eatons' Ranch and he willingly shared many of them with me. Frank and his wife Kathy both read the manuscript in various stages and provided me with insightful comments and many photos. Thank you Frank and Kathy for your generosity and cooperation in this effort.

Jeff Way, general manager of the Ranch, also read the manuscript and provided important perspectives in many areas. He also facilitated my access to research material and graciously agreed to write the foreword to the book. Thank you Jeff.

Doyl and Jaci Fritz proved to be meticulous editors and they made important contributions to the quality of this book. In addition, they provided me much valuable material and told me many stories that enriched the manuscript. Thank you both for your openness and total support.

As with my other books, Roberta Sankey was gracious enough to read the manuscript. I am always relieved when my work passes muster with Roberta for I value her opinion. Thanks, once again, to Roberta.

I received help with this project in many forms from many other people including Mary Eaton, Billy Ferguson, T. J. Ferguson, Kim Ferguson, Jack Fritz, Susan Van Allen, David Van Allen, Juli Kerns, and Wendy Martin. On the Pelissier side of the family I am indebted to Willis Pelissier, Jack Pelissier and Suzanne Pelissier Hill.

Several people granted me entertaining interviews and for their time and wonderful stories I would like to thank Nan Wertman, Martin Koether, Keen Butcher, Bots Young, Bobby Cagnina, Dippy King, Irv Alderson, Bob Gaskell, Holland Duell and Jim Niner.

As usual, as with all my research projects, I am indebted to the staff of the Sheridan County Fulmer Public Library's Wyoming Room. Karen

Woinoski, Andy Wenburg and Judy Slack rendered invaluable assistance. Thank you all.

Also, Jean King, the curator of the Don King Western Museum, Sheridan, Wyoming, generously allowed me to make use of the museum's superb photograph collection. Thank you Jean.

This is my fourth collaboration with Annette Chaudet of Pronghorn Press, Greybull, Wyoming. It's always a pleasure to work with Annette because she always offers encouragement and sound advice and helps me produce a product that we can both be proud of. Thank you, Annette, once again.

I also want to thank Jo Massey, Sarah de Souza and John Belobraidic for their contributions toward preparing the book for print.

PART ONE

Pittsburgh and Medora

CHAPTER 1
The Eatons

Ancestry

In 1845, in Pittsburgh, Pennsylvania, two families were joined together by the marriage of Franklin H. Eaton and Josephine W. Alden. This marriage, which lasted forty-five years, until Josephine died in 1890, produced nine children. The four brothers, Howard, Willis, F. Alden, and Charles, would go west and found a legacy that lives on today at Eatons' Ranch in Wolf, Wyoming.

The Eaton lineage was impressive, more on Josephine's side than Franklin's, for Josephine's ancestry reached back to John Alden, a ships carpenter employed in Southampton, England. When a ship called the

Mayflower—which was transporting "Pilgrims" to America in their quest for religious freedom—put in for repairs, John decided to join them on the voyage to America. When the *Mayflower* landed at Plymouth Rock in 1620, John was supposedly the first passenger to set foot on land.

John became one of the founders of the Plymouth Colony after he signed the Mayflower Compact. That document was the original basis for true democracy in America. After an impressive career with the Colony, John died in 1687, the last male survivor of the signers of the Mayflower Compact and with one exception, the last survivor of the Mayflower Company.

Timothy Alden, Josephine's grandfather, was a descendant of John Alden. Timothy was a 1762 Harvard graduate and Congregational minister who made frequent religious pilgrimages, one of which was to western Pennsylvania in 1814. There he founded a new village called Aldenburg, about ninety miles from Pittsburgh, and founded a college in its center. In 1815, he also founded Allegheny College in Meadville, Pennsylvania.

Timothy Alden's son, Timothy Fox Alden, went to Pittsburgh in 1831 and became a prominent member of the legal profession. It was his daughter, Josephine, born in 1827, who married Franklin Eaton in 1845. Franklin had emigrated some years before from Massachusetts to Pittsburgh and set himself up in the dry goods business. Other details about his background are not known.

The Family

What is known is that Franklin became a successful entrepreneur. A newspaper account in later years reported that he was a "pioneer businessman and a well known and much esteemed citizen," and that he was "noted as perhaps the earliest dry goods man who maintained his store along modern lines." His place of business was on Fifth Avenue near Market Street and his business was listed in the Pittsburgh City Directory as "Eaton, F. H., Trimmings, Laces, Hosiery, Gloves, Notions, etc."

Franklin prospered. In the United States Federal Census taken in 1860, Franklin listed twenty-four people in his household, including his wife and, at that time, five children. Only a prosperous man could support a household of that size.

Franklin's prosperity enabled him to house his family in a fair amount of affluence at the family mansion called "Erin Hill" on Center Avenue. In 1870, Franklin and Josephine celebrated their twenty-fifth wedding anniversary. The occasion prompted the local newspaper to report on the "Pleasant Anniversary" which described not only the residence but also the social standing of the Eatons in Pittsburgh. The social reporter wrote:

> *Erin Hill, the capacious old family mansion, was the setting for the anniversary of our well-known citizen, Franklin H. Eaton, Esq., and his estimable lady. Several hundred elaborately engraved invitations were sent out but few regrets could have been sent in, as the attendance was exceedingly large. Never before have we seen drawn together in social assembly so large and fair a representation of our refined and cultured society.*

Just as the Eatons of Pittsburgh were well-established pillars of society and successful in business, they were equally successful in producing and raising a family. They raised nine children.

When they married, Franklin was twenty-eight years old and Josephine only eighteen. They proceeded to have children on a rather regular basis. The oldest, Josephine Alden, was born two years after the marriage in 1847. A sister, Mary Brewer, was born in 1849 and the first son and brother, Howard, followed her in 1851. A second son, Willis, was born in 1852 followed by two daughters, Alice Dilworth in 1854 and then Lizzie Parker in 1856. Three years later, in 1859, the third son, F. Alden Eaton, was born followed by the last brother, Charles Stone, in 1861. It would be eight years later, in 1869 that the youngest daughter, Harriet Arthurs, would arrive on the scene.

Regrettably, the childhood years of the Eaton brood are not documented. We can only assume that they led lives normal to people of their standing in Pittsburgh society, received an adequate education and were involved in some way in the family business.

Two of the boys were definitely involved. Howard was listed in the 1870 Pittsburgh City Directory as a "cashier" and in later years, when the family business became "Eaton Bros & Co." Willis was listed with the firm. Alden and Charles probably worked for the firm at one time or another, but in city directories, they were listed as "machinists."

The girls all married. In later years, some of them would be connected in various ways with a grand western adventure—an adventure instigated by their brother Howard

CHAPTER 2

The Eatons Go West

Howard Leads the Way

Howard first visited the West in 1868 when he was only seventeen years old. The accounts of why he went, or where, are vague and conflicting. One states that "Mr. Eaton came west *(Note: Probably somewhere in Kansas according to some sources.)* in 1868 prospecting for gold and fighting Indians during that year, and returned to Pittsburgh in 1869." The account further states that he then went west, ten years later, to the Badlands of North Dakota. Several other accounts echo that view.

In fact, according to a 1908 Eaton Ranch brochure, Howard journeyed back and forth between Pittsburgh and the western climes on a regular basis until he actually pulled up his Pittsburgh stakes and immigrated to the Badlands of North Dakota in 1879 when he was twenty-eight years old. Howard's trips were most likely a series of adventure vacations to various parts of the West since he probably worked in his father's business. It is curious though that in the 1880 United States Census, when Howard was twenty-nine, he was still listed as a member of his father's household with the occupation of "merchant." Perhaps, that was because he was simply visiting his father in Pittsburgh when the census person stopped by the Eaton mansion.

At any rate, Howard was a permanent fixture in North Dakota at least by 1879 (*Note: Other accounts state both 1876 and 1878.*) Why did he choose the Dakota Territory? The most plausible answer is found in a 1931 newspaper article in the *Bismarck Tribune* written by George Hawley and based on an interview with Howard's youngest brother, Charles.

Charles recalled that there was a famous physician from Washington, Pennsylvania, named F. Julius le Moyne who is reputed to have erected the first crematory in the United States for private use. Dr. le Moyne had a son, an Eaton friend, who had visited the Dakotas earlier and established a ranch near the Badlands. Supposedly, young le Moyne persuaded Howard to put down his roots in the Dakotas.

Where Howard went is one thing, but *why* is another. While he may have wanted to settle permanently in the West anyway, because he certainly was enamored with the West, there was another contributing factor: The Eaton family in Pittsburgh suffered a serious financial reversal.

Howard's niece, Mary Covington, the daughter of Howard's youngest sister, Harriet (Hattie), wrote about her life in North Dakota in an unpublished 1967 manuscript. Mary wrote, "Howard Eaton, my mother's eldest brother, went west from Pittsburgh after his father failed in business, having co-signed a note for a 'friend' who defaulted on paying the debt." Other sources also mention that the Eaton family fell on "reduced circumstances."

When Howard went to Dakota Territory, the time was ripe for enterprising men to make their fortune. Their path was cleared when the Indians—the Sioux, Crow, and Blackfoot tribes—were subdued and banished to reservations for the most part, although there were still sporadic "Indian problems." In addition, the American bison were well on their way to extermination. The vast expanse of the Dakota open plains with its free grass was there for the taking, and consequently, thousands of Texas Longhorn cattle were herded north to take advantage of the grass on open range. Then too, the Northern Pacific Railroad completed its expansion across the Dakotas and Montana in 1880 creating was alluring opportunity for ambitious and energetic young men to turn quick profits if they put their backs to the wheel and were willing to take a chance.

Though the Dakota Badlands were desolate and life was hard, many hardy souls were unable to ignore the plentiful nutritious grass that made for ideal summer grazing and the bottomland cottonwood groves that were well adapted for wintering livestock. Howard was one of those willing to take a chance, as were his three brothers, though not all at the same time.

The most repeated story about when the Eaton brothers made their way to take up permanent residence in the Badlands is that Howard arrived in 1879, followed by his two brothers, Alden and Willis, in 1881 and 1882 respectively. The actual facts are probably different.

We know from a documented interview with the fourth and youngest brother, Charles, that he arrived in the area when he was only nineteen years old. Another brother, Alden, arrived soon after, most likely in 1891. Willis, who is widely reported to have arrived with the first Eaton contingent, probably didn't arrive until sometime in the early 1890s. His niece, Mary Covington, who was in North Dakota, wrote that Willis did not appear until about 1891. Further, the obituary for Willis's mother Josephine, who died on February 11, 1890, states that Willis was connected with the Fuel Gas and Engineering Company in Pittsburgh at the time.

Willis's exact whereabouts for the first decade or so of the Eaton operation in the Badlands is not clear. If he did visit his family in the Badlands during the intervening period, he didn't bother to sign the Custer Trail guest book, as did other family members. It's possible that Willis was on an adventure in Mexico in between his employment in Pittsburgh and his arrival in North Dakota. His sister-in-law, Mary Eaton, Alden's wife, specifically mentions in her memoirs that Willis arrived at the Custer Trail Ranch from Mexico in 1892.

What, then, was there when the Eatons arrived in the Badlands?

According to the 1931 interview with Charles Eaton, the railroad had not yet arrived in the area "and their baggage, outfits and trinkets were borne thither in the famous 'freighter' drawn by the sturdy ranch horse, frequently for two hundred miles or more." The Northern Pacific Railroad was under construction and just west of the Little Missouri River, opposite the site of the future town of Medora, was a cantonment of United States soldiers. Their mission was to protect railroad workers from any possible Indian troubles.

The town site on the west bank was called Little Missouri, or by some, "Little Misery." Herman Hagedorn described the place in his 1930 book *Roosevelt In The Badlands*. He colorfully described the place as it was in 1882, after the railroad had arrived, and a couple of years after the first Eaton arrival.

> *The "town" of Little Missouri consisted of a group of primitive buildings scattered about the shack, which did duty as a railroad station. The Pyramid Park Hotel stood immediately north of the tracks. Beside it stood the one-story palace of sin of which one, who shall, for the purposes of this story, be known as Bill Williams, was the owner, and one who shall be known as Jess Hogue, the evil genius. South of the track a comical, naïve Swede named Johnny Nelson kept a store when he was not courting Katie, the hired girl in Mrs. McGeeney's boarding house next door, or gambling away his receipts under Hogue's crafty guidance. Directly to the east, on the brink of the river, the railroad section-foreman, Fitzgerald, had a shack and a wife who quarreled unceasingly with her neighbor, Mrs. McGeeney. At a corresponding place on the other side of the track, a villainous gun-fighter named Maunders lived (as far as possible) by his neighbors' toil. A quarter of a mile west of him, in a grove of cottonwood trees, stood a group of gray log buildings known as the "cantonment," where a handful of soldiers had been quartered under a major named Coomba, to guard the construction crews on the railroad from the attacks of predatory Indians seeking game in their ancient hunting grounds. A few huts in the sagebrush, a half-dozen miners' shacks under the*

butte to the south, and one or two rather pretentious frame houses in process of construction completed what was Little Missouri...

The town of Medora, on the eastern bank of the river, didn't exist in name when the Eatons arrived, although there were three or four buildings on the site. It was described by Hagedorn as a "paradise for jackrabbits" before it was established as the town of Medora in April 1883, by a twenty-four year old French nobleman, the Marquis De Mores. He named the town for his bride, the former Medora Von Hoffman, the daughter of a wealthy New York City banker.

There were some other cattle ranches in the area, notably the Chimney Butte Ranch, often called the Maltese Cross Ranch because of its brand. Joe and Sylvane Ferris and their partner, William J. Merrifield, operated it. In 1884, a blustery New York politician named Theodore Roosevelt persuaded them to take him on as a partner and after that, the ranch was always known as the Maltese Cross.

Ranching at Medora

The Eatons were squatters. The practice was common in those days, since the land had not yet been surveyed. They squatted in a location about five miles upstream from what was to become the town of Medora in the fertile alluvial bottom of the Little Missouri River. The site was actually an old stage station on what had been the first mail route between Fort Abraham Lincoln, Dakota Territory, and Fort Keogh, Montana Territory. Hagedorn described the first Eaton abode:

Custer Trail Ranch, Medora, Dakota Territory. *Courtesy of Eatons' Ranch.*

> *...the two-room shack of cottonwood logs and a dirt roof, which had been the station, was inhabited by calves and chickens that were kept in bounds by the stockade, which only a little while before had served to keep the Indians at a distance.*

Howard named the new enterprise the Custer Trail Ranch because General George Armstrong Custer and his regiment had camped nearby on the way to their last battle in 1876 on the Little Big Horn in Montana Territory.

As the Eaton boys developed their livestock operations, they found other ways to make cash money. In addition to putting up wild hay for the nearby army cantonment, they killed wild game and sold the meat to the railroad work gangs.

Wild game was plentiful and offered enormous opportunity. Newspapers in Dakota publicized the country as a "hunter's paradise." *The Bismarck Tribune* in February 1880 claimed, "...2 hunters in 6 weeks time killed 90 deer and antelope and 15 elk." Allegedly, the hunters shot eleven of the elk in about fifteen minutes.

The Northern Pacific Railway really opened up the area for game hunting when it reached the Little Missouri River in September 1880. Howard Eaton was right in the thick of it. Howard, together with another local named E. G. Paddock, formally established a professional guide service and ran continuous advertisements in the *Mandan Pioneer.* (*Note: In one source, Paddock is credited with helping Howard establish the Custer Trail Ranch. The truth is not clear. Possibly the writer assumed because they cooperated in a guide business that they were ranching partners, as well.)*

The Eatons prospered enough to build a two-story log house at the Custer Trail Ranch. This became their base of operations for several endeavors, one of which was to extend their hospitality to their "endless procession of Eastern friends who came for the hunting." The Eatons, it seems, virtually kept an "open house." Hagedorn described the phenomena and Howard Eaton:

> *Travelers wrote about the hospitality that even strangers were certain to find there, and carried away with them the picture of Howard Eaton, "who sat his horse as though he were a centaur and looked a picturesque and noble figure with his clean-shaven cheeks, heavy drooping moustache,* sombrero, *blue shirt, and neckerchief with flaming ends.*

Indeed, history has been very kind to Howard Eaton. While he was an equal partner with his brothers, over the course of time Howard garnered, unwittingly or not, the lion's share of historical attention concerning those early days.

For instance, Lee Silliman wrote an article about Howard Eaton in the *American West Magazine* in 1979. Silliman described the time that George Shields, a writer, made his first hunting trip to the West in 1880 and met Howard. According to Silliman:

> *...he (Shields) met Howard Eaton at a railroad construction camp on the Little Missouri River. The previous day a detachment of soldiers had gone hunting and returned with four geese. Sensing an opportunity to play a practical joke on*

Howard Eaton in Dakota Territory in early 1880s. *Courtesy of Eatons' Ranch.*

the soldiers, a neighboring rancher solemnly demanded reparations for the death of his "pet" geese. When a guilt-ridden lieutenant actually paid damages, the event was celebrated the next evening at the railroaders' mess, in an extemporaneous song by Mr. Howard Eaton of Pennsylvania, which brought down the house, and some more cigars. Howard Eaton and his talents were well received in the Little Missouri country.

And, again, on another hunting trip Shields found himself boarding the same train as Howard, and described Howard in a *Harper's Weekly* article:

...He was dressed in a regulation costume of the craft—canvas trousers and jacket, leather chaparajoes, *blue flannel shirt, and a broad-brimmed white felt hat. His loins were girt about with a well-filled cartridge belt from which hung his six-shooters—a weapon that may almost be termed a badge or order. Large Mexican spurs rattled at his heels as he walked...*

Shields realized that the other passengers were alarmed at the presence of the "terrible cowboy," so to allay their fears, he introduced Howard to some of the travelers and:

...they were agreeably surprised at his polished manners, his fluent and well-chosen language, his handsome though sun-browned face, and his kind, genial nature.

Silliman then summed up the general impression that Howard eventually made on everyone he met:

...the gentlemanly cowboy from Pittsburgh was hardly your average cowhand. In fact, Howard Eaton was probably a good representative of the refined Easterner-turned-rancher who dressed and worked as hard as his less-polished cowhands.

From the beginning, the Eatons' primary goal was to make their mark in the cattle business, but for that, they needed financial investors. They found them in eastern acquaintances. One was a wealthy Pennsylvanian, and lover of horses, a man named A. C. Huidekoper.

Huidekoper was well established as a gentleman farmer from Pennsylvania. Since he was a descendant of a very wealthy ancestor, he had plenty of money and led a very comfortable life.

Together with three friends, Huidekoper journeyed to the Custer Trail Ranch in 1881 to hunt buffalo and Howard made quite an impression on him. Silliman described the hunt:

> *Eaton's verve was quite in evidence on this hunting expedition. One morning they saw a Black Hills stagecoach in the distance transporting soldiers. Eaton quickly had the party drape Red Indian blankets about their bodies and fire their rifles in order to give the soldiers something to write home about. To the merriment of Eaton's guests, the stage driver played his whip and the soldiers shouldered their guns as the coach careened out of sight. The action that most impressed his guest, however, occurred the day they finally approached a herd of a thousand buffalo. Eaton generously loaned his favorite pony, "Lady," to Huidekoper in order that he might take the lead in the chase. This advantage permitted Huidekoper to shoot the biggest buffalo—and to form the opinion that Howard Eaton was "as kind and generous a host as ever lived." Huidekoper was only the first of countless guests to appreciate Howard Eaton's hospitality: "We were a merry, happy crowd, and I shall never forget it."*

Silliman also described how the favorable impression made by Howard worked to the Eaton brothers' financial advantage:

> *Indeed, Huidekoper did not forget Howard Eaton. At the end of the hunt, the wealthy guest made a business proposition. Huidekoper would purchase a cattle herd and all the necessary supplies, the Eaton brothers would provide the labor and management necessary to run the stock on the open range,*

and the profits would be divided equally. A verbal agreement consummated the deal. Immediately the Eaton brothers began construction of sheds and stables, while Howard went to Minnesota to direct the overland drive of one thousand cattle to the site of the newly created Custer Trail Cattle Company. Two years later, in 1883, Huidekoper himself moved to the Little Missouri to share in the adventure of cattle ranching. The Eatons were now operating on a sound financial basis.

By 1885, the Eatons had a sizeable herd. The census records of Billings County, Dakota, list Howard Eaton as one of the larger livestock owners with sixteen hundred head of cattle (*Note: The census doesn't say what kind, i.e. bulls, steers, cows, etc.*) and three hundred calves worth a total of $4,500.

In 1891, Howard recorded several brands to mark the livestock at the various Eaton ranches. Among those brands recorded were the V Bar, the Quarter Circle Open A Bar, the SO, and the TV. These were recorded in the state of North Dakota. However, Howard recorded two other brands earlier in the territory of Montana. In 1886, Howard recorded the HE Backward, and in 1887, he recorded the Arrowhead brand. The Arrowhead brand became the predominant Eaton brand and is still used by Eatons' Ranch in 2010.

The Eatons' livestock operation wasn't confined to cattle. They tried their hand in the sheep business as well. In February 1884, A. T. Packard, the owner of the local paper *The Badlands Cow Boy,* wrote that:

…On the other hand, look at some of the successful sheep raising in the Badlands. Howard Eaton has some large, long-wool variety that also labored under the disadvantage of being driven upon the new ranges late in the fall, but they have done as well as cattle.

Packard didn't mention the size of the Eaton flock, but he did mention another interesting, but unrelated, tidbit, and that was that the Eatons shot a huge bull buffalo that winter within "twenty rods of the Custer Trail home ranch."

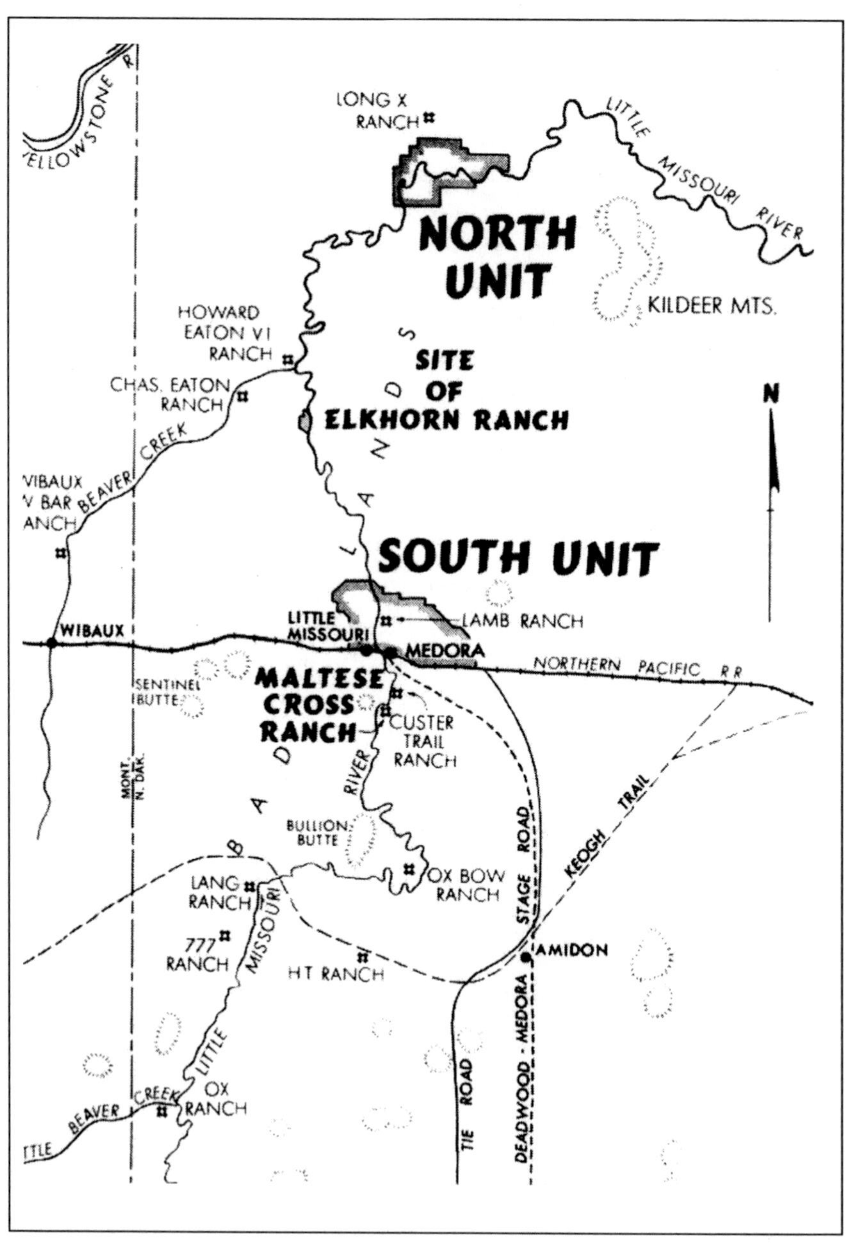

Map of Bad Lands Ranches in the 1880s. *Courtesy of the National Park Service.*

Later in the year, in June, Packard wrote in his paper that Howard Eaton and Lloyd Roberts came into Medora driving a thousand head of cattle for the Badger Cattle Company.

Most versions of the Eaton story mention only the Custer Trail ranch. Actually, there were other ranches, and other financial backers. One was named Van Brunt who backed the Eatons in the establishment of a ranch called the VI (Vee Eye) about forty miles down the Little Missouri River at the junction of Beaver Creek. And Charles Eaton had the help of a certain Chris McGee, described as "a somewhat smoky light in the murk of Pennsylvania politics" that helped him put together a ranch twelve miles up Beaver Creek above the VI ranch. This ranch, the SO Ranch, was named for Soho in Pittsburgh, where McGee lived.

Curiously, Charles Eaton mentioned in an interview that there was another ranch, the 76 Ranch, located forty-five miles down the Little Missouri River from Medora. Evidence as to whether or not this ranch existed is not available, and from its location, there is a possibility the interviewer confused this ranch with the VI ranch, since they would have been almost in the same location.

According to Hagedorn, the Custer Trail ranch was the headquarters for all the outlying operations. This point of view is conflicted by an interview with Charles Eaton who stated that:

> *All of these ranches were operated by the Eatons, one or more, at the same time and that for many years the Eatons lived on the ranches north of the railroad, and, although the Custer Trail ranch was operated, the only members of the family who reportedly resided there were the father and mother and a sister, during the summers.*

This may all be a question of timing. In the early days, the Custer Trail ranch may not have been the hub of the Eaton ranching network, but it certainly was later on as the names "Eaton" and "Custer Trail" are synonymous. There are no records about the operations of the other ranches. Indeed, they are rarely mentioned. And, certainly, whatever happened to the financial backers is hidden in history's shadows except in the case of A. C. Huidekoper.

In addition to his investment with the Eatons, Huidekoper bought enormous tracts of railroad land available in a checkerboard pattern, leaving every other section in the public domain and open to homestead or timber culture claims. He then did something controversial with his holdings—he fenced them! This in effect closed off access to other legitimate claimants. (*Note: Years later, in 1906, Huidekoper would be forced to remove his fences, and make the land he didn't own available to homesteaders.*)

In the meantime, Huidekoper invested heavily in the cattle business himself and with the Eatons until the disastrous winter of 1886-1887. After that dreadful experience, he sold off his remaining cattle and went into the horse business. He was a prominent Dakota horse rancher until 1906 when he sold his horses, a herd said to number more than four thousand animals, and his ranch because he became fed up with the land laws of the time.

As for the Eatons, there is no record of what happened to their other ranching operations, but it's not hard to imagine. Most likely, the disastrous winter of 1886-1887, which reduced the cattle herds considerably, (the Eatons are reported to have had only 150 head of cattle survive from a herd of 1,500), caused the Eatons to abandon their other enterprises and shrink their operation down to the Custer Trail ranch.

For the Eatons, the horrible weather was not the only hardship they endured, for that same winter their house burned down. Esther McWilliams described the event:

> *...They had a fire the same year that burned the ranch house. They did a lot of hunting then, and there was so much ammunition stored in the house that it was impossible to fight the flames. They lost everything in the house. There isn't much of anyplace to go after a catastrophe like that except up, so up they came again.*

Many years later, the same thing would happen, but in a different setting.

Neighbors

In the first half of the 1880s, the Eatons and the rest of the community acquired two new notable neighbors—the Marquis de Mores and Theodore Roosevelt. They both arrived on the scene in 1883 but the Marquis got there first, in March. Roosevelt didn't show up until September.

Hagadorn, author of *Roosevelt in the Badlands* described the scene:

> *When one day in March, 1883, a striking young Frenchman, who said he was a nobleman, came to Little Missouri with a plan ready-made to build a community there to rival Omaha, and a business that would startle America's foremost financiers, the citizens of the wicked little frontier settlement, who thought that they knew all the possibilities of "tenderfeet" and "pilgrims" and "how-do-you-do-boys," admitted in some bewilderment that they had been mistaken. The Frenchman's name was Antoine de Vallombrosa, Marquis de Mores. He was a member of the Orleans family, son of a duke, a "White Lily of France," remotely in line for the throne. He was an unusually handsome man, tall and straight, black of hair and moustache, twenty-five or twenty-six years old, athletic, vigorous, and commanding. He had been a French officer, a graduate of the French military school of Saint Cyr, and had come to America following his marriage abroad with Medora von Hoffman, the daughter of a wealthy New York banker of German blood. His cousin, Count Fitz James, a descendant of the Jacobin exiles, had hunted in the Badlands the year previous, returning to France with stories of the new cattle country that stirred the Marquis' imagination.*

Howard Eaton played an indirect role in the arrival of the Marquis, in that, according to Hagedorn:

> *...The Marquis arrived in Little Missouri with his father-in-law's millions at his back and a letter of introduction to Howard Eaton in his pocket. The letter, from a prominent businessman in the East, ended, it seemed to Eaton, rather vaguely: "I don't know what experience he has had in business or anything of that kind, but he had some large views."*

Howard's exchange with the new arrival went like this, according to Hagedorn:

> *The Marquis enthusiastically unfolded these views. "I am going to build an abattoir. I am going to buy all the beef, sheep, and hogs that come over the Northern Pacific, and I am going to slaughter them here and then ship them to Chicago and the East."*
>
> *"I don't think you have any idea how much stock comes over the Northern Pacific," Eaton remarked.*
>
> *"It doesn't matter!" cried the Marquis. "My father-in-law has ten million dollars and can borrow ten million dollars more. I've got old Armour and the rest of them matched dollar for dollar."*
>
> *Eaton said to himself that unquestionably the Marquis' views were "large."*
>
> *"Do you think I am impractical?" the Marquis went on. "I am not impractical. My plan is altogether feasible. I do not merely think this. I know. My intuition tells me so. I pride myself on having a natural intuition. It takes me only a few seconds to understand a situation that other men have to puzzle over for hours. I seem to see every side of a question at once. I assure you, I am gifted in this way. I have wonderful insight."*
>
> *But Eaton said to himself, "I wonder if the Marquis isn't raising his sights too high?"*

Well, to make a long story short, his sights were much too high and terribly off the mark. The Marquis formed the Northern Pacific Refrigerator Car Company. Two brothers named Haupt became his partners and guides. The Marquis "plunged into his dream as a boy into a woodland pool" but "it did not take him long to discover that the water was cold." In a word, the enterprise was a miserable and spectacular failure both because of the foolishness of the endeavor and because the interloper and his wife were mostly despised by the locals for their haughty behavior.

Mary Covington, the Eaton brothers' niece, provided a good example of why the "transplants" annoyed the locals:

> *The DeMores weren't too popular around there. They tell of one time when the DeMores rode up to a ranch at mealtime and were invited to eat. The Marchioness asked that her plate be brought out to her, and not dismounting, (she rode sidesaddle) she turned her horse so that her back would be to the hostess, and ate her dinner.*

There was another example that directly involved Howard. According to the interview with Charles Eaton, the Marquis had built a store in Medora but he made a mistake when he tried to take advantage of Howard Eaton:

> *The Eatons always had a large and complete supply of provisions, etc., on hand, and the Marquis drew upon their stores as he pleased, but made no payment.*
>
> *When his store was completed and packed with provisions, Howard Eaton made out a list and sent a cowboy to Medora to get the order filled. The Marquis refused, unless cash was paid, and the cowboy returned empty handed. Howard Eaton had lived too long in the West to accept such discourtesy—it might be said insult—and so he forthwith galloped to Medora and confronted the Marquis in his store. The explosions of his just wrath angered the Marquis and he retorted, reaching for his six-shooter in the drawer of his desk.*

"This is the way I meet an insult."

But, Howard Eaton was not to be outwitted by this tenderfoot, after his many years of experience, and, in the twinkle of an eye the Marquis was looking down the barrels of two faithful bludgeons, and received the reply non-courteous, "This is the way I handle crooks." And the Marquis melted in humiliation and remained a friend ever after, and he paid his obligations to the Eatons in full.

Though the DeMores departed, their grand scheme in tatters, they did leave their mark, which still exists today because the Marquis named the town he established after his wife, Medora. As Hagadorn declared, "On April Fools Day, 1883—auspicious date!—he pitched his tent in the sagebrush and founded the town of Medora." By 1886, the Marquis' venture had utterly failed and he and his wife moved on to engage in other spectacular schemes in other far-flung places. They failed, as well, and eventually the Marquis was murdered in a foreign clime.

Theodore Roosevelt arrived on the heels of the Marquis, and Howard Eaton was indirectly responsible. Howard had written a letter to a New York newspaper extolling the country and the plethora of wild game available for hunting and Roosevelt swallowed the lure. In 1883, he took off for Dakota Territory to hunt a buffalo.

Roosevelt, the twenty-four year old son of a wealthy New York family, led an extraordinary life. When he stepped off the train at Little Missouri, he had already graduated from Harvard, *magna cum laude,* and a member of Phi Beta Kappa. He entered Columbia Law School but did not take a degree. Instead, he married Alice Hathaway Lee of Chestnut Hill, Massachusetts on his twenty-second birthday, and joined the Republican Party. In November 1881, he was elected to the New York State Assembly, from New York City (the youngest man ever elected to the Assembly), and served three one-year terms. In 1882, he published his first book *The Naval War of 1812.* In the same year, he joined the National Guard and was commissioned a Second Lieutenant in B Company of New York's Eighth Regiment.

Roosevelt continued his political career. In 1883, he was re-elected by the widest margin of any legislator in New York by a two-to-one majority and he became the Minority Leader.

With these credentials in hand, Roosevelt made his way to the Dakota Territory to hunt buffalo. He was introduced to two men, Sylvane Ferris, and Bill Merrifield, partners in the cattle business. Apparently, according to Hagedorn, Ferris and Merrifield greeted Roosevelt: "...without noticeable enthusiasm. They admitted later that they thought he was just another Easterner, and they did not like his glasses at all."

But Roosevelt had cash in hand and used it to prevail upon Joe Ferris, Sylvane's brother, to serve as hunting guide. Roosevelt proved his mettle. A National Park Service document tells the rest of the story:

> *Once Roosevelt found someone willing to loan him a horse (actually he had to buy it before it was made available to him because as a "foreigner" he wasn't trusted) and finally began his quest, Ferris found he hardly had the energy to keep up with the dynamo from N.Y. who had hired him. Undeterred by nasty weather or bad luck, Roosevelt pressed on, much to the exasperation of his hunting guide. Finding a buffalo to shoot proved difficult, because commercial hunters had killed most of the bison in the area mercilessly in recent years. Unknown to Roosevelt, a herd of ten thousand had been killed nearby just a week before his arrival. Each evening at Gregor Lang's ranch, an exhausted Ferris often left Roosevelt squeezing Lang for every drop of conversation he could provide. During their conversations, and maybe as a result of them, Roosevelt expressed interest in cattle ranching in the badlands* [sic].

In the end, Roosevelt got his buffalo and became involved in the cattle business. He arranged to purchase a herd of cattle, tended by Sylvane Ferris and Bill Merrifield, for $14,000 (after they managed to extract themselves from a cattle management contract with another party), and they agreed to tend Roosevelt's cattle. In his absence, they built him a cabin named the Maltese Cross Cabin.

With his prized buffalo head in tow, and an investment in the cattle business consummated, Roosevelt returned to New York and his legislative career. But, the winter of 1884 was filled with tragedy.

The joy of the birth of his daughter and first child, Alice Lee Roosevelt, on February 12, 1884, was trampled on two days later when his mother, Martha Bulloch Roosevelt, died of typhoid fever. Then, only hours later, Roosevelt's wife, Alice Hathaway Lee Roosevelt, died from Bright's disease, a chronic kidney infection that had been masked by her pregnancy.

Roosevelt's utter grief, but also his remarkable spirit, was reflected in a private letter written in March 1884: "It was a grim and an evil fate, but I never have believed it did any good to flinch or yield for any blow, nor does it lighten the blow to cease from working."

Sad but undaunted, Roosevelt picked up the pieces and got on with his life. Between March and June of 1884 he signed a contract to build a new home in Oyster Bay, performed his duty as chairman of the Committee on Cities by presenting a report that resulted in vital changes in the Charter of New York City, and was a delegate to the Republican National Convention in June.

In the same month, Roosevelt returned to the Maltese Cross Ranch and made further heavy financial investments in cattle. One of the problems he found, though, was that he had little privacy in the Maltese Cross Cabin. Hagedorn explained:

> *Roosevelt's first weeks at the Maltese Cross proved one thing beyond debate, which was, that the cabin seven miles south of Medora was not the best place in the world to do literary work. The trail south led directly through his dooryard, and loquacious cowpunchers stopped at all hours to pass the time of day. It was, no doubt, all "perfectly bully," but you did not get much writing done, and even your correspondence suffered.*

So, Roosevelt set out to find another ranch and Howard Eaton helped with the search:

On one of his exploring expeditions down the river, he met Howard Eaton riding south to the railroad from his VI Ranch at the mouth of the Big Beaver, to receive a trainload of cattle. He told Eaton the object of his journeying, and Eaton, who knew the country better possibly than any other man in the Badlands, advised him to look at a bottom not more than five miles up the river from his own ranch.

Roosevelt took Howard's advice. The place was ideal for him. With the help of two men he imported from Maine, Roosevelt established his "home ranch", the Elkhorn Ranch, and built a residence suitable for his purposes.

Later, Howard visited Roosevelt at his new ranch and Chris McGee, an Eaton ranching partner and Pennsylvania politician, accompanied him. Hagedorn described the exchange:

Roosevelt had heard of McGee, not altogether favorably, for McGee was the Republican "boss" of Pittsburgh in days when "bosses" were in flower.

"Are you going to stay out here and make ranching a business?" asked Eaton.

"No," Roosevelt answered. "For the present I am out here because I cannot get up any enthusiasm for the Republican candidate, and it seems to me that punching cattle is the best way to avoid campaigning."

Eaton asked McGee on the way home how Roosevelt stood in the East. "Roosevelt is a nice fellow," remarked McGee, "but he's a damned fool in politics."

Roosevelt was involved in his Badlands enterprises until 1887. During that time, in amongst his many hunting and ranching adventures, he managed to track down a thief almost single-handed and deliver him to justice (for a reward of $50), and became active in the Little Missouri Stockmen's Association, which would become an affiliate of the larger Montana Stock Growers Association.

Many area ranchers had recognized the need for a stockmen's

organization to enforce range rules. Early in 1884, Howard and several others initiated the necessary action. The local newspaper, *The Badlands Cow Boy,* editorialized:

> *We are glad to see that Mr. Howard Eaton has taken the initiative in the one thing that is now most important to our cattlemen. We refer to the subject of a cattle organization... This is a matter of vital interest to every stockman of the Badlands. Subjects continually come up that should be settled by a vote of the majority of our cattlemen. At present, there is no organization and each man must decide all questions for himself...*

Roosevelt played a major role in organizing the Little Missouri Stockmen's Association and served as its chairman and president. He also played key roles in the Montana Stockgrowers Association until 1887.

Roosevelt was absent during the winter of 1886-1887 on a European honeymoon with his new wife. The National Park Service provides a good description of that devastating winter:

> *The winter of 1886-1887 proved to be extraordinarily harsh, compounding the already difficult circumstances created by the vicious summer. Unable to feed their cattle, ranchers were forced to turn them out to fend for themselves. One blizzard after another quickly buried what was left of the grazing land, and cattle were found "frozen to death where they stood" in temperatures as low as minus forty-one degrees Fahrenheit. Hardier cattle survived long enough to eat the tarpaper off the houses in Medora before succumbing to the elements. Others were found dead in trees after the snow melted, having climbed massive snowdrifts to reach the edible twigs before expiring amid the branches. Tens of thousands of cattle died in the Badlands in the winter of 1886-1887, around 80% of the total population... In the spring, the Little Missouri swelled onto its floodplain, surging with melt water. The carcasses of innumerable cattle bobbed down the river.*

Roosevelt, who had been abroad for the winter, was unaware of the horrors that befell the area until he returned in late March 1887. He was shocked to discover he had lost more than half his herd:

> *The blow proved disastrous for Roosevelt, who had lost over half of his $80,000 investment, the equivalent of approximately $1.7 million today. As for the future of the Elkhorn and Maltese Cross Ranches, Roosevelt wrote his sister Bamie, "I am planning to get out of it."*

He did. And as the history books record, he went on to do many other great things, including being elected as governor of New York, and vice president of the United States, a position from which he would assume the presidency of the United States on September 14, 1901 after the assassination of President William McKinley. Roosevelt died in his sleep at age sixty on January 6, 1919.

He would always fondly remember his days in the Badlands and maintained links with several who were there at the time, including Howard Eaton. Howard had fond memories of Roosevelt as well, and said of him in later years:

> *...Roosevelt was a great visitor...When he first came out there, he was a quiet sort of fellow, with not much to say to anybody, but the best kind of a mixer I ever saw.*

Today, there is still physical evidence of the Eaton-Roosevelt relationship at the Eaton Ranch in Wolf, Wyoming. One is an inscribed photograph of Theodore Roosevelt that hangs in the Ranch office. The other is a reproduced set of andirons made from a railroad track. The original was made for Roosevelt's Elkhorn Ranch and was presented to the Eatons as a gift. Later, in 1924, the original set was needed for the Roosevelt Memorial at New York City. The museum replaced the original with a reproduction, and it is used in Howard Hall at Eatons' Ranch today.

CHAPTER 3

Family, Dudes and Change

Family

In spite of conflicting accounts about whether three or four brothers settled in the North Dakota Badlands in the early 1800s, we definitely know the roles played by Howard, Charles and Alden.

Howard's role is not in doubt. He did go west first, as previously described, and was the impetus behind the Eaton western movement. Howard's base of operations was in North Dakota from the beginning until the Eatons moved to Wolf, Wyoming in 1904. He was frequently absent. He had a passion for travel and loved to take guests on extended hunting trips and pack trips to far-flung places. He guided his first trip to Yellowstone Park in 1883, and over the rest of his life, he would take hundreds of extended trips to many other places. But through it all, in the Medora days, the Custer Trail Ranch was his base of operations.

There is also little doubt about the role that Charles Eaton, the youngest brother, played, although in most versions of the Eaton story he is not even credited with being in Medora. He most definitely was. Charles, the youngest brother, arrived on the scene as a nineteen year old and established the SO Ranch. He was a major player in the Eaton operations and was an important figure in the Medora scene.

His obituary, written in 1946, when he died at age eighty-five, described his time in Medora:

> *At the age of twenty (he was really nineteen) he went west to the Dakotas on the advice of his brother Howard. There he built his first cabin with logs hauled from the bottoms. He engaged in various types of business in the West including blacksmithing, "breaking" horses and hauling hides to the railroads for hunters. He was well acquainted with former President "Teddy" Roosevelt, who lived on a ranch neighboring his, and whose unbroken horses Mr. Eaton helped to tame.*
>
> *Mr. Eaton recalled clearly the celebration when the golden spike was driven into the Northern Pacific Railroad, marking completion of the rail link to the West.*

Charles was one of only two Eaton brothers to have a family. In 1886, he married Elizabeth Clarke from Pittsburgh. It was Elizabeth's family who recorded their first visit in the Custer Trail Ranch guest book in August 1883, and it's possible that some members of the Clarke family accompanied Howard on his first pack trip to Yellowstone Park.

Details of the courtship between Charles and Elizabeth are not available, but they married in 1886 and moved to Charles' SO Ranch for a brief period of time, at least through that fall. We know they were there through part of the fall because Charles related in an interview many years later that when they left for Mandan, North Dakota, to spend the winter—because of the impending birth of their first daughter, and only child,

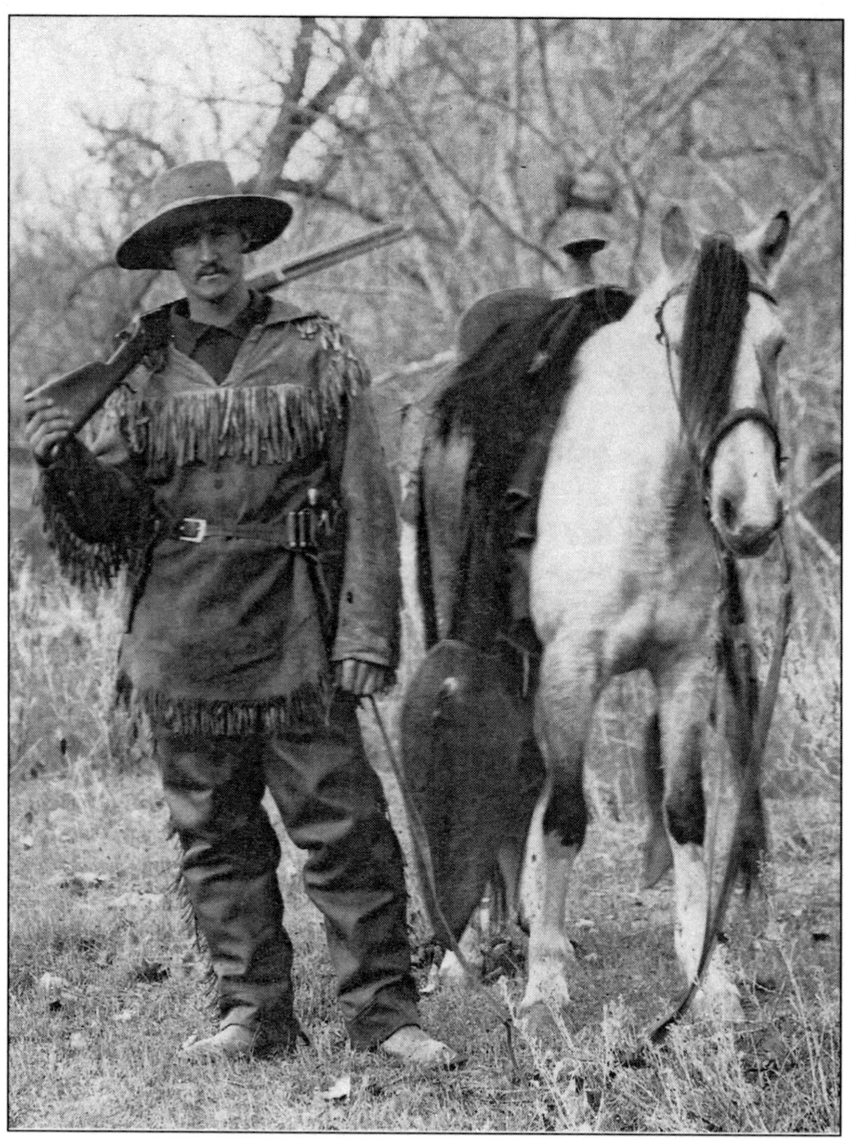

Charles S. Eaton at Medora in early 1880s. *Courtesy of Eatons' Ranch.*

Elizabeth Clarke Eaton—someone broke into their house on the SO Ranch. Apparently, a "wanderer" had not only the audacity:

> *...to open the locked piano, but he had stolen and absorbed a large part of the preserves which Mrs. Eaton and her mother had put up in the fall of 1886 in the cellar.*

The baby was born in Mandan on February 24, 1887. The family probably did not return to the SO Ranch in the spring. It had been devastated, livestock wise, by the famously horrible winter and as Mary Covington revealed, "Charley's wife did not care for the West."

Charles and Elizabeth returned to Pittsburgh in 1887 where Charles became a successful businessman. In 1918, they moved to Geneva, New York, where they occupied the Clarke family home. In 1936, Elizabeth was struck by an automobile and died.

Their daughter Elizabeth married Foster P. Boswell, who became a professor of philosophy at Hobart and William Smith Colleges in 1922. Elizabeth became a recognized watercolor painter, especially of Geneva homes, and lived to be eighty-eight years old. She died in 1975.

Charles only returned to Medora twice: once in June of 1897, when he signed the Custer Trail guest book, and then many years later in 1932.

Alden was the only other Eaton brother to have a family. His progeny was the sole lineage for the Eaton enterprise that exists today.

Alden was by Howard's side in all the ranching endeavors at Medora up until the time that they delivered a load of horses to Will Brown in Kingwood, West Virginia, in 1889. It was six weeks before his sister, Mary Brewer Brown's, nineteenth birthday. In Mary's own words, she and her friends were having an annual Halloween spook party and this is what happened:

> *While waiting for the witches' hour, we asked old Aunt Susie to tell our fortunes. She had been a slave in the Fairfax family and seemed about a hundred years old to us. She looked at us, then gazed off into space and said, "Miss Mary will be married before any of you. She will marry a man out of the*

Alden Eaton in Dakota Territory in early 1880s. *Courtesy of Eatons' Ranch.*

West and he will have blue eyes." Then she refused to go on. All of the girls, including myself, laughed about it, and it did seem a real joke.

The next day, when five of us trooped into our house about suppertime, two strange men were there with my brother, who had been on a hunting trip in North Dakota earlier in the year, and had purchased a carload of unbroken western horses. The two men had offered to bring the horses east when they came on their annual visit to their mother who lived in Pittsburgh. The men were Howard and Alden Eaton, and both had very blue eyes. We dug out a guitar for Howard, and with one of the girls at the piano, we had quite a gay evening. When the men went to their room that night Alden said to Howard (as I learned some time afterwards), "I've always said I would never marry a girl with red hair, especially curly red hair, but I am going to marry Mame (Mary's nickname) if she will have me."

Alden and Mame agreed to marry and while preparations for the wedding progressed over the next few weeks Alden kept himself occupied. Mary described the scene:

It was a three-ring circus around our place for several weeks. Alden volunteered to break, or at least bend, those twenty-two broncs, and every farmer and town boy at some time contrived to be at the taming. Plenty of girls, also. Howard said that Alden was one of the best riders in the West at that time and had never been thrown. There were many thrills and spills for the novices, but Alden lived up to his reputation.

Alden and Mary were married on December 19, 1889, five days after Mary's nineteenth birthday. Alden was thirty years old. It was a large elaborate wedding, and afterwards Mary and Alden set out for their honeymoon, which took them to various places before they arrived in Pittsburgh for Christmas when young Mary met the Eaton family.

> *...they were all there to meet us. A few had been to our wedding, but the rest were all strangers and much older than I. I was scared to death, but they were so kind, and there were so many parties, shows, strange and fascinating things for a little country girl to do and see, I really had a wonderful time.*

Alden and Mary didn't return to North Dakota immediately. Mary's mother had withheld her consent to the marriage unless they stayed in the East "at least for a while." So, Mary and Alden stayed on the Brown place and kept the "home fires alight" while Mary's mother was visiting in Florida.

Nine months later, in September 1890, Mary gave birth to their only child, William Alden Eaton, a nine-pound son who would come to be known as "Big Bill."

Bill's birth was quite an event according to Mary:

> *I weighed only 118 pounds then, and was quite proud when all was over, that mother—whose room adjoined ours—never wakened, and our doctor gave no anesthetic. Alden rushed up town as soon as it was daylight to telegraph to Howard, whom my brother was visiting in Dakota at the time: "It's a boy with a voice like a foghorn and a head like a scoria butte." (In Dakota, all the hills were called buttes, and if covered with red shale, they were "scoria buttes.")*

Alden, Mary, and their new son may have stayed in West Virginia indefinitely, but circumstances dictated otherwise. They had even built a house and were ready to move into it in the spring of 1892. But word from Howard changed that:

> *...Howard wrote Alden that things were not going so well at the ranch. He had a broken ankle and could not ride as long and hard as was necessary to look after the horses and cattle. There were no fences—it was all open range with plenty of various kinds of rustlers.* (Note: This seems to further the case that Willis was not yet in North Dakota in partnership with his brothers.)

And so Alden, Mary and their young son Bill set out for North Dakota. Mary described the scene:

> *I was sorry to leave all the home ties, but the romance and lure of the West was strong, and to me it was starting on a Great Adventure. We came on the Northern Pacific, and at Mandan, I saw my first Indians. They were in buckskin and feathers on the platform—just scenery, but to me real and scary. The ranch home was five miles from the station, Medora. We arrived in the evening. Alden's sister, Hattie Pelissier, her husband, three children and Josephine Gillespie, and Howard were there. Also several cowboys. We all sat at one long table, and the men seemed to do most of the waiting and dishwashing, and it was all very new and strange. That night I had my first coyote serenade, and if there is any sound more horrible to a strange girl in a strange land, up to that time I had not met up with it. Everyone was kind and thoughtful, and I soon learned that most of the things I dreaded never happened. No one was bitten by a rattlesnake, and no horses bucked. If you got into quicksand in the river, some way you came out alive, and Indians did not go on the warpath.*

Harriet (Aunt Hattie) Eaton, the youngest Eaton sister, visited her brothers at the Custer Trail Ranch with her father several times. On one of those visits, she met and married Peter Pelissier who at one time worked for the Eatons.

Peter was born in Brandon, Minnesota on March 11, 1865 but moved to Jamestown, North Dakota in 1873 when his father, Antoine Pelissier II, moved his family. The two hundred mile trip took three weeks with oxen and wagons.

Peter was an interesting character. In 1884, when he was only nineteen years old, Peter was foreman of the Little Missouri Horse Company. This was the Huidekoper operation, and was thought to be the largest horse raising operation in the world. Peter held that position until

1888. He was also the Sheriff of Billings County in 1897 and had a Wild West Show from 1897 to 1908 or longer.

Years later, a nephew, Louie Pelissier, wrote about his uncle:

I had an uncle who was a great horseman—Pete Pelissier. He was a great roper. He was also a gambler. He was perhaps the best horseman in this part of the state. When I was a kid, Pete would take his horse wagon and a crew of men every spring and go from Medora to New England City, across Cedar Creek and down on the Grand River (fifty or sixty miles east of Bowman) to gather horses. They would come back in about three weeks with around four hundred head of the best-looking horses anyone ever looked at. I've been to the Denver Stock Show and have never seen any there that matched these. These horses ran as to color—red bays with black manes and tails, and a few browns. None of those sore-eyed pintos or palominos or other off-colored ones were in these bunches. This type of horse you could ride a hundred miles in a day if he didn't buck you off in the morning.... He had a good stud called Steeldust Monte.

Peter and Harriet were married in December of 1887 and had three children: Willis, born in August 1888; Elsie born in June 1890; and Mary, born in July 1891. They also had a second son, John, but he died at a young age and was buried on the Pelissier ranch south of Medora.

Mary, the youngest daughter, wrote her unpublished memoirs when she was seventy-six years old in 1967. It gives a remarkable glimpse into the life and times of the Eatons and Pelissiers in the early days at Medora:

We never lacked for food, clothing or love. In fact, as I look back on those days, we were a spoiled bunch. However, my parents believed in spanking and other punishment. My parents deserved a crown in Heaven, for there was rarely a time when we didn't have one or more youngsters in our home, due to illness of their mother, divorce, or death. There was always room for one more. Bill Eaton lived a mile and a half from us, and as he was an only child, he spent most of his days at our house...

For the first few years of schooling, the school was held at our house. Uncle Alden made a long low table, marked off in one-inch squares. Our paste was made from Mellin's Food, a powder for baby formula. Clay was dug from some nearby creek bank. The school was held in one of the bedrooms of our house at first. Later a small building was erected out of bridge timbers, and we had regular school desks and a desk for the teacher.

Our first teacher was a Mrs. Emma Brown from Kingwood, West Virginia. She taught kindergarten and first grade. She wore her hair with three long curls hanging down the front sides of her head, and the rest on top of her head in a knot. Bill's mother had known her back there. We called her "Aunt Emma"...Uncle Howard was always offering us prizes for our spelling. One year it was a .22 rifle. We won it, and what a time we had with that gun.

Eaton family members at Custer Trail Ranch in the early days. Identity of the women is uncertain, but the woman with the baby is believed to be Harriet Eaton Pelissier with her son Willis. The other woman may be Mary Eaton Gillespie. Howard and Alden Eaton are to the right.
Courtesy of Don King Western Museum.

The Eaton and Pelissier children at Medora. Bill Eaton is in center and Willis Pellissier is behind him. Elsie Pelissier is on the right and Mary Pelissier on the left.
Courtesy of Eatons' Ranch.

The Pelissier children and Bill Eaton had many adventures and got up to all sorts of youthful shenanigans:

> *We went to school in Medora for a while. Uncle Alden, the handy man, put a back seat on a one-horse buggy for us to drive in with. Bill would start out and drive to our place, then we would join him, with Willis driving, and off to Medora we would go. There was no top to the buggy, and in very severe weather, we would very often have to turn around and go back because we were so cold from driving against the north wind. Many times mother would have hot boiled eggs for us to hold in our mittened hands and warm bricks, which had been heated on the back of the cook stove all night, for our feet, and blankets to put over our laps. We had a long, steep hill to come down on the way home, which ended with a short steep dip into the creek at the bottom. We would come down that hill with Willis driving and Bill whipping, the poor horse fairly running, and when we hit the creek at the bottom Bill was usually bounced out, but he was so bundled up he never got hurt. He led a charmed life. Once he got a whole little orange stuck in his mouth and Willis had to borrow a buttonhook to get it cut in pieces so Bill could get rid of it.*

When Uncle Willis had come up from Mexico in the early nineties (*Note: This corroborates Mary Eaton's statement that Willis was not around during the first years when the Eatons founded the ranching operation.*) he brought some of those strong Mexican cigarettes wrapped in cornhusks. Evidently, after he got there, the Mexican cigarettes did not please his taste, so they were stored in a desk drawer in the living room of Custer Trail. Bill would snitch a few of these and we three would ride down to the riverbank and smoke them.

> *My father was very strict about firearms, we weren't supposed to point a stick at another kid and yell, "Bang." ...Willis was usually keeper of the gun, and he had to use all care in handling it. He loaded it for the rest of us. When we got*

Young Bill Eaton riding his tricycle at Custer Trail Ranch. Circa mid 1890s.
Courtesy of Eatons' Ranch.

too pesky at home, we would be sent to the nearby prairie dog town to shoot prairie dogs. Anyone who has ever tried to shoot a prairie dog knows how almost impossible this is, but it worked off a good deal of steam and gave my mother a rest. Uncle Howard furnished animals for zoos, and he had us trap prairie dogs with wrapped traps, so their legs would not be broken. We went over our trap line every day. One morning we found that we had caught a small animal full of fight that was not a prairie dog. We hurried to the house after mama, and she came out and helped us get the animal in a box and home. When Uncle Howard came over, he identified it as a black-footed ferret. Among those to whom Uncle Howard sold animals was W. T. Hornaday, I think he was the keeper of the New York Zoo, and he visited the Custer Trail when we were young. I most remember him for his beard.

(Note: According to the Custer Trail Guest Book, Mr. Hornaday and his wife visited on November 4 and 5, 1900. He wrote in the book, "Two golden days, the glories of which will never be forgotten, by W. T. Hornaday, New York Zoological Park.")

There was another game we used to take part in, which was cut short by our misunderstanding parents. At Custer Trail there was a building consisting of five or six bedrooms, which opened on a walk to the main house. Bill Eaton, being the only one with red hair—and it was so red that it was almost bright orange—would get in one of the end rooms, and the rest of the bunch would get in the other end rooms. Bill would stick his red head out for a minute and someone in the other end would take a shot at him. Luckily, someone discovered the game we were playing, and the gun was retired for a while. I forgot to mention that after the shot was fired Bill would again stick his head out and announce, "you missed me that time." We were certainly a bunch of irresponsible youngsters, in spite of all the lectures on the careful use of firearms.

And so life went on at Medora.

Perhaps the Eaton sibling who visited Custer Trail Ranch most frequently, if the guest book is any indication, was the second oldest daughter, Mary Brewer (Aunt Mary.) She married Thomas Gillespie, who was well off and died early. Mary Gillespie would eventually find herself a permanent resident of the Eaton Ranch in later years and she never needed any financial support. She had a deaf daughter, Josephine (Cousin Josie), who also spent time at Medora and often looked after the Pelissier children and Bill Eaton.

Another member of the extended family was Aunt Minnie, Mary Eaton's (Aunt Mame's) sister. Actually, though their maiden name was Brown, they were not really the Browns' children. Their mother died leaving a houseful of children, and so the Browns took Minnie in to help. (*Note: Whether they took her in to just "help" or adopt is not clear.*) But Minnie cried constantly because she was so homesick, so they exchanged her for Mary. When Mame moved to North Dakota with her new husband Alden, Minnie followed for a visit. She met and married a man by the name of Reid, who unfortunately died of acute appendicitis only a short time after they were married. Aunt Minnie then took in boarders in her house in Dickinson, North Dakota, but had a hard time making ends meet. When the Eatons moved to Wyoming, Aunt Minnie went to visit and never left. She worked as the ranch housekeeper for years.

The Eaton parents, Josephine and Franklin, passed away in 1890 and 1893 respectively. Josephine and Franklin made several trips to Custer Trail Ranch. Franklin's last trip was in September 1892 when his daughter Elizabeth (Aunt Lizzie) and her husband Arthur Cullum took him west to see the boys and his daughter Hattie Pelissier. When he died a year later, he was seventy-six years old.

Dudes

A dude is a non-derogatory term, supposedly coined by Howard, and assigned to paying guests from the East. According to Mary Covington:

> *The name "dudes" as applied to the guests, was what Uncle Howard called them because of their ideas of the correct western dress, and after the Palmer Cox Brownie by that name.*

(Note: Palmer Cox was a Canadian illustrator and author. He was best known for his humorous verse books and comic strips about the mischievous but kindhearted fairy-like Brownies. The Brownies were always dressed rather absurdly and, obviously, Howard believed some of the dudes dressed in the same way.)

When exactly, as Hagedorn wrote, "The Eatons forsook the punching of cattle, and engaged in 'dude' ranching on a grand scale" is subject to conjecture. There are various theories about when the Eatons launched into the dude business. Without question, it seems that the first person to pay for his keep was, as mentioned before, Mr. Bert Rumsey of Buffalo, New York, who, in 1882, insisted on paying so he wouldn't have guilt feelings about his extended stay with the Eatons.

Mary Covington's theory about when the dude business got started was that:

> *As young men in Pittsburgh, the Eaton brothers had many friends, and after they were settled, they invited some of their friends to come out and enjoy ranch life. Among these friends was a Mr. Clark, who was interested in the Anaconda copper mines. During the mid-eighties* (Note: 1886-1887)*, the severe winter proved fatal to a great number of cattle in North Dakota. The Eatons cut the top from cottonwood trees to feed their cattle, but suffered some losses. When Mr. Clark was ready to*

return to Pittsburgh the next summer, he insisted on paying for his vacation, stating that he realized that the previous winter had not been profitable for the Eatons, and that by being allowed to pay for his entertainment it would also allow him to bring friends along to enjoy the West. Thus was the Dude Ranching business born.

Mr. Clark may have paid and others, too occasionally. This correlates with an anonymous note found in the Custer Trail Guest Register that states "Occasional paying guests up to 1888." The note also says that:

> *F.A. E. (Farley Alden Eaton) went to Virginia in 1889. When he returned in 1891, the regular dude business was started. Leonard Graham and George Flinn first dudes after 1891.* (Note: Leonard Graham's son, of the same name, eventually became a dude at Eatons' Ranch at Wolf. He was notable because although he was a paying guest, he still pitched in and worked. He eventually ranched near Eatons' Ranch and still lives in Sheridan, Wyoming.)

Perhaps the most viable information about the matter comes from Aunt Mame, Alden's wife, who was, after all a firsthand observer and family member. Aunt Mame wrote:

> *The Eaton boys had taken one paying guest before I came into the family* (Note: She arrived in the spring of 1892.), *so after several hard winters and dry summers, they decided to add some buildings and make it a business...although for a while, we invited so many to visit, it was about half and half. Another brother, Willis, returned from Mexico about that time and started a bookkeeping system. We never balanced the budget, but we had fun. As usual, we had boys, and they would go on the roundups, camp through Yellowstone Park, hunt antelope and prairie chickens (no game laws in those days), fight grass fires, ride half-broken horses, eat and sleep.*

Perhaps the "boys" that Aunt Mame refers to were the same boys mentioned in an article in *The National Hotel Reporter* on July 12, 1910:

> *While one of the Eatons was paying a visit to his home in the East, (Probably Howard) and old friend asked him, as a personal favor, to take charge of his younger son, a wayward youth, in the hope that in the West, away from metropolitan temptations, he might make a man of himself. Eaton readily agreed.*
>
> *This gave him an idea as to the possibilities of the dude traffic. Many Eastern families of wealth had sons who were giving them more or less anxiety and worry at home, and a summer in the West appealed to them as a good thing. Thereafter, the Eatons looked out for such visitors.*
>
> *The young men looked upon it as a great lark and came west in droves. The Eatons boarded them, furnished them with horses, guns and all the necessary accoutrements and organized personally conducted excursions in the way of hunting, range riding, round ups and the like.*
>
> *Upon the ranch, they erected a great, long building, divided by partitions into small rooms, in each of which were a bunk and whatever furniture was necessary. This became known to the cowboys as the "dude pen" and here the visitors slept.*
>
> *Sometimes one summer was enough for them, but some of them remained, secured capital from home and today are among the substantial men of the State. They were a constant source of amusement to the cowboys of the range, largely from their fondness for immense hats, big revolvers, rattlesnake belts and leather "chaps."*

The dudes, as Hagedorn wrote, "...became a notable factor in the Badlands. You could raise a laugh about them at Bill Williams' saloon when nothing else could wake a smile."

The Eatons and their Custer Trail Ranch in the Badlands became a "notable factor" in the lives of many easterners. The ranch made an indelible impression on visitors and was the subject of many articles.

Donald G. McCaskey in *The Pennsylvania School Journal* wrote one, which reveals the flavor of the place and time, in 1902:

> *Custer Trail Ranch can accommodate fifty or sixty people, though not all in one house. There are probably two dozen buildings of one kind and another. There is a windmill with large tank and running water and plenty of trees—in fact, everything to make up a big, comfortable business ranch. The visitor is expected to make himself thoroughly at home. No rules as to dress as long as you are comfortable and enjoy yourself. Inside, you find a fine library of several hundred volumes, with latest magazines and newspapers, letter-writing materials, pictures upon the walls, and a fine guitar to be used by anybody who plays. In the evenings, I took this, and, as luck would have it, happened to know nearly all the tunes anybody called for. Mrs. Gillespie, a sister of the Eaton brothers, has traveled widely. She enjoys music and sings many of the best of the older songs.*
>
> *The ranch has a large corral, with stables, and cattle and horses roam at will. In all, I am told, there are from five hundred to six hundred horses. Most of the guests here do more or less riding. The charge is fifteen dollars per week, which includes all the horseback exercise wanted. There are all sorts of horses, from gentle, well-broken animals to vicious buckers and quick side-steppers...*

Mr. McCaskey also described some of the people who made up the Custer Trail staff:

> *There are people of unique personality here. The Eaton brothers are all men of force, with the strong stamp of individuality. "Texas Jack" and others are fine horsemen and good fellows. "Uncle Billy" is a little Englishman, an old-timer from Land's End, whose health is as sound as his face is wrinkled and weather beaten. He's great on short yarns, very apocryphal, and you laugh loud when his contagious smile lights up the wrinkles. You pat him on the back and want*

another of his Western fairy tales, and you get it if he is in the humor. His chief business is gardener to the ranch, and he has hosts of friends.

"Danny Kerr" has been here four or five years, looks up the football and sporting news and stock reports, enjoys music, plays the guitar some and suggests pieces to play and sing. He lends a hand at almost anything, often presides at one of the tables, tells a good story and laughs a good laugh, and when you say goodbye, gives you a grip that warms you to him and makes you glad you've met him.

Another favorite at the ranch is Mrs. Kinley. In matters culinary, she is the most useful person in the place. In fact, she comes near being "the whole thing," for she is the cook. What Mrs. Kinley says "goes" and without comment. She weighs about 260 pounds, and carries it all very easily. She can dance as lightly and run as swiftly, for a short distance as the younger people. She is strong, quick, efficient, jolly and big-hearted. In disposition, she has endeared herself to those working around her, but if anybody comes around the kitchen hunting trouble, he finds out very quickly that Mrs. Kinley is "it."

The population base for the Eaton "dude business" was Pittsburgh. Certainly, there were dudes from other cities who visited Custer Trail during the Medora years, but the largest number of dudes came from Pittsburgh and many on a repeat basis. Many of them were followed by successive generations of Eaton devotees. The guest book from 1883 to 1903 reveals the names of hundreds of people who enjoyed Eaton hospitality, either as a non-paying guest in the early years, or as a willing paying guest in the later years when the Eaton hospitality had become a viable, paying business.

Many loyal Pittsburgh followers made multiple visits to the Custer Trail Ranch, and are too numerous to list here. However, some should be recognized for their loyalty to the Eatons and some tribute should be paid to them because, as Bucky King wrote in 1973, they "loved the country and the scenery better than inside plumbing, and pioneered the dude ranch business." Among them, and the number of times they visited, were:

W.M. Kennedy (5); Theo. R. Hodtetter (5); James King and Mabel Clarke (5); Frank W. Kennedy (6); Colonel Henry Hall (8); Samuel Stottler Steel (5); John G. Magee (6); Mary Eaton Gillespie (4).

Change of Venue

As the century turned, Howard, Willis and Alden were well established at the Custer Trail Ranch. Their dude business enjoyed a national reputation and they had a huge following of people who considered themselves as part of the Ranch family. For many families, the trek to Medora was an annual ritual ingrained in their lives.

By 1903, the Custer Trail Ranch had been in operation for twenty-four years. Howard, the impetus behind the operation, and its founder, was fifty-two years old. His brother Willis was fifty-one and Alden was forty-four. Alden's wife, Aunt Mame was thirty-three years old, and their son, Bill, was thirteen.

By all rights, there seemed to be no reason for the family to leave Medora. But they did. In 1904, they packed up lock, stock and barrel and moved to Wolf, Wyoming.

Just as there are many theories about exactly when the Eatons entered the dude business, and there is probably a trace of truth in all of them, so, too, have many theories been advanced about why the Eatons moved from Medora.

In her book *Eatons' Ranch* Esther McWilliams states that:

> *No one is sure exactly why the Eaton brothers decided to look for another place for their home ranch. It was possibly just to be closer to Yellowstone Park as Howard was taking pack trips to Yellowstone, the first in 1883.*

Another unknown writer penned the following in an article about Eatons' Ranch:

> *While the Medora ranch, which was called the Custer Trail Ranch, was highly popular, the reasons for the added attraction the new location has for visitors is not hard to find. In North Dakota, the range alone offered the exercise and enjoyment the visitors sought, while in Wyoming, fine fishing and mountain climbing are great features. Then the entrance to the famous Government reservation of Yellowstone Park, a mecca for tourists, is but a few score miles away...At Medora it is true that the ranch owned by ex-President Roosevelt in his early years was close at hand, but it offered little beyond ordinary ranch scenery.*

Yet another theory, advanced by Jane Holler, who was a dude at Eatons' and eventually married one of the cowboys, Rusty Holler, wrote that:

> *The land along the Northern Pacific was getting crowded with homesteaders, and the Eatons felt the new country, with its mountains and rolling hills, would be a better location for a dude ranch. Also, the summer and winter temperatures would not be so extreme...*

But once again, we must rely on Aunt Mame, for a firsthand account of why the Eatons really moved to Wolf, Wyoming: "Some men came along one day and wanted to buy the ranch. We had never thought of selling, but the offer was cash and too good to refuse."

A few years earlier, the Eatons would not have been able to sell because they didn't actually own the land. But by 1900, the land had been surveyed and those present could file on the property on which they lived and worked.

And so the Eatons made a deal. How much the ranch sold for, or how many acres were involved isn't known, but it is known that six years later the place was sold again for $30,000.

Aunt Mame continued with her account of the situation:

> *We started packing our personal belongings, while Alden started to look for a new location. We wanted to stay on the Northern Pacific, as we knew all the officials and it was a main line, but something was wrong with every location visited. A Pittsburgh friend wrote he had a friend who had located in Sheridan (Wyoming) some years before, and had written what beautiful country it was.*

At about this time Alden was almost in despair because he couldn't find a suitable place, so he journeyed to Sheridan to meet with a friend of a friend, Mr. Edward A. Whitney. (*Note: Mr. Whitney had established the first bank in Sheridan in 1885 and had become a successful businessman, investor, landowner and developer, and public benefactor. His legacy was an estate that would eventually provide over $20 million in student loans [as of 2009] and many other amenities to the Sheridan community.*)

Alden had never been to Sheridan, although he had visited the nearby Crow reservation a number of times. When he arrived in Sheridan he found, according to one account, "… the Sheridan Inn jammed with cattlemen, financiers, promoters, and traveling salesmen." He felt very lucky to secure a room.

It happened that Mr. Whitney was traveling in Africa and not available, so Alden was directed to John Helvey, a local real estate broker. A 1935 *Sheridan Press* article takes up the account:

> *…Helvey described to him the Oscar Devol* (Note: His name was really Austin O. Devol.) *place, which he had listed. The description appealing to him, Uncle Alden asked to see it.*
>
> *The roads, a bottomless mixture of snow and mud were very bad—a sharp contrast to the all-weather highway of today. Helvey, not wanting to make the trip on the slim chance of selling under such conditions, offered to split the commission with "Shorty" Beckwith, if he would take Eaton out to the ranch. Beckwith readily agreed.*
>
> *After a long and wearisome trip—with many a stop to pry*

the chunks of gummy mud from the buggy wheels—the ranch was reached. Mr. Eaton was not long in realizing that the Devol ranch "filled the bill completely."

The Devol place was in an ideal location, about eighteen miles west of Sheridan at the foot of the Big Horn Mountains where Wolf Creek tumbled out of Wolf Creek Canyon. The altitude at the Ranch was 4,500 feet and the land consisted of 1,240.77 acres in two tracts of 160.03 and 1,080.47 acres each. Included with the land were:

...all ditches, laterals, water-rights, (including the water rights belonging thereto from the Red Canyon Ditch, the Wolf Creek Canyon Ditch, the Red Canyon Ditch No. 2 and the Windy Canyon Ditch) easements, privileges or heriditaments and appurtenances thereto belonging or in any wise appertaining.

In addition to the superb location and lay of the land, Alden recognized other amenities that suited the needs of the Eaton brothers. For one, the place had a large cut-stone ranch house heated by hot water and had running water on every floor. In fact the brochure for that year would praise the dwelling as "one of the most comfortable structures in Wyoming."

The place was also connected with Sheridan by telephone and there was a post office, with daily mail, at the Wyoming State Fish Hatchery just two miles down the road. Even though Alden knew that the place was not ideally configured for the dude business and it needed a lot of hard work, he was impressed with the enormous potential. It could work.

Pleased with his discovery, Alden secured a thirty-day option on the place and returned to North Dakota to tell his brothers about his find. Ten days later, all three brothers returned to Sheridan to inspect Alden's discovery. Supposedly, Colonel Hall, who had been a guest at Medora every year since 1893, accompanied them and helped them in their deliberations.

Everyone agreed with Alden that the Devol place had all the potential needed to develop a fine ranch, for dudes and otherwise. They liked what they saw and so on March 14, 1904, signed a five-year note with Austin O. Devol through the State Bank of Sheridan for $5,000 with an interest rate of 6% per annum.

With the deal done, the Eaton brothers returned to Medora to fetch their family and their belongings.

The Eatons were moving to Wolf…

PART TWO

Wolf

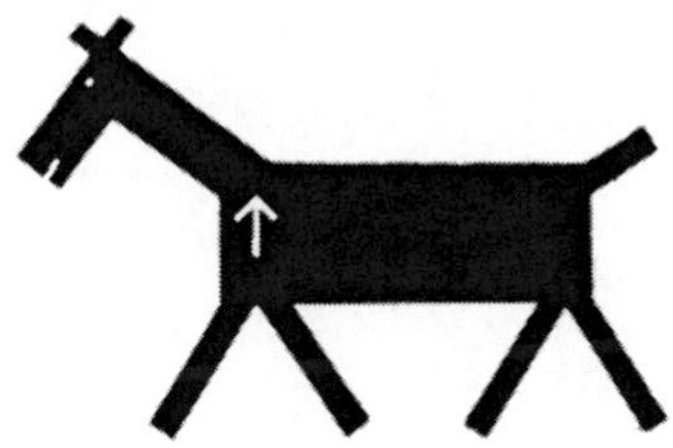

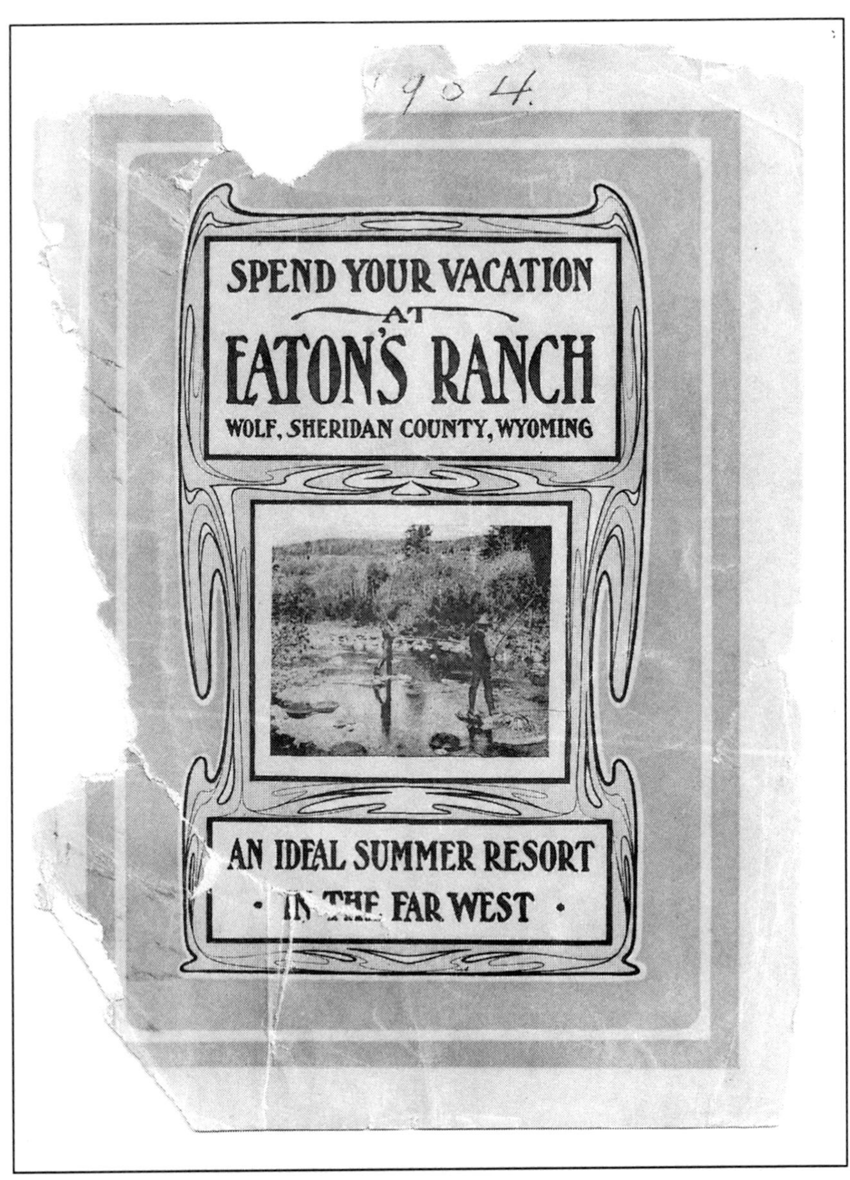

1904 Eaton Ranch brochure. *Courtesy of Eatons' Ranch.*

CHAPTER 4

Eatons at Wolf 1904-1920

The Move

Aunt Mame described the move:

The men came ahead with the horses and a few household treasures. Bill stayed in Dakota to finish his school year with the Pelissier cousins and go on spring roundup. Alden's sister, Mary Gillespie, her daughter Josephine and I came by train in early April 1904.

The Eatons must have broken out the guest book the moment they arrived. Howard Eaton was the first one to sign it on April 18, 1904 followed by Willis Eaton, and a J. S. Ferguson. Ferguson was most likely the John S. Ferguson, Jr., from Pittsburgh who signed the guest book in October of 1903 at Medora. It's entirely possible he stayed on at Medora and accompanied the Eatons on their trek to Wolf Creek. The other person to sign the book on April 18 was Henry O. Colt of LaJolla, California. Esther McWilliams told Henry Colt's most interesting story:

> *Some of the guests have always kept private horses here, and the first one listed is Henry O. Colt of LaJolla, California. He came as far as Nebraska where he bought a blue roan and a bay. Henry rode them from Nebraska to North Dakota, some six hundred miles, camping along the way. Traffic and fences did not slow a man down much in those days. The next year, 1904, Eatons moved, so Harry rounded up his horses and followed along, again riding alone. It was a four hundred mile ride this time, and Harry was the first dude to register here at Wolf Creek.*

On April 19, Uncle Alden arrived, and shortly thereafter, on April 24, Mary Gillespie, the Eaton brothers sister, and her daughter Josephine (Cousin Josie) arrived as well as Alden's wife, Aunt Mame. Aunt Mame described their arrival:

> *...It was a beautiful sunny Sunday. The mountains were gorgeous, road dry, grass green, some trees budding. The Duvols had a warm welcome and a delicious dinner for us and we immediately fell in love with the place...*

The next to arrive, a month later on May 24, was fourteen year old Bill Eaton, who had by then finished school and the spring roundup at Medora. The Eaton family was well and truly in place on Wolf Creek.

According to Aunt Mame, they had not intended to take in any dudes for the next year so that they could get the place in shape and build proper accommodations. That idea didn't last very long, because, "...the dudes decreed otherwise and seventy of them arrived despite our 'standing by to repel boarders.'"

It's curious that the Eatons professed that they did not intend to take on guests the first year on Wolf Creek, since that same year they produced a comprehensive marketing brochure. In the brochure, they announced:

> *Eaton Brothers announce to their friends and patrons, and to the public, their change of location from the Badlands of North Dakota to the Big Horn Mountain region of Northwestern Wyoming. Their new ranch is situated at the very foot of the mountains and but a few rods from where Wolf Creek, a typical mountain stream, fed by continual snows and clear as crystal, emerges from a rocky canyon and flows through mesa and plains into the Tongue River.*

Perhaps they merely succumbed to the inevitable and decided that since their "dude operation" was going to happen whether they were ready or not, they might as well make it official and put out a brochure.

Another article written in 1935 described the scene as well:

> *The brothers had no intentions of taking any guests the first summer in order that they could make adequate preparations for the season of next year. However, many of their old guests of the Custer Trail Ranch thought differently about it. They did not intend to be cheated out of a whole summer with the Eatons. So they came, some sixty strong. True sports, they accepted all the necessary deprivations with the best of humor. Memories of those happy, busy days still bring chuckles from Uncle Alden as he tells about the first summer when the guests had to eat off ironing boards, card tables and what have you. To make matters worse, the kitchen was small. The "dudes," as Howard named them, slept in tent houses. Kerosene lamps were their only source of artificial light. These lamps were the bane of Mrs. Alden's life for the fear they would cause a fire.*

There is ample reason to believe the stories, which allege that the Eatons didn't intend to take guests for the first year, and that multitudes of dudes arrived unexpectedly may be the stuff of Eaton Ranch lore and subject to conjecture. There is certainly another version of the story. Only three days after Howard arrived the following article appeared in *The Sheridan Post* on April 22:

Eaton Brothers Here

The three Eaton brothers, Howard, Alden and Wm. (Willis), who bought the Devol ranch and summer resort, arrived Sunday from North Dakota, and took possession of the ranch the following day. Mrs. Alden Eaton and two other ladies will arrive next Sunday, and make their home at the Devol place. The gentlemen brought in two carloads of horses, and will drive through several hundred head of pack and saddle horses, for the use of tourists and pleasure seekers, who will stop at their resort. Twelve new buildings, cottages, dining hall, etc., will be erected at the resort at once, and by June, the "Eaton Ranch" will be in condition to receive the many eastern people who are coming to spend their vacation in the Big Horn Mountains.

Howard Eaton departed Wednesday night, for the Flathead reservation, from where he will ship two carloads of buffalo to the east. The Eatons have a buffalo ranch on the reservation.

Somewhere in between the two accounts lies the truth. Most likely, it was all a question of timing, the planned buildings were not completed before the onslaught of the dudes, and so there was a lot of improvisation required to accommodate everyone. It is doubtful that all the dudes showed up unexpected.

The Eatons' had to improvise and used tents to accommodate dudes until a crew of carpenters completed the construction of a series of "little square rooms made from logs with no foundation at all." The carpenters were paid one hundred dollars for each cabin. This first row of dude cabins was dubbed "The Pike." An article in the *Sheridan County Heritage* Book, 1983, explains a possible origin of the name:

Guests on the The Pike in the first days of Eatons' Ranch at Wolf.
Courtesy of Eatons' Ranch.

> *...a current dude from St. Louis tells us that the World's Fair at St. Louis that same year (1904) had a "Freak Show" along a street called The Pike, and although we are unable to verify it, choosing that name certainly fits the Eaton style of humor.*

As soon as cabins were completed, the dudes cleaned them so they could move in. Undaunted, the dudes also helped with the beds, dishes, and anything else that needed to be done. As Aunt Mame said, they "paid for the privilege."

While all the people who signed the guest book in 1904 were important to the Eatons, one deserves special mention because he was to be a significant fixture on the Eaton Ranch for the next thirty-nine years. His name was John Lyons Fleming from Pittsburgh.

Angela Buell, who joined the Eaton operation several years later, and became yet another dedicated lifetime Eaton employee, explained in a 1970 reminiscence how John Fleming became associated with the Eatons:

> *In the late nineties the brothers were smart enough to realize that were not talented as BUSINESSMEN* [sic], *although they had the engaging personalities etc. to carry on the dude business from the public relations angle. So they asked John Fleming to join them as business manager. He was honest, upright, an accountant, and qualified in every way.*

It is not totally clear how or when John Fleming became associated with the Eatons. Patty Eaton said many years later that John Fleming went to North Dakota for health reasons and subsequently became the business manager. He would play a major role in the Eaton operation until he died at the ranch on April 22, 1943, aged sixty-five, six years after the last Eaton brother, Alden, had passed on.

Expansion

From the beginning, the Eaton brothers took advantage of every opportunity to acquire land contiguous to their property. They certainly took advantage of the Homestead Act whenever possible and many members of the family filed homesteads in their own name and then signed the property over to the ranch. They were also able to purchase stone and timber leases. All the Eaton brothers filed homesteads and, in addition, Mary Eaton, Josephine Gillespie and Minnie Reid filed, as well. During the period 1908 to 1911, members of the Eaton family filed for seventeen land patents. By 1911, the family had managed to obtain over

1400 additional acres to raise their total acreage to just over 3,561 acres.

Included in the expansion, by 1909, was a purchase from E. A. Whitney for 960 acres. Whitney had purchased this acreage from C. L. Decker in 1900. E. A. Whitney, the vice president of the Sheridan County Savings Bank and Sheridan Banking Company, offered to sell the land to the Eatons. But because they needed to borrow money for the purchase, Mr. Whitney wanted to make sure they understood the ramifications of the deal since he was the one who suggested it. He encouraged them to do it, but wanted to make sure that they knew that:

> *...No farmer can take the place on borrowed capital at 8% and win out...Whatever the place fails to show as a net profit.... must be made up from your other resources, or be met by the rise in the value of the land as the years go by...*

However, he concluded that they were "of mature age" and had shown "good business qualities." Since they were not speculating, but rather pursuing a solid business transaction, Whitney agreed to the deal. But he first had them sign a statement to "assure me that you know where the money is coming from to pay your obligations and that you have no dread of the burden to be assumed."

To complete the transaction, the Eaton brothers refinanced all of their existing obligations in the form of a security bond for $35,000 consisting of seven notes of $5,000 each to be repaid during the period from 1911 to 1917.

The acreage purchased by the Eatons surrounded the Wyoming State Fish Hatchery. The Fish Hatchery consisted of 1.47 acres "...and right of way and improvements thereon." The official Wolf, Wyoming Post Office was also located on the property. On May 11, 1909, the governor of Wyoming, B. B. Brooks, advertised for bids for the property because the Fish Hatchery was being moved to Story, Wyoming.

The Eatons must have known what was up, for on April 24, they wrote to the governor and made their case:

> *We are the owners virtually of the land surrounding the fish hatchery near Sheridan...We enclose you herewith a plat*

Wyoming State Fish Hatchery and Post Office at Wolf, Wyoming.
Courtesy of Eatons' Ranch.

> *showing the surroundings of the fish hatchery, and the contract for the 960 acres of land which we have...*

They enclosed copies of all the documents that proved the chain of ownership from C. L. Decker through Whitney to them and then stated:

> *By examining the deed to the state, you will find that there is contained therein a proviso, that when the state ceases to use the land for a fish hatchery, that then the land shall revert to "grantor, his heirs and assigns." In as much that we are the assigns, the land should revert to us. In any event, on account of the ownership of the entire surrounding land, it would be an injustice to sell the property to anyone else, and let a private person have a little strip of land right in our midst...it would be highly undesirable to sell this fish hatchery to any person who might be a continual annoyance to us. We are prepared*

and willing to pay more for the property than the actual worth thereof.

In the end, the governor sought advice from the attorney general about the legality of a private sale without the solicitation of bids. The attorney general's opinion, plus input from several politicians, and the fish hatchery superintendent, C. W. Morgareidge convinced the governor that the Eaton bid of $3,000 was appropriate and legal and, in the words of Mr. Morgareidge, "…it would be in the best interest of all parties concerned to close the deal with Eaton Brothers." And so, they did.

The Eatons acquired not only the property, but they obtained the Post Office function as well. In a letter written shortly after the purchase, the Eatons wrote to the Honorable Frank Mondell, the Wyoming Representative to the United States House of Representatives. The letter said, in part:

…We understand Mrs. N. V. Morgareidge is resigning the position of postmaster and will recommend Mr. W. L. Eaton for appointment….If you can add your good word in Will's behalf it will be deemed a great favor to us all. We will endeavor to care for the efficiency of the office in such a way as to meet the approval of the department….

Willis did receive the appointment and was postmaster of the Wolf Post Office for many years.

Today, Billy Ferguson, the great grandson of Alden and Mame, and his wife Karen live on the old fish hatchery property

By December 31, 1911, the Eatons had acquired yet more property. Their balance sheet for that date stated that they possessed 4,175.68 acres, including associated buildings, valued at $98,185.19.

Their land acquisitions didn't stop there. Other opportunities presented themselves and the Eatons were quick to seize them. For instance, in 1915 and 1916, two state school land parcels of 440 acres and 480 acres were released for sale. The Eatons leased this land for grazing and were obviously anxious to acquire it. They were the successful bidders and the land was added to their holdings.

Then, in 1917, E. A. Whitney died. Whitney had extensive holdings, one of which was 953 acres adjacent to the Eaton ranch and the Eatons were able to purchase that land. Finally, in 1919, the "Merrifield Place," which comprised 560 acres, was put on the market and was purchased by the Eatons.

Thus, in the span of fifteen years, the Ranch on Wolf Creek increased from the original fourteen hundred acres to approximately seven thousand acres. Even though there would be two minor transactions in the future—one land patent in 1921 and the purchase of a small acreage as late as 1955—Eatons' Ranch has been essentially the same size since 1920. The present size of Eatons' Ranch is approximately seventy-two hundred acres—about one third of that acreage was derived from land patents and two thirds from land purchases.

Their property ownership was not restricted to acreage on Wolf Creek. In 1906 and 1907, they purchased property in Sheridan that included several lots in town, some with houses on them. Whether or not the purchases were for speculation is not known, but by 1917, they had sold some and owned at least two houses in town, which were for family use.

The Eaton expansion was not limited to land since they had a pressing need to build facilities to keep pace with the growth of their burgeoning dude business.

When the Eatons arrived in Wolf in 1904, the main house was already there. In addition, there were the usual sort of outbuildings and corrals found on any working ranch. By 1906, the Eatons had constructed the main barn that exists today and reorganized the system of corrals, torn down some buildings and added or modified others.

In 1908, just four years after their arrival, the Eatons were able to state in their annual brochure:

> *On the home ranch, open throughout the year, Eaton Brothers have provided many comforts for visitors. Pleasant cottage, tent or cabin rooms afford wholly healthful living quarters, and, when preferred, the regulation round-up bed*

Eatons' Ranch in early days. Exact date unknown, but after 1911 when Howard Hall, in lower left corner of photo, was constructed.
Courtesy of Eatons' Ranch.

> *may be used for outdoor sleeping. Bathrooms with all conveniences—running water, hot and cold. An open-air swimming pool, tennis court and a well stocked library with current magazines and daily papers. A large central dining room provides amply for the limited number of visitors.*

The "open air swimming pool" sounds rather grand but in fact, according to Esther McWilliams who wrote in 1981:

> *...The swimming pool used to be just a dirt hole with some of the creek diverted through it, and it wasn't heated or anything. It has been improved over and over again, and is now a nice, modern pool...but some wonder if the old one might have been more fun!*

The main Ranch House was a popular gathering place in the early 1900s.
Courtesy of Eatons' Ranch.

The interior of the main ranch house.
Courtesy of Eatons' Ranch.

The first swimming pool at Eatons' Ranch. *Courtesy of Eatons' Ranch.*

The local newspaper, *The Sheridan Post,* commented on the "Wolf Creek Development" and among other things said that:

> *On the Eaton ranch, the house is a handsome stone one, and every convenience and comfort was looked after in the building of it. The spacious dining room is one of its good features. The walls are covered with a collection of mounted buffalo, elk, deer, bear and other wild animal heads that would rank well in any collection. They also have a good office building and about twenty cabins. A number of prominent people are arranging to build homes of their own on the Eaton ranch and will spend several months each year there.*

Eatons' Ranch in 1915. *Courtesy of Eatons' Ranch.*

Horses saddled for the morning ride in about 1915.
The scene is the same in 2010.
Courtesy of Eatons' Ranch.

One of the first guests to build a cabin at the Ranch was Colonel Hall, the perennial Eaton guest and friend at Medora who traveled to Sheridan with the three brothers when they looked at the Wolf Creek place. His cabin was just one big room. The Eatons wanted him to build a bathroom but he refused. He didn't mind walking all the way over to the bathhouse.

A few other guests—Moss, Elliot and Louer—were allowed to build cabins. But, then the Eatons had second thoughts about the practice. The Eatons believed it was wrong to rent the cabins owned by guests when they were not in residence, although this was common practice in some other resorts. As a result, the cabins lost a lot of use, which was not good business. If the Ranch owned the cabins, they could rent them at will whenever they chose.

A summary of the construction dates of the buildings that were either in place when the Eatons bought the Devol place and the buildings, as they are known today, erected during the period 1904 to 1920 is as follows:

Building	Construction Date
Original Main House	1894
Dining Room, Kitchen/Laundry	Unknown
Office	1896
Original Pike	1904
The Hennery	1905
Horse Barn & Saddle Rooms	1905
Pack Shed	1905
Bachelor Quarters 73 & 74	1906
Colonel Hall Cabin	1906
Cow Barn	1907
Little Antlers Cabin	1909
Wigwam Cabin	1909
#69 Cabin	1910
Alden Eaton House	1910
Rinehart Cabin	1910
Howard Hall	1911
Wolves Club	1911
Rotten Row	1911
Duryea Cabin	1914
#68 Cabin	1914
Pike Bath House	1917
Ferguson House	1918
Big Graham Cabin	1919
Stevens Cabin	1919
111-112-113 Cabin	1919
Applegate Cabin	1919
Stoner Cabin	1919
Mellon Cabin	1919
Nimick Cabin	1920
Bryan Cabin	1920
Blanchard Cabin	1920
#48 & 49 Cabins	1920
Arbuthnot Cabin	1920
Gentry Cabin	1920

Terrace Cabins	1920
#53 & #54 Cabins	1920
Lawton Cabin	1920
Robbins Cabin	1920
Duncan Cabin	1920

In future years, these structures would be revamped several times over and some were rebuilt because of general deterioration and destruction by fire. However, the original names were maintained.

A cabin at Eatons' Ranch in the early rustic days.
Courtesy of Eatons' Ranch.

Incorporation

On February 11, 1907 the Eaton brothers—probably upon the advice of their business manager, John Fleming—incorporated as Eaton Brothers Incorporated—for the purpose of becoming a body Corporate and politic, under and by virtue of the laws of the State of Wyoming concerning corporations." The charter named each of the brothers as a trustee and declared the issuance of capital stock worth $100,000. The capitalization consisted of one thousand shares and the par value of each share was $100. Each Eaton brother received 333 1/3 shares.

When the Eaton brothers incorporated, they transferred most of the assets and liabilities from their old organization to the new one, but not all. Some highlights of the asset and liability statement they declared on March 31, 1907 are as follows:

Total Assets	$124,702.22
Total Liabilities	$ 24,702.22
Net Value of Property	$100,000.00
Three properties in Sheridan	$ 5,450.00
Eatons' Ranch 1,400 acres @$25/acre	$ 35,019.25
Main Ranch House	$ 14,000.00
Improvements from 1904-1907	$ 14,501.97
8 Buffalo at Ronan, Montana	$ 1,600.00
Livestock as follows:	
26 draft horses	
140 saddle horses	
105 cattle	
100 cattle in North Dakota	
Poultry—Estimated Low	$19,350.00

The statement also included $4,460.21 in accounts receivables. Their main liabilities, worth $19,000.00, consisted of four notes owed to various people and illustrate that they had relied on family and friends to help finance their operation. They owed Mary Gillespie, a wealthy sister, $7,400.00 and a William Flinn, a dude from Pittsburgh, $5,000. The remaining notes were the $5,000 owed to Mr. Devol, from whom they bought the property and $1,600 to the First National Bank of Missoula, Montana.

A few years later, in 1911, the D. W. Jones Company in Sheridan audited Eaton Brothers and produced a condensed balance sheet. By this time, their assets had increased to $147,747.38, and their liabilities, including the capital stock, were listed as $147,747.38. The liabilities also included $43,184.87 in debt secured by real estate.

The nature of the ranching and resort business created frequent demands for more cash and credit. For example, in 1913, the corporation needed more money and so the following resolution was approved at a meeting of the board of directors that empowered them to:

> *...issue certain certificates of indebtedness to the amount of $25,000 to be known as Special Preferred Stock...The Special Preferred Stock certificates being a special form of loan giving under certain conditions the right to the holder thereof the privilege to convert the same into common stock of the corporation which right the said corporation must recognize unless the certificates are called in and paid off.*

In exchange for investing in preferred stock of the Eaton Brothers Corporation, the certificate holders were guaranteed semi-annual dividends at the rate of six per cent per annum, before any dividend was declared to the common stockholders. There would be many future years when the proviso for dividends constituted only false hope, as the Eaton Brothers were rarely in a position to pay dividends. However, when they could, they did.

The preferred stock, unlike common stock, gave the holders no voting rights in the management of the Eaton Brothers Corporation. Many years later, as both common and preferred stock filtered down by inheritance through successive generations of the Eaton family and loyal employees, the Eaton Brothers Corporation would face challenges in managing the stock and maintaining control of the corporation.

The Eaton brothers occasionally found themselves in the position where they became indebted to several loyal employees for "services rendered" and gave them stock in exchange. By 1916, two employees, John Duncan and John Fleming, became small stockholders (six and fifteen shares respectively.) In addition, Alden's son Bill received six shares under the same conditions as the other employees.

Others had also been allowed to creep into the Eaton Brothers Corporate tent as stockholders although in very minor positions. The 1916 stockholders list included an Eaton niece, Josephine Gillespie, and five dudes: Henry Hall, Howard Irish, W. H. McClung, W. S. Elliott and F. B. Nimick.

Eaton Brothers Corporation kept rather meticulous records of their corporation meetings. The minutes provide glimpses of some of the challenges that the three Eaton brothers faced. For instance, in September 1911, they realized that the three of them, jointly, were not doing an adequate job of managing their business, and therefore passed the following resolution:

> *Resolved that the following duties and authority be forthwith vested in the secretary* (Note: Alden Eaton). *The entire direction and management of all the business of this corporation, including all branches of work relating to the resort, general store, ranching and any other enterprise now followed, together with the undivided final authority over all expenditures pertaining thereto. That he is herewith instructed to make full use of this authority for the purpose of furthering any possible economy and that during the continuance of this resolution he shall plan only for regular maintenance work above the current operations of the corporation.*

Therefore, business wise, Uncle Alden was in charge. However, John Fleming was the steady presence behind the scenes. During the next few years, it became increasingly apparent that John Fleming needed a stronger role. As a result, in 1919 the Eaton brothers gave him sweeping authority to put and keep the Eaton house in order. They adopted a resolution to put the new policy into effect:

> *With the desire to encourage more effective and more cordial co-operation and to provide a method of prompt adjustment of all misunderstandings that may impede such aims we hereby appoint J. L. Fleming as Business Agent of Eaton Brothers Incorporated with full authority to act in all general operation of this business not specially prohibited by law or corporate usage. Memorandums made and approved by us from time to time during the past ten years will provide him with an adequate guide as to our wishes and in fact it is our feeling that we have not effectively carried out such plans that lead us to test the value of more concentrated control. We realize that nothing can be done unless we personally support our appointed agent, aid him directly and indirectly at all times and convey to all others the impression of sincere cordial co-operation while earnestly seeking to make such co-operation real...*

John Fleming's appointment was originally to be effective for one year. In fact, it remained in effect for the next twenty-four years and would transcend the lives of all three Eaton brothers.

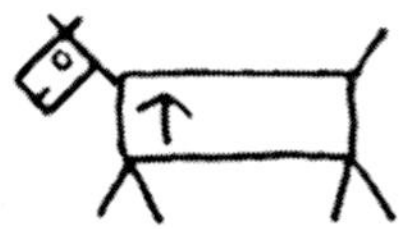

Family

Any discussion about the Eaton family during this period must begin, as usual, with Howard, the man who started the whole Eaton western adventure when he went west to North Dakota. He was an impressive man —so impressive that Mary Roberts Rinehart, the author and journalist and inveterate Eaton Ranch guest, wrote an entire book about her experiences as a member of Howard's first pack trip through Glacier Park in 1914. At the time, Howard was sixty-three years old. In her book *Through Glacier Park: Seeing America First With Howard Eaton,* Mrs. Rinehart wrote:

> *Howard Eaton is extremely young. He was born quite a number of years ago, but what is that? He is a boy, and he takes an annual frolic. And, because it means a cracking good time, he takes people with him and puts horses under them and the fear of God in their hearts, and bacon and many other things, including beans, in their stomachs.*
>
> *He has taken foreign princes and many of the great people of the earth to the tops of high mountains, and shown them grizzly bears, and their own insignificance, and one and the same time. He is a hunter, a sportsman, and a splendid gentleman. And, because equipment is always a matter of much solicitude on the part of the novice, I shall tell you what he wears when, on his big horse, he leads his long line of riders over the trails. He wears a pair of serviceable trousers, a blue shirt, and a vest! Worn by Howard Eaton, believe me, they are real clothes. He has hunted along the Rockies from Alaska to Mexico. He probably knows Montana, Wyoming, and Idaho as well as any man in the country.*

Mrs. Rinehart also said about half of the forty-two people who went with Howard on the first Glacier Park trip were women, and they all had one thing in common: the philosophy of true adventure. That is probably the one word that best sums up Howard—adventure.

Adventure was common fare for Howard. He never tired of it, and by the time the year 1917 rolled around, Howard Eaton had taken eighty-three pack trips to Yellowstone National Park since his first trip in 1884. His insatiable need to travel and explore, and, most importantly, share it with others, led him to other venues besides Yellowstone National Park.

In 1909, he wrote to his many friends and proposed a trip to visit Old Mexico in 1910. It was not to be a camping trip, but rather a train trip. Howard had planned on using a private Pullman car, using regular trains and stopping at regular meal stations en route, but then he changed his mind and wrote:

> *...but after studying the matter and considering the annoyance of traveling on regular trains, and being desirous of making the trip a most enjoyable one, I have decided to arrange with Gates Tours to handle our car on one of the Private Train Daylight Mexico Tours...By this arrangement we are not obliged to travel on regular trains—stopping over an entire day, when a few hours would be more satisfactory—dining at inferior eating houses at irregular hours, or being subject to any of the discomforts or delays to which passengers on regular trains are liable...*

No, Howard's guests were going first class with a special train complete with separate dining car, club car, observation car and baggage car. The train left Chicago on February 15, 1910 and guests joined the procession at Chicago, Kansas City or "any place en route." Included in the itinerary was the Petrified Forests and Grand Canyon of Arizona on the return from Mexico and an optional trip to California for those who wanted to visit the Pacific Coast before returning to the East.

This attention to the care and comfort of his guests extended to his lengthy camping trips. These trips presented major logistical challenges but Howard's experience and organizational flare caused them to be routine and well-oiled operations—usually.

One Glacier Park trip was, according to Esther McWilliams "little short of disaster." Esther compiled a book called *Eatons' Ranch*, first published in 1981. Esther described the event:

> *...Howard Eaton had been back east drumming up trade, and with his wonderful personality, he simply oversold the trip. They had around a hundred people on that one. Glacier wasn't even a park yet, but a man named Brewster had a concession of some kind so they had to use his horses. This meant they couldn't use the regular Eatons' dude horses, so they couldn't predict the behavior of the animals. Some of the horses were completely unbroken and had never even had a saddle on before. The broncs were packed with supplies and immediately started bucking all over the place. A few of the packs came undone, scattering belongings everywhere. The guests' clothes and personal things were packed in "war bags," which were just flour sacks. The boys went about gathering everything up and jamming it together every which way because they couldn't tell what belonged to whom. It was a real mess, and if there had been many like that, Howard would have had quite a different reputation.*

The best "insider's view" into one of Howard's camping trips was provided by Dorothy Dodge Duncan who, when she was seventeen, was hired by Howard as a camp maid to "make up the tepees" for a sixteen day camping trip through Glacier National Park. She shared her experiences with Barbara Ketchum who published them in an article titled "Camping 1916 Style" that was published in the *Old West Magazine* in the summer of 1985. Dorothy related that the sixteen day trip for 110 people:

> *...required a lot of supplies and help. Staff included the camp manager, John B. Duncan, a cook with several assistants and waiters, a doctor, an official photographer, and a guide for each ten guests. It also included two camp maids, Alice Mettler and me, to make up the tepees.*

Dudes took the train to East Glacier where Howard met them with horses and all the accoutrements needed for the trip. The supplies were carried by wagons, as opposed to the first two trips that used packhorses. There was also a stagecoach called the "hearse," drawn by four horses for anyone who suffered an injury or just wanted a break from riding.

The ride to the first camp, Two Medicine Lake, was twelve miles and, according to Dorothy, to ride into the camp:

> *...was a never forgotten experience. The huge tents, called big tops, and the tepees were already set up for the guests. Buckets of warm water were on the campfire to be taken for washing our hands and faces.*

Dorothy then described the camp, and how it operated:

> *There were eighty-four tepees divided into three groups—one for single women, one for single men, and the third for married couples. Each morning, Alice and I would eat breakfast early so we could make up the beds while the guests ate breakfast. The tepees had canvas bottoms with flaps that came up over the beds. Each tepee had room at the head of the bed for a suitcase or duffel bag. Good feather pillows with checked gingham pillowslips added the final touch.*
>
> *Most of the women wore riding skirts. My attire consisted of a Stetson hat, which had cost five dollars, a blue denim blouse and full bloomers made of blue denim to take the place of a riding skirt, I could not have crawled around the tents otherwise.*
>
> *Howard Eaton, whom everyone called "Uncle Howard," knocked on the tepees each morning telling us to get up. Breakfast was at 6:00 a.m. and we hit the trail by 8:30. Breakfast included hot mush, pancakes, eggs, and a "pail" of bacon that Uncle Howard personally served to the guests.*
>
> *The kitchen and dining room were large tents. In good weather, the sides were tied up. Long tables covered with oilcloth tablecloths sat on folding sawhorses. The aromas that came from the tents were enticing, and the meals were delicious. When Uncle Howard yelled, "Grub pile, come and get it or we'll throw it away," the guests hurried to the Big Top, where waiters served them.*
>
> *Food for the noon meal was carried on packhorses, which were taken ahead and prepared while the riders were*

> *sightseeing. The noon meal consisted of sandwiches...delicious canned fruit, and coffee. Loaves and loaves of bread had to be sliced. Uncle Howard gave me my first lesson in making sandwiches. I was putting butter on one side of the bread only when I felt his hand on my shoulder. "Young lady," he told me, "my dudes get butter on both sides of the bread."*
>
> *I felt this was an indication of how guests were to be treated. When I asked Bill Arthur, who had been on the trip the year before, what else I should do, he said, "Say yes-us, yes-um. Do whatever they ask and they'll ask for strange things."*
>
> *When the campers left a site, there were no Brownie Camera wrappers or any kind of debris left. Uncle Howard was a stickler for leaving the camp absolutely clean.*

Dorothy described the rest of the trip and ended with a nostalgic look back:

> *I look back on that trip as a magic time filled with long days in the saddle, up mountains, over passes, and riding through beautiful meadows. Nights around the campfire found Uncle Howard telling stories and reciting poetry, with occasional special additions from dudes. There was much singing. Uncle Howard recited all nine verses of Casey d'hôte by Eugene Field.* (Note: The true title is Casey's Table d'hôte and there are eight verses.) *The House of Shupe was one of Uncle Howard's favorite stories, and years later, a dude printed this delightful story, and a copy was given to me for Christmas. We all knew when the evening was ending, for all at once Uncle Howard would stand up with his back to the fire, and say, "We're going to hit the trail early."*

The next year, 1917, Dorothy returned to work on another Glacier trip. When the trip was over Howard gave her a book of poetry, *Out Where The West Begins*, by Arthur Chapman. In the book, Howard wrote a special verse for her and it tells us something about Howard:

To Dorothy Dodge

Dear Dorothy, we know you
by the smile upon your mug
you are always gay and jolly
like a happy tumble bug

When you open your sweet kisser
and smile a little smile
it's a cinch you would be happy
even while drinking caster 'ile

When next we strike the Glacier Park
if you are not with us
the camp will be plumb full of gloom
Lord how the boys will cuss

If this does not kill you
I'll try strychnine next time

Yours to a Frazzle
H. Eaton

Dorothy graduated from Flathead High School in 1918 and hired on at Eatons' Ranch for the summer. That summer turned into a lifetime relationship for Dorothy who said that her first trip to Glacier "opened up a whole new world for me." On that trip, she first met John B. Duncan, the camp manager, who was her boss.

Our friendship spanned seventeen years until "I grew up to suit him." We were married June 10, 1933, and we lived at Eatons' Ranch until his death in 1956. I continued to live at the ranch until 1966, when I moved to Sheridan, Wyoming, where I still live.

Howard did not confine his horseback camping trips to Yellowstone and Glacier. He ventured through the "Southwest Indian Country," as well. In September and October of 1914 and 1915, Howard had, as he wrote in a 1916 brochure that described a future trip:

> *... the pleasure of showing some Indian country in Arizona and New Mexico to a party of riders, many of whom had ridden through the Glacier and Yellowstone Parks with me on some of my annual excursions through those Wonderlands.*

On the Southwest trip, Howard and his party visited the Navajo, Hopi and Zuni Indians "riding and camping through their country for twenty-seven days." Then, as if that wasn't enough, they:

> *...went to the Grand Canyon of Arizona, where we spent three days, riding down the Hermit Trail, sleeping at the Hermit Camp, riding to the Bright Angel Trail, up to Hotel El Tovar and gazing at the wonders seen from the canyon's rim.*

In the prospectuses that Howard wrote to invite his friends to join him in yet another adventure, Howard was at his descriptive best. In a 1916 invitation, he penned:

> *The Grand Canyon of Arizona at El Tovar is thirteen miles wide and six thousand feet deep. It is firmly established among our natural wonders, and draws travelers from all parts of the world. It will prove a fitting close to a journey through a land of wonders.*
>
> *Think of ruins with over five hundred rooms; canyons with hundreds of cliff dwellings, high up in the rocks; tribes who still practice Sun worship; a land of witchcraft and the home of the Aboriginal Suffragette; a country high and clear; wind-swept plains, canyons, starlit nights in camp and sunny days in saddle...*

Howard's other passion was the maintenance and reintroduction of wildlife in areas where it had ceased to exist, for whatever reason. He was largely responsible, for instance, for the preservation of buffalo in Yellowstone Park and was able to place buffalo in many zoos across the United States.

He managed to gain control of part of a large herd of buffalo in about 1907 when the Flathead Indian reservation in Montana was opened for settlement, and contained what Howard described as "the last large band of buffaloes in the United States" and "one third of all the buffalo in the world." Howard was concerned that the buffalo would be "scattered to the four winds or else removed to the Blackfeet reservation farther north, or into the Milk River country of the Canadian provinces." Howard was chagrined that some of the herd did indeed go to Canada, but was consoled by the fact that he was able to purchase about four-fifths of the interest of one of the two men who owned the herd and then sell them off to cities and private individuals across the United States.

One of his customers was the United States Government, which bought two bulls and eighteen cows for the Yellowstone Park. In two years, the herd increased to forty animals and became the foundation of the buffalo herd in Yellowstone Park today.

One Denver, Colorado, newspaper described the extent of Howard's buffalo distribution effort:

> *Mr. Eaton has furnished more buffalo for the zoos and parks of North America than any other one man has. He furnished the new shipment of buffalo through his friend, W. F. Kendrick, to the City Park of Denver this season, and has supplied parks from Winnipeg to Texas, and from New York to San Francisco. Every zoo man in America knows Howard Eaton.*

Howard was rewarded for his efforts to save buffalo and distribute them across the United States for all to see. His old friend and Medora neighbor, President Theodore Roosevelt, appointed Howard to a National Park commission to "prevent the extinction of the buffalo."

Howard was also interested in elk. In 1911, Howard and his brothers

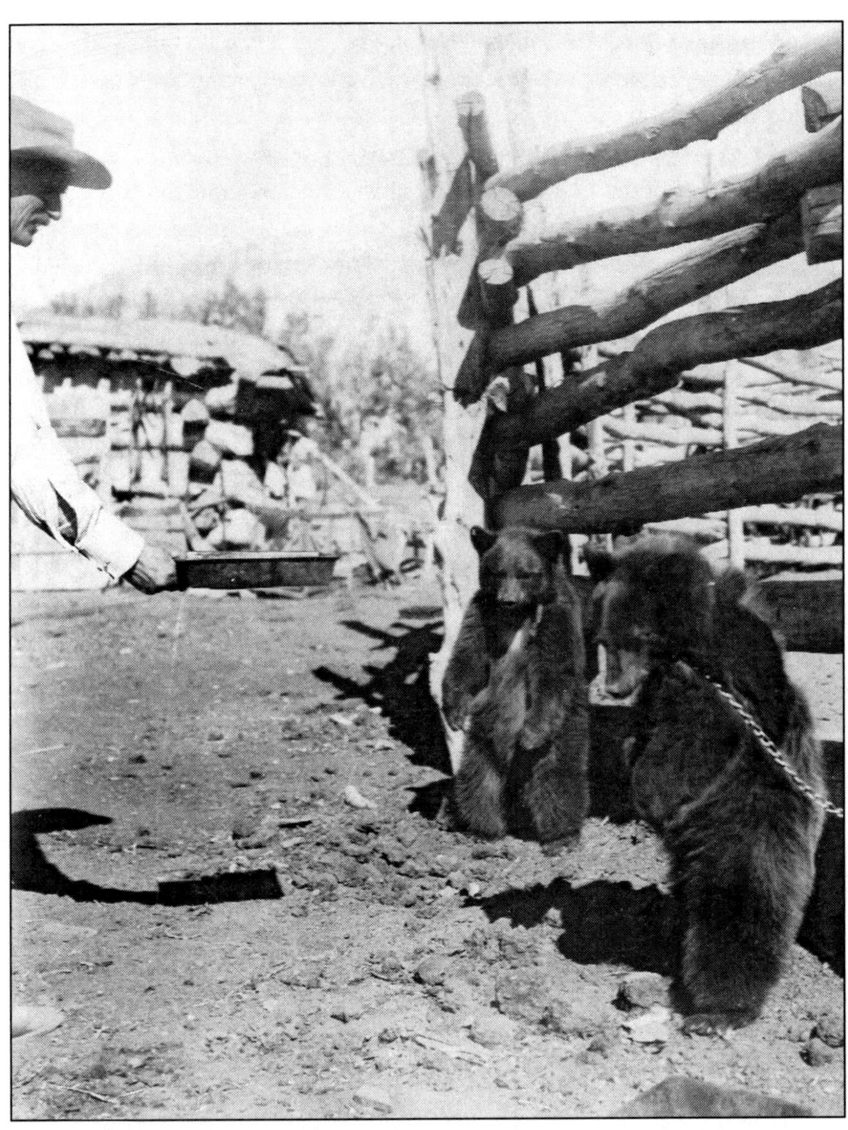

A pair of Cinnamon Bear cubs kept at Eatons' Ranch in the early days.
Courtesy of Eatons' Ranch.

Alden and Willis, took action to restore elk in the Big Horn Mountains where the animals had ceased to exist by the turn of the century. The Eatons worked closely with the Game and Fish Department and managed to secure a herd of elk that was trapped at Gardiner, Montana. The elk were shipped by train, which was met by the Eatons with a wagon for transport to the ranch. There the elk were held overnight in a corral, and then released in the mountains the next day. They repeated the exercise the next day and that was the beginning of the present elk herd in the Big Horn National Forest.

Howard also exported elk back east to his native Pennsylvania. Elk had been native to Pennsylvania, but died out, so Howard, in 1913, arranged the shipment of fifty elk (ten bulls and forty cows) from Yellowstone Park to the Pennsylvania Keystone State Forest. Howard accompanied the elk himself to make sure they arrived safely. They did, and a local newspaper reported that "…he brought them safely through without accident and the elk reached here in fine health."

Howard did not confine his wildlife efforts to just buffalo and elk. He was interested in fish as well. In 1910 or 1911, he planted thirty thousand Black Spotted Trout in the Big Horn National Forest and repeated the act in 1914. In 1915, he got notice that the fish hatchery was going to make 495,000 Trout Fry available for distribution and he requested 100,000 brook trout for planting on Wolf Creek, Soldier Creek and Little Tongue River "above the falls." In the end, he was allotted only fifty thousand fish, which he planted in the appropriate areas himself. It was a labor-intensive effort, as he had to transport the fish in iced cans by wagon and packhorse over a large area. Nevertheless, he got the job done.

In addition to large game animals and fish, Howard captured other kinds of wild animals for exhibition and sale to zoos around the country. It was a common experience for Eaton guests to encounter mountain lions, bobcats and bears either caged or tied up around the Ranch.

By 1920, Howard Eaton was sixty-nine years old and had, if one reads his press clippings, crammed several lifetimes into one. In addition, there is no doubt that he was famous throughout the United States. He was once said to have known more than ten thousand people. He was definitely a charismatic figure on the Western landscape and was described in one newspaper article as "A splendid mimic and versatile talker, well read and with a memory stored with legends and tales dear to the old-timer." Howard cut a swath wherever he went.

A colorful example of Howard's "larger than life persona" was illustrated during the First World War in a 1918 article in the *Denver Post.* It pretty much sums up the man:

Howard Eaton Would Settle Kaiser Grudge
Western Sportsman and Ranchman,
Wants to Fight the Huns

Howard Eaton, sportsman, ranchman and guide, resident of Wyoming and South Dakota for fifty years, who has conducted more than 100 tourist parties through Yellowstone and Glacier National Parks, and on hunting expeditions through Yellowstone and Glacier National Parks, and on hunting expeditions through the Rocky Mountains from Alaska to Central America, life-long pal of ex-President Roosevelt, and a personal friend of prominent members of European nobility, is 68 years old, and wants to fight the Huns.

He is a Denver visitor and declares he has a personal score to settle with the Kaiser—or the sometime German ambassador, Von Bernstorff. This is how it came about.

In 1904, Count Ernest Bernstorff and his son, Count Arthur, cousins of the ex-ambassador, came to Wyoming to inspect the Yellowstone country. Howard Eaton offered to take them and their party through the park. The trip was made. Afterwards, the noble party wanted to hunt big game, so Eaton conducted a hunting expedition for them.

Of course, he became well acquainted with them. He liked them and they liked him. So he permitted them to kill one of his largest buffalo...They parted warm friends.

Since the war, Eaton's friendship for the Bernstorff family has cooled rapidly, and his animosity has rapidly become hot. So, partly because he feels like getting even, in some way, with the Bernstorffs, but mostly because he is 100 percent patriotic,

> *Eaton went to Washington recently to see if he couldn't get into some branch of the war service, preferably abroad. But they wouldn't let him fight in the trenches because he is past the age limit, and they haven't been able to find anything for him to do on this side of the ocean.*
>
> *"I wanted them to make me a dollar-a-year man, but they said they didn't have anything for me to do. So then I told them I'd work for nothing, but they haven't given me a job yet," he said.*

That was Howard. He never went to war, but he would have, if given half the chance.

The three Eaton brothers.
From left: Howard, Willis and Alden. Circa 1920s.
Courtesy of Eatons' Ranch.

Willis and Alden were not as visible as Howard was. While Howard was away on his exploits, his two brothers stayed at home and ran the ranch.

The 1912 Eaton Ranch brochure explained how the Eaton brothers division of labor worked:

> *All the work of directing the Yellowstone Park trips rests entirely upon Howard Eaton. The management of the resort is under Willis L. Eaton. The regular ranch business—livestock, dairy, poultry, etc.—is now conducted from a separate center (2 1/2 miles from the resort proper) known as the "Lower Ranch," and is under the personal supervision of F. Alden Eaton.*

Willis was a superb host to Eaton dudes and was beloved by them all. He was the first to greet them when they arrived at the ranch. He always took the first couple of rides with newcomers to show them the trails and the lay of the land before they were allowed to ride by themselves. He was always around the corral or the living room of the main house and made himself constantly available for guidance and help.

Apparently, Willis had an eye for the ladies. According to Patty Eaton, Willis was briefly married once for two years and there were no children. There are no known records with the details of the marriage. Therefore, being single and available, Willis was not necessarily passive when it came to seeking the company of available dude women who might have an amorous bent. Willis, it is rumored, was something of "a lad."

Willis also took a drink now and then—in fact, quite often. One of his duties was to drive the Ranch stagecoach to nearby Ranchester and meet guests when they arrived by train. Apparently, Willis often got to Ranchester early and took the opportunity to socialize at a few "waterin' holes" while waiting for the train arrival. Naturally, his socializing involved "tipping a few" and so it was a fairly frequent occurrence that an exuberant Willis was a bit worse for wear when he met the guests. As a result, some of the rides back to the ranch with Willis at the reins were singularly hair-raising events that shredded the nerves of many Eaton guests.

Eatons' Stagecoach that transported guests from the train station in Ranchester.
Courtesy of Eatons' Ranch.

Alden, in addition to operating the ranch part of the Eaton Brothers enterprise, with his wife, raised their son, Bill. Bill was fourteen years old when the Eatons moved to Wolf, the only child among a sea of adults. Esther McWilliams wrote that:

> *It is interesting to speculate what it might have been like to be young Bill Eaton, the only chick growing up among all of those gracious and hospitable elders. Some teenagers would have felt obligated to rebel, but for whatever reasons, Bill did not.*

Instead, Bill took to the ranch like a duck to water and spent the rest of his life maintaining the "old traditions of hospitality" established by his father and uncles.

Nannie and Walter Alderson had four children.
Clockwise from top, Mabel, Fay, Patty and Walter. Nannie (Domo) is in the center.
Courtesy of Eatons' Ranch.

Another old tradition of the Eaton family, hunting, was imbued in him, as well. He developed into an avid hunter. He shot an elk when he was only ten years old and its mounted head still hangs on the end wall of Howard Hall.

School interrupted Bill's life at the ranch for when he arrived at Wolf he was still only fourteen years old. He may have seemed older than that because of his size. Well over six feet tall and powerfully built, Bill Eaton grew up to be an imposing figure, especially when he wore his high crowned Stetson hat. When Bill Eaton entered a room, you knew he was there.

Bill attended high school in Sheridan, eighteen miles away. It was not practical to make the round trip every day so Bill did what most kids from outlying ranches did—he boarded in Sheridan and rode home for weekends. It was while he was a student at Sheridan High School that he met his future wife, Patty Alderson.

Patty lived in Birney, Montana, sixty miles away. Like Bill, she rode into Sheridan and boarded for the week, and returned home on weekends.

Patty recounted her life many years later in an article, *Patty Eaton Reminisces*. Patty was born in 1891 on the Cheyenne Indian Reservation in southern Montana, not far from the Wyoming border, on a place called Muddy Creek. Her parents were Nannie Tiffany and Walter Alderson.

Nannie's husband had arrived in Montana with a trail herd from Texas some years before and decided to homestead on Muddy Creek. It was there he brought his young bride, Nannie Tiffany, from West Virginia to set up housekeeping one hundred miles from Miles City in a log cabin with a dirt floor.

When Patty arrived on the scene, her mother had already given birth to her two sisters, Mabel and Fay, who apparently were terribly disappointed that Patty was a girl. Patty recounts the scene: "Mother said they had to watch me closely as Mabel and Fay did not like me and would pinch me when Mama wasn't looking."

However, the sisters' prayers were answered two years later when their brother was born. Patty wrote that:

> *...my sisters were so delighted that Fay wrote to Albert Brown at Birney and said, "Dear Albert. We have a little brother. His name is Walter. He is a boy." Mrs. Brown kept that letter from Fay for years."*

After the hard life on Muddy Creek, the Aldersons moved to Miles City so Patty's sisters could attend school. Patty's first recollections were of Miles City where they lived until she was ten years old. Unfortunately, her recollections included the memory of a tragedy. In 1895, a horse kicked her father in the head and killed him.

Left on her own with four children and living in a rented house, Nannie took some of the money she had from Walter's insurance and built her family a house. To make a living, Nannie took in boarders and because she was, according to Patty, a "wonderful cook," she also served dinner at night to her boarders and others, including Mr. L. A. Huffman, the well-known photographer and his wife. She also cooked lunch for the schoolchildren of army officers at nearby Fort Keogh and catered for the local Masonic Lodge when they had dinners.

The upshot of it all was, according to Patty, that "Mama was working very hard and not making a dime. All her friends told her she was putting all her money in her boarders' stomachs because she fed them so well."

Something had to change, and it did when Captain Brown of the Three Circle Ranch and Mr. Brewster of the Quarter Circle U Ranch at Birney, Montana, made her an offer. Nannie and the children had spent the summers since Walter's death at the Three Circle Ranch and so the Birney community was acquainted with Nannie. Brown and Brewster asked Nannie to move to Birney, start up a store, and be postmistress at the Birney Post Office.

Nannie, as usual, worked very hard to run the store and cope with the mail. All the children pitched in and helped her. Patty had fond memories of her time in Birney:

> *...Some of the happiest years of my life were spent in Birney. I grew up with the three Brown children, Albert, Joe and Natalie. Natalie and I were devoted friends, and loved to go to the Three Circle Roundup when it was anywhere near.*

Patty and Natalie would:

> *...leave early in the morning and get to the round up before they had dinner, and ride home after supper in the long evenings. Mr. Brown was always nice to us and seemed glad to see us, as were the cowboys who worked for him, but Albert and Joe were not so pleased and would always say, "There are those darned kids again.*

Patty never mentioned it, but others testified that Patty was a useful hand around a ranch and unafraid of hard work:

> *Although she never learned to rope or to ride a rough bucking horse, Patty did everything else. She pitched hay, built fence and worked in the corral holding down colts or calves for branding.*

According to Patty's mother, her brother Walter said, "...she was the best hand on a horse I ever saw for a lady, though she was a little wild." The fact that Patty was, like her mother, a tiny person (they each weighed less than one hundred pounds) did not deter her or her mother from hard labor. Esther McWilliams wrote, "...they both worked hard and long at whatever needed to be done, and both managed to stay completely feminine and dainty through all of it."

Patty attended her first year of high school at Birney school, which was unusual because normally eighth grade was the highest grade taught. However, when the regular teacher quit, the replacement had the qualifications to teach the first year of high school and offered to do so for Patty if she wanted to stay in Birney. Patty said that, "I always thought he was the best teacher I ever had."

By the time Patty finished her first year of high school, her sisters Mabel and Fay had moved from home. It was then that Nannie and Walter bought a small ranch on Young's Creek, not far from the Crow Reservation, but still in Montana and about eighteen miles from Sheridan. It was also close to the ranch that Mabel and her Eastern husband had bought. Nannie and Walter made this decision because, once again,

Nannie, who had no head for business, was not making a living. Patty wrote that:

> *...Mama had foolishly given credit to a lot of people who never paid, and she left Birney and the store, with thousands of dollars on the books that she never collected a dime for. Mama was no businesswoman and was too trusting of too many people.*

In addition, her son, Walter, had become old enough to help his mother on a ranch. He had worked for Mr. Brown on the 3 Circle Ranch as a horse wrangler and had turned into a "real hand."

Patty hated to leave Birney and her friends for Young's Creek but she learned to love it and it gave her fond memories. She wrote:

> *We were always poor but we had a very happy childhood and my mother always made all of my friends welcome. She had built a large living room on the small house that was on the place when we bought it and we used to have wonderful country-dances, as the room was big enough for two sets of square dancers. People came from miles around in buggies, spring wagons or on horseback and we danced from seven in the evening until daylight the next morning as people could not go home until it got light and there was no place they could sleep. My mother was wonderful and a great worker, though she was just five feet tall and never weighed more than one hundred pounds in her life. She would have supper for the people when they arrived, and again at midnight and always gave them breakfast before they left. She said she hated to make sandwiches but thought nothing of making biscuits for fifty to seventy-five people. Now I don't know how she did it, but at the time, we just took it for granted.*

Patty continued her high school education as a sophomore in Sheridan. Young's Creek was only eighteen miles from Sheridan, but she still had to board in Sheridan during the week. The first family she boarded with was well off, but miserly, and worked Patty very hard. Patty resentfully remembered, "They were the only people I ever knew who would cut a fried egg in two for breakfast, and as I scorned eating only half an egg, I went to school hungry." Later, Patty's circumstances improved when she boarded with a friend's family who treated her decently.

Patty's mother allowed her to keep a horse in town although Patty doesn't know how her mother managed to do it. She wrote:

> *I don't know how my mother let me have a horse in town, as we were always poor, but I did have one and kept him at Mr. Boot Power's Livery Stable.* (Note: This was across the street from the Western Hotel.) *Bill rode in from the ranch at Wolf, and since we both had horses, that is how we met.*

Bill and Patty developed a close friendship and maintained it even though they did date other people. Patty once reflected that she sometimes thought back to all of the other boys she was sure that she was crazy about at the time, and thanked her lucky stars she didn't marry any of them.

The spring of Patty's third year in high school, Bill invited her to a dance at Eatons' Ranch. That was her first visit and she remembered that:

> *...He came for me in a spring wagon and I spent the weekend there and met all of the family for the first time. They were always lovely to me. That was the beginning of many visits to Eatons. For several years, Bill would ride the thirty-five miles through the hills to Young's Creek to see me. He would leave after work and would visit until about midnight, then ride home to get there in time to wrangle the horses before breakfast. Mama would never allow us to have company late, but she liked Bill and felt he came such a long way that she made an exception for him.*

(Note: Patty went on to graduate from high school, but Bill did not graduate. Perhaps it was because of his "schedule." According to one source, Bill's school schedule was to ride into Sheridan on Monday, attend school on Tuesday, play pool on Wednesday, attend school on Thursday, and ride home on Friday.)

For some reason, in her reminiscences, Patty did not mention a freak accident that happened to Bill on one of his visits to see her. However, Esther McWilliams discussed it in her book:

On one of Bill's trips, he and Walt Alderson were planning to go to the Cheyenne Indian Reservation to buy ponies. They intended to go the following day, and in the meantime, there were colts in the corral to be broken. Bill was about nineteen years old and was an excellent rider. He had just finished riding a colt, and everyone was sitting in a row on the corral fence, including a neighbor boy who had been out hunting prairie chickens. The boy tied his horse to the fence and propped his 12-gauge shotgun against it. The horse pulled back and somehow the gun exploded. The shot went up through Bill's leg and face.

Walt leapt down and grabbed the boy's horse to go for the doctor while the rest of them helped Bill walk to the house. He was covered with blood, but made it under his own power. No one really knew what to do for him, but they bedded him down on the couch in the living room and applied towels wrung out in the ice-cold spring water. The doctor later said they couldn't have done a better thing.

Bud nearly killed the horse, as he had to ride twelve miles uphill and down to Monarch for the nearest doctor, but when he arrived, the doctor was gone. So he rode to Kearneyville (afterward called Kleenburn, which isn't there anymore, either) before he found a doctor. The horse was worthless after the long ride. The next challenge was that the doctor had a buggy with only one horse, making the long ride on a rough road even longer. He went as quickly as he could, but it was hours and hours before he reached the ranch. When the doctor arrived, he did what he could, dressing and bandaging the wounds to stop the bleeding. There wasn't any electricity, so Patty held the lamp. It was a gruesome sight, and she was only eighteen. After a bit, the lamp began to wobble and she had to give it up. She almost fainted but managed to hold it together. Bill was a big, husky young man, and because he was in such fine physical condition, he pulled through in spite of the loss of blood.

Eventually, Bill's parents, Alden and Aunt Mame, were notified and after a long and arduous journey were able to get Bill to Sheridan and into the hands of a fine surgeon. McWilliams wrote that:

...he did the best repair job he could. Bill's jaw had been broken, and the whole side of his face was gone. The doctor said just a sixteenth of an inch farther and the shot would have hit his jugular vein. Bill had some buckshot left in his face all his life, although they took out quite a lot. The leg wound was not serious, except for the loss of blood.

There are other versions of this episode. Notably, *The Sheridan Post* reported that the doctor journeyed by car from Sheridan. However, the important thing is that Bill did recover, but was left deaf in one ear.

Bill and Patty were married October 28, 1914, at Aunt Hattie's house in Sheridan at 231 West Loucks. Patty was twenty-three and Bill was twenty-four. In preparation for their marriage, the Eatons built them a nice house not far from the main buildings, but, as Patty wrote, "...Bill was only getting $50.00 a month, so we didn't have any money for a honeymoon. Nevertheless, they did have a honeymoon, which Patty described:

That summer, Uncle Howard Eaton had lost three horses when they went through Yellowstone. A friend at Mammoth had found them and put them in a pasture, so Bill and I went to get them. We took the train to Gardiner, picked up the horses and rode them home. I rode the same horse all the way but Bill would ride one and lead the other. It was November, but we were very lucky and had beautiful weather, and enjoyed every minute of the trip.

In another more detailed account, Patty related how they suffered a two-day delay during the trip because of a snowstorm and how awful the food was in a hotel in Big Timber, Montana. She wrote:

Bill Eaton in World War I uniform.
Courtesy of Eatons' Ranch.

I will never forget the dining room or the food. Both Bill and I were big butter eaters, and the butter was so strong we expected any minute to see it walk off the table! And the rest of the food was just as bad, but we did stay over a day, as we were in no hurry to get home, and the weather was beautiful. And, after all, we WERE on our HONEYMOON.

When they returned from their honeymoon, Bill and Patty settled down to life on the ranch. In the next few years, they would have two children. Their son, William Alden Eaton, Jr. (Billy) was born in 1917 and their daughter Nancy Jane Eaton was born on February 28, 1921.

There was one occasion during this period when Patty and Bill were separated for a time and that was when Bill served in the Army during the First World War. When Bill tried to enlist, he was turned down because of the injuries he'd received from the accidental shooting. Still, Bill was determined to serve and so his Uncle Howard intervened by traveling to Washington. He prevailed upon his friend, the famous writer Mary Roberts Rinehart, who had been on Glacier Park trips with him, and she was able to use her influence so that Bill could enlist.

Bill entered the service on April 1, 1918 at age twenty-seven. He was assigned to the 308th Ammunition Train, sailed overseas in May, and saw frontline action in the Meuse-Argonne offensive and elsewhere. For several months after the close of the war, he served with the American Expeditionary Force. Bill was discharged on May 16, 1919. He returned to the Ranch, where he lived the rest of his life.

The Pelissier family from Medora, North Dakota, Peter and the Eaton sister Hattie and their three children, Willis, Elsie and Mary, eventually followed the Eatons to the Sheridan area.

Mary first visited the Eatons at Wolf when she was only thirteen years old. Willis visited when he was seventeen in 1905 and Elsie did not visit until she was seventeen in 1907. At the time, Elsie listed her residence in the Eaton guest book as Dickinson, North Dakota, where she attended business college.

Peter and Hattie visited Hattie's brothers at the Eaton Ranch about 1909 and then made a permanent move to Sheridan in 1913. What prompted the move is not really known, but the most likely reasons

Bill Eaton confers with his father, Alden, on left, and his Uncle Howard.
Circa 1920.
Courtesy of Eatons' Ranch.

were that ranching business in North Dakota turned sour and Peter was not very stable as a provider.

Many years later, Angela Buell, a long time employee of Eatons' Ranch, observed, "Uncle Pete was a professional gambler, and horse trader, and they lived sort of a 'feast or famine' life." When Pete and Hattie moved to Sheridan, they rented a house at 231 West Loucks. Later, in 1919, the Eaton brothers bought the house for Hattie to give her some security. According to Angela Buell they "did many other things for her" as well to help the family survive.

Whether or not all the children went with them at the same time is uncertain. But they all did eventually move to Sheridan. In 1914, their son Willis married Ethel Bryan in Soldiers Grove, Wisconsin and then moved to Sheridan where their first son, George P. Pelissier, was born on May 27. They had a second son, Willis E. Pelissier, ten years later on February 26, 1924. Willis worked at Eatons' Ranch until the mid-1920s.

By 1914, Elsie was working in Sheridan as assistant clerk of the district court, a position she held until 1918, which turned out to be a challenging year for her. Unfortunately, Elsie, who was not married, became pregnant. She escaped public scrutiny by taking a leave of absence to Billings, Montana, where her son, Jack M. Pelissier, was born on July 5, 1918.

Elsie covered up the whole episode by inventing the story that she adopted the child. It worked, because it was not until many years later that the truth came out. Indeed, her son Jack did not learn of his birth status until much later.

With her reputation intact, and a new son to support, Elsie made a bold move and decided to run for the office of clerk of district court. She was well qualified for the office. The local press wrote that Elsie was an "…efficient deputy—thoroughly familiar in every way with duties—expert stenographer—trained in many duties of that office." Elsie won the election and held that office for the next six years.

Elsie's sister Mary worked as secretary to J.J. Early, the superintendent of schools, for several years until she married Roy Haywood, a miner, on September 10, 1920. Coincidentally, some years later, Mary followed in her sister's footsteps, and was elected clerk of the district court.

During this period, from 1904 to 1920, the Eaton Ranch on Wolf Creek was a popular visiting place for members of the extended Eaton family and many of them signed the guest book multiple times through the years. Frequent visitors were the Browns (Aunt Mame's relatives) from Kingwood, West Virginia, and an Eaton sister, Alice D. McFarlane (Aunt Lizzie) and her family. Charles Eaton, the brother who had been with Howard at Medora at the beginning, visited in 1917.

Some family members visited Eatons' and never left. Aunt Mame's sister, Minnie Reid, went for a visit and stayed on as the Ranch housekeeper for years. The one with the longest tenure was the Eaton sister Mary (Aunt

Mary.) She and her daughter Josephine (Cousin Josie) visited the ranch once for two weeks. They liked it so much that they decided to make their home there. Aunt Mary lived there until she died in 1935. Aunt Mary was quite well off, financially, and could have lived any place she wanted, but Eatons' was the place she loved. Aunt Mary and her daughter, Cousin Josie, traveled all over the world, but when they weren't traveling, they were home at the Eaton Ranch.

In 1919, another family member came to spend the rest of her days at the Ranch. That was Patty's mother, Nannie Alderson, known to all as "Domo," (a name she supposedly acquired when a grandchild mispronounced her name). Domo explained the circumstances surrounding her move when she wrote in her book *A Bride Goes West*:

> *The end of ranching for me came in 1919. That was the terrible year of the drought and the crash, which spelled disaster for so many in our country. Walter had built up our herd, by 1917, to 250 cattle, and after that, under the influence of the war boom, we had bought seven hundred head on money borrowed from the bank. When the market dropped, we lost them all, and everything else with them.*
>
> *And so we were broke again. It was hard for Walter to lose what he had worked so hard to build up, but he was young, and he still had his life ahead of him. While as for me, I was sixty years old, and I'd been broke so many times before that, I could face it. When you have lived without money as much as I had, it loses a great deal of its power to hurt you.*
>
> *Besides, all my children were married now except Fay, and she was teaching, and I had no one but myself to worry over. Instead of worrying, I went to live with Patty on Eatons' Ranch...*

Domo lived there for the rest of her life until she died in 1947 at age eighty-seven.

Employees

Over the years, thousands of employees have worked at Eatons' Ranch. Many were transitory and only worked for a season, or maybe a few seasons. Indeed, there have been instances where an employee worked for only a few hours or days before either the employee or management decided that the fit was not a good one.

But in the early years of the Eatons' operation on Wolf Creek, when the dude season really lasted all year long, there were opportunities for year round employment. Many employees went to work for the Eaton brothers and literally found a home. Many worked there year round for decades and others worked there for decades but only during the summer season. In many cases, the employees were treated more like family than employees and the employees equaled the sentiment with unstinting loyalty to the Eatons.

In 1981, Esther McWilliams chronicled some of the early employees when she wrote, "The list of the faithful begins with Uncle Billy, who came to Wyoming from North Dakota with the Eaton brothers." Esther quoted Patty Eaton who said that Billy was:

> *...a little bit of an old Englishman that Uncle Howard picked out of a snowdrift in North Dakota when he was half frozen to death. We never knew how old he was or even what his last name was. He worked here until he died.* (Note: Exact date is unknown.) *In the early days, the Ranch had chickens, ducks and pigs, even guinea hens and peacocks, and they always had pet deer or some bears or mountain lions and things like that. Uncle Billy cared for all of those animals.*

At the same time, in 1904, John Fleming arrived from North Dakota with the Eaton brothers and, as has been discussed previously, spent his entire life with the Eatons until he died in 1943. John married a woman named Mae, but no details about their marriage are available. They did have a son named John Alden Fleming, who was named after his father and Alden Eaton. John was born in approximately 1915.

Then McWilliams mentions Emil Jacobs who came from Nebraska in 1908. She wrote that:

> *He is the one who holds the record for being employed for the longest time.* (Note: The exact duration of Emil's employment at Eatons' is not available.) *Big Bill said when he picked Emil up at the train station, he had on bib overalls and a derby hat and was a farmer boy who didn't know anything about riding. Apparently, the long ride from Sheridan just about killed him off.*

In 1911, Tommy Butler arrived at the Ranch and stayed until 1966, a period of fifty-five years. Tommy was a "jack of all trades" and eventually performed just about every job on the Ranch. His first job was as a waiter and he had one experience that illustrated how important it was to the Eatons that the ranch atmosphere be one of "we're all friends here." McWilliams related the story:

> *Tommy told about one guest who came and was "shooting orders" in a most autocratic way, treating Tommy like a servant. Tommy resented it, but wasn't too sure how to cope with it, so he went to Uncle Howard. Howard went up to the guest, put his arm around his shoulders and said, "We understand you don't like the atmosphere of Eatons' too well. If you need any help packing, I'll come along down and do it for you." The guest sputtered in surprise, apologized and stayed on to become a valued friend.*

Tommy's wife Anna also worked at the ranch and was in charge of housekeeping until they retired. His brother Jeff served as the baker for a number of years.

John "Dunc" Duncan went to work full time at Eatons' in 1912 when he was forty years old, but before that had worked for them on and off as an independent guide and also helped to build Howard Hall in 1911.

John loved the outdoors. He had arrived in Wyoming with his parents in 1899 and returned to Colorado, where he was born, to attend Colorado A&M at Fort Collins. After school, he worked for a number of cattle companies in Wyoming.

In 1903, Dunc became the first deputy game warden in Sheridan County. He held this position for eight years. One of his biggest achievements was bringing a herd of twenty-eight elk to the area in 1910 after the elk herd in the Paintrock and Shell Creek areas near Cloud Peak was wiped out by winter storms. The elk were trapped in Yellowstone Park, where they were starving, brought to Sheridan by sleighs, wagons and railroad on a trip that lasted for nineteen days. After the elk were rested in Kendrick Park in Sheridan, they were released and wandered behind the ranch, up South Red Canyon and into the Big Horns. Howard Eaton was heavily involved in this exercise, and usually gets most of the credit.

As described earlier, Dunc met Dorothy Dodge on a Howard Eaton pack trip to Glacier Park when she was sixteen years old. They later married and spent the rest of their lives at Eatons'.

John had a whimsical nature. Sometime during this period, with the approval of the Eatons, he established the "John Duncan School for Riding." While the instruction was most certainly serious, the brochure that advertised the school was most certainly not. John referred to himself as "Professor John Duncan" and other members of the ranch family as "Riding Professors" and "Associate Professors." One section of the brochure described special lessons as follows:

Special Etiquetical Lessons

How to ride with your wife
Associate Prof. Hon. F. Alden Eaton
How to ride when with some other man's wife
Associate Prof. Hon. Howard Eaton

How to ride with your fiancée
Prof. William Eaton
How to ride with your would be fiancé
Associate Prof. Hon. Willis Eaton

Dunc's humor extended to the advertised rates. For example, with tongue in cheek he wrote:

Children, age 1 day to 2 years with nurse (good looking) 9¢ per hour.

Children 4 to 6 years of age ...not taken.

Young ladies, 16 to 20 years of age...lessons free mornings

Young ladies, 20 to 30...free at any time

Tenderfeet (Know it all)...$100.27 per hour

Cranks...Absolutely barred

Harry Fulmer worked at Eatons' for years. He didn't make Eatons' his life's work, but did keep up a lifetime acquaintance. Harry first worked at Eatons' in 1911 as the corral boss. Patty Eaton said that Harry went to work there the day after he graduated from high school. Harry was born on April 22, 1891, on the PK Ranch where his father was foreman. The PK Ranch was established in 1876 and is "just down the road" from Eatons'. It is now called the Cato Ranch. At one time, Harry was also the PK Ranch foreman.

The first year that Harry worked at Eatons' he met Margaret Scully, a dude from Philadelphia. This must have been one of the first "dude ranch romances" for Harry and Margaret were married on January 27, 1915. Margaret's circumstances enabled them to acquire and operate ranches in southern Montana and Northern Wyoming until 1956 when they retired and moved to Big Horn, Wyoming. Margaret died one year before Harry. Just before Harry died in 1972, he donated

$300,000 towards construction of a new public library in memory of his wife. In her honor, the library was originally named the Margaret S. Fulmer Memorial County Library.

Angela Buell was another employee who virtually dedicated most of her life to the Eatons. Angela was born in Whiteside, Illinois on October 3, 1897 but sometime after that, her family moved to Sheridan and lived on Big Goose Creek. She hired on at Eatons' when she was twenty-two years old in 1919.

Angela left Eatons' in 1958 when she was sixty-one years old and had been an Eaton employee for thirty-nine years. Through her many years at Eatons', Angela would prove to be a pivotal person in the operation of Eatons' as an understudy to John Fleming and when he died, she and Tommy Butler assumed his duties. Angela was also the long-time editor of *Wranglin' Notes* from the mid-1920s.

Julia Segoski's career with Eatons' began in 1914 when she was only fifteen years old. She only worked at Eatons' during the summer season. In the winter, she worked in Sheridan at the J. C. Penney store. Julia became an institution because of her compelling supervision of the dining room and staff. One article written about the ranch in 1943 said that Julia was:

> *...now in charge of guest seating in the dining room and known from coast to coast. No one on the place would think of usurping Julia's right to ring the dinner gong, a huge steel tire from a locomotive wheel sent to the Eatons by a guest, a railroad executive.*

George Gentry went to work at Eatons' because he met Bill Eaton during the First World War. George was a Nebraska boy who found his way to Big Horn, Wyoming, where he trained polo ponies for the Gallatin Ranch. George enlisted in the Army and crossed paths with Bill Eaton. Bill Eaton apparently said, "If we come through this alive, George is going to come and take over the corral." Well, they did get through it alive. George never went overseas and spent most of the war at Fort Lewis,

Washington while Bill was in France. But, when the war was over and George was discharged in 1919, he went to Eatons' and worked there during a large part of the year for over fifty years.

Curly Witzel also arrived on the scene during this period. Curly, whose real name was Erwin Fay, was nicknamed "Curly," because of his curly hair. He was born in South Dakota but his family moved to Broadview, Montana, where he was raised. When he was eighteen, in 1918, he took a job at the PK Ranch, but by 1920 had moved to Eatons' where he learned to ride saddle broncs. Curly worked at Eatons' off and on during the next seventeen years. When he wasn't working at Eatons' he found time to compete in rodeos, work in motion pictures, and become an accomplished aviator. Curly would have a connection with Eatons', in one way or another, for the rest of his life.

Arthur "Pete" Dailey was another early employee. His life became intertwined with Eatons' Ranch over a period of sixty years. Pete was born in Omaha, Nebraska and first appeared on the Eatons' employee rolls on June 23, 1912. It was quite by accident. According to McWilliams, Pete was attending the University of Illinois and majoring in journalism. Eatons' had hired four boys to work in the dining room as waiters, but one of them dropped out and Pete took his place. Pete would eventually hold about every job from waiter to wrangler and would later be a seasoned dude as well as world-renowned photographer, advertising executive, author and radio personality in Chicago.

Many others worked at Eatons' for significant periods and they are too numerous to mention here. But during the first years of the Eaton operation at Wolf, from about 1904 to 1920, there were some notable people—John Fleming, Tommy Butler, John Duncan, Angela Buell, and George Gentry—who devoted their lives to the Eatons and were like family. These people provided constancy, continuity, corporate memory and guidance for the new generations of the Eaton family as they took their rightful places in the Eaton Brothers Corporation.

Dudes

After the Eatons moved to Wolf, their faithful followers didn't desert them. Rather many of them just bought a train ticket to a different destination and continued their association with the Eatons at Wolf.

Many families who visited Eatons' during this period would still be represented by family members on the Eatons' Guest List decades and generations later. For example, many families that visited Eatons' between 1904 and 1920 were represented by descendents on the 1952 guest list. Those 1952 guests and the year a family member was first a guest at Eatons' are:

Mr. and Mrs. B. Botsford Young, Lake Forest, Ill (1909)
Mr. and Mrs. Howard Butcher, Jr. Ardmore, Pa. (1909)
Mrs. Julian Hill and Jeff, Wilmington, Del. (1910)
Mr. and Mrs. Charles Buffum Jr., Charles III and Sally, Louisiana, Mo (1915)
Mr. and Mrs. Howard Butcher III, Howard IV, McBee and Jonathan, Villanova, Pa. (1916)
Mr. and Mrs. W.S. Stimmel Jr. and Billy, Pittsburgh, Pa. (1917)
Mrs. Dorothy Douglas, Wolf, Wy. (1918)
Mr. and Mrs. Thomas H. Graham and Annie Laurie, Evanston, Ill (1919)
Mr. and Mrs. Dewey Ericsson and Becky, Chicago, Ill (1919)

Several families that make their annual, or at least periodic, pilgrimage to Eatons' Ranch today (2010) can trace their family connection to the early days at Wolf. One of those is the Young family from the Chicago area, who now has a fifth generation that enjoys Eatons' Ranch.

It all started when Mr. and Mrs. Caryl B. Young and their son, Botsford Young, from Chicago, signed the guest book on July 1, 1909. Their grandson, Bots Young, recalled in his revised memoirs in 2008 (ninety-nine years later) that:

> *They had survived a three day train trip from Chicago, and were met (probably by Alden Eaton) at Ranchester. The Eaton Stage (still owned by the Ranch, and displayed during Sheridan Day parades), headed for the Ranch on Wolf Creek Road, past Shreve's, past Kane Ranch until it arrived at the Main Gate…On to the final destination, the Gazebo where today's covered phone is near the main house, to receive greetings from old friends, new friends, and surely members of the family. Everyone on the ranch turned out to meet and greet new guests. Grandmother and Grandfather first stayed in an old Army platform tent located on The Pike…Patty Eaton once reported to Annie and I* [sic] *that Grandmother was a popular guest because she cooked little cookies and cakes on a coal stove in their tent and was always passing them out for treats…*

The Youngs returned often in subsequent years and later their son, Bennett Botsford, returned with their children, Botsford Jr. (Bots) and Montgomery (Monte) as early as 1937. In turn, Bots and Monte worked at Eatons' in their early years. Bots met his wife, Annie, at Eatons' and they brought their children and their grandchildren to Eatons'. They still do. Many of the children, and grandchildren, not only are dudes, but worked at Eatons' as well. Eatons' is a family tradition for the Young family from Chicago.

The Rinehart family from Pittsburgh also established a generational relationship with Eatons' Ranch. Dr. Stanley Marshall Rinehart first signed the Eaton guest book on July 9, 1916. Not only was he a physician, he was also a partner in the New York publishing firm of Farrar and Rinehart.

Dr. Rinehart was accompanied by his wife and two sons. His wife was Mary Roberts Rinehart, a nurse, who, by that time claimed some fame as a writer even while she worked in her husband's medical practice and raised their children.

As mentioned before, Mary Roberts Rinehart accompanied Howard Eaton on a pack trip through Glacier Park the first year the Rinehart family visited Eatons' and wrote an entire book about her experience. In addition, her close association with the Eaton Ranch provided ample fodder for many future articles in prominent magazines. Her family remained Eaton devotees for several future generations. In recognition of her loyalty to the Eatons', the cabin in which she stayed, and which had an extra room built on for her maid, was named the Rinehart Cabin.

Mary Roberts Rinehart.
Courtesy of Eatons' Ranch.

Probably the greatest differences between the dudes of today and those of this period were that in the latter they stayed longer and rode farther. For instance, McWilliams wrote that:

> *In 1908 and 1909, and for a number of years thereafter, there were fifteen to twenty-five dudes at the Ranch during the winter months. The Pike and Rotten Row, which were then about the only cabins, were almost as active as midsummer. There may have been some competition as to who should shut the windows, start the fire and break the ice in the water pitcher in the mornings, but everyone had a good time riding almost every day. They also helped with the feeding and the work around the corral...For a long time there was a major upheaval every fall because the main dining room was transferred into what is now the sunroom of the main ranch house, and the huge kitchen range and sinks were transferred to the front room of the main house.*

And they definitely rode farther:

> *The guests used to ride much farther and harder than they do now during their stays at Eatons'. Of course, everyone traveled by horse in those days so were already used to horses, and that made a difference. Many times, the guests rode into town, had lunch and rode back to the Ranch again in the afternoon. They organized long rides up to Custer's Battlefield, Buffalo or across the mountain to the Basin country. Often they went on to Tepee Lodge or to Horton's, and those ranches came to Eatons' at times, even the entire Ranch would visit for "play days." The things they dreamed up for entertainment were something to see. Musical Chairs on horseback can be quite exciting! Guests were often invited to local ranches for lunch or dinner, and they took more and longer pack trips. They used to go to all of the famous spots in the mountains such as Solitude Lake, Geneva Pass, and Medicine Wheel. One group stayed on a pack trip for fourteen days. Harry*

McCormack and his Roughriders were pretty vain about how much ground they could cover. They often rode eighteen to twenty miles in a morning and were back for lunch...Of course, the land was more open then—there weren't as many fences, roads or closed-off places.

Esther McWilliams also told one story that was more typical than some would like to believe:

There used to be a place in Dayton called Mrs. Temple's. It wasn't a regular restaurant, but one could get a party together, call to make arrangements and she would feed the people great dinners. She had a specialty called tipsy pudding that she put port and sherry into, and it was the guests' favorite dessert. She also made a dandelion wine that was really something. It was quite a thing to ride over there for dinner and come back by moonlight, but now and then, something would happen. Once they went over and forgot about the eclipse of the moon, and on the way home, it got so dark that a rider couldn't see the horse's ears. The boys had to break the people up into small groups and keep in touch by voice...

Tommy Butler told about a time where there were fifteen or so in the party, and they got more than a little high on that dandelion wine. It started to rain that night, too, and was black. One of the guests was an opera singer from Chicago, and after they had been riding for a while, they realized she was missing. Tommy told them all to wait right where they were while he went back to hunt for her. He found her back a bit, lying on the ground by a little stream. She had just rolled off her horse and was lying there peacefully. He got her back onto her horse, but when he got back to where the rest were supposed to be, they weren't there. Henry Leyendecker had decided he knew the way home and took off. Tommy found them eventually, headed up toward the mountain just as he expected they would go. He and Henry got into a big argument about which was the right way to go, and each thought the other was wrong. They wandered all over the country until about two o'clock in the morning when they should have been in at least four hours sooner. It was quite a night. Tommy said there wasn't anybody waiting up for them, though, because if one of the boys was with the guests, nobody got worried...they just figured the guests would be taken care of. When that group of guests returned so late, they all threw their saddles down on the cement and stalked off to bed.

That's how it was in the early days of Eatons' at Wolf...

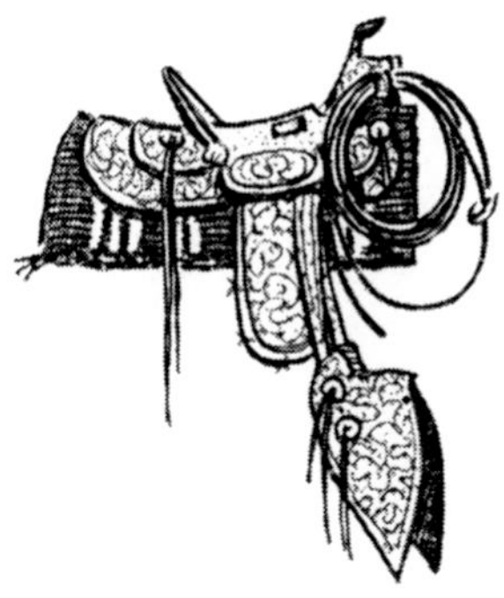

CHAPTER 5

The Twenties

Ranch Business

The Eaton brothers were meticulous about holding and documenting necessary corporate meetings. At their first one of the decade, on January 5, 1920, they elected officers: Howard Eaton, president; W. L. Eaton, vice president and treasurer; and F. A. Eaton, secretary. During the meeting, they gave a ten percent pay raise to themselves as well as John Fleming, Tommy Butler, John Duncan, Bill Eaton and Willis Pelissier and allowed them to use the wholesale buying power of the business to reduce their living expenses. The directors also extended John Fleming's appointment as business manager for another year.

John Fleming continued to be the central point for ranch management, and gained so much confidence from the Eaton brothers, that in 1921 they called a special meeting, to offer him a four-year contract as general manager. The contract gave him sweeping powers for every aspect of ranch management as well as his salary, room and board. They also awarded him an increasing percentage of net profits. John continued to hold quiet sway over the management of the Eaton Brothers Corporation for the next twenty-two years.

The action to give John Fleming so much authority was prompted by a letter from the Sheridan Banking Company to the Eaton Brothers in March 1921. Essentially, the letter said, "it has been our pleasure to continue through these years a pleasant and satisfactory business relationship." However, the letter suggested that if the relationship were to continue then the Eaton Brothers, Inc. should do two things: centralize responsibility and form a voting trust of those who owned 51% of the company stock.

For unspecified reasons, the Sheridan Banking Company believed that the Eatons needed to tighten up their operation. They obliged. They gave John Fleming centralized authority and formed a voting trust which consisted of the three Eaton brothers and John Fleming.

The Sheridan Banking Company asked for the voting trust because the list of stockholders by this time had extended beyond the three Eaton brothers. Others either had been gifted stock or were allowed to buy it. The stockholders and amount of stock they owned in 1921 were, in addition to the Eaton brothers, John Fleming (90), Bill Eaton (26), Tommy Butler (3), Willis Pelissier (3), F. B. Nimick (10) and Henry Hall (2).

Throughout the decade, there would be other corporate challenges and the Eatons would be required to make several administrative and policy changes to cope with the situation.

Uncle Howard Dies

On April 5, 1922, Howard Eaton died. He was seventy-one years, one month and twenty-seven days of age and the first of the nine Eaton Siblings to die. The local newspaper, *The Sheridan Post,* proclaimed:

ONE OF NATURE'S NOBLEMEN IS DEAD

Howard Eaton, Sportsman, Hunter
and Lover of All Out-of Doors, Dead;
Was More Widely Known
Than Possibly Any Man in Western Country

"One of Nature's Noblemen"—when that phrase was invented, the sage who framed it must have had in mind Howard Eaton, for no term more aptly describes the man, and no man does it more fitly describe.

Rancher, ranger and Boniface, he claimed no high position, but dignified every avocation in which he might engage. When gathered around the campfire or before the open grate as an entertainer and raconteur, his wit and wisdom won him admirers, but his real friends, those who loved him in life and now venerate his memory, are those who knew him, and those who knew him best loved him best...

Howard died of peritonitis. He took ill March 21 and was admitted to Sheridan County Memorial Hospital, where he underwent an operation for appendicitis. He did not recover. Funeral services were conducted in Sheridan before his body was sent to Pittsburgh for cremation.

The newspaper also noted that Howard was a member of Sheridan Lodge No. 8, A.F & A. M., a member of Kalif Temple and a member of Sheridan Lodge, BPOE. No. 520.

Howard received tributes from all quarters. Charlie Russell, the

"Cowboy Artist" and one of Howard's greatest friends, wrote:

> *Like one of the big hills he loved and lived in, he was the West. His trail was plain and clear, and no man could backtrack him to a crooked place. Many men cache their sins, but those who raised a cache that Uncle Howard made found it filled with kindness.*

Another old friend was George Bird Grinnell, who wrote:

> *I suppose there never existed a man who had a sweeter nature. He never thought of himself or his convenience, but was always trying to help others.*

Mary Roberts Rinehart, who had been to Glacier Park with him and a frequent guest at Eatons', wrote in tribute:

> *I have never known anyone so truly fine and yet so gentle and self-effacing. Outside of public life, I know of no one so widely known and generally beloved.*

Perhaps the most touching testimony came from his niece, Josephine Gillespie, who lived at Eatons' with her mother. Josephine, who was deaf and attended the Clarke School for the Deaf in Northampton, Massachusetts, wrote an article about her Uncle Howard in her school alumni newspaper, *The Clarke School Bulletin* in October 1923:

> *In later years, my uncle became very deaf, and could not enjoy general conversation, but he was kind and jolly as ever, never letting his limitation make him morose or selfish, or allowing it to interfere with his activities. During that last winter he was planning another long trip through the wildest part of New Mexico, but when the time for that journey came, he had gone on a still more distant one, "The long, long, trail"—leaving a gap that nothing can fill, but leaving, too, the splendid heritage of a noble, useful life.*

In the same article, Josephine also described how her uncle was honored by having a trail named after him in Yellowstone Park. Josephine wrote:

The Howard Eaton Trail was formally opened July 19, 1923, with a simple but impressive ceremony. From Eatons' Ranch, Wolf, Wyoming, went eighteen of the family and friends for the occasion. We reached Mammoth Hot Springs in the morning, and after lunch motored over to Sheepeater's Cliff, seven miles away, where the trail starts. This site was chosen because the Eaton parties made their first camp at this place. It is a lovely spot—the steep, rugged cliff at one side, many trees around, and a green meadow sloping to a beautiful stream close by. The ceremony was opened by a group of Shriners in uniform, and then a large picture of my uncle on his favorite horse, Danger, was unveiled, and speeches were made by Mr. Allbright, Superintendent of the Yellowstone Park...Nearby were two tepee tents, and after the trail had been formally pronounced open to the public, a number of riders and pack-horses passed along it for a short distance, reminiscent of "Howard Eaton Parties." To me, who had taken three of these trips, this had a touching significance, remembering the pride my uncle felt in arranging and conducting a successful camping party. The picture of him returns vividly, and I see him at the head of a long line of riders, sitting so straight and easily, turning to say a word of warning or encouragement to the "tenderfeet" to whom he was showing the wonders of his beloved West, or perhaps spurring ahead to see if the road was clear. He looked so vigorous and manly, square-shouldered, carelessly dressed, (he despised "dude" clothes) but with an elaborately carved saddle and bridle, heavily silver-mounted saddle. In the evening when the campfire was lighted, he was the center of attraction with his stories of the old West and hunting adventures for he had shot every species of big game...

Dedication of the Howard Eaton Trail in Yellowstone Park.
Identity of people is not known.
Photo by J. E. Haynes, St. Paul.
Courtesy of Eatons' Ranch.

The Howard Eaton Trail is 157 miles long and reaches the most interesting and beautiful sections of the Park. It is marked by about two hundred signs and one tablet that is inscribed:

Howard Eaton

Celebrated Western horseman and guide on his favorite mount, Danger. He conducted over one hundred horseback and camping parties through the Yellowstone Park and other scenic regions of the Rocky Mountains from Canada to Mexico. Died April 5, 1922

Another old friend, Dr. William T. Hornaday, a visitor at the Custer Trail Ranch in the early days at Medora, had some final words as well:

This is the tangible memorial to Howard Eaton. But he has left an intangible and endearing mark upon the hearts of the many hundreds who have known him, and who are indebted to him for their introduction to the great outdoors.

Howard was gone, but not forgotten. In his honor, the Ranch clubhouse, which was built in 1911, was renamed Howard Hall, a name it maintains to this day.

Howard's departure created a vacancy on the board of directors of Eaton Brothers, Inc. Therefore, at a meeting on May 10, John Fleming was elected as Howard's successor.

In Howard's Last Will and Testament, recorded in 1907, he left his entire estate, which consisted mostly of Eaton Brothers, Inc. stock, to his two brothers. Therefore, the control of the corporation remained in the hands of the Eaton brothers.

In the early 1920s, the Eatons formed the "Wolves Club." It was simply an informal organization and anyone who had been a guest at or worked on the Ranch could join. The Wolves Club even had a summer convention in 1923 and a pre-season meeting in 1924. Pete Daily published the minutes of this meeting complete with photos and tidbits of information about the Ranch.

Then, after the summer meeting, *Wranglin' Notes of the Wolves Club* was published. Again, it contained Ranch news and photographs taken by Pete Dailey and drawings by Joe DeYong. This four-page publication was the forerunner of what was to become a remarkable journal of life at Eatons' Ranch and has lasted to this day eighty-six years later.

In September 1924, Pete Daily issued the first *Wranglin' Notes.* The intent was to publish and distribute it several times a year to everyone who was interested about the latest "goings on" at the Ranch. Ranch personnel, notably Pete Daily and Joe DeYong, created a daily *Wranglin' Notes.* This informal version was only published at the Ranch during the dude season. It contained the latest "happenings" and announced information that would be helpful to dudes. It was not devoid of humor and gossip, either.

Pete Daily designed a distinctive masthead with a cartoon of himself, drawn by Joe DeYong, and a cluster of wooden stick horses. Today, this same masthead still adorns the publication.

The figure was adapted from southwest Indian drawings of horses and the Eatons adopted it as the Ranch logo. Eventually it appeared on just about everything and everywhere. It was, and still is, the pattern for the Ranch china. It is the form used for napkin rings and appears around the grounds in the form of foot-scrapers and weather vanes. The Eatons also painted it on the barns and gates.

To some, it looked more like a dog than a horse. Indeed, the first issue of *Wranglin' Notes* announced that at the summer meeting all Wolves Club members would be presented with the "popular little silver Ranch horse pins for their membership emblems." The article then said:

> *And here it is: (drawing of horse). It's a horse. So now that ought to answer for all time, one of the questions usually asked several hundred times a week, according to the tabulation of the store and office staff. The question, of course, is, "Are these little things horses or dogs?" And now, let's talk about the weather.*

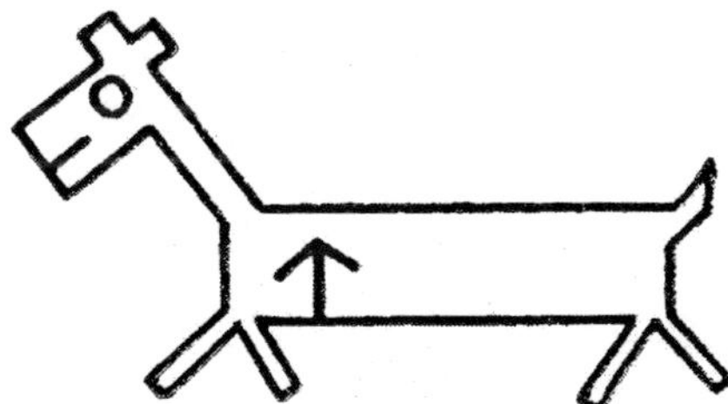

The stick horse led to other things. When new dudes arrived, they had to have their assigned saddles fitted. Rather than put the saddle on a real horse, it was easier to mount the dude on a stick horse to adjust the saddle stirrups. So someone built two stick horses, a large one and a small one, and they were dubbed "Big Brownie" and "Little Brownie." Even today, every new dude goes to the Wolves Club and climbs aboard "Big Brownie" to have their stirrups adjusted. (*Note: "Little Brownie" was put out to pasture years ago.*)

In the beginning, Pete's partner in crime in writing and editing *Wranglin' Notes* was Joe DeYong whose pen name was Kid Currycomb, a cartoon character he had invented earlier.

Joe met Howard Eaton in 1919, accompanied him on a Glacier trip and as a result became a dude wrangler and semi-official artist for the Ranch. When they met, Joe was twenty-five years old, only five feet, six inches tall, a protégé of Charles Russell, and deaf.

Joe was born in Webster Grove, Missouri on March 12, 1894. He was an only child and was fascinated by cowboys. His godfather and namesake was Joe Bartles, who was the last hereditary chief of the Turtle clan of the Delaware Indian Tribe. Bartles had met Joe's father in a military school and encouraged him to move his family to the Indian Territory. Eventually the family moved there and Joe learned to ride and draw horses at the ranches on which his father worked. He learned to be a cowboy at a very young age.

By accident, Joe got a bit part into the movies when he met Tom Mix in 1910. This adventure gave him the thirst to be a cowboy actor. Unfortunately, when he was filming the movie *The Law and the Outlaw*, he contracted meningitis. The sickness left him totally deaf and physically impaired in other ways to the extent that he decided he couldn't be a working cowboy. Instead, he turned to art.

When Joe saw a collection of Charlie Russell's art at Cheyenne Frontier Days, his interest in art was rekindled. Joe was inspired to meet Russell and so sent Russell a portfolio of his drawings and a photograph of his first model. His audacity paid off—Russell sent back encouraging words.

In July 1914, Joe visited Russell in his Great Falls, Montana, studio for the first time and by the end of the year Joe and his very supportive family moved to Montana to be near Russell. On January 3, 1916, Joe began work in Russell's studio. This was the beginning of a teacher-student relationship, which lasted until Charlie Russell died, ten years later. In addition to honing his artistic skills under the tutelage of Russell, Joe also developed and refined his ability to communicate through sign language or "hand talk" at which Russell was adept.

Eatons' proved to be an ideal place for Joe during this period since it opened a "fruitful market" for his artwork. Throughout the 1920s, Joe capitalized on the dude market and entertained them in his tepee with rope tricks.

Wranglin' Notes, hereinafter referred to as *WN,* was a success from the first issue. It provided all the details of Eaton Ranch life—activity at the corral, the weather, the results of the tennis and horseshoe tournaments, the status of Wolf Creek with regard to fishing, and often how many states were represented at Eatons' that summer. Two announcements were of special interest:

> *One of our boys, Arthur ("Pete") Dailey, has made some attractive photographic landscape studies around the Ranch country that will probably be entered in a few of the international photographic exhibitions during the coming winter. While we are not in the habit of commercializing the circulation list of the* Wranglin' Notes, *we believe that Ranch folks will appreciate Pete's pictures, so by way of helping him place his pictures before the members we are permitting him to insert his announcement card with this edition of the Notes.* (Note: This was the beginning of Pete's career as a photographer. He was swamped with Christmas orders from dudes, some of his photos were sent to photographic exhibits and two of his photos were used in a full-page advertisement of a "well-known make of camera." Fame was to follow.)

And then there was this startling announcement:

> *More than likely the pictorial sections of the larger city newspapers will publish a picture of a group of Ranch girls wearing overalls, the Ranch riding habit they adopted by practically unanimous consent. It is an interesting feature item when a group of attractive girls cast aside expensive tailor-made riding suits of exclusive cuts for the comfortable, inexpensive, and plebian blue overalls. What'll they do next?*

Eaton guests loved *WN*. They lapped it up. To them it was akin to receiving a chatty letter from a long lost relative in which no detail was too mundane. Written in an informal and entertaining style, the early editions used "ranch lingo." For instance, the April 1925 issue contained the following:

Uncle Will is still EAST [sic] *and havin' a fine time visitin' but seems kinda anxious to get back, and says he's going to break all records ridin' with his big family from all over these United States 'cause he knows the weather will be fine."*

Northern Wyoming seemed to have gotten its share of winter by Christmas as the weather has been fine most of the time since then. Spring showed up ahead of schedule, so any dudes plannin' to come early can count on green grass and wildflowers, and plenty of fat ponies to pick from. Bein' anxious to have everything ready for the first arrivals the whole outfit's been scramblin' around busier than a one-legged man at a sword dance.

In the April 1925, issue, Kid Currycomb (Joe DeYong) announced that Pete Dailey's career was taking off and he was in Egypt. So, Kid Currycomb assumed the duties of "editor-in- chief" and wrote:

But Wranglin' Notes *has got to be published regardless, 'cause there's a whole flock of folks that writes in to the effect that this here sheet is THE* [sic] *bright spot in an otherwise smoke clouded existence...But you'll just have to make allowances since the Kid's ideas on grammar and punctuation are from the Catch-as-Catch-Can School, bein' gathered in accidently like the burs in a horse's tail.*

Joe DeYong continued to write *WN* for a time, and sometimes Pete Daily would show up from his world travels and help with an issue. But in the September 1927 issue, there appeared a short history of the publication *and* then this:

So Wranglin' Notes *has become an institution. About four times a year—there is no regular date—the postman delivers copies of it to friends all over the country, some of whom have not visited the Ranch for twenty years or more but are still interested in the doings of Ranch folks. Pete Dailey edited the first few numbers. But the editor of the sheet for some time past, Angela Buell, has decided to come out of the sagebrush where she's been hiding for a good many years, and take the responsibility for it all...*

Unstintingly, Angela took responsibility the next thirty years and over one hundred issues thus providing a remarkable chronicle of life at Eatons' Ranch.

Improvements

From the earliest days at Medora, Eaton guests seldom complained about any accommodations shortfalls: in fact, they prided themselves on their ability to cope with Eaton Ranch rusticity. It was simply a part of the Eaton experience and the Eatons more than made up for any hardship with a robust and genuine brand of friendly hospitality.

But the Eatons believed it was their duty to maintain a program of constant physical improvements for the comfort of their guests. In a 1929 issue of *WN* the Eatons expressed their philosophy this way:

Each year a remarkable percentage of Ranch guests are friends who have been with us before, and each year we like to feel that these folks are noting physical improvements here and there and that they are conscious of an improvement in the general trend of the place.

Up until the 1920s, the Eatons struggled to make the necessary improvements just to keep up with the increased demand for accommodations. But by the 1920s, the Eatons had reached the point where, as they expressed in *WN*:

The Ranch plant as a whole has reached the point where it is big enough but it is not good enough. So we're working back polishing off the rough edges and putting on finishing touches to the places that we rushed over the first time.

In the 1920s the Eatons evolved from the primitive to the modern. Their first move was to eliminate the need for kerosene lanterns. In 1923, they constructed a hydroelectric plant. The project involved the construction of a circular wooden flume about twenty-four inches in diameter that extended from an upstream water diversion point off Wolf Creek down to a specially constructed stone powerhouse that housed a turbine. The turbine produced DC current; therefore, all appliances that required AC power required converters. Details about the construction of the wooden flume are not available, but the workmanship that went into its construction was impressive. It remained in service until the 1960s when the Eatons were able to obtain commercial power.

In the mid-1920s, the Eatons installed sewer and water lines throughout the Ranch which made it possible for them to build bathrooms in some of the cabins. Up until that time, there were no private baths attached to the cabins, rather guests used a series of modern bathhouses "conveniently placed about the grounds."

While the addition of bathrooms to cabins seemed like a groundbreaking improvement to some, to others it was disgraceful. Mary Roberts Rinehart wrote an article called "The Cavvy" in the September edition of *The Saturday Evening Post.* She first described her introduction to the bathroom installed in her cabin, and then noted the amusing reaction of some regular die hard dudes when, on their arrival, they learned that bathrooms had come to the Ranch:

"Bathrooms!" they say. "What next? We'll be having an orchestra with our meals before long."

And they go firmly to the familiar bathless cabins, and can be seen ever and anon, towel over arm, and clutching their dressing gowns together against the wind in search of a vacant tub.

As the years unfolded, the Eatons maintained a constant program of cabin improvements. They added porches, bedrooms, and sitting rooms, for instance, and, of course, there was the constant need for regular maintenance and "paint up/fix up."

In 1929, *WN* Angela Buell made note of the annual spring maintenance program:

> *Seems as if we buy enough paint every spring to put a dozen coats on the White House but we're getting just as much as ever this year and it will be disposed of in short order. Following the painting jobs will be carpenters with hammers and nails to fix the scores of little things that work loose or need replacing. And then there will be lots of hot water and soapsuds and a thorough cleaning.*

Domo, who had come to live with her daughter Patty in 1919, also made some improvements in order to help her daughter, Fay. McWilliams described the situation:

> *...Fay never married and spent her life teaching. Her first school was out on Prairie Dog, near Sheridan. She was eighteen years old and just out of high school. Her eighth grade boys took her to the country dances on weekends. Fay was ambitious, though, and saved her money to go to summer school, eventually getting her degree from Berkeley. She was county superintendent of schools at Forsyth, Montana, for three terms, also spending one term at Hardin, Montana. Patty worked in her office at Forsyth for a couple of years, and Fay also taught a couple of years in Hawaii. While she was teaching in Berkeley, she developed tuberculosis and had a complete breakdown. Mrs. Alderson was living with Patty and Bill at that time, and the doctor said Fay shouldn't be near the children because tuberculosis was contagious. So Mrs. Alderson fixed up the old cabin that was standing empty on the lower Ranch...It has just been a cook shack for hay hands at one time and was a wreck, but she built on a bedroom, put a fireplace in the living room,*

Dudes often stopped by to visit with Nannie Alderson (Domo) at her cabin.
Circa 1920s.
Courtesy of Eatons' Ranch.

and added front and back porches, making it quite a charming place. The cabin was the perfect place for Fay because in those days, there was no cure for tuberculosis, only good care and bed rest. When she arrived at Eatons' she weighed less than one hundred pounds. She was kept in bed for a year and stuffed like a Thanksgiving turkey, as Patty put it; at the end of that year, she weighed 135 pounds and had to wear Aunt Mame's clothes, but she was completely cured...

When Fay was cured, she went on to teach school in Sheridan for the next twenty-five years and Domo continued to live in the cabin for the rest of her life. The cabin became a popular stopping place for dudes whom Domo plied with lemonade, cookies and cake. After Domo died, and Fay retired from teaching school, Fay moved to Eatons' and lived in her mother's cabin for many years.

Unfortunately, a fire caused a major unplanned improvement to the main ranch house in 1927. The fire gutted the stone house. The event rated a special edition of *WN* (Number 14, February 1927) in which Angela Buell described the event:

February 2, Ground Hog's Day, found the resident Ranch family pretty small, with Bill, Patty and the children just leaving California overland, the Flemings also in California, Uncle Will in Pittsburgh, and only a dozen folks, all told, living at the Ranch. And as Fate would have it, the few at home were scattered early in the afternoon when Mrs. Alden Eaton smelled smoke and stepped out hurriedly in her kimono to investigate.

Smoke and flames were pouring from around the dining room chimney. Mrs. Alden rang the gong but the fire had a good start, was fanned by a wind from the canyon, and the few folks within reach of the alarm didn't have a chance to check it. We only regret that the photographer wasn't on the job, for Mrs. Alden can throw away her shoes and skim up a ladder quicker than a flash, and she was the first person on the roof with extinguishers and the big fire hose.

The first phone call reached our neighbors, the Grahams, and by telephone and horseback, they in turn notified all the ranchers near us who left their teams in the field and rushed to help. Within half an hour twenty or twenty-five men had joined the handful of fire fighters at the Ranch, in time to save clothing from the main house, bring out most of the furniture and keep the fire from reaching other buildings.

The flames were greedy, and urged on by the wind, they swept not only kitchen, dining room, milk room, laundry, heating and hot water plants and all their contents, but they jumped the narrow passageway onto the roof and into the windows of the main house and took everything remaining within its stone walls.

Yes, Uncle Alden saved his stogies unlighted; Miss Josephine got her toothbrush out (though was unable later to identify it among the scrambled belongings on the lawn); Pete lost all his milk pails and the cows are still bewildered; Mrs. Alden finally took time to put on a dress, finding it difficult to clutch a mattress with one hand and hold a kimono around her with the other; Tommy Butler is thinking of joining the trapeze artists in the circus after his practice with the fire hose on the dining room roof; and Aunt Mary holds the record for finding and tying up bundles of clothing for the men to carry out. After dark, Bruce (Brockett) made such a hit scrambling eggs and making coffee for the fire fighters on the embers of the burning coal pile that he's been offered a permanent job in the kitchen next summer. But, he's thinking of quitting the outfit because he lost his best silk shirt and his other union suit in the laundry.

Angela then reminded the readers that the Eatons had suffered another fire in Medora in 1887 but that, "Before the ashes were cold plans were being made, ways and means figured for starting over again." And so, she wrote:

...with the same courage that rebuilt the Ranch in 1887, Eaton Brothers are going ahead now in repairing this comparatively small loss. With several months to pass before the first friends arrive this season, there is ample time for the important task ahead of us, and by early June, we hope to be better equipped than ever before to care for Ranch visitors.

The Eatons had to make creative adjustments in temporary living and dining arrangements while they rebuilt the main house, but with their usual resilience, they did, and that summer they took dudes, as usual.

Main ranch house after it was gutted by fire and rebuilt.
Courtesy of Eatons' Ranch.

There was another fire, a year later, which McWilliams described:

Then in 1928, the very next year, Bill and Patty's house burned to the ground. They had been on vacation in California and just arrived at home. They put their belongings in the house, including a suitcase containing all of their silver that had been kept in the bank while they were gone, and drove up to the main house to greet the rest of the family. The house must have been struck by lightning because it simply burst into flames. Patty and Bill didn't save as much as a teaspoon...

Patty and Bill never rebuilt their home. That was the year the Eatons bought the Rimrock Ranch in Arizona, and for ten years Bill and Patty were gone for six months each year to run that ranch. While they were here, they lived in the cabin where T. J. Ferguson's family now lives...

Expansion

In the 1920s, the Eatons purchased two ranches to expand their operation. They bought a winter place for their horses in 1925, and a winter place for their dudes in 1928.

By the mid-1920s, the Eaton horse herd had grown to about five hundred animals and the Eaton place on Wolf Creek did not have enough pasture to see them through the severe winters that typically haunted the foothills of the Big Horn Mountains. To solve this problem the Eatons purchased a place of approximately ten thousand acres near Echeta on Wild Horse Creek, a tributary of the Powder River. In time, the acreage would more than double as the Eatons leased adjacent land. The winters at Echeta, which was one hundred miles from Wolf Creek, were milder with less snow. When the snow did fall, the wind usually scoured the snow from the ridges. Also, even if the country was covered with snow, the horses could paw down to the cured grass below. Only a few weaker horses needed extra feed during the winter.

With the purchase of Echeta, the Eatons began an annual ritual. In the fall, they drove the horses from Wolf to Echeta and in the spring, they drove them back to Wolf Creek. The trip takes three days each way. This bi-annual event, to this day, always draws a crowd as the horses thunder through Sheridan on either their way to or from Echeta.

The purchase of Echeta brought the need for a manager. Luckily, the Eatons found Ben and Claire Sittler who managed the place until the late 1930s.

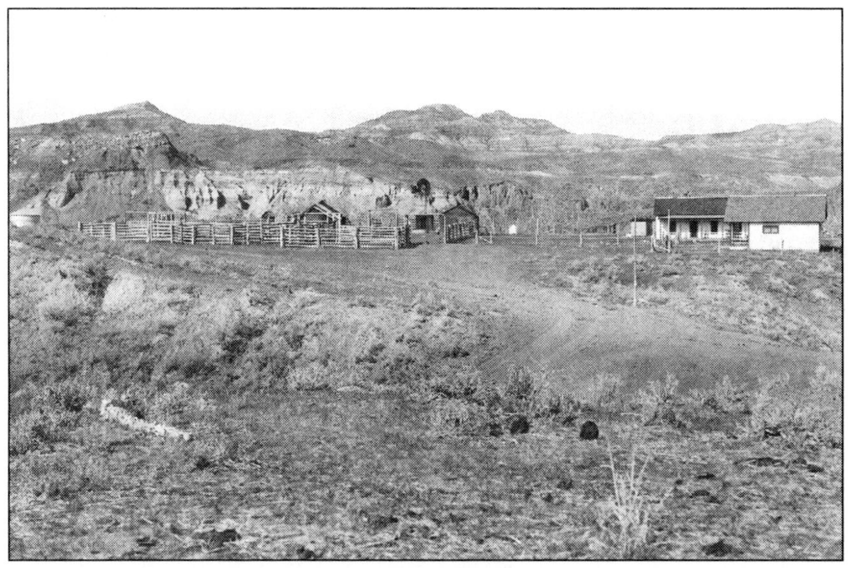

Eatons' Bar 11 Ranch in Echeta where the cattle summer and the horses winter. *Courtesy of Eatons' Ranch.*

For some years, the Eatons wanted to find property in the Southwest to establish a "winter place" which could host a limited number of dudes. In fact, while he was still alive, Howard made several overland trips to the Southwest country and southern California in his "rough riding" Dodge touring car. He never found a suitable situation.

After Howard died, Bill and Patty Eaton and their attorney, Chuck Schlegel, resumed the search. They finally found what appeared to be an ideal building site near Elgin, Arizona. Unfortunately, they found it was not ideal because, as *WN* noted, "...Wells that were thought to be sufficient were found to be short..." and so that site was abandoned. However, in the fall of 1928 they did find the right place.

Bill, Patty and Chuck discovered Rimrock Ranch, near Cottonwood, Arizona, and it was what they were looking for. It was, as Angela Buell wrote in *WN* "…new but it has been in operation a part of one winter and there is no question as to sufficient water or the practicality of its location and operation."

Patty wrote her mother Domo and described the trip she and Bill made to inspect Rimrock and described it. John Fleming, and his wife Mae, accompanied Patty and Bill. Between them, they reached the conclusion it was the ideal spot for the Eatons' southwest ranch. Patty described it:

> *The buildings sit right on top of a hill and when you first see it, you wonder why in the world anyone would build a house on a place like that. But when you get up to it and see the beautiful view from every direction, and realize how attractive the little house is with its green lawn and pretty little patio, you decide that the Lowdermilks* (Note: The owners) *have an eye for beauty, and knew what they were doing. …At first we all felt a little strange. Everything was on such a small scale in comparison with the Ranch and the country was all so different.*

In spite of the "strangeness" of it all, the Eatons bought the place and it proved to be an ideal situation for the Eatons' winter operation for the next ten years. In October 1928, Bill and Patty returned to the Ranch and gathered up their children and with a convoy of people, including Dunc and Domo, and supplies, left to get Rimrock Ranch ready for the first winter guests.

Angela Buell informed all who read *WN* that: "We must, however, warn all friends that the Ranch is very small—only nine guest rooms—and no one should come unannounced."

The Rimrock Ranch in Arizona.
Courtesy of Eatons' Ranch.

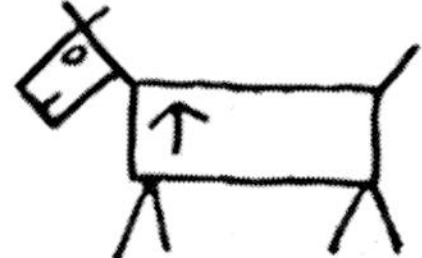

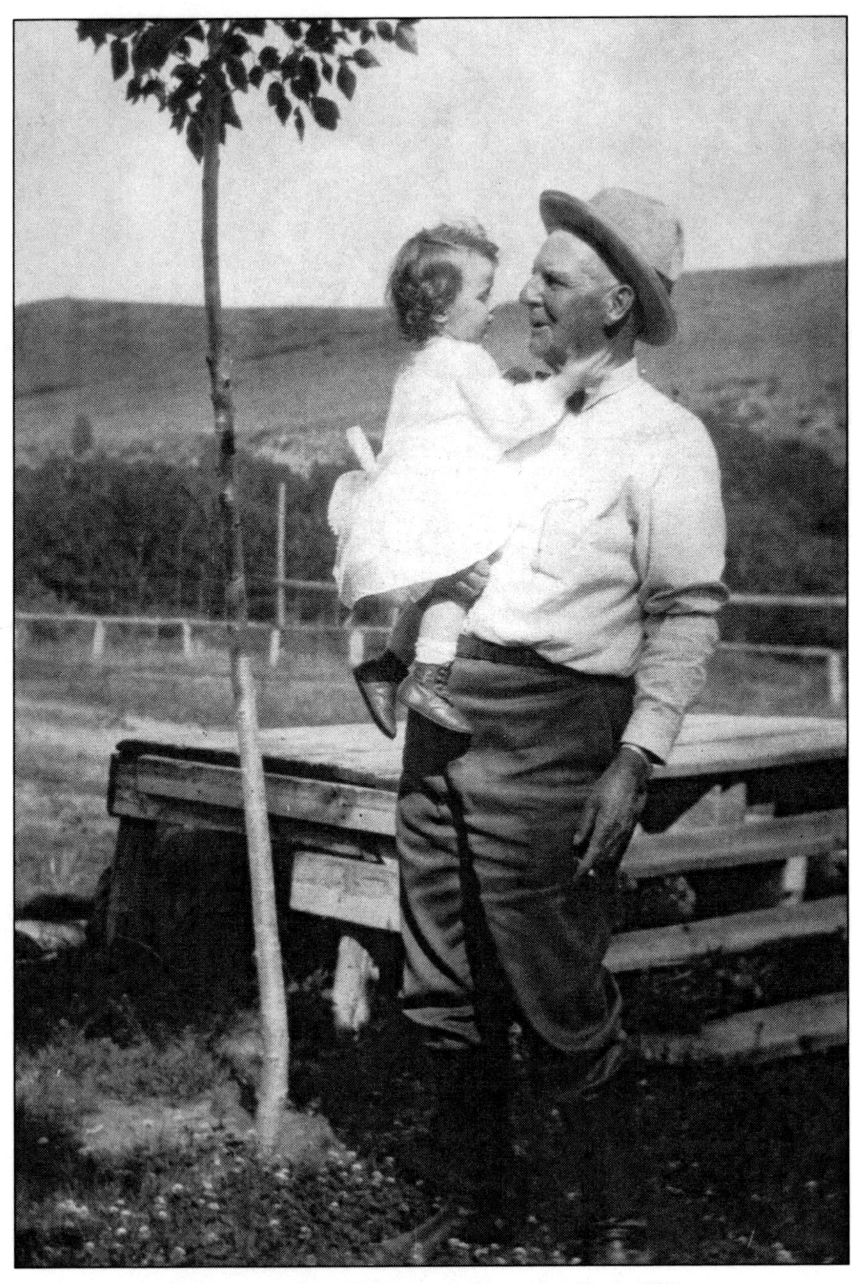

Baby Nancy Eaton in the arms of her great Uncle Willis.
They are next to the old stagecoach platform. Circa 1922.
Courtesy of Eatons' Ranch.

Uncle Will Dies

The following spring, after the Eatons set up housekeeping at the Rimrock Ranch, the second Eaton brother, Uncle Will, died. Angela Buell prepared a special edition of *WN* to note his passing:

Willis Langstaff Eaton
1852-1929

With a feeling of deep sorrow and great loss, we must tell Ranch friends of Uncle Will's death on Thursday, May fourteenth, at Louisville, Kentucky.

His illness came very suddenly and did not last long—as he had always hoped it might be—and we had time to wire only a few of his many friends of his serious condition. And because Uncle Will was always so deeply interested in the Wranglin' Notes *and was so pleased when folks spoke appreciatively of them, we believe he would wish the message of his passing to go to his friends in this very simple form.*

Uncle Will left the Ranch early in February for his annual visit to Pittsburgh, his old home and the home of several sisters, as many Ranch friends know. It was a cold blustery day, lots of snow, and we last saw him as he sat up very straight on the front seat of the open bobsled, enveloped in a huge fur overcoat, smiling and waving goodbye as they started the long pull through the drifts toward Sheridan and the train. He wrote often, telling of his trip, and always of meeting this friend or that friend, how kind they all were to him and how much he enjoyed seeing every one. From Pittsburgh, he went on up to Geneva, New York for a short visit with Uncle Charley Eaton…

Willis Eaton in barn door. Circa 1920's.
Courtesy of Eatons' Ranch.

Uncle Will visited various other friends in New York City and Trenton, New Jersey before returning to Pittsburgh to gather his things for his return home, but not before a side trip to see his close friends Ed and Ida Belle Thompson in Louisville, Kentucky.

No sooner had he arrived in Louisville than the Thompsons wired that:

> *...Uncle Will had been taken ill shortly after reaching their home, had apparently suffered a sudden heart attack, and that the doctor advised against his continuing the journey alone. Uncle Alden was on his way east within a half hour. The following day Ed and Ida Belle wired that Uncle Will was apparently much better but they were glad Uncle Alden was on the way. But the improvement in his condition was only temporary, and when Uncle Alden reached Louisville the evening of May eighth to join Mrs. McFarlane and Dr. Clem Flood of Pittsburgh, his sister and nephew, who were already there, his message home was that Uncle Will's condition was very alarming indeed, although everything in the world had been, and was being done for him. He passed away shortly after noon on Tuesday, May 14. After very simple services in Sheridan, he now rests there, the beautiful Big Horns and the Ranch country he loved spread out before him...*
>
> *Looking back, we truly believe Uncle Will had a life full of happiness. He loved the Ranch and his life here, he loved the people who visited the Ranch and called on him constantly for guidance and help. His only apprehension was that the time might come when he could not do his full share of the Ranch work and would not be able to ride morning and afternoon with his friends. He was spared that realization and to the very last was surrounded with countless friends in whose memories he will live for many, many years.*

Uncle Will's Last Will and Testament, which was recorded about five years before his death, contained a provision that could have made the control of Eaton Brothers, Inc. a bit difficult in future years. While

Howard had left his shares of the corporation to his two brothers, Willis left his shares to Alden, but with a twist. The twist was that the shares Willis left to Alden were the 169 shares Willis had inherited from Howard, and these shares were left to Alden in a life estate. The provision was that Alden could vote the shares as long as he lived, but when he died, he was to leave the shares to their sisters and Hattie's son, Willis E. Pelissier. Willis did not specify any shares to his sister Josephine A. Conway or his brother Charles, because they apparently did not wish to be included in his will.

Willis was well aware that there was a need for the Eaton brothers to maintain control of the corporation. In fact, he stated in his will that the sisters, once they inherited the shares, should give the corporation the opportunity to purchase the shares back because, as he emphasized:

> *...the business conducted by that corporation is a peculiar one, differing greatly from other kinds of business in many respects, and its best interests, which are of much importance to all those mentioned in this Will, are best served by the control thereof being held in a few hands and by those directly concerned in the management and on the ground in control of the operation thereof...*

As it turned out, this provision of Uncle Will's estate plan was rendered moot about a year before at a corporation meeting when the stockholders (Uncle Will, Uncle Alden, John Fleming, John Duncan, Tommy Butler and Bill Eaton) called for a special meeting to increase the authorized capital stock from $125,000 to $200,000. The additional stock was "preferred stock"—that is, stock that did not give the holder voting rights in the affairs of the corporation but did qualify for annual dividends from any profits.

It was through this preferred stock mechanism that the corporation was able to keep control of the corporation in the hands of those immediately engaged in the operation of Eatons' Ranch and at the same time recognize Uncle Will's desire to provide for some of his siblings. The Ranch issued preferred stock to all concerned and paid dividends when appropriate. This preferred stock was not fully redeemed by the corporation until the 1990s.

Uncle Will's death left a vacancy on the board of directors. It was only natural that the heir apparent and only member of the second generation of the Eaton brothers fill the vacancy. William A. Eaton, ("Big Bill"), the only child of Uncle Alden and Aunt Mame replaced Uncle Will on the board of directors. Bill was thirty-nine years old and a key member of the management team, especially with regards to all livestock matters and corral management. Now he was not only a stockholder, but also a member of the corporate team headed up by his father, Uncle Alden, who was chairman, and the rock of the whole operation, John Fleming, secretary.

Family

The 1920s was a transition decade for the Eaton family. With the death of Uncle Howard and Uncle Will, near the beginning and end of the decade, Uncle Alden and Aunt Mame became the sole representatives of their generation in the Eaton Ranch activities as their son Bill, and his wife Patty, assumed larger roles.

Uncle Alden and Aunt Mame were inveterate travelers and when the dude season ended each fall, they were apt to take off on long distance motor trips for all parts of the United States. Often, Uncle Will went with them. In fact, in 1928 *WN* reported that they had just completed their "eighth annual overland journey" to California. Two of their traveling companions on the 1928 trip were Walter and Kathleen Louer. Supposedly, according to *WN*, Walter said that:

> *...the men at the gas stations along the way have come to know Uncle Alden and his stogie so well that he says "Hello*

Jim," "How are you Tom," "So long Harry," as casually as if he'd been past the day before and would probably see them again tomorrow.

One year, in 1926, Aunt Mame wrote a letter from California for the Christmas *WN*. The delightful and humorous letter described their annual trip that year which included many members of the Eaton family. She wrote:

There were so many nice people at the Ranch when we left last October it was difficult to make the break, but Grand Canyon and Zion Park, like all great beauties, are temperamental. So, for fear they would hide their beauties under a mantel of snow, we had to leave early. As it was, we were overtaken at 8,800 feet by a pouring rain which turned to snow a few hours later, but we had seen the canyon and park at their very best, and the drive thru beautiful Kaibab Forest was worth braving any or all elements.

Back to Salt Lake, and then up thru Idaho, Washington, Oregon and into California, meeting many ranch friends and old pals of Howard's along the way. At Santa Barbara, Joe DeYong is doing some fine work in bronze, and there we had a ranch reunion, which included Ed Borein, Frank Linderman, Mrs. Holden and Mr. and Mrs. Smitheran. On to Hollywood and Long Beach, where the Lows and Harry McCormick hang out, and, after a few rounds of dinners, movie studios and sightseeing, we motored on down the coast near San Diego, where the Flemings have a charming little Spanish house.

Surrounded by orchards and delightful neighbors, we settled down for a few weeks and sent for Patty, Bill and the children, but something about the Ranch seems to reach out and find you wherever you may be, and Uncle Alden is casting around for a good excuse for starting back. The latest is that there is no smoke coming from the chimneys, and it makes him feel lonesome in the mornings. Now, that is something we have plenty of at the ranch this time of year. So, as soon as Nancy learns to swim, Billy catches a few fish, Uncle Will finishes the back numbers of the Saturday Evening Post, Domo meets a few more movie sheiks, Patty and Bill see some of the big races over at Tijuana, and Santa Claus heads back North, we will break a few speed records getting home, bringing pleasant memories of old friends met and new ones made, old trails revisited and new ones traveled, happy to settle down and await the return of the Ranch Family...

Uncle Alden and Aunt Mame continued the California trips even after Uncle Will died. They also took trips back east to see family in Pittsburgh and visit dudes in various other parts of the East.

No matter how much Uncle Alden enjoyed his trips away from the Ranch, he was always glad to return. He cherished his days at the ranch whether they were in the summer or winter. In 1928, Angela Buell described a typical winter day with Uncle Alden at the Ranch:

Scores of folks spend active days with Uncle Alden in the summer time and he continues his activities in the winter whether or not there are friends to go along for company. Uncle Alden is the first to eat Mrs. Link's good coffee and bacon in the morning, and breakfast is a pleasant meal in the "winter dining room" (what summer friends would call the "sun room" in the Ranch house.) Before he has finished breakfast Aunt Mary, Cousin Josie, probably Mrs. Reid and other members of the family are drifting in and the sun has peeked over Chocolate Drop and is flooding the room through its big southeast windows with warm winter sunshine. Folding his book or magazine to be resumed in the evening, Uncle Alden wrangles his hat and coat, gloves and overshoes, and starts for the "work" part of the Ranch—the office, the barn, the shop, corral, and garage. The smoke of a freshly kindled fire is curling from the chimney of the office and Tommy Butler can be seen inside working away with the business end of a broom before going on to his miscellaneous array of winter jobs. Whit is busy around the cow barn. Emil has fed the saddle horses, and is getting

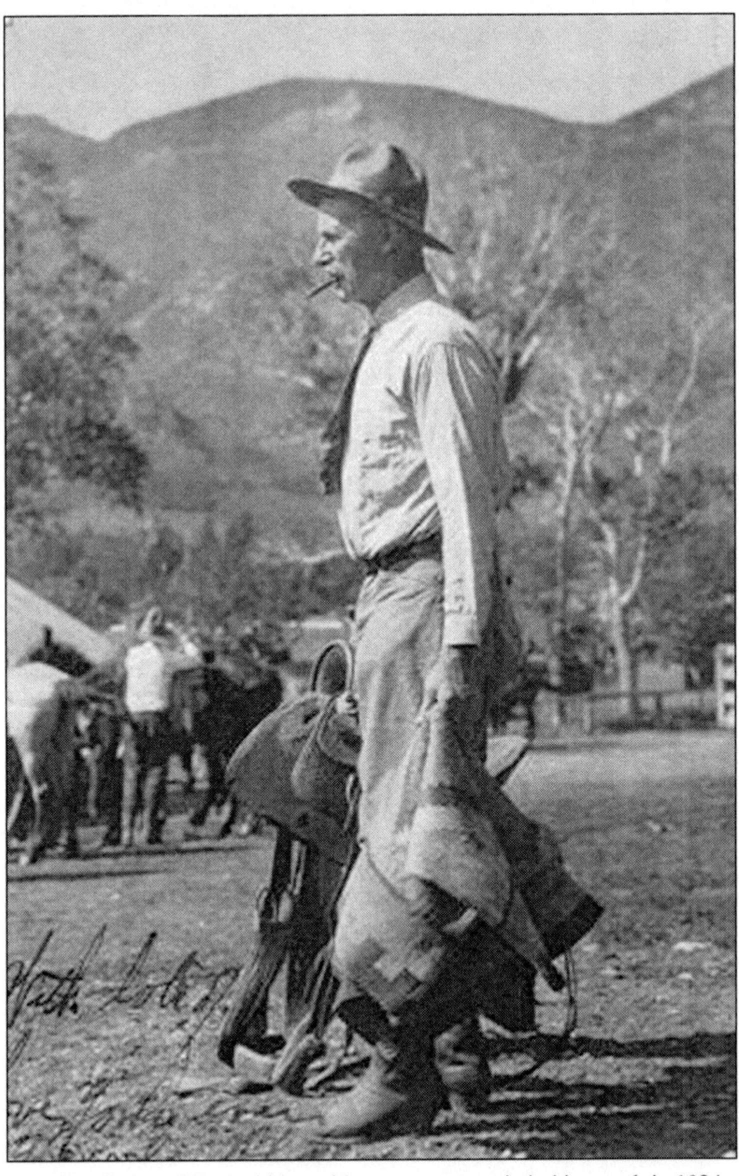

Familiar figure of Uncle Alden with permanent stogie in his mouth in 1924.
Photo by Arthur Dailey.
Courtesy of Eatons' Ranch.

ready to harness the team for a trip down the creek for a load of hay. Red, Hammer and Darkey look up quickly from the corral, thinking it is Ed Boaler coming up to choose one of them for his morning ride. But Uncle Alden goes on into the shop where there is a morning's job sharpening and getting in shape all the ice tools.

After lunch, Uncle Alden finds his horse saddled and bridled waiting in the barn, and he crosses the ford below the Ranch house on his way down the meadow to the lower ranch where the PK cattle are being fed the hay brought from the Ranch last fall. They look fat and contented but they don't stray far from the feeding grounds where the boys are scattering good alfalfa hay for them. Across the small stream to Domo's where the porches are covered with untracked snow and drawn shades mean that Domo is not there to welcome visitors, and on down to the ice house for a look at the pond. Only three or four inches of ice—not enough yet to cut. The mountains are beginning to throw their shadows although it is not yet three o'clock, so Uncle Alden heads for home riding back on the "lease" side of the creek. Following the Domo Trail for a short distance, he startles the family of deer that has spent the past year in the woods between the lower and upper ranches, that any number of guests will remember seeing there last summer when they rode the Alden or Domo trails. Every Ranch hunter protected them during the open hunting season last fall, and the deer continue to seem entirely at home and probably are missing the frequent visits of summer rides.

By the time Uncle Alden reaches the barn, the sun has long since set at the Ranch buildings, but can be seen down the valley beyond the reach of the mountains. Winter days lack most of the activity and excitement of summer days at the Ranch, but folks accustomed to Wyoming winters find a certain pleasure in them just the same—and that's only a little bit of sour grapes...

Uncle Alden's horizons extended well beyond the Ranch and his travels. He was a conscientious citizen and active in the community.

He particularly cherished his membership in Rotary International and seldom missed a Friday Rotary meeting if he was home.

Uncle Alden also entered politics for a time and was elected as a Republican to serve in the 16th and 18th Wyoming Legislatures in 1921 and 1925 respectively. His fellow legislators held him in high esteem and when the main house burned in 1927, the Eatons received the following telegram from Uncle Alden's friends in the Wyoming state capitol in Cheyenne:

> *The House of Representatives of the Nineteenth Legislature taking note of the serious loss sustained through fire by the far famed Eaton Ranch and appreciating the loss to not only Eaton Brothers, but also the State of Wyoming and the entire West offers to you its sincerest sympathy.*

In the 1920s, Bill and Patty Eaton came into their own as a family and as an integral part of the Eaton Ranch operation. In 1920, Bill was thirty years old. His wife Patty was just a year younger. Their only child at the time, their son, Billy, was only three years old. Billy's sister, Nancy Jane, would be born one year later on February 28, 1921.

Even though she was capable of doing just about anything that needed doing around a ranch, Patty could not be of immediate help in the Eaton Ranch operation because of her familial duties. Patty focused on raising her young family and providing a home for Bill. As Patty said in her memoirs:

> *When we were first married, I did what I could to help around the ranch but after the children were born, I was pretty tied down for awhile, keeping a seven-room house, getting three meals a day, washing and ironing for four people and taking care of two small children...*

But by 1927, Patty was able to help on the Ranch. The *WN* in March of 1927 proclaimed that:

> *Now that Nancy is six years old and quite capable of setting out for the corral early in the morning and ordering her horse for a ride, we are seeing more of Patty and we can promise her presence at the corral very regularly once more. She will be ready to ride with Ranch guests this season any time they want a guide or counselor, and she'll be most anxious to help any newcomers in any way she can.*

Then Angela Buell declared in *WN,* "If you are coming to the Ranch this summer and miss meeting and knowing Patty—you are the loser."

Another *WN* written in 1927 described the second Eaton generation. Bill Eaton, it said, "…is more and more taking over the burden of the Ranch…" It then discussed Patty Eaton and the children: "…Billie [*sic*] who is growing up into the best fisherman and hunter on the Ranch and small Nancy Eaton who rides like a seasoned cowboy in her diminutive leather skirt…"

And another passage, which again discussed the coming of the second Eaton generation, said:

> *Bill Eaton leads them, sitting the saddle easily from many years' experience and a lifetime of riding and roping. North Dakota friends who remember the little boy of six at the Custer Trail Ranch riding the roundups and roping calves, a few years later hunting elk, deer and bear, and realize that at thirty-five Big Bill, six feet, one inch tall, weighing 220 pounds, is ready for the burden we must shift to him…*

Bill Eaton, like his father and uncles, was interested in Sheridan community affairs and made whatever contributions he could. In 1921, for instance, he willingly accepted a position on the newly formed Sheridan County Fair board and then later worked to make the Sheridan County Fair a success. In 1924, he arranged and directed a "Dude Day Rodeo" which included participants from not only Eatons' Ranch, but the surrounding resorts as well. It was reported that the crowd was "noisy but good natured" and "was the largest to attend a county fair in Wyoming's history."

Nancy Jane Eaton.
Courtesy of Eatons' Ranch.

William Alden Eaton, Jr., (Billy).
Courtesy of Eatons' Ranch.

Bill had a natural affinity for horses and it was his goal to make sure that Eatons had a first class dude string. He took pride in being able to select the right kind of horses for any dude—regardless of whether the dude had ever sat a horse, or was an expert rider. The *WN* throughout the years often referred to Bill's activities with regard to the Eaton dude string. In April 1925, *WN*, which at that time was written by Joe DeYong, proclaimed that:

> *The Ranch saddle bunch is workin' up quite a REP*[sic] *for itself, it bein' Bill's aim to make this here cavvy the best collection of western range horses on the map. They're a mighty reliable bunch of ponies, too—well broke and well cared for—a dern sight better than the usual run and getting' better all the time.*

Some dudes became besotted with their horses and bought them for their exclusive use at Eatons' for which they paid pasture charges. Others bought their horse and took them back home. In April 1925, the *WN* made note of this:

> *Big Bill is scatterin' his tracks wide and reckless these days as he's plannin' a shipment of saddle horses to some folks in Pittsburgh...These ponies bein' almost human it's not surprisin' that folks often find they've lost their heart to their Summer Side Pardner, so Bill says he's going to take a special interest in helpin' any Ranch folks to get a serviceable horse for home use, though he won't be able to make up any more shipments until after the summer's work.*

Inveterate Eaton dudes took an enormous interest in the dude cavvy, especially if they owned some of the horses, and so *WN* was careful to make notice of the status of the horse herd. One entry in 1926 was that: "A number of the Ranch friends have bought horses that they ride during the summer and range during the winter with the main cavvy at the Bar Eleven." Then, *WN* listed each of the many owners, and where they came from.

Efforts to keep the Eaton dude clientele informed about the cavvy led to one humorous exchange that was noted in the March 1928 *WN*:

> *A few days ago we wrote to Ben Sittler, who manages the Bar Eleven Ranch on Wild Horse Creek, some hundred miles away from the home Ranch where the cavvy spends the winter, and asked him if he'd run across lately and noticed especially any of the privately owned horses, and that if he had, perhaps it would interest Ranch folks to hear about it in the next* Wranglin' Notes. *Ben was apparently a little nervous about writing anything for publication, for this is his reply:*
>
> *You know, if I was the praying kind, I would pray to be able to write and tell things like Will Rogers and James and some of them fellows do. Of course, you understand maybe I've got my sights raised high but if I could do that, I could write and tell a lot of things that would probably interest folks. As it is, I guess I'm one of the most uninteresting things that ever happened.*
>
> *Now if I get you right, you want this dope for* Wranglin' Notes *so I will do my best. Maybe you can take out some in places, and add to in other places and make it sound like something.*
>
> *We have a pretty good lineup on all the horses here, as we just moved them on to another part of the range where there's fresh feed. We noticed a lot of the private horses—Laddie, Wyo, and Paint all hanging together (the Louer string), Firecracker and Twenty Minutes (belonging to Buddie Harries), the Wilson horses, Ruth Leyendecker's sorrel horse, Henry Leyendecker's horse Glory, and the Stoner horses. All the private horses seem to be in good shape except Harry McCormick's white horse Soldier. He is not very poor but he don't look as good as the other's. Liz Ludlow's blue horse is all out of shape and, you know, if I was Liz, I'd sure trade that horse off. Here he is on a range with four hundred and forty some odd head of horses and they won't any of them notice him. But he's real chummy with Bill Eaton's mule. Something's sure wrong with a horse that has to pal with a mule under them conditions. My advice would be to get rid of the horse or buy the mule.*

Ben then proceeded to make some more pithy comments about the situation at the Bar Eleven:

> *The going here is not so good. A shod horse balls up bad. Just enough snow and ice to make the north hill rides bad, and a bare-footed horse is just about as good as a shod one. All the Ranch horses are looking fine, and with fresh feed, they'll be fattening up good.*
>
> *The weather is great overhead and it suits us fine, too, as we're trying to get a new house started, then put a roof on the old one, so a warm spell will sure be appreciated. We have the gate for the new corrals just about ready to put up and they'll go in just as soon as the cement gets set.*
>
> *Reid (Kochel) brings in a coyote or a bobcat every once in a while, we see deer most every time we go out, but the antelope have drifted out of the Twenty Mile country. We have not seen the antelope for some time. Gone to lower country, I guess, but when the sun gets to shining on both sides of the fence, they'll all be back.*
>
> *This is getting pretty long so I will close. Best regards to everybody.*
>
> *Ben Sittler*

It is doubtful that anyone would have agreed that Ben Sittler was "one of the most uninteresting things that ever happened."

Bill Eaton was known as a "cowboy's friend" and people like Ben Sittler were his kind of folks. McWilliams made note of this aspect of Bill Eaton:

> *He found it difficult to be at ease with easterners, with crowds and with strangers, so some aspects of his job must have been hard for him. Yet he was completely at home with westerners and ranch folk. Bill was at his best sitting around with a bunch of cowboys, yarnin' about all those things cowboys have always told tall tales about. He had such a way with the*

kind of people he knew as his own that he inspired a worshipful article in Western Horseman *magazine. A cowboy who had accidentally killed one of Bill's horses wrote the article, and the cowboy couldn't get over how Bill accepted what happened without blaming anyone.*

There are many examples of Bill Eaton's compassion toward cowboys. A young dude boy named Martin Koether remembered two prime examples.

Martin first visited Eatons' in 1926. He was eleven years old and his brother Herb, who was with him, was thirteen. The boys traveled by themselves on a train from Detroit and the Eaton Ranch driver met them in Sheridan with the Eaton Studebaker limousine.

Martin and his brother visited Eatons' three years in a row, from 1926 to 1929. Two incidents occurred during Martin's first years at Eatons' that typified Bill Eaton's compassion for cowboys. One occurred in the Wolves Club, the cowboy bunkhouse.

Cowboys like to gamble and one day during a break, they put three big double beds together to make a crap table. There were several cowboys, and Martin remembered that three of them were Scorp Neeley, Reid Kochel and Kid Curry (*Note: Not the same as Kid Currycomb, Joe DeYong.*) Martin and his brother, young as they were, were "allowed" to join the game, probably because they were thought to be easy marks. But they weren't easy. In fact, they were extremely lucky and managed to win about $60.00.

Flush with success, the boys gathered up their money and left. In the meantime, Bill heard about the game and later encountered the boys in the dining room. Bill had a conversation with them that went something like:

Boys, I hope you know that you won every cent those cowboys had to their name. That's all they had and it's not right. You don't really need that money. Now I want you to go back and give them a chance to win it back.

Chastened, the boys complied. They kept their twenty-dollar stake back and got in another game with the cowboys, and, sure enough, the cowboys won their money back. No doubt, if the boys had won again, Bill would have sent them back into the fray until they lost.

In 1928, the Koether boys were involved in another incident. Again, Bill taught them a lesson. In 1928, Mr. and Mrs. Morgan of the neighboring PK Ranch staged a huge rodeo. (They staged another one in 1929.) The rodeo took place in a natural amphitheater alongside two prominent hills called Dot and Dash and people came from all over the country to sit on the hillside and watch the show. One rodeo day, in fact, almost all the Eaton dudes rode over to watch the show.

Martin and his brother rode horseback on their way to the rodeo and encountered a cowboy who had paid his entry fees to ride in the rodeo, and was camped out waiting for the rodeo to begin. Martin and his brother stopped to talk to the cowboy. When one of the boys wrapped his horse's reins around the bumper of the cowboy's car, the horse jerked back, broke the reins and took off.

The cowboy sprang into action. He jumped on the remaining horse and tried to rope the loose horse. Alas, his loop fell short of the mark. The loop missed the horse's head and fell over the saddle horn instead. The situation turned into a serious wreck in a hurry. The cowboy lost control and was jerked to the ground. As the cowboy sat there rubbing his seriously injured shoulder, the two horses took off for parts unknown, still connected by the rope.

As the two young boys trudged dejectedly back to the Ranch on foot they could only think about and dread their inevitable meeting with Bill. In the meantime, the two horses returned, one dragging a saddle. When the boys finally showed up Bill asked them, "What happened?"

After the boys described what had happened, Bill impressed on them the fact that the cowboy had been trying to help them, and as a result lost his entry fees because he was unable to compete in the rodeo with his injured shoulder. Bill told the boys that they should pay the cowboy for his lost entry fee. It was the only right thing to do. The boys certainly agreed to do this since it only meant adding the fee to their Ranch bill that their father paid, anyway. But, they learned a valuable lesson from Bill.

The lessons learned from Bill remained fresh in Martin's memory for his whole life. Eighty-one years later when he was ninety-six years old and was still a guest at Eatons' Ranch in June of 2009, he was eager to recount these lessons in an interview with the author.

Young Martin certainly did not know when he was learning those lessons from Bill over eighty years ago that one day he would have a granddaughter named Kimberly (Kim) Koether. And, Bill could not have imagined that his young daughter Nancy, who was only about seven years old at the time, would eventually marry a man named Tommy Ferguson with whom she would have four surviving children. One of them would be named T. J., and neither Martin nor Bill could imagine that one day Martin's granddaughter would marry Bill's grandson. It's all pause for thought about the grand order of things and the "Eaton connection."

Martin was not the only one to gain a lifetime of memories from his stay at Eatons'. So did his brother Herb. On June 25, 2007, Herb wrote his grand niece, Kim Ferguson, a thank you note for a gift she'd sent him. The note read:

Dear Kim:

Thank you so much for the 125th Anniversary Edition of Eatons' Ranch. What a thoughtful gift—just like you! And thanks to T.J., too. The book brought back many memories as I read it.

In one way, there are people from Pittsburgh and New York State who know more about the Eatons than their next-door Wyoming neighbors do. That is a certain kind of friendship hard to describe.

Marty and I did a certain amount of growing up during those three summers at the ranch. Our parents offered to take us to Europe on the Grand Tour with them in the summer of 1929. We chose to go back to Eatons'.

There are many stories I could tell you about our summers at the ranch. It was all a part of a life I'm glad we were fortunate enough to live. Please give my best to T.J. and to Nancy.

Love,
Herb

While Bill had a compassionate nature for cowboys, he also had a rough physical side as well. He loved to play practical jokes on "the boys" and roughhouse with them. McWilliams described his nature:

> *Bill was quite the prankster, too. You still hear about some of his escapades...how he put alum in the open mouth of a cowboy who was snoring a bit too spiritedly...how he was going to throw Shorty in the horse trough (a common enough occurrence for any number of reasons) and got creative when he found it frozen over—instead of giving up, he just picked Shorty up, used his head for a battering ram to break the ice and threw him in anyway...how one of the rooms on The Pike was full of bullet holes where Big Bill playfully shot at the mice that stuck their noses out. Pete Daily told about how he (Pete) had such a hard time getting up in the morning that they used to throw him in Wolf Creek. When that didn't cure him, Bill roped Pete's tepee (with him inside) and dragged him all over the fairgrounds where they were camped at the time. Pete managed to get up on time after that.*

It wasn't a one-way street. The boys took every opportunity to reciprocate. Once, Bill and Curly Witzel had a historic rough and tumble fray in the Wolves Club. There are many versions of this oft-repeated story, but generally, the story revolves around the fact that Curly bet Bill that Bill could not eject Curly from the Wolves Club in less than twenty minutes. Bill took him up on the bet. When he entered the Wolves Club, he found Curly underneath one of the iron beds with his arms and legs curled around the frame and metal springs. One version of the story claims that Curly had even nailed the legs of the bed to the floor. Big, powerful Bill was determined to break Curly's death hold on the underside of the bed and Curly was equally determined to hold tight, no matter what. The pitched battle seemed to go on forever, but eventually, in just over twenty minutes, Curly, and possibly the bed, were forcefully ejected from the room. Curly won the bet, but the Wolves Club was shattered. Today, Curly and Big Bill are both gone, but the bed remains in the Wolves Club as a lone silent witness to the scuffle.

Bill and Curly found many ways to torment each other and could carry it to extremes. Curly absolutely did not trust banks and hated even to go in them. He was notorious for not cashing his paychecks, so the Ranch had to direct deposit his checks so he had to go to the bank to get his money. Because he did not use banks, Curly carried a lot of money in his pocket. According to legend, one day Bill was talking to Curly and for some reason Curly pulled a big wad of bills from his pocket. Bill suddenly grabbed it from him and tore it into little pieces as he declared, "Aw, hell, that's all counterfeit." Quite an expensive prank, for Curly, anyway.

Frank Eaton, Bill's grandson, loves to tell the following story about Bill and Reid Kochel in the Wolves Club. One year they were in there and got into a friendly argument that resulted in Bill chasing Reid around the room, which had a potbellied stove in one corner. The stove was burning hot. Bill managed to corner Reid with the stove in between them, and from the other side reached around both sides of the stove and encircled Reid with his long arms. Big Bill gradually pulled Reid closer and closer to the hot stove. As he did so, Reid's eyes got bigger and bigger as he got hotter and hotter. Eventually, Bill let Reid go, but not before he had Reid's total attention.

Bill was also impetuous and took action with little regard for the consequences. Once, the barn roof needed repairs and one of the employees was assigned the job. The steep slope of the roof required that the employee rig up some sort of harness so he could do his work without falling off. In this case, the employee took a long rope and secured it to the corral on one side of the barn and he suspended himself on the other end of the rope on the other side of the barn roof. Apparently, Bill passed by and shouted something to the employee on the roof. Whatever Bill said evoked the wrong reply. Bill casually sauntered over to the other side of the barn where the rope was tied, and cut it. The employee tumbled to the ground and Bill casually strolled off. Whether or not the employee was hurt is uncertain, but we do know he must have learned a lesson—don't mouth off to Big Bill.

Bill's toughness and propensity for roughhousing and practical jokes was just his nature. Irv Alderson explained it. Irv Alderson ranches on the family ranch, the Bones Brothers Ranch on Hanging Woman Creek near

Birney, in southern Montana. Irv's great uncle was Walter Alderson who married Nannie Tiffany Alderson, the mother of Patty Eaton who was Irv's second cousin.

Irv said, "Bill wasn't a mean man." Irv explained that though Bill was rough and tough, and he and his friends liked to torture each other, he would never extend that behavior toward someone who couldn't take it or give back as good as he got. Bill never wanted to hurt anyone.

He felt that way about the dudes and horses as well. In one *WN*, Angela Buell wrote a fictitious incident to describe Bill's attitude about safety. In the story, Patty is showing a new dude the ranch and when they get to the corral, the dude asked Patty:

> *... if there was a chance of the boys bringing out a bucking horse for a dude as a joke, but instantly regretted the question for Patty was horrified. She said that one of Bill's greatest concerns during the busy midsummer season was that of safety for every rider. It would be absurd of course for anybody to guarantee against accidents with horses, although everyone connected with the work of the Ranch, and especially with the corral, took every precaution they knew against the liability of something going wrong and someone getting hurt.*

That was, always has been and still is Eatons' attitude about safety.

Peter and Hattie Pelissier continued to live in Sheridan but Peter died at the age of fifty-nine years on December 1, 1924. Peter suffered a paralytic stroke about five months before he suffered a second stroke, which killed him. When he was stricken, Peter was a member of the Sheridan Police Department. His obituary in the *Sheridan Post Enterprise* described Peter as "one of Sheridan's best known men." His widow Hattie continued to reside in their house at 231 West Loucks and it became a kind of headquarters for other members of the Pelissier family.

Willis, the oldest child of Peter and Hattie, worked at Eatons' Ranch until the mid-1920s. Why he left is not certain. It may be because he and his wife Ethel had a second son, Willis E. Pelissier, on February 26, 1924 and they needed more income. In 1924, the Sheridan City Directory listed Willis and Ethel living in the Anderson Apartments and Willis employed as a bookkeeper at the Sheridan Commercial Company. Later, Willis, Ethel, and their two sons moved in with their mother Hattie. Willis was associated with Sheridan Commercial for the rest of his life.

Mary continued to work and live in Sheridan with her husband Roy Haywood. Unfortunately, Mary was widowed by the time the decade ended. After her husband died in 1929, Mary stayed in Sheridan and lived, at times, with her mother, Hattie.

Elsie was elected as clerk of district court in 1918 and served three, two-year terms. She did not run for a fourth term in 1924. Why she chose not to run is not clear, but it may have been because of family circumstances. A year earlier, on December 10, 1923 Elsie had married Augustus H. Beidler. She had known Beidler for some time as he and members of his family were frequently guests at the Eaton Ranch. For reasons unknown, the marriage was short lived and Elsie and Augustus were divorced just one year later on December 12, 1924, just after Elsie's father died.

After the divorce, Elsie and her son, six year old Jack, moved to Denver, Colorado, where Elsie raised her son and served as deputy clerk of the United States District Court for forty years.

Dudes

Dudes, both old and new, flocked to Eatons' Ranch in the 1920s. Sometimes, like in 1925, Eatons' had to turn people away. The September 1925 *WN* declared:

> *We are mighty sorry that we didn't have places for everyone who wished to come in July and August—but there*

were just more friends than there were cabins this year and we had no choice—we were tied up early in the summer and were obliged to write and wire "no room."

In 1925, the Eatons planted the seed for an informal competition for tenure honors—in other words, which dudes had bragging rights for the longest history with Eatons' Ranch? Their first declaration was in 1925:

Someday an "Old Timers" list at Eatons' Ranch will be the subject of friendly rivalry. One friend boasts of twenty-nine visits in thirty-one years. Families tell of three generations traveling from the East over a period of forty years to ride with the Eaton brothers. In the fall of 1884, Mr. James B. Stevenson of Pittsburgh wrote his name in the guest book of the Dakota Ranch, and in 1924—forty years later—and this loyal friend rode again with Eaton Brothers, this time on the Wyoming ranch.

As time went on, *WN* continued to publish lists of Eaton dudes and how long they, or other members of their family, had been guests at Eatons' Ranch. It was a point of pride. In 1927, *WN* proclaimed that:

About once a year, we allow ourselves the pleasant privilege of boasting in Wranglin' Notes *about the many friends who return, season after season, for their Ranch vacation. Colonel Henry Hall of Washington, D. C., heads the list with a credit of twenty-two visits to the Wolf Creek Ranch out of its total of twenty-three seasons, and Harry Hayward of St. Louis comes next with sixteen summers.*

The lists became longer and longer, and not only did they list who had been guests for a particular year, they also provided information about who had made reservations for the next year. After publishing one list of people who had made reservations in 1928, *WN* stated that:

We know that this list is incomplete and that we'll probably have indignant letters telling us of omissions, but that's just what we want, for the new lists have a good start. And we are anxious to hear from all old returning friends, who have pet cottages and cabins, and horses that they want again. Then we can go ahead and arrange for the many new friends—most of them friends of friends—who have already written for places.

Occasionally, in addition to the long lists of dudes who visited the Ranch the last year, or those who had reservations for the next, *WN* featured news about a particular person. The occasion of Mary Roberts Rinehart's fifty-third birthday party at the Ranch is a good example:

All who have visited the Ranch in midsummer the past twelve or thirteen years have very promptly become acquainted with and a personal admirer of one of the Ranch's most faithful and best loved dudes—Mary Roberts Rinehart. It took only the slightest suggestion to interest everyone in plans for a celebration of her birthday on August 12, in which all were to take part and to which many guests from neighboring ranches and other friends were invited.

Bill Eaton and the corral boys arranged the afternoon entertainment—races, roping and bucking. There were potato races for the cowboys, for the dudes, and for mixed cowboy-dude teams. There was a maverick race which George Gentry won in short order, a chair race, a quick change race, fancy roping by Joe DeYong and Dave Edwards, and last of all some exhibition bucking.

After dinner in the evening, there was a lull when everyone scattered to their cabins to dress for the costume dance. The orchestra arrived from town, a family of Crow Indians came in from the Reservation to add their bit to the pleasures of the day, spectators gathered in Howard Hall. With smothered giggles and many "ohs" and "ahs," horses and chickens and monkeys and dogs, hula dancers and savages from the jungles, ladies of the Gay Nineties with eighteen inch waists and inscrutable smiles, a man upside down who turned out to be a girl, contortionists, H. R. H. the Prince of Wales, three small Goops, beautiful ladies and charming gentlemen—many fantastically dressed figures—trooped from The Terrace, The Pike, Rotten Row, Butler Boulevard, and the outlying cottages of the Ranch to the brightly lighted porch and interior of Howard Hall where they paraded around and around for the pleasure and delight of Mrs. Rinehart and the crowd.

The judges, Mrs. Kenneth Mygatt and Colonel Marshall, (Note: Colonel Marshall would become Chief of Staff of the United States Army and direct the Army during World War I. He also served as Secretary of State after the War and was awarded the Nobel Peace Prize in 1953.), *were dismayed at the job ahead of them, but they carried it off well.*

Mr. Graham was a fine major domo of the whole affair. Presented by friends as a remembrance of the day, Mrs. Rinehart has a model of her horse, Kaycee, carefully worked out from life by Joe DeYong—complete to the last detail of bridle, saddle and rope. She said it was one of the finest birthdays she had ever had, and surely no one enjoyed it more than those who planned and helped make it a success, which includes just about everybody.

One of those in attendance at the party was young Martin Koether. Eighty years later, Martin still remembers the party and Mrs. Rinehart, whom Martin describes as a "very genuine and handsome lady." Martin also remembers the words that Mrs. Rinehart used to express her sentiments about her party. In a rather emotional thank you speech she said, "In my life, this is high tide."

While some dudes had records for longevity at Eatons', others had different records of achievement of which they were most proud and would do literally anything to maintain them. Sometimes it proved to be a difficult task. The September 29, 1929 issue of *WN* described one such difficulty:

Edwin Boaler, Jr. of Oak Park (Illinois) sustained his reputation by again being the first dude to arrive, coming up from the Rimrock Ranch in March. Uncle Alden met him in Sheridan and they left town for the Ranch in great style traveling by automobile. Then, according to schedule, the automobile was left at the Half-Way House in Beckton and passengers, groceries and load transferred to a lumber wagon. But not according to schedule. The lumber wagon was abandoned half a mile farther on when it unexpectedly turned into a stone boat that six horses couldn't pull through the mud, and Ed reached the Ranch on the final leg of his journey, horseback.

Keen Butcher has another record that might stand. Keen may be the oldest living person who first visited the Ranch at the earliest time and youngest age. Keen was only seven years old on his first visit in 1923. From Philadelphia, he was one of six children. During a full lifetime, including five years in the Army in North Africa and Italy during the Second World War and extensive travel in Europe on vacations, Keen visited the Ranch often. He still recalls as a young boy what was almost a "rite of passage." That was on the grand day when he was riding with Uncle Willis and Uncle Alden and they actually allowed him to open the gates. To a young boy, that gesture was a signal honor. Keen still visits Eatons' and organizes large family reunions for his extended family. Eatons' Ranch is a Butcher family tradition.

Employees

Just as dedicated dudes returned year after year, so did dedicated employees. The Eatons considered them family members. News about their activities and whereabouts was interesting to the thousands of *WN* readers.

There was one sad item not discussed in *WN*, surely at John and Mae Fleming's request, and that was the death of their son, John. His death was noted in the local newspaper, which explained that young John died on June 8, 1925 after a short illness. He was fifteen years old and had just completed his sophomore year at Sheridan High School. He died of complications from a bout with influenza that resulted in pneumonia. Apparently, he had a heart condition, as well.

But there was lots of good news. For example, the September 1926 *WN*:

> *Curly Witzel and Minnie Hiser were married in Sheridan the first part of August. The bride is Mrs. Reid's assistant in the Ranch housekeeping department. The groom, for years one of the corral boys, returned the first part of the summer after working with the Universal Corporation in Hollywood where he played the "hero" in many of the western movies. Curly has the leading role in*—The Fighting Strain, Double Trouble, The Whirlwind Driver, When Bonita Rode, Western Bound, The Law of the North, The Hollywood Dude, *and* On The Lone Prairie…

(Note: When Minnie and Curly married, she was only twenty years old, and Curly was twenty-three. Sadly, in 1930, Minnie died two weeks after giving birth to a daughter, Elizabeth "Betty" Fry Witzel. Curly was unable to care for the baby and put her in the care of his good friends from Banner, Earl and Ethel Harper. They raised Betty as their own along with their son Bill, who was about the same age as Betty. When Betty grew up, she married George Nimick—a former Eaton dude—of Buffalo, Wyoming and had six children.)

...Harry Fulmer, corral boss at the Ranch a few years ago and later a rancher near Dayton, Wyoming, is now selling Dodge automobiles at the main sales room in St. Louis...

...Ben and Claire Sittler (who was Claire Curran) are in charge of the Ranch saddle horses near Echeta, Wyoming...

...Bill Graham is now a corral hand...

...Bruce Brockett is driving the Ranch car, meeting all trains to welcome Ranch friends...Bill is limping a bit from the bad fall he got in last year's Frontier Day bucking contest, but otherwise he's the same jovial, likeable laughing cowpuncher he's always been. (Note: Bruce was also a poet and contributed often to WN. He also later wrote articles for western magazines and published a book of poetry)...

...Pete Jensen is still the "dairy boss" for the thirty Holstein and shorthorn dairy cows that supply the Ranch table with milk and cream...

And later there was other news, like in the 1926 Christmas Issue of *WN*:

...George Gentry has been shivering and wishing the climate would change so all the country would be tropical. Curly has been working at the P.K. this fall. Reid Kochel is back on Powder River near Miles City. Bruce and Neeley are over at the OW Ranch in Montana. Russell Burgess is in the Big Horn Basin helping with the Sheriff's office. Bobby Espy and Everett Chetham are at Hot Springs, Arizona, hunting for waterholes and shade. Emil is staying at the Ranch helping Tom Butler keep Wolf Creek from freezing up—but when green grass starts, they will be drifting back to the home range...

And then, in 1927, more typical news:

...Then there was Jack Burgess who was badly hurt while wrangling the cavvy early one morning. The doctors couldn't help him much and Jack is still laid up at home—Littleton, Colorado. Whenever the home folks get down that way they drive

out to take him for a ride. Curly and Minnie stopped on the way to their winter work at the Seven Dash Ranch at Johnson, Arizona. Bill and Patty have seen him recently, too...

In March of 1928, another employee update read:

...Bruce Brockett is home again, mighty glad to be here—and best of all, his ankle coming along in fine shape and promising to be as good as new. Chuck Schlegel will be here the first of July as usual. Miss Lulie McGregor will be here of course, and Mrs. Ralph Denio expects to be with us. Donald Knapp will be back in the office. Mrs. Reid will have your comfort always in mind, and John Duncan and Emil Jacobs will be ready for pack trips. Down the road, Domo Alderson will be waiting at her cabin for you to call, and once you taste her good cookies you'll be going back for more...

In February 1929, Angela Buell published a special edition of *WN* and told a fictitious story about two new dudes, named Tom and Mary, and their first experience at Eatons' Ranch. It described a typical day at the Ranch and, of course, featured some of the employees:

...There was the corral boss, George Gentry, who knew every horse in the cavvy and solemn looking Ewin Neely, whom everyone called "Scorp," and who turned out later to be far from solemn. And Curly Witzel (as far as everyone knows he was baptized "Curly") who could get a job clowning in the circus any day. Reid Kochel, who was easily fussed when addressed as "the sheik of the creek," and Bobbie Espy who seemed to be a general favorite, and also, Everett Cheetham, who Patty said was the only musically inclined cowboy on the Ranch, so far as she knew...

Joe DeYong still showed up at Eatons' when he could and his presence was noted in September 1929:

...Joe DeYong was with us again, as everyone was reminded when they read the daily Wranglin' Notes *on the bulletin board with his clever illustrations of horses, cowpunchers and dudes, all in action. The demand for the daily issue as a souvenir was so great that the boys had to list and take them in order...Joe delighted folks again with his rope tricks and Indian stories told in sign language. He says he'll be in Santa Barbara again this winter, and extends an invitation to wandering dudes to look him up there...*

Many other old long-standing employees were mentioned as well:

...There were familiar faces on every hand—Mrs. Reid always at the door to greet newcomers and make them comfortable in their cabins at the Ranch, Mrs. Butler taking the same excellent care of the laundry, Julia ringing the bell right on the dot as she has done for the past twelve years, and so on down the list..

Then *WN* gave a brief historical review and how certain people, family and employees had contributed to its success:

...The building up of the Ranch, covering, to date, a period of fifty years, has already absorbed the lifetime of a number of people. And there are some of the second generation, who figure they have put in a good many years at it, themselves. Changes in management are so gradual they are hardly noticed. It has been almost fifty years since Uncle Alden helped found the Ranch. Bill Eaton has known the Ranch his entire lifetime and has been active in its affairs for twenty years, John Fleming twenty-five years, and his assistants, Tom Butler, eighteen years and Angela Buell, ten years...

In those days—the 1920s—most of the old-timers who worked at Eatons', especially in the corral, were "hands." In western parlay, a "hand" is someone who knows how to do whatever it is that has to be done and knows when to do it. They don't need a lot of supervision and don't need much direction, except maybe to be pointed in the right direction and told to get the job done. In the West, to be described as a "real hand" is a supreme compliment.

Bill Eaton wasn't much for giving directions and had unique ways of dealing with those who needed them. Irv Alderson loves to tell the story about Bill and Curly Witzel and the paint thinner.

In the very early 1920s, when Curly first went to work at Eatons', he was not yet a fully-fledged hand. One day, he asked Bill, "What do you want me to do?"

Bill said, "Come with me," and led Curly over to a shed and gave him a can of paint and some paint thinner. "Thin this paint," said Bill, and left.

Curly sat down and began to thin the paint. He poured some thinner in the paint and stirred until he thought he had it to the right consistency. When Bill came by, Curly asked him if it was thin enough.

"No, thin it some more," said Bill, and left again.

This routine went on all day. Curly kept thinning the paint, and Bill kept telling Curly to thin it some more. At the end of the day, Bill returned again, and Curly showed him the paint, which by now was almost pure thinner, and asked, "How's this?"

Bill looked in the can and said, "That's okay."

"What do you want me to do with it?" asked Curly.

"Pour it out," Bill said, and walked away.

That was the last time Curly ever asked Bill Eaton what to do. Possibly, this was one of the reasons that Bill Eaton, with his wry sense of humor, once stated that "Having Curly around was like having four good men gone!"

Another incident involved Bill Eaton and Irv Alderson's father and uncle. Irv's father was Irving N. Alderson, called "Little Bones," and his uncle was Allen R. Alderson, called "Big Bones" There was also a third brother, the oldest, whose name was Floyd Taliaferro Alderson. He was called "Skin and Bones," and became a western movie actor. In the silent movies, he performed as an extra (often with Tom Mix) under the name Wally Wales. Supposedly, his name was derived from the fact that he looked like the Prince of Wales. When sound movies arrived, he used the name Hal Taliaferro and starred in several movies.

Big Bones and Little Bones grew up in Montana and "worked around." They worked as horse wranglers for the Three Circle Ranch for some time and then went to work for Bill Eaton. At Eatons' they met Mary Roberts Rinehart. She asked them if they would take her on a roundup because she thought it would be a good subject for a book. The brothers took her to one on the Tongue River in Montana and the result was *No Man's Land.* One chapter in the book, "Riding the Circle," featured her experiences on the roundup with the Bones Brothers.

Rinehart encouraged the brothers to start their own dude ranch and they took her advice. In 1923, the brothers left Eatons' and homesteaded on Hanging Woman Creek near Birney, Montana. They joined forces with two cousins, Percy and Ned Cox, whom they later bought out. Thus was born the Bones Brothers Ranch, which operated as a prominent dude ranch until 1969 and still is a family owned working ranch today.

When the Bones brothers went to work for Eatons' they were already "hands" but not yet familiar with the Eaton operation or Bill Eaton's style of management. They soon learned.

One day, out of the blue, Bill pulled up in his car and ordered them to "load up." They jumped at Bill's order and quickly did as they were told. After they had put their saddles, saddle blankets and bridles in the car, they climbed in themselves and Bill sped off.

The Bones brothers had no earthly idea where they were headed and Bill wasn't exactly forthcoming. In fact, he didn't say anything at all. They learned their destination when Bill finally stopped one hundred miles later at Echeta where the Eatons wintered their horses. Bill just dropped them off and left. As Bill drove away, the boys just stood there with their saddles—no change of clothes, no personal items, like a toothbrush, no money—no nothing! They survived and learned a lesson. Be ready for anything.

With that in mind, the Bones brothers vowed to be ready the next time Bill beckoned. They made up contingency kits with a little food and other personal items and clothing for any conditions.

It wasn't long before Bill and Patty drove up, and Bill told them once again to get in the car. The boys asked no questions. They just gathered up their gear (including their contingency kits), hopped in the car and departed for parts unknown.

The Bones brothers found themselves on a leisurely drive to Birney, Montana where they had a nice chicken dinner with Ned and Percy Cox's mother, Mrs. Cox, and then returned to the Ranch. That time the Bones brothers didn't need their emergency kit, but, by God, they were prepared!

For the Eatons, the decade of the 1920s had its sad times and challenges. Howard and Willis died and left an enormous gap in the family, fire gutted the main ranch house, and there were some economic hurdles to leap. But those family members who remained—Alden and Mame and Bill and Patty—were resilient. In addition, the Eaton brothers' foresight in hiring John Fleming as the business manager many years before paid untold dividends. John Fleming and his assistants did their best to keep the Ranch affairs in order.

At the end of the decade, there was room for optimism. Bill and Patty had produced a third generation—Billy and Nancy—who were coming into their own. In addition, the Ranch expanded its operation when it acquired the Bar Eleven at Echeta for winter horse pastures and the Rimrock Ranch in Arizona for a winter place for dudes.

However, there was also room for concern. The stock market crash on October 29, 1929, "Black Tuesday" was an ominous signal for Eatons' Ranch. Even though it was in far off Wyoming, it couldn't escape some suffering. The Great Depression, along with some troublesome internal Ranch matters, made the 1930s a challenging time.

CHAPTER 6

The Thirties

Early Thirties—Troublesome Times

The early 1930s were difficult for everyone, and the Eatons were no exception. They needed to borrow money to keep the operation alive. The first people they turned to were relatives.

In January 1932, the Eatons secured a loan from the Bank of Commerce in Sheridan, Wyoming for $5,000, and the collateral was stock shares provided by Mary Gillespie, a sister, and Mary Eaton, Alden's wife.

Then, in late October, they needed money again. They had used their "Dude Ranch Fund" to buy cattle and needed to borrow money to replenish that fund and finance "carrying expenses." In their loan application letter, they stated their case:

After fifty years of dude ranch and livestock work, we find ourselves in one of the most difficult periods we have known in that time. Our operations have always been conservative, and with strict attention to our business, which yields only modest profits, we have gradually built up a plant and a reputation, which is known all over the country. A great many people depend upon our dude ranch and livestock operations for a livelihood. For many years, we have taken part in any plans for the betterment of our community, and we believe that our whole record entitles us to favorable consideration of this application.

Eatons needed more than cash infusions to keep the Eaton ship afloat during the difficult early years of the 1930s. John Fleming believed there was much room for improvement in ranch management practices—or lack of them—and expressed his views in a three-page memorandum to the staff in January 1932. John opined:

We need an increase in income and a reduction in expense for 1932 after the two dwindling years just passed. This is quite a challenge, but I believe is worth trying for, and much will depend upon good teamwork and careful planning…

Most any year we need to do better in trying to chart our way by use of actual figures rather than take the much easier course of "guess"…

The ideal would be a general storeroom with all supplies under lock and withdrawals supervised. Accounts would probably judge our commissary and store control almost fair but all other spots weak. Stuff gets terribly scattered and waste occurs. Everybody Orders…

And there is never any doubt in my mind as to the value of the simplest style and service and menu, etc. in the commissary. I would far prefer merely an extension of the winter simplicity into the summer as far as possible. And to continue the effort for better cooking (home style) and for cleanliness. To Smoke or Not to Smoke?...

Advertising becomes of more and more importance as so

many others join in the chase for business in the dude ranch industry. We are glad the Dude Ranch Association promises to work more quietly and to omit the ballyhoo. Each one of us should endeavor to enlist particular friends in our "campaign" this year by personal letters, etc., and we must all try to remember that new names for the address file are most welcome...

The Bar Eleven seems fated to be an outlay proposition for we see no way to make it directly self supporting.

The venture in the Rimrock is marking time for lack of capital. These very poor years here affect its chances for early progress unless some way opens to secure "new capital." Perhaps with the turn of business, which all hope for, a way will be found to finance the needed enlargement and thus avoid a long wait. We surely hope so, and believe it well worth a real effort.

(Note: Two years later, in 1934, Eaton Brothers, Inc. took out a $10,000 loan from the Bank of Arizona and the loan was secured by promissory notes and their real estate, the Rimrock Ranch in Yavapai County, Arizona.)

Private horses should be here under a definite, understood in advance by the owner, plan...

Poor old store. I fear it is likely to continue its downward way, but we would welcome any proposals to restore its position as an important factor. Can we all very seriously remember the importance of fully completing any sale—particularly if to be "Charged"...We have never found any satisfactory way to overcome the losses through carelessness and due to easy access to the store in off hours. And, again such losses are not due to dishonesty in any way but almost 100% due to carelessness. "I meant to tell you."...

Fleming then launched into his philosophy about some other things that preyed on his mind.

The auto and plane are symbols of the more important change and this is increased speed in living. Time in which to do things always seemed short in the old slow motion days, but, now, with the use of speed, we are lost to know how to fill in the hours we have gained. People need to escape to a slower tempo and be able to stretch out simple tasks to form a quiet, restful day—but we find it harder and harder to make them see the real opportunity the ranch affords. (Few factors have injured the ranch more—as I see it—than Speed.)...

It is difficult for me to change (sign of years) and so I am still reluctant to alter my "no order" system of management and to revert to the usual "do this or do that." But I sometimes leave the wrong impression and receive credit for density that is not really deserved. I usually know the weak spots and I generally expect to see them corrected, but I won't insist upon correction. I feel it is up to the younger folks to really study things—really plan their work—and then force improvements upon me that they will personally uphold.

John finally implored the staff and family:

You who read this are entrusted with a personal responsibility to try to lend a special hand in 1932. I can vouch for our need for such aid and can assure you that I am now just making up a poor song—the way grows very hard. And a thousand tendencies inimical to this business arise which are beyond the weaknesses of our own work. So it is only in bettering the daily routine that we can provide the margin, to meet the drain so imposed from without. Your chance to help lies largely in efforts to simplify and to follow the guidance of the facts as fast as we can obtain them. If our forecast shows poor business for May or for June, please adjust your plans accordingly. Consider carefully all expenditures, check up before buying, try to reduce the number of items on inventories, cut the employee list at the beginning and end of the season by planning long in advance, and generally proceed as if facing a very difficult year...

It is worth noting here that John believed that they wouldn't have had all the management problems if the operation weren't so big. Years later, Patty Eaton said in an interview that John Fleming told her: "…it was too bad they ever let the ranch get bigger than to accommodate fifty people."

Business was in a serious decline and in an attempt to keep it flowing Eatons lowered the rates in 1932—twice! In the May 1932, issue of *WN* Angela Buell discussed the rates:

An appreciable cut was made early this spring for the 1932 season, but with the continuance of dropping prices and unfavorable business conditions, we're going to make the 1932 rates even lower. We believe that fair value has always been received for the money exchanged for a Ranch vacation, but this year it looks like a tremendous value...the general rate is reduced and the customary extra charge for single rooms in the midsummer season has all but disappeared. The further discount of 10% for a stay of three months or more reduces the rate to a very modest figure for the friends who can be with us throughout the season…For us this further drop in rates means added economies, and the hope that somehow everything will come out all right. Needless to say, there's no building program this year. But there's activity on the Ranch just the same…

Angela then described the activity, which was mainly a "paint up, fix up" operation on cabins, and other Ranch buildings and she discussed the road:

Down through the "first and second woods" below the Ranch house, something has been happening to the road. Under Uncle Alden's direction, the boys have blown out the biggest boulders, dug out and rolled away many smaller rocks, graded up what remained, and made a real road. Beckton Hill (Note: A steep hill on the road between the Ranch and Sheridan.) *has been surfaced and the gravel is now slowly creeping on toward the Ranch gate. As one of the dudes wrote—with the passing of the gumbo there's nothing left to kick about—we'll really miss it. But the road improvement is a step forward for the Ranch, and if nothing else were accomplished this season, we could look back on that with satisfaction.*

(Note: John Fleming had a different view of the road situation. He believed that fixing the road would only encourage "gawkers" from town to "come out and poke around the Ranch.")

The rate reductions and the loyalty of Eatons' clientele helped Eatons survive the horrible year of 1932. In May 1933, *WN* expressed optimism for the future:

Before we close our remarks on behalf of Eatons' Ranch for the season 1933...we want to be deadly serious for a moment. We want to say that we are obliged to the many friends of the Ranch whose kindness toward us has never wavered, whose constant support has kept us pushing along regardless of the increasing odds against us. Now that it's well past, we'll admit that last summer was a tough one for us, and still we believe we succeeded in our earnest effort to make it the best and happiest vacation of all time for the friends who could come. We're not yet clear of the woods, but now we positively believe that things are getting better here and everywhere, that burdens will soon be easier all the way around...

During the remainder of the 1930s, the Eatons faced other challenges but, as always, they proved their resiliency and survived. John Fleming, Tommy Butler and Angela Buell were instrumental in that effort.

Ranch Operations

During most of the thirties, Eatons' Ranch operated on three fronts: Wolf, Rimrock and Echeta. At Wolf, even though the first few years saw a precipitous decline in business, Eatons' was somehow able to keep afloat. And then they managed to return to something near the pre-Depression pace. In fact, the 1934 season, according to the September issue of *WN*, was:

> *...more like those busy summers we remember in the years before 1930, when every cabin was occupied and the cavvy really earned their long winter rest, when The Pike was the busy hub for a group of energetic young people who apparently required no rest at all in the bracing altitude and pure dry air of Wyoming, when the watering trough was used on occasion for purposes other than the watering of horses, and when Emil, the veteran camp cook of the Ranch, figured no less than eighty plates, cups, knives, forks, spoons and large juicy steaks, plus incidentals and a couple hundred hot corn fritters, would be needed for the weekly all-day rides and picnics back in the mountains above the Ranch.*

Even though the 1930s presented challenges, Eatons' didn't appear to change. Angela Buell always presented an upbeat face to the thousands of people who regularly received *WN* and thrived on the news. In July 1932, Angela wrote:

> *We hope this issue of* Wranglin' Notes *will remind Ranch friends that we are thinking of them...We are mindful of the problems on every hand, the obstacles that in some cases may be insurmountable this season, but we just want folks to know that we'd be happy to have them anytime if they can come. And if we continue to receive the friendly encouraging letters that have*

been coming in from here and there all season, we'll survive this disappointment of empty cabins in midsummer this year and will be ready to work all the harder and to make every effort to do better next year.

In the same issue of *WN*, Angela dished up the kind of fare that dudes loved to read when she wrote:

> *The little block horse that has been a Ranch symbol for many years makes a new appearance every now and then. He's been worn by Ranch riders in the form of a silver pin for many seasons, and at the corral "Brownie," the wooden horse on whom every new dude has his saddle fitted, was patterned after him. Just as* Wranglin' Notes *goes to press, the* Saturday Evening Post *comes out with "Brownie" himself, big as life on the front cover...Several years ago the little horse appeared on automobile plates labeled with "Eatons' Ranch, Wolf, Wyoming" and many friends told us of friendly hails in the traffic of some eastern city from another "rancher" who recognized his form. He appears on the Ranch dishes, and last year he came to the table in the form of napkin rings. And, by the way, now that the traditional "no smoking" in the Ranch dining room has become a thing of the past, some artistic person might put him to work in the form of an ashtray. This year the little horse showed up on the Ranch barn. He also serves as a foot-scraper in front of the office, besides marking the direction of the wind on a weathervane. Originally, he came from the Southwest, the creation of an artistic Indian, but he has been adopted so long by the Ranch that we sometimes forget that he migrated, and was not born here.*

(Note: The wooden horse figure had become such an institution at Eatons' that the Ranch applied for a patent from the U. S. Patent Office. The request was summarily denied.)

Then Angela Buell fessed up to her authorship of the publication when she wrote:

> *Folks are mighty kind to be interested in* Wranglin' Notes—*to write of having received them—and now and then to send suggestions. Because there seems to be an interest in what member of the Eaton Ranch Outfit throws together the* Wranglin' Notes, *authorship of former issues is admitted (not without misgivings) and this issue is signed by Angela Buell For the Eaton Brothers.*

From that point on, until she left the Ranch in 1958, the masthead of *WN* listed Angela as "Editor."

Eatons' always looked for ways to improve Ranch operation and safety. One change they made, in 1930 was to the rodeo arena. According to *WN*:

> *...For a good many years, the bucking exhibitions and shows at the Ranch have been held on the Plaza in front of Howard Hall and the main house, a space too small for safety with the extra hazard the boys had to take riding their broncs downhill toward a fence topping a sharp drop. Sometimes the best hazers couldn't hold the bronc from banging into the fence and tipping his rider over it and down the slope. All hands got busy this spring and built the new bucking chutes and corrals around the ridge from Howard Hall, back of the Fleming house* (Note: Where Jeff Way, the current Ranch manager, lives today.), *figuring on using the old vegetable garden site for a rodeo grounds....The ground is practically level, well, fenced, no rocks, and there's no end to the bleacher seats on the hillside below the ridge...Of course you can't sit in a rocking chair on the shaded porch of Howard Hall in your best dress and watch the bucking as you used to do, but who wants to sit in a rocking chair anyhow when it's a question of more safety for the boys?*

Bronc riding in front of Howard Hall was great entertainment
for the dudes and corral boys. Rider unknown.
Courtesy of Eatons' Ranch.

Curly Witzel entertains the dudes in front of Howard Hall.
Courtesy of Eatons' Ranch.

Earlier, Angela wrote, "It's a little early to say just which name will stick to it but 'Gentry Field' seems to be heading the list right now." Eventually, that's how it turned out for she later wrote: "There's plenty of room for roping and bulldogging in Gentry Field, which wasn't the case with the Plaza."

The new area also gave Billy Eaton, who was thirteen at the time, a chance to prove that he was becoming a hand:

> With the added interest in roping that has sprung up around the Ranch lately (no doubt winters in Arizona have helped), young Billy Eaton sticks a tie-rope into his belt every morning as regularly as he pulls on his boots. And Billy got the biggest hand of the day one Sunday in early July when he roped and tied his calf ahead of Big Bill and the other boys.

There were other improvements made during the thirties as well. For one, in 1933 they built a new swimming pool.

...The IDEA of a new pool had been on the hook for a long time (one of the many improvements we wanted to make when we could), but when the weather turned against us we stretched a point, let the boys loose on the job, and before you could say "Jack Robinson" there was a fine cemented pool, 70'x35', 7 1/2 feet deep at the lower end, fed from the power line with pure mountain water, a lifeguard on duty for safety, all a tempting invitation to dive in and get cool... "What an uplift that gives you on a warm day," Nancy Eaton said, "I've moved over to the pool. You'll find me there every afternoon"...

Eatons made improvements inside as well, and some of them were not planned. One occurred in 1934 when refrigeration (other than blocks of ice cut from the pond on the lower place) came to Eatons'. The weather "prophets" had predicted a horrible winter, as bad as the winter of 1886-1887, but it turned out to be a winter of "...warm sunshine, dusty roads, no snow to mention, plenty of wind..." These conditions caused the "calamity of calamities, for the first time in the history of the Ranch, no ice crop!" *WN* reported how the Ranch was forced into action:

Finally one summer day in February, the Frigidaire man came out from Sheridan to see us, his hands filled with pamphlets and his head full of ideas. And then the artificial ice folks in town began to be interested in us. So now, we have a new Frigidaire in the kitchen and an icehouse full of very fine but somewhat expensive ice. We mention this so everyone will properly appreciate their iced tea and cool salads this summer.

Weather was always a factor in Ranch operations. For instance, the winter of 1932 was awful—so awful that:

For the first time since its installation eight years ago, the hydro-electric light plant of which we are so proud has frozen up, and we are back temporarily, to the early days on the Ranch when candles and kerosene lamps furnished the only illumination...

In the winter of 1931, Eatons' couldn't take the whole cavvy to Echeta because "it forgot to rain last summer, so streams were low and grass short on the Bar Eleven." Consequently, only half the herd went to Echeta. However, that same year Eatons' was able to put two hundred head of horses on the lease at Wolf because "...last winter was so mild that little snow fell in the mountains" and Eatons' had plenty of hay to feed the horses through the winter.

Nineteen thirty-six was different. It was the year of the "Great Drought" when there was little moisture and grasshoppers and Mormon crickets took over the pastures and stripped the alfalfa meadows. The Eatons were short of feed both at Wolf and at Echeta. The situation was news fodder for *WN*:

> *The drought of 1936 struck the Bar Eleven country as well as Wolf Creek, and lack of normal feed there made it necessary to arrange for the horses elsewhere—in Garvin Basin across the mountains from us. Try to picture about forty thousand acres of broken grassy land in the shape of a triangle. The long side of the triangle is bounded by cliffs that rise precipitously, about three thousand feet, to form a wall of the Big Horn Mountains. The swift, treacherous waters of the Big Horn River hem the second side of the triangle. Another natural barrier is formed on the third side of the triangle by the Devil's Canyon, sheer red walls that drop abruptly several hundred feet. Only a few strands of barbed wire are necessary to close the half-dozen narrow trails leading into the Basin and thereby hold stock in this huge stretch of good pastureland. These natural boundaries have made the Basin so inaccessible that not many years ago outlaws held it as a hiding place for stolen horses and cattle...*

There was a small primitive cabin in the Basin and Curly Witzel and "Hawk" Schaeffer spent the winter there looking after the horses. The Eaton herd was not the only one in Garvin Basin that year. Other dude ranches, mainly the HF Bar Ranch near Buffalo, Wyoming, and probably Tepee Ranch in the Big Horns, had the same pasture problem as Eatons'.

These ranches drove their horses along the face of the mountain, picked up the Eaton herd, and approximately a thousand horses spent the winter in Garvin Basin. The next spring, the ranches picked up the horses and drove them back to their respective home ranches.

While 1936 was certainly a drought year, it must have rained at least once during the summer for a Mrs. Ward wrote the following poem during her stay:

What a joy it was to snuggle
In my cabin's good warm bed
And listen to the patter of the
Soft rain overhead.

My heart was filled with happiness
As I settled for my nap,
Though the paths were muddy rivers
I didn't care a rap.
Uncle Alden was a smiling
Aunt Mame was laughing too,
Bill and Patty were a grinning,
So why should Dudes feel blue?

They are sure of hay for winter,
Let not a soul complain,
All should hurrah with glee and praise
This God sent blessed rain.

Let's not look cross, nor pout, nor frown
It really is not raining rain,
It is raining fodder down.

Unfortunately, Mrs. Ward's optimism was unfounded. One rain did not cure a drought.

In the thirties Bill Eaton continued to be the focal point for the "cavvy" and *WN* reported his activities because all the dudes who read *WN* thirsted for news about the horses, especially if they owned some of them. The following, written in the October 1936 issue was typical:

> *There's plenty of news about the cavvy, which is ever changing. Every fall some of the older horses are pensioned or sold. Every spring young horses are bought to take their places. In May and June Bill Eaton combed northern Wyoming and southern Montana for good saddle horses, which were scarce—but he found what he wanted, and some fifty new horses, all of them gentle, well broke, young, and suitable for Ranch riders, arrived to join the arrowhead cavvy...*

And in the February 1939 issue, Angela wrote:

> *For a number of years Bill has had a definite program for culling the cavvy each fall or spring, disposing of the older horses that are passing the period of best service to Ranch riders, selling others that have not proven best for the work they're asked to do, and buying new horses to take their places. Although Bill Eaton has a real knowledge of the horse market within five hundred miles of the Ranch, most any direction you want to turn, it's not always easy to find just the horses he wants. So he's always on the lookout for strong, sound, safe, broke saddle horses for the Ranch cavvy. He's found some of the thirty or forty horses that we'll need this year, but there are still many to be bought that when he gets home from the trip East he'll have to continue his scouting...*

Angela put a good face on the horse buying operation. Apparently, it was not always that pretty. What she did not write about, of course, was that Bill Eaton, according to Irv Alderson, often bought horses in bulk—by the truckload. He only knew what he really had when the corral boys tried them out. Then he found out which ones would make dude horses and which ones were unsuitable. The unsuitable ones—the really bad buckers and the ones with bad habits, like rearing up and falling over backwards, or the ones that were just plain outlaws—were disposed of.

Often, when there was a glut of horseflesh on the market and horses were worthless, the unsuitable horses were fed to the pigs because horseflesh was cheaper than pig food.

Bill didn't get rid of all the buckers. He kept some at the Ranch for the corral boys to ride and entertain the dudes at Ranch rodeos. At various times, Eatons' provided horses for the Sheridan-Wyo-Rodeo.

The Sheridan-Wyo-Rodeo was established in 1931. Bill was one of the charter members of the board of directors and a lifelong supporter of the event. The arena director of the rodeo the first year was Harry Fulmer, but Bill Eaton took over the second year and held that position for thirty-five years until he retired from the board of directors in 1966.

Horses were central to the Eaton dude operation and in the spring of 1938, *WN* described how the system worked:

> *It's a rare occurrence when the cavvy fails to come up from Echeta in good shape, but this year with a mild winter behind them they'll probably have to waddle those hundred miles. A few days rest on the grassy hills of Wolf Creek and they'll all be ready to go (after the boys top them off). And right here we might say that the cavvy of three hundred-odd saddle horses offers a sure-fire selection for riders who come to Eatons'. You can't pick your own horse, for you wouldn't know by looking at one of these western horses whether he was unbroken, or green, or a bronc, or someone's "private," or what. But Bill Eaton and George Gentry know every horse in the cavvy, what he can be counted on to do, whether he's the right mount for a five year-old youngster who's taking his first horseback ride, whether he'll interest the experienced rider with a string of his own horses at home, whether he'll bring confidence to grandmother who has come to the Ranch to prove to herself and her children's children that she's still able to sit on a horse and get the joy from riding that she remembers from her youth. The boys are careful with the horses. They select them with thought and care to the experience of every rider, and few friends visit the Ranch and fail to be satisfied with the mounts that are chosen for them.*

Big Bill throwing the "Big Loop."
Courtesy of Eatons' Ranch.

Not only did Bill Eaton and George Gentry know every horse in the cavvy, they were expert at roping them in the corral and bringing them to the saddle barn to be saddled. Irv Alderson still marvels at Bill Eaton's skill with a rope. In the corral with a sea of horse heads before him, Bill could spot the horse he wanted and sail the loop halfway across the corral to land gently over the horse's head and shoulders. Then with a flick of the wrist, he would flip the loop up the horse's neck, tighten it just behind the horse's head, and lead the horse out of the corral at a high speed. Bill

Eaton and George Gentry were masters of their craft and together could probably rope more horses in a given amount of time than any other two cowboys. Irv Alderson says that, "There are very few cowboys today that can rope like those two."

Bill used his roping skills to entertain dudes. According to McWilliams, "He used to take a ninety foot lariat (thirty-five feet is the average length) and build a big loop for six or seven cowboys galloping at top speed to ride through abreast." He caught them all. Bill also could stand on top of his horse and twirl a huge loop around him and the horse and a couple of other mounted men on each side. It was all good stuff.

Family

The thirties was a transition decade for the Eaton family. Only one of the Eaton brothers, who founded the operation on Wolf Creek, Uncle Alden, remained. In 1930, when Alden was seventy-one years old and Aunt Mame was sixty, they celebrated their fortieth wedding anniversary at the Rimrock Ranch in Arizona. The revered couple continued to be essential figures in the Ranch activities and inveterate travelers during the winter months. *WN* reported their travels in detail:

> *Uncle Alden and Aunt Mame left the Rimrock in late January, followed out their original plan for a short visit in Tampico, Mexico, then drove up to Fort Benning, Georgia, where Colonel Marshall ordered out the Army in their honor and where they enjoyed every minute of their stay...*

WN then described the rest of their trip and concluded:

The closer they came to the Ranch, the faster the car went. Not even Beckton Hill slowed them up. But they'd driven more than ten thousand miles by that time and after five months away from the Ranch, Uncle Alden and Aunt Mame were surely glad to get home...

On all of their trips, Alden and Mame acted as good will ambassadors for the Ranch. In May, 1935 a special issue of *WN* was prepared, complete with Alden's photo and mailed to all concerned to announce that "Alden Eaton Is In Town."

Uncle Alden is in town to visit his sister Mrs. McFarlane, and to greet the many Pittsburghers who have been at the Ranch. Wyoming has been HOME to him for many years now, but he holds Pittsburgh "in fond remembrance" and for several years has looked forward to this renewal of old acquaintances and friendships. He can't stay long—must be back at the Ranch ahead of the summer season—but he'll be in Pittsburgh for a week or two. In that time, if you see a blue-eyed Westerner with a Stetson hat and an unlighted stogie walking down Fifth Avenue, you're safe in calling, "Hello, Uncle Alden."

Though he was still a vibrant man in his seventies, Alden occasionally had health problems. The December 1931 issue of *WN* alluded to one of his sick spells:

Out in California Uncle Alden has been busy calling on the doctors and taking treatments as they prescribe. But they have had good reports for him and now he feels much better and is hoping for dismissal soon. If everyone followed Uncle Alden's example, they'd be pushing right ahead in spite of personal worries, they'd be smiling and cheerful through the deepest depression that could come their way...but we do know we're fortunate to have Uncle Alden at the head of the Outfit, spreading strength and good cheer and leading the way over all sorts of obstacles...

Uncle Alden also took ill during the winter of 1935. *WN* used the incident to reflect on a story he often told about the old days:

> *Uncle Alden is home from Denver, where he had several uncomfortable weeks in the hospital with some pleurisy pains to plague him. He says that just getting home again has put him right back on his feet. Uncle Alden contrasts the everyday comforts of 1935, the radio that brings New York and San Francisco right into the Ranch living room, the heated car that slips him quickly and comfortably over a good road to town...with the drafty log cabin in North Dakota that was his first ranch home—the long evenings with a book or a week-old newspaper by the dim light of a kerosene lamp, when it was several cold hours on a saddle horse through snowdrifts to the nearest settlement. He tells us of fifty below zero, short feed, and horses turned out on the range to drift and get through the winter as best they could. Chills run up and down our spines when we hear about the time his saddle horse broke through the ice of the Cannonball River when he was far from the Ranch hunting horses. It was a cool swim to shore but his horse carried him through safely. By the time he reached the nearest settler's home, twenty-five miles distant, the sun had dropped and it was twenty below zero. And when he rode up to the cabin and called for help he was so stiff with ice that they just lifted the saddle off with him and set them both beside the fire to thaw. That's a true story!*

In spite of some sickness and family problems that will be addressed later, the thirties were good for Uncle Alden and Aunt Mame. They had much to be thankful for including two grandchildren, Billy and Nancy, and they enjoyed watching them grow up. But Uncle Alden was to die before the decade was over.

Bill and Patty were busy. Not only were they raising their children, but they also had to stretch their energy between Wolf Creek in the summer and Rimrock in the winter.

Nineteen thirty was a typical year and *WN* reported the move and trek from Wolf Creek to Rimrock:

> *As October advanced and the first chilly winds swept down Wolf Canyon, traveling cases, trunks and saddle sacks came out of the storerooms at Eatons' Ranch and a good part of the Outfit prepared to go south to Arizona for the winter. Lew Crews was the first one on the road and by the time the rest of the crowd reached the Rimrock, he had painted all the floors and done lots of odd repair jobs. On October 20, Archie Brammer and Bobby Espy set out on the big truck, which was loaded down with trunks and saddles and whatnot. Behind them was Reid Kochel driving the girls—Agnes and Hazel, Millie and Mac—in the station wagon. Bill and Patty and the children left the 21st, planning a few days stopover in Denver. John Duncan pulled out on the 27th. Angela Buell left on the 3rd of November, and on the 8th the few folks left at the Ranch—the Flemings, the Butlers and the Schlegels—said goodbye to the last to leave Wolf, Uncle Alden and Aunt Mame, Aunt Minnie and Domo...*
>
> *Bill and Patty Eaton reached the Rimrock a few car lengths ahead of the first dudes, Gil and Dorothy Dunham, who followed them down from Wyoming. The Rimrock seems like home to the Dunhams for they were charter dudes its first season. It was only a short time before every room at the Rimrock was occupied—dudes quickly claiming the few places not needed by the Family, and Christmastime finds us with a household overflowing with friends...*

(Note: The Eatons never had to transport horses to Rimrock. Bruce Brockett, who worked for the Eatons at Wolf, had gone into partnership in a ranch near Rimrock. Bruce's partner got killed in a poker game and Bruce inherited his partner's interest. Bruce kept horses for his use in the summer, but in the winter, the horses were used at Rimrock. Another interesting sidelight about Bruce is that he married Angela Buell's sister, Fredrika [Fritzy].)

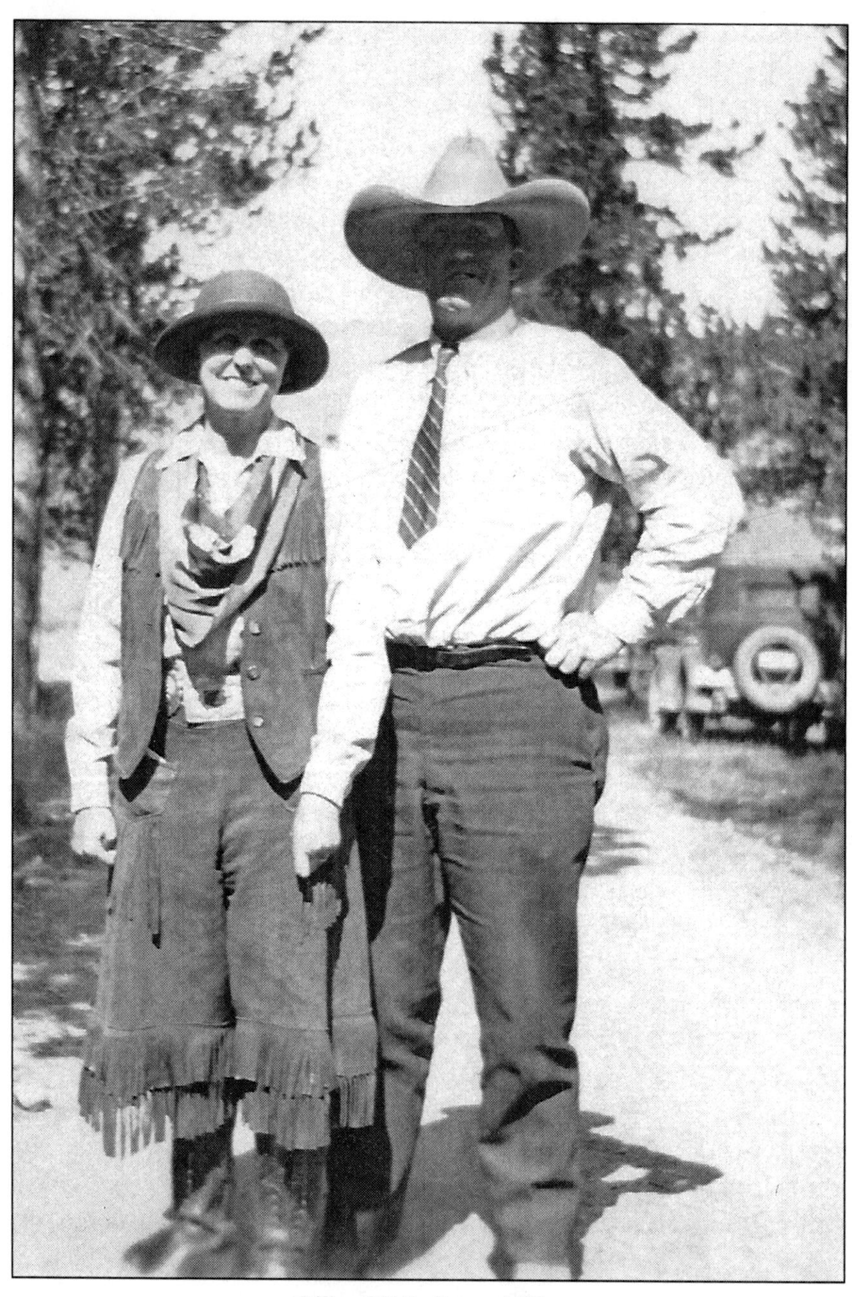

Bill and Patty Eaton, 1931.
Courtesy of Eatons' Ranch.

Apparently, both Fritzy and Angela vied for Bruce's affections when he was at Wolf, but Fritzy won out and they married. Perhaps that is the reason that Angela never married—her unrequited love for Bruce.)

WN reported further:

As soon as they arrived in Arizona, Bill and Nancy Eaton joined the children at the little white schoolhouse within sight of the Rimrock Ranch. There are several full-blooded Apache Indian children among their schoolmates and this is the story Nancy brought home recently: The schoolteacher was asking the children what they most wished to be when they grew up. There were the usual number of cattlemen, ranchmen, policemen and aviators represented in their replies. When she came to Jack, one of the Apache boys, he said very earnestly, "When I grow up I want to be a dude at the Rimrock Ranch."

The annual trek back and forth to Rimrock for Patty and Bill ended in 1938 when the Eatons sold Rimrock to Chuck and Honora Schlegel who had:

"...been associated with the Eaton Outfit for a number of years, spending their winters at the Rimrock and becoming as much attached to the little place as any of the Eaton family."

Rimrock had been on the market for two years but when it finally sold, the Eatons had a slight case of sellers' remorse. However, they were glad to rid themselves of the financial burden and the onerous logistics workload. The Rimrock Ranch sold for $35,000. According to John Fleming, the Ranch used the proceeds "...mostly on debt but also to take care of a few long needed renewal items..."

Like any family, the Eatons had their challenges. However, one problem was especially troublesome—Bill was a gambler, and by all accounts not a very good one.

The problem first surfaces in Eatons' Ranch records in a memo John

Fleming wrote to Bill Eaton on October 19, 1922. The purpose of the memo was to sort out how Bill and the Ranch were going to redeem eighty-four shares of Ranch stock that Bill had signed over to a W. H. Spear to satisfy a gambling debt incurred at Camp Sherman, Ohio, in 1918.

The solution to the problem was to use resources from the estate of Bill's uncle, Howard Eaton, and then repay the estate. Fleming figured that the size of the debt, with interest, was approximately $6,500. This was an enormous debt in 1918, equal to approximately $92,000, in 2009 dollars. Fleming was very stern with Bill and instructed him to provide:

> *A list of all items of indebtedness you are now responsible for, whether secured or unsecured.*
>
> *A statement from you in respect to your knowledge of gambling on the ranch this summer, whether you took any part in it—and a statement of your future and final attitude on this subject as long as you are employed by the Eaton Brothers.*
>
> *A statement from you as to your intention in regard to outside personal deals—involving in any way, shape or form the use of Eaton Brothers payroll, or its feed or pasture or any of its property, and the keeping of special private horses requiring extra care and attention, or in fact any form of operation whereby you or any outsider is to profit directly or indirectly at the expense of the firm.*

Fleming then gave Bill a withering written lecture:

> *If anyone of this place owes utter and unfailing loyalty to the welfare of the firm—you are the leader. Most has been done for you and most is still being done. You are easily the highest paid individual on the ranch, considering regular salary and expenses—and if your experience in deals, etc., teaches you anything, it must be that if you are to have any show to get along in the world, it is by fighting, first, last and all the time to see that the firm of Eaton Bros. gets its just dues and its reputation be protected.*

Bill Eaton complied with John Fleming's instructions and agreed to a long-term contract to make restitution to Howard's estate. Whether or not he fulfilled his pledge is unknown.

Fleming did not hesitate to discuss the situation with others. In January 1931, John Fleming wrote a letter to Mr. John Parker in Philadelphia. Mr. Parker seems to have been a stockbroker who handled John's personal finances, but he may have done some work for the Ranch, as well. Mr. Parker was obviously a confidant of John's, and John unloaded his frank thoughts. With obvious frustration when he wrote:

> *Each year I think things will be easier as regards the ranch and my part. Each year they seem a little more difficult and more uncertain. You can guess that I would regard the loss of Uncle Alden as one of those things that cannot be met—for most, unfortunately the heir apparent is weak material and lives a sort of Jekyll and Hyde existence with one side pretty good and the other very poor stuff. I think (between us) that it always hinges on his inveterate love of gambling—plus the fact that he must be the world's worst player. But this weakness provides no background to support the old traditions of this institution and I would not know where to turn to graft on a new and promising shoot. I can get clerks and office men, etc., but no western gentleman of sterling worth and who referably* [sic] *does not know a lot about the moneychangers.*

Bill's behavior plagued John Fleming throughout the decade. There is no record that John discussed the situation with Bill's parents, Alden and Mame, or with Patty, but the discussions must surely have occurred. John certainly did not hesitate to discuss the problem in writing with other members of the family. One letter, written in 1939, to a sister, Elizabeth Cullum, was painfully frank:

> *...One matter I must mention to you and know you can see it all and know about the family and us and how Alden worked and how much he wanted to have his son Bill take the entire responsibility. I never give up working with Bill, for I feel that he*

has what we need—if he can just settle down to it and be frugal and live within his income...He owes the firm $2,500 and wishes to turn over some of his stock (25 shares) to take up the overdraft and I hope it is all right to do this. I've asked the others and believe they agree, though, of course, all wish he would just get with it and try to make a real record...

John Fleming wrote another letter to Josephine Gillespie, Mary Eaton Gillespie's daughter, who lived most of the time at the Ranch with her mother. Fleming laid it all on the line:

Little by little but at the last you will just have to assume that I do what I can with the character problems within our ranks.

Lord bless you I never pay a gambler a cent nor ever have a thing to do with the direct and dire stuff that my big fellow gets into. No doubt he owes them all. My problem is a fellow who never knew self-denial, never saved a cent in his life, wandered along spending more than he earned—kept overdrawing. His folks—his father could not stop it; his mother could not—tough for anyone to say to me just crack down and stop it. Anyone else not named Eaton would be gently bounced long ago... I say that some way and somehow it has to be stopped. The brunt of the trouble will fall on me. But I simply cannot pull any Hitler stuff. He is the product of years of wrong living—others, entirely innocent, are involved—I have to try to stop it without wrecking everyone, making the innocent suffer most....

In reply, Josephine expressed the opinion that:

...I think if you let Bill's friends know he has no money, and E. B. (Note: Eaton Brothers) *will not pay his gambling debts, they won't be so crazy to play with him. I can hardly imagine Mame would want to make up the amount herself, and if they had a grand row about it among themselves, it might give Bill a settling...*

But, even though this problem constantly lurked below the surface, life at Eatons' Ranch did go on.

For one thing, young Billy and Nancy Eaton were growing up. *WN* often described Billy's exploits.

By the time Billy was thirteen years old, in 1930, *WN* noted his enthusiasm for roping. Once George Gentry and John Duncan brought some goats back from Arizona and *WN* explained why:

> *...For a number of years young Billy Eaton has headed a gang of youngsters here at the Ranch who were learning to rope. It takes hours of practice. A post or an ash can or a good natured grandmother are excellent objects to rope at first, but pretty soon you get to the point where you want something a bit more animated than any of these are likely to be. So the gang would head for the calf lot at the Ranch and deal out some misery to the calves. Unfortunately, this has never made a hit with the men responsible for the well-being of the calves, and it didn't seem to make the calves any fatter either. There are plenty of goats in Arizona and they are fine objects for the rope of the future cowpuncher. They'll twist, turn, run, buck, and jump. No one cares whether they get fat or not, and the goats themselves aren't over sensitive...*

Practice on the goats worked, and by 1933, Billy had become an accomplished roper and *WN* proclaimed Billy's performance at a Ranch rodeo: "The Eaton delegation yells and claps when Billy Eaton ropes and ties his calf in the best time of the afternoon..."

Billy also became an accomplished hunter. In December 1930, Angela Buell wrote that fourteen year old Billy Eaton:

> *...was the hero of the hunting season at the Ranch. Billy got his deer in short order and a few days later set out for an elk. While trailing an elk up over the mountains near the head of the Cattle Trail, he was startled by a noise in the bushes just above the trail, and all thought of an elk immediately left his head—for there, hardly a rifle's length away from him, was a big old brown*

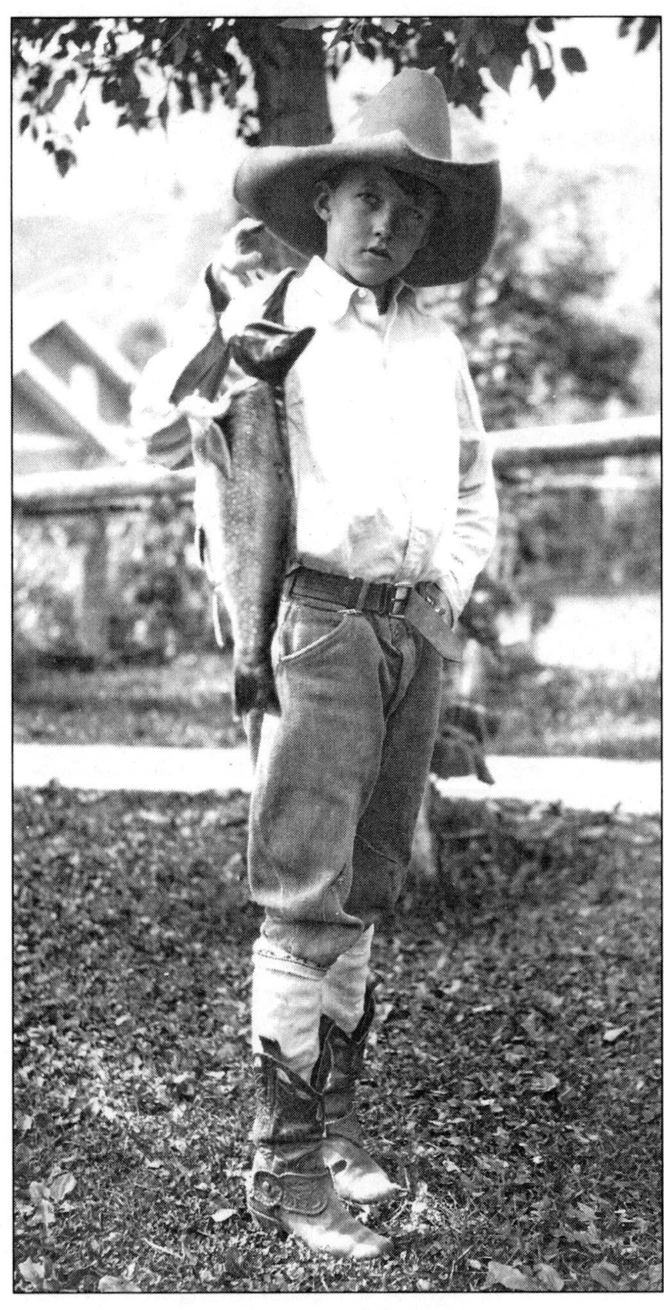

Billy Eaton was a hunter and fisherman at a young age.
Courtesy of Eatons' Ranch.

bear, scratching away busily in the leaves, preparing to hole in for the winter. Billy is only fourteen and he was alone, but he's been John Duncan's pupil all his life and knows his way around when it comes to hunting. The bear hadn't seen or gotten a whiff of him, so Billy crept around above him before taking aim...and the bear fell dead at the first shot. He was an unusually big one for the Big Horns, too. Next summer Billy will show you the hide, which is now in Denver being mounted.

In 1936, Billy and Dunc were still hunting partners, and *WN* noted: "Billy Eaton and Dunc have been chasing coyotes. Billy shot one from the car on his way to school (*Note: The high school in Sheridan.*) one morning. Dunc has brought in five."

Billy attended grade school at the Wolf Creek School, just down the road from the Ranch and then went to high school in Sheridan even though he spent some time during the winters in an Arizona school near the Rimrock. For some reason, he didn't begin high school until he was sixteen years old. He was active in high school and belonged to a number of school clubs. Billy was very interested in acting and was a cast member in two school plays. In the 1936 school play, he played Howard Davidson in a play called *Hawk Island.*

Billy was a popular boy. He was selected for his homeroom "Hall of Fame," and listed in the class "Who's Who" as a "tall, soft spoken debater." Billy also represented Sheridan High School at the Wyoming State Debate in 1936 where he spoke in the affirmative for the resolution:

Resolved, that the several states should enact legislation providing for a system of complete medical care to all citizens at public expense.

Because of his debating ability, Billy received a scholarship to Drake University in the Department of Speech but did not take advantage of the opportunity. After high school graduation in 1936, Billy attended the University of Arizona in Tucson in 1937 and the University of Wyoming the following year. That was the extent of his college career. Rather, Billy chose to return to the Ranch to live and work. It wasn't

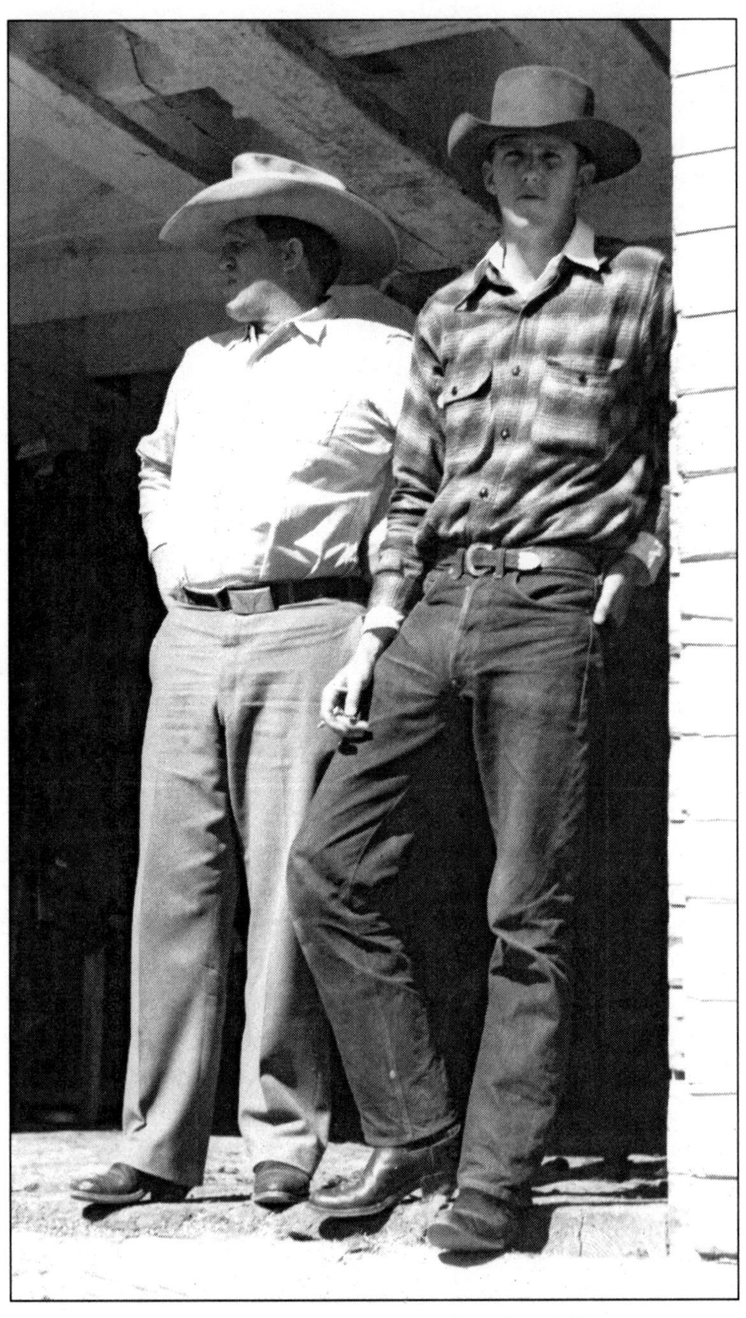

Big Bill and young Billy Eaton. Circa late 1930s.
Courtesy of Eatons' Ranch.

long before he became a married man.

Nan Baker came into his life. She first visited Eatons with her parents, Frank and Gladys Baker of Philadelphia, in 1931 when she was fifteen years old. The reason they went to Eatons' was Zane Grey, the western author. Frank Baker had read many of Zane Grey's books and became intrigued by the West. He had also heard about Eatons' Ranch, and knew they required personal references. Frank Baker had a friend who was a former Eatons' guest who provided a reference for the Baker family. The Bakers thoroughly enjoyed their first trip to the Ranch.

The next year Nan became ill and needed the kind of climate afforded by Rimrock in Arizona, so her parents sent her there with a nurse, to recover. Billy was there at the time, but he and Nan were only casual acquaintances.

Nan has one vivid memory of her time at Rimrock. Rimrock was very close to an Indian village and Rimrock guests often rode through the village. Nan remembers two things—the great number of dogs that always wandered around the village and how much the Indians liked to play baseball with the Rimrock team.

The problem, for the Indians, was that they always lost. However, one day, miracle of miracles, the Indians won. The Indians were so overcome with their maiden victory that they went back to the village and launched an exuberant celebration. From their vantage point, the Rimrock people could hear the noise and see the smoke from what was obviously a barbecue. The Indians had a good time.

The next day Nan and other Rimrock guests rode through the village and witnessed the aftermath. They could not help but notice the obvious absence of dogs.

The next year Nan's parents allowed her to go to Eatons' Ranch at Wolf with a girlfriend, but only on condition that they stayed in the main ranch house, where Aunt Mame could "keep an eye on them." That year Nan and Billy became better acquainted and during the next winter Billy, who was in college, corresponded with Nan at some length. The next year Nan and her sister returned to Eatons'. This time they were allowed to stay in a cabin by themselves.

It wasn't long before Nan and Billy fell in love, and Billy asked Nan to marry him. Nan was fully prepared to marry Billy, but first Billy had

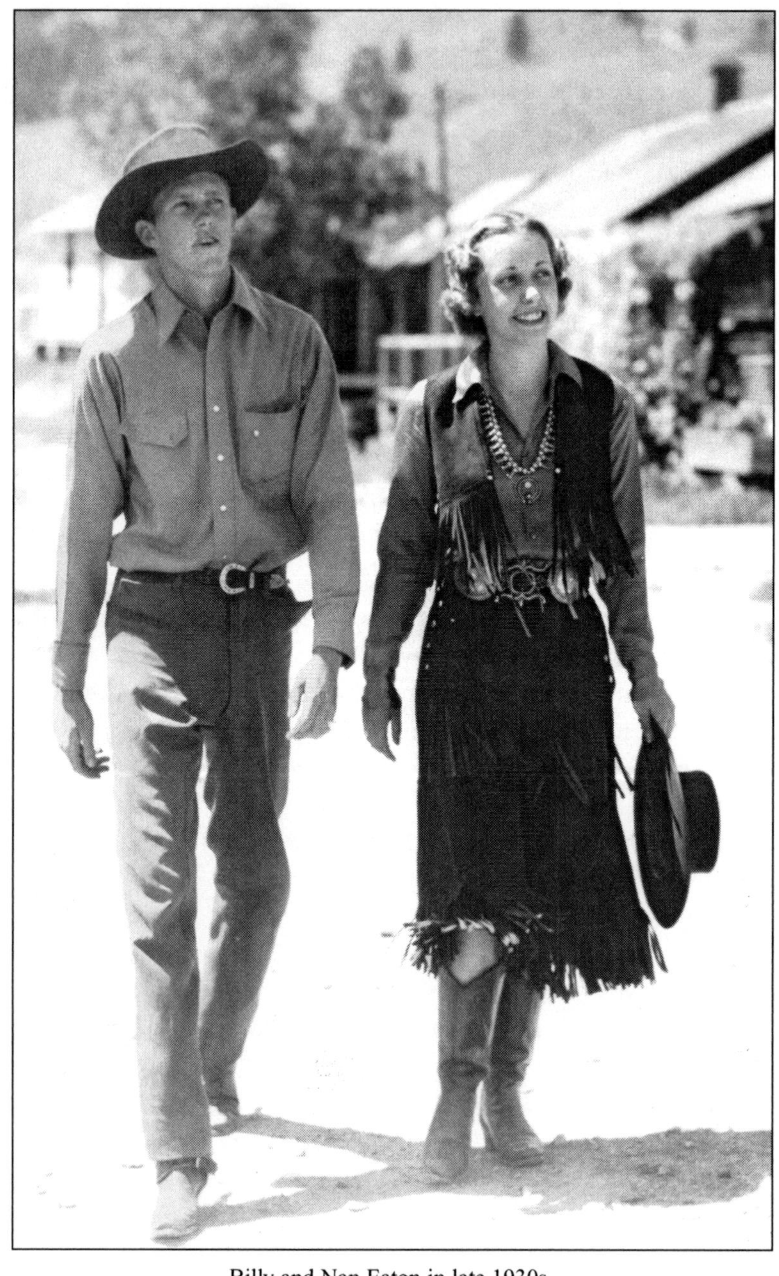

Billy and Nan Eaton in late 1930s.
Photo by W. Thomas McGrath, Sheridan, Wyoming.
Courtesy of Eatons' Ranch.

to pass muster with her parents. Frank and Gladys Baker liked Billy but didn't really know him that well. In order to get better acquainted, and to make sure Billy was the right man for their daughter, Nan's parents took Billy and Nan to on a cruise through the Panama Canal in the spring of 1937.

The cruise was a success and Billy passed muster. Gladys Baker was especially impressed because Billy didn't get seasick. Everyone in their party suffered from seasickness except for Gladys and Billy. While Nan and her father sat on the deck covered in blankets and eating tiny sandwiches in an attempt to keep seasickness at bay, Billy and Gladys enjoyed huge meals in the dining room. Then when the ship docked at a port, and Billy and the Bakers went ashore, the table was turned on Billy. When he left the ship, he kept his sea legs, but they didn't operate too well on land, and Billy fell ill at lunch.

Nan recalls that the Eatons could not have been nicer to her, especially Aunt Mame and Aunt Minnie, and with the approval of the Eaton and Baker families, Billy and Nan made plans to marry at the Ranch in September of 1938. Because her family was in Philadelphia, Nan had to organize the wedding. She remembers specifically going into Sheridan to arrange for the wedding cake. When she told the baker how many people were to attend the wedding, the baker told Nan, with some alarm, that such a cake would cost the grand sum of five dollars!

Billy and Nan were married on September 12, 1938 with her family from Philadelphia in attendance. Billy and Nan only had a one day honeymoon in Billings because Nan had to get back to the Ranch to see her family off and Billy had to get back to work.

Nan's parents gave Billy and Nan a wonderful wedding present. Because they were married at the Ranch and Nan had made all the arrangements, Nan's parents used the money they would have spent on a large Philadelphia wedding to build a house for Billy and Nan. Billy's parents, Bill and Patty, provided the building site. It was a spot they had chosen for their own use, but instead they gave it to Billy and Nan. Frank Eaton, Nan and Billy's son, and his wife Kathy, occupy the house today.

Nan has fond memories of those early years at Eatons' and of the Eaton family. She remembers Patty Eaton as a wonderful, gracious hostess who knew the name of every guest, even the children. Moreover, she remembers how nice Uncle Alden was to her mother, who was terrified of horses. Uncle Alden kindly drove her up on the mountain so she could see the scenery she could not see from horseback. Someone had advised her that you could tell what a horse was going to do by watching its ears, and she was so terrified that she never looked past the horse's ears.

Billy and Nan settled in to life at Eatons' Ranch and before the decade was over, their first child, William Francis Eaton, was born on October 11, 1939. The October *WN* proudly announced the arrival of the first fourth generation Eaton:

> *Fall visitors have just been introduced to a new member of the Ranch Family, William Francis Eaton (named for his father and two grandfathers) who arrived on October 11, just in time to make news in this issue of* Wranglin' Notes.
>
> *Uncle Alden's great-grandchild has come to join a large family in his Western ranch home. Aunt Mame and Domo, the great-grandmothers, will be here to watch the new rancher grow and develop—imagine Bill and Patty being grandpa and grandma—but then there's Aunt Nancy too (who is going to school in Philadelphia this winter), not to mention great-aunt Fay, John Fleming, Dunc and Dorothy, Tom and Anna, Angela Buell, Uncle George Gentry, Aunt Minnie, Cousin Josie, all the "home folks" welcome the newcomer to the Ranch. About this time next fall* Wranglin' Notes *may publish a picture of the youngest William taking his first horseback ride, working right into the life of the Ranch...*

Angela didn't wait a year to show *WN* readers a photo of the new Eaton baby. the December 1939 issue of *WN* sported a picture of William Francis Eaton, who by then had acquired the nickname of "Beaton." The following accompanied the photo:

> *...here's the first picture to be published of William Francis Eaton, taken on the day he was eight weeks old. We had to make*

a special appointment with him for he sleeps about twenty hours a day, but he was out on the front porch in the sunshine, waiting for us, when we arrived with the camera. He's full of health and growing fast. At the moment, he bears little resemblance to either the Eaton or Baker families. His eyes are inclined to be blue, although Grandma Patty still has hopes that eventually they'll be brown like Nan's.

For Domo's 80th birthday the family assembled for a photo.
Frank, the only great grandchild at the time, sits on his mother's lap.
Clockwise from top: Billy Eaton, Frank Baker (Nan's father),
Big Bill Eaton, Domo, Patty Eaton, Nan and Frank,
Gladys Baker (Nan's mother) and Aunt Mame (Big Bill's mother).
Photo by W. Thomas McGrath, Sheridan, Wyoming.
Courtesy of Eatons' Ranch.

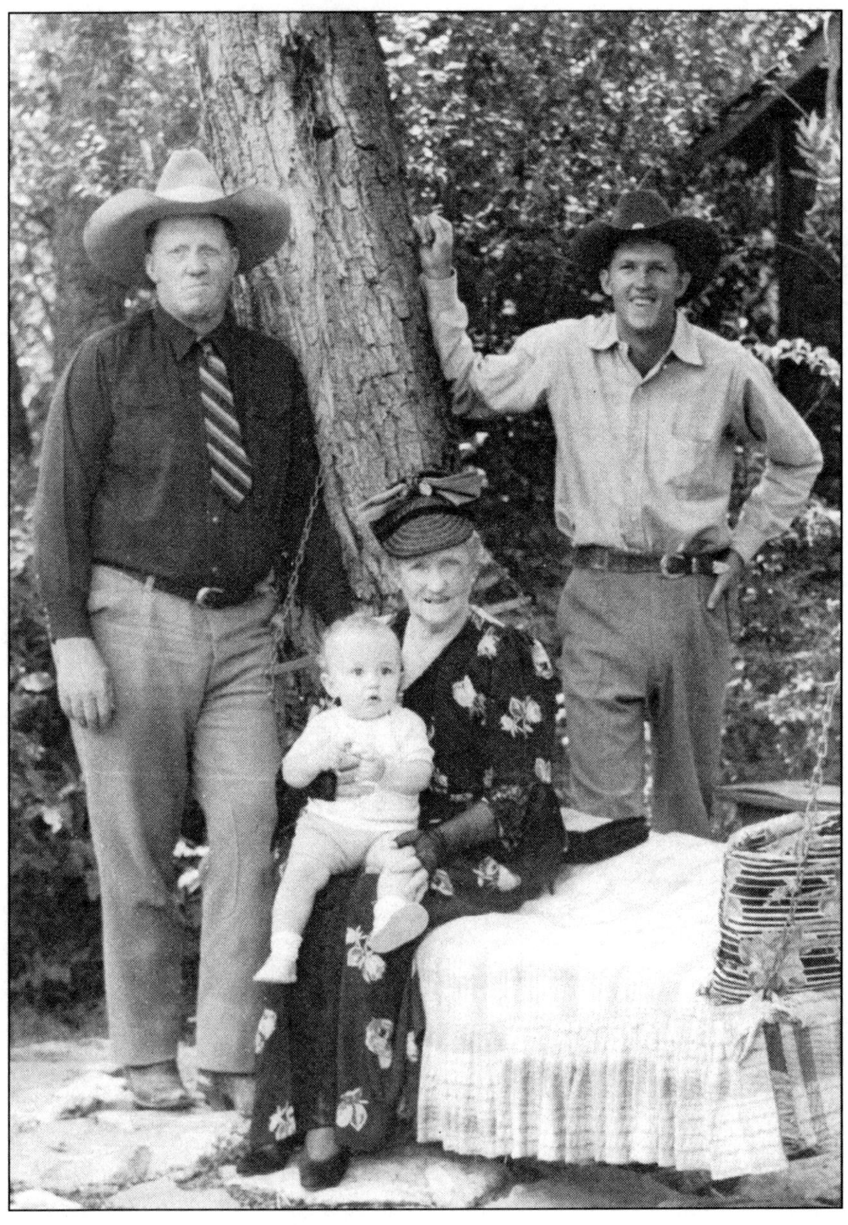

Four generations of Eatons.
Clockwise from top: Big Bill Eaton, Billy Eaton, Aunt Mame and Frank Eaton.
Photo by W. Thomas McGrath, Sheridan, Wyoming.
Courtesy of Eatons' Ranch.

Appropriately enough, Bill and Patty Eaton asked George Gentry and Curly Witzel to serve as Beaton's godfathers. Curly's wife, Annie Laurie, who he married in 1933, served as godmother. No one knew it at the time, but "Beaton,"—who later chose to be called Frank, because there were already too many "Bills" around the place—would be the last of the male children with the Eaton name descended from Alden Eaton.

After attending Wolf Creek School with her brother, Nancy Eaton began high school in Sheridan in 1934 when she was thirteen years old. She graduated only one year after Billy, because Billy started high school late. She graduated as a member of the Sheridan High School Class of 1937 when she was sixteen years old.

Nancy was active in high school. Like Billy, she had a thespian side to her and appeared in two school plays. She was a member of several school committees, was a good student, and was elected to the National Honor Society in her senior year. She also became a Flag Bearer for the Sheridan-Wyo-Rodeo.

Each year, the Sheridan-Wyo-Rodeo selected a Queen, together with an attendant Lady in Waiting and a Flag Bearer. The system was that in subsequent years, when the reigning Queen completed her one-year reign, the other attendants would move up one notch and each year would require the selection of only a new Flag Bearer. So when Nancy was selected as Flag Bearer, she was assured of being crowned Sheridan-Wyo-Rodeo Queen in 1939, unless something happened to alter the succession chain.

Nancy was a fitting candidate because the Eaton family was well known and Nancy was the genuine article when it came to horsemanship. It probably helped that her father was a charter member of the Sheridan-Wyo-Rodeo and the Arena Director. It was a natural fit.

In between summers when Nancy was involved with her duties as part of the Sheridan-Wyo-Rodeo Queen Court, she attended college. During 1938, Nancy attended the University of Wyoming and the next year the University of Arizona. In the summer of 1939, Nancy reigned as the Sheridan-Wyo-Rodeo Queen.

That same year, Nancy also had a serious romance that could have led to marriage except for the fact that some members of the family objected to the suitor. Josephine Gillespie commented on the matter in a letter to John Fleming when she wrote:

> *I told Nance I would give her five shares* (Note: Of her preferred Ranch stock.) *for an engagement gift, but now her grandmother says WAIT, she hasn't announced her engagement, and I suspect they would like her to be free to look further...*

Others suggest that the objection may have been a bit stronger. Bill is purported to have said that the marriage would take place "over my dead body." That kind of edict prevented any possibility of a marriage. Instead, Nancy went to live with Nan Eaton's parents in Philadelphia and attend school. While she was there, Nancy had an appendicitis operation, and Bill and Patty traveled to Philadelphia to be at her side. The next spring, she returned home to Eatons' Ranch.

From time to time *WN* often contained news about other members of the family. One of them was Uncle Charlie Eaton, the fourth Eaton brother, who had initially been with Howard in Medora North Dakota.

Charlie visited Eatons' in 1930 and the July *WN* noted that: "Uncle Charlie's heart was almost broken when a bad foot kept him away for a few weeks, but he's on hand at the corral again now..." He visited the Ranch again in the summer of 1934 when *WN* noted that:

> *Uncle Charlie Eaton of Geneva, New York, was at the Ranch the greater part of the summer, riding with new dudes and initiating some of the most attractive girls into the secrets of manufacturing horsehair hatbands for the Stetsons.*

One of those girls was eighteen year old Nan Baker, the future Mrs. Billy Eaton. Nan specifically remembers when Uncle Charlie attended the weekly dances in Howard Hall. All of the attractive wranglers danced with the older women while Nan and her friends sat on the sidelines just hoping one of the wranglers would ask them to dance. Then they spied Uncle Charlie striding toward them in a very colorful shirt. They cringed and hoped that the old man (who actually was only sixty-three at the time) wouldn't ask them to dance. It was only later that Nan realized Uncle Charlie was just being kind and trying to save them the embarrassment of sitting on the sidelines "not danced with."

Other members of the extended Eaton family—Nannie Alderson (Domo), Patty's mother; Aunt Mary Gillespie, an Eaton sister and her daughter Cousin Josephine; Aunt Minnie Reid, Aunt Mame's sister; and Aunt Fay Alderson, Domo's daughter and Patty's sister—who made the Ranch home, were mentioned. Most of them spent the summer season at the ranch at Wolf Creek, but in wintertime were likely to scatter around the United States on visits to either Rimrock or to visit friends in California. Aunt Mary and Cousin Josephine had a house in Sheridan where they lived during the worst weather or when they weren't traveling, and Domo often went on extended visits to relatives in Kansas.

The family did have one loss in November of 1935. *WN* reported that:

> *One place will be empty this year—that of Uncle Alden's sister, Aunt Mary Eaton Gillespie, who passed away last month. An invalid in recent years, she was unknown to many guests of the past few seasons. But to those who knew her through the many active years of her long residence at Eatons' Ranch, Aunt Mary was one of the "home folks" who contributed very much to their pleasure here.*

Hattie Eaton Pelissier continued to live in Sheridan after her husband Peter died in 1924. Hattie died eight years later on December 19, 1932, at age sixty-two, in Denver after an illness of only one week. When she died, her children, Elsie, Willis and Mary were at her bedside.

Elsie continued to live in Denver and raise her son Jack. Jack, who attended grade school in Sheridan, attended junior high and high school in Denver and graduated from East Denver High School in 1932. He then matriculated at the University of Colorado and studied accounting.

While a student, Jack met and married a fellow student, Helen Kettering. He graduated in 1936 with a bachelor's degree in accounting, ans obtained a position with the firm of Dun and Bradstreet in Denver, where Jack and Helen had their first child, a son Jack, in 1937. After their son was born, Jack applied for training in 1938 as an agent with the Federal Bureau of Investigation (FBI). In those days, a candidate had to have either a law or accounting degree to qualify. Jack successfully completed the training, he became an agent of the FBI. His first assignment, in New York City, was the beginning of a twenty-seven year career with that organization.

Willis Pelissier, his wife Ethel and their two sons, George and Willis continued to live in Sheridan in Hattie's house at 231 West Loucks while Willis continued his career with the Sheridan Commercial Company.

Mary Pelissier Haywood followed Elsie's footsteps and was elected clerk of district court in November 1932. Mary had a checkered tenure. Internal audits periodically revealed errors in the court books, and once, the auditor suggested that Mary be replaced if her performance didn't improve. That never happened. The voters continued to elect Mary for successive two-year terms and again in 1938 when the term was changed to four years. However, on December 11, 1939, a bombshell dropped. Mary suddenly resigned with no reason given. The story was the headline of the day in the local paper. but there were no follow on stories to explain the situation. Perhaps the answer lies in a letter John Fleming wrote to Josephine Gillespie two days after Mary resigned:

> *...Much as I might be sorry for her, I would not do a thing for Mary. We do not have it (money) and have troubles plenty. Her uncles did things for her. A few years ago, Uncle Alden rescued her, and he really could not afford (it). Now none of us can. She is just another gambler as far as I ever hear, though I do not know about her as I do about Bill. No—I don't know of a person in the group that would make any sacrifice. You need not. And I simply can't get mixed up at all, as the poor devil who tries to keep this outfit afloat, and I can't do a thing for her personally.*

The details remain mysterious.

Uncle Alden Dies

Uncle Alden did not live to see the marriage of his only grandson or the birth of his first and only great grandson, William Frances Eaton. Alden died two years earlier on January 4, 1937. *The Sheridan Press* marked his death on the day he died with headlines and a story:

> *PIONEER IN DUDE RANCH INDUSTRY SUCCUMBS AT 77*
> *Death Closes Colorful Career of Prominent Citizen*
>
> *Farrelly Alden Eaton, whose name for more than a half-century has been synonymous with the picturesque dude ranch industry, died this morning after a lingering illness at his nationally famous Eatons' Ranch in the Wolf Creek valley.*
>
> *Known and loved as "Uncle Alden" by hundreds of friends from all walks of life—notables from the East, Wyoming wranglers, business and fraternal associates, and acquaintances —he both fathered and typified the industry which brought the East to the West in search of an unusual summer playground...*
>
> *Although in poor health for several years, he was not confined to bed until late in July. Death came to him almost exactly thirty-three years from the time he came to Sheridan...*

The Sheridan Press published a special editorial in tribute to Uncle Alden:

> *A personality both fine and charming is missing from the West tonight. Uncle Alden Eaton has left his beloved Wolf Creek Valley, never to return, but we like to think of him as a bold-spirited pioneer once again starting along a westward trail, which will unfold into a land of eternal peace and beauty...*
>
> *Friends gravitated to him from all walks of life. Rich in humor, he possessed a personal magnetism that was his own*

naturalness. Affable, courteous, and kindly, he personified the sympathetic spirit and hospitality, which we associate with the mountains and the rolling sagebrush hills...

Now he has followed "Uncle Howard" and "Uncle Will" down the last long trail—the trail which mortal man must ever follow...

And no man had more friends!

One of those friends was Mary Robert Rinehart, who sent a telegram to *The Sheridan Press:*

In the death of Alden Eaton, America has lost a fine citizen and many people a dearly beloved friend. The last to go of three great pioneer brothers, I know he will ride this new trail as bravely as he rode the old one. My deepest sympathy and personal sorrow at his passing.

Alden's passing was, of course, mentioned in the March 1937 issue of *WN*:

Since friends left Wyoming in the autumn, sadness has come to the Eaton Ranch family, distant members as well as the home folks. We refer to the death of beloved Uncle Alden Eaton. He would not wish us to dwell on that event. His example was always to go forward courageously, to look back only upon pleasant happy recollections. He wished everyone always to be cheerful and just as joyful as possible. So we will only say, very briefly, that in the Eaton name Mrs. Alden Eaton (Aunt Mame), Bill and Patty, Billy and Nancy, will carry on the tradition of Eaton hospitality and kindness to all guests under their roof...

The article then offered some assurance to Eaton guests:

We wish also to say that there will be neither interruption nor change in the administration of business affairs of the

Ranch. Beginning in North Dakota more than thirty years ago, Howard, Willis and Alden Eaton depended on their friend and associate, John Fleming, for the management of their business affairs, and his quiet, capable guiding hand is in its accustomed place on the tiller of the Eaton Ranch ship. Characteristically he protests even this slight mention of himself and insists that his loyal assistants, Bill Eaton, Tom Butler and Angela Buell, be included in any reference to him. In these hands, friends will be interested to know that this new chapter in Ranch history promises to go forward as a happy continuation of the pleasant story so well known to everyone....

Uncle Alden named John Fleming as executor of his Last Will and Testament that was prepared in 1933. Alden's estate consisted of $48,300 in Eatons' Ranch capital stock, clothing and personal effects worth $50.00 and Eaton credit worth $684.21. Alden left all of this stock to his wife, Aunt Mame, and on her death, to his son Bill. The will provided that Aunt Mame could sell the stock with Bill's consent.

The will made no provisions for an income for Aunt Mame and so she petitioned the estate for a payment of $150.00 a month. The estate was unable to produce the income and so Fleming arranged for her to receive a Ranch salary of $90.00 per month. He commented on this arrangement in a letter two years later when he wrote Josephine Gillespie that the Ranch "Had to give her a salary when Bill stripped them bare." Aunt Mame received a salary from the Ranch until she passed away twenty years later.

Dudes

In the thirties, *WN* continued to provide an inexhaustible flow of information about the Eaton dude family. Each issue was replete with information about which dudes either had been a guest the last year, or had made reservations for the next. *WN* even discussed which dudes did not come and which dudes had corresponded with the Ranch for any reason. The dudes lapped it up and eagerly awaited each issue of *WN*. The dude readership by 1930 had become extensive. In May 1930, for instance, the Ranch distributed seven thousand copies of *WN* to Eaton contacts.

The following are some typical examples of "dude news" during the 1930s:

1930

We're definitely holding places for the following list of old-timers. The year notation means that was their first season at the Ranch...

...Colonel Henry Hall (1893) and Mr. Harry Hayward (1907) will be here again...Dick Baum (1909) who says to hold Number 2 on The Pike for him...Harry McCormick (1909) usually arrives before the end of May...General and Mrs. Harries (1921) hope to be here by mid-May...Then there's Mrs. Wilson Low (1909) who hasn't missed a season since 1913...Colonel G. C. Marshal (1929) will arrive in July... Herbert and Martin Koether (1928) say they'll be here as long as they possibly can...The Frank W. Kennedy family (1922)for the "family" but 1893 for Mr. Kennedy...

...Harry McCormick, as everyone knows, owned the Forbes Ranch years ago and still loves every inch of those wide spreading acres on Big Goose Creek. Recently Mr. W. Cameron Forbes (who is now ambassador to Japan) has put our friend

Charley Long, an old time cattle and sheep man of this country, in charge and the place is undergoing a renovation of fences and buildings with a view to making it a first class polo ranch in addition to its customary position high up in the ranks of cattle and sheep ranches...

...Mr. S. L. Nicholson returned to the Ranch this season after seventeen years absence—rather apprehensively, he said because he'd heard rumors that the Ranch had expanded tremendously and that folks now brought all their best clothes. Before leaving, he told us that he'd had a wonderful time and that he'd been particularly pleased to find the place little changed, and to notice several ancient hats and overalls that he remembered seeing on duty back in 1913...

1931

Looking back over 1931 for the benefit of the folks who missed Wyoming this season, there were many Ranch riders on hand, but we could have found places, provided horses, and good times for more. We missed the folks who've been faithful visitors for so many seasons and who for varying reasons couldn't make it this year. Mr. and Mrs. Fred Ayres couldn't come, but they sent Anne and Fritz. Betty Gould was the representative of the Gould family, and the Kennedys missed a season at the Ranch for the first time since 1922. Everyone asked for Doctor and Mrs. Rinehart. Harry Hayward put a black mark on a mighty wonderful record...On the other hand, Frank LeMoyne and Harry Singer came twice, first in the spring and again in September, all the way from Pittsburgh...

1932

...Mr. A.G. Uptegraff, a friend of the outfit since his first visit in 1916, says: "Sometimes I feel like sitting down and

writing, 'Don't send me Wranglin' Notes *any more for it is next to impossible to resist the urge to jump on a train and head for the Ranch.' Sometimes I hide the* Notes *just to avoid the agony."*

Mr. and Mrs. Albrecht were here in 1930, but this year they returned with Ginger, Phyllis, and Freddy so now their acquaintance with the Ranch is a family affair. As this is being written they're on the way into the mountains with a string of pack horses for a several days camping trip. Dunc and Emil are the guides, Nancy and Billy Eaton went along, too, with Bob and Dorothy Whitney Stevens... Since Bob and Dorothy met here eleven years ago, many things have happened—not the least important being four small Stevenses, whom we figure are potential ranchers, even if they are getting their start in New Jersey...

Walter and Kathleen Louer were here among the first dudes of the season as usual...

...Harry McCormick heads his roughriders as usual...

...Sherman Burns from New York was here again in September....

...Harry McCormick (his Ranch visits date from 1909) will be insulted when we call attention to the fact that he now mounts his horse from the wall...

Mrs. Hull is wearing one of her prized collection of "corral-boy" hats. She spent the season buying new Stetsons and trading them to the boys for the used variety. It seems there is considerable personality attached to a battered Stetson that has been worn three or four years by Scorp or Curly or one of the other boys.

1933

We have had cards and letters from friends whose Ranch visits date twenty, thirty and forty years ago. Miss Nella Marble writes of her acquaintance with Uncle Howard 50 years ago when she went with her father on hunting trips in the

North Dakota country...

Mr. Harvey S. Dyer writes, "Although it is over twenty-three years ago I can recall events and friends' faces as clearly as though it were yesterday, and believe me it is with the utmost pleasure that I do recall them...

..."Pete" Dailey writes that he will be out again this season, to catch new pictures of Ranch scenes and the Ranch folks with his camera. In the meantime, he's busy with photographs for advertising as his main work, when he's not instructing at Northwestern University on the subject of "Radio Writing," or planning new radio programs.

The June number of Wranglin' Notes *mentioned the return of a dear friend of many years standing, Mary Roberts Rinehart. Mrs. Rinehart's visit was a pleasure to everyone at the Ranch, and when she left in September all felt that the summer had indeed been a happier one for her presence here...*

There were many friends who returned after an absence of several seasons, and at the head of the list belongs Mr. Fay Ingalls of The Homestead, Hot Springs, Virginia, who last visited the Ranch in 1906. Mrs. Ingalls came with him, also Susie, Abbie, Polly and Dan. When Mr. Ingalls passed through Chicago on his way home, he saw Mr. Cecil Barnes, here in 1906 and 1907, and as a result, Mr. Barnes stopped in at the Ranch with his boys, Edward, Ben and Cecil, Jr., in August. It was fine to become re-acquainted with these friends of earlier days, and we believe that Mr. Ingalls and Mr. Barnes enjoyed the Ranch as much in 1933 as they did when room-mates in 1906...

We doubt if Mr. Julius LeMoyne, who visited the Eaton boys at their Custer Trail Ranch in North Dakota in 1884, had any idea that his great grandson would be riding with the Eatons in 1933. Following in the footsteps of his parents, his grandparents and his great-grandfather, Frankie LeMoyne Schmertz, aged four, came all the way from Pittsburgh to ride at Eatons' Ranch...

... Sherman and Dotty Burns, Ossining, New York, brought

the three boys out with them this year. Sherman (Note: Of Burns Detective Agency.) *was busy working on an important case while here, solving the mystery of Nancy Eaton's cat's kittens, but he found time to go fishing and managed to snatch a few days for a pack trip in the mountains...*

Joe DeYong's visit in August and early September was a shorter one that we had hoped, but while he was here, the daily Wranglin' Notes *again blossomed on the bulletin board... It was impossible to supply the demand for copies to take home for souvenirs.*

1934

Here's a crowd of Pittsburgh people whose names come along pretty close in the alphabet: Mr. and Mrs. Frank J. LeMoyne, who have been here every season since 1915 (that's a remarkable record), and will be out again in August for the late summer and early fall season...Mrs. George W. Laughlin (formerly Miss Elizabeth Shaw), who was here in 1913 with her parents, is returning with her three daughters. She has pleasant memories of the Ranch twenty years ago...

Howe Nimick plans to join his family at the Ranch this year. Mrs. Nimick was here last summer with the three children—her first visit at the Ranch since 1912 when she herself was small...We've also heard form Mr. Francis Nimick who is considering the Ranch again for his family and a friend or two...Looks something like a family reunion of the Nimicks at Eatons' Ranch this summer...

..."Sylvia" Jameson opened the social season for dude dogs by giving a hilarious party in Howard Hall, which was attended by all the Ranch canines from big Pal Butler to little Rosie Moss. Refreshments were served, including a delicious raw hamburger pie with sugar frosting. There were caramels for dessert, which probably explains why the party did not break up in a general dogfight as some predicted it might. Probably the

most striking costume was worn by matronly Mrs. Pepe Pell, who made a dramatic entrance late in the festivities and almost missed out on the food...

We don't often mention the passing of friends in Wranglin' Notes *but there's an exception this time, and we tell Ranch friends with great sorrow of the recent death of Colonel Henry Hall. He first came to the old Custer Trail Ranch of the Eatons in North Dakota in 1893, and from that year to the time of his serious illness, he missed hardly a season at the Ranch. We cannot fail to give particular mention to the passing of that loyal friend, Colonel Hall, who has been numbered for many years as one of the most esteemed friends of the three Eaton brothers and their associates...*

1935

Hank Leyendecker spent the entire winter with us in Wyoming, and his visit has extended almost a year now. We think he has enjoyed it. Anyway, we'd match him against anyone for a picture of health and contentment...

Mrs. Charles J. Graham, Frances Graham Luke and her children, Jean and Nancy, and Tom Graham, were also June arrivals...Billy Graham drove up from Arizona to join them here for a few weeks—and incidentally helped out the Eaton ball team in their games with Tepee Lodge and Bones Brothers. To date we've held our reputation for never winning a ball game...but we're getting better...

1936

Shortly after Christmas, Russell Kettell came all the way from Boston just for a few days at the Ranch. It was one of those "hello-goodbye" visits, but he managed to get in several horseback rides with Bill Eaton, some calls on his friends in the neighborhood, and a trip to the second-hand in Sheridan where he managed as usual to pick up something of interest to him. This time it was a bobcat skin. His Ranch visit rivaled that of Rogers Lamont who drove to the Ranch alone from New York last August, stayed here for six or seven days, drove back again—all within the space of a two-week vacation. But he said he wanted to get back to the Ranch, if only for a fleeting visit, and we guess Rusty Kettell had the same feeling...

...we truly believe Anne Hull spoke for practically all the dudes when she said over her newspaper one day, "I can't understand it. When I'm at the Ranch, the Spanish situation means nothing to me and the president's activities pass entirely unnoted. If Curly is bucked off, or the cook cuts his finger, or one of the Ranch horses is lost—that makes the headlines and nothing else matters so far as I'm concerned."

(Note: The October 1936 issue of *WN* was the first issue to have a separate insert that listed the names of all the Eatons' guests for that year. Among those listed were Nan Baker, who would marry Billy Eaton and Mrs. E. G. Clapp, Bud, Marge and Dorothy from Fargo, North Dakota. Dorothy [Dippy] would later meet her future husband, Don King, at the Ranch.)

1937

...Al Harter came out on the 19th (of May). Right here we'll have to digress a bit and say that Al packed his duffle bag during May and helped the boys drive the horses out of Garvin Basin where Curly had been riding herd on them all winter. Al told us he rode fifty miles on the first day, changing horses six time, and when the roundup cook called "come and get it" at 3:15 the next morning, he was so stiff and tired that by the time he had crawled out of his tarp and pulled on his boots the boys had all finished breakfast and were saddling up. Al wondered at that moment whether he could possibly live

through the day, and he added, "Just think, and this is what I call my vacation."

An old friend of the Eaton family and of John Fleming's, Mr. G. B. Bosworth, last here in 1906, stopped in during June with Mr. Chandler Weaver...

...Botsford and Ruth Young were here...

1938

The Rinehart family will be represented at the Ranch by Alan and his two daughters...Not a season passes that we don't recall the many happy summers spent at the Ranch by Mary Roberts Rinehart and her family. Her cheerful presence at the Ranch and her encouraging words in difficult times has ever been an inspiration to the Eaton Outfit. We value the friendship of the Rinehart family and greet the fourth generation of Rineharts as we have greeted other third and fourth generations at the Ranch—with appreciation of their loyalty to us...

(Advertisement.) It's true that Eatons' Ranch was the first so-called dude ranch, dating from back in 1879 when Howard Eaton settled in North Dakota Territory. The grandchildren and in one or two instances great grandchildren of some of the men who rode with Howard, Willis and Alden Eaton in those days, are now riding with the second and third generations of Eatons. John A. Murtland, Stanley M. Rinehart, Francis B. Nimick, Charles J. Graham, Julius LeMoyne, Howard M. Fry, are the names of some of the men who rode with the Eatons years ago, whose grandchildren will be at the Ranch this season carrying on the family tradition that a summer vacation at the Ranch is not only good health insurance, but a pleasure to be enjoyed every summer if possible. So one little warning—don't come to Eatons' Ranch unless you're ready to run the risk of forming that habit for your descendents in the generations to come...

Newest candidates for membership in The Eaton Ranch Ex-Dude Club are Mr. and Mrs. Tom Moss of St. Louis. They've been faithful friends and visitors at the Ranch for fifteen years, spending usually from two to three months here every summer. A permanent home in the ranch country has been in the back of their minds for some time, and this season they returned in October after their usual three months' visit to complete arrangements for the purchase of the Edward S. Moore Jr. ranch, located some twenty miles from us as the crow flies...We're sorry to lose Tom and Kathryn Moss as dudes but glad to have them as neighbors...

Pete Daily writes that he has every issue of Wranglin' Notes *but one, which he missed while world cruising some years ago. Unfortunately, we're unable to supply it, having only our one file number—and we're hanging on to that ourselves, for it may become a museum piece and help lift the mortgage some day...*

1939

There were old –timers back this summer who had gotten out of the Ranch habit, but we hope the season's visits have reawakened their interest and they'll come again soon. Mrs. Belknap came with her grandsons, her first visit since 1925. Mrs. Elliott, Russell Kettell, John Keenan, Anne Hall, Mary Jane Dunivan, Ralph Woodley, were here again after several years absence. Kate Ludlow Jones came again (last visit 1925) bringing her small daughter Betsy. Others were Paul Platter (1922), with his son Niel, Mrs. Welch (1914) with Tom, Whitney Baker and Ann (1931). John McMillan recalled his last summer on the Ranch in 1924. Mr. and Mrs. Gilman came in 1913, Gordon Wood in 1929 and Mrs. Forker in 1923. Ruth Leyendecker Quinn was last here in 1930. Robert Lyman Grant had made the Glacier Park Trip with the Eaton Outfit in 1922...

Employees

In the thirties, John Fleming was still the stabilizing force behind the Eaton Ranch operation. He organized the solutions to the difficult financial problems brought about by the Depression and Bill Eaton's gambling, and he served as a conduit between the various Eaton family members. For all practical purposes, John was a member of the Eaton family.

The sadness in his life caused by the death of his young son in 1925 was deepened by his wife's death noted in the December 1931 *WN*:

> *...The Ranch family—headed by John Fleming—is small. We have written "John and May Fleming" for so many years that we stumble and pause here, realizing afresh the vacancy made by the loss of any one of the Ranch home folks. Mrs. Fleming had been a part of the Ranch since its early days in Wyoming, and the cheer and joy of our Christmas Season is dimmed by her absence...* (Note: In WN, Mrs. Fleming's name is spelled both "May" and "Mae.")

Angela Buell's importance to Eatons' Ranch grew with her tenure. Aside from her prodigious production of *WN* three or four times a year, she was a valued apprentice to John Fleming. John recognized her value to him in May 1931, when he wrote a memorandum for the corporate records. The memorandum noted:

> *...that her present salary of $150 per month with board and room is regarded as a good salary considering the difficulties of seasonal work and the handicaps that seem to beset this particular business. It cannot be guaranteed but is subject to change up or down.*
>
> *Stock Bonus. For the five years beginning Jan. 1, 1931 an annual stock bonus of five shares of common stock to be issued*

> *to her regardless of the amount of her monthly salary and regardless of general business conditions.* (Note: This is a belated recognition of some very good work in the past several years as well as a reward for future effort.)

In addition, John gave Angela permission to buy an equal number of shares of common stock and set up a cash bonus plan in which her bonus was tied to the profitability of Eatons' Ranch.

Angela was John's understudy and involved in all aspects of Ranch business. In this capacity, she was witness to much "behind the scenes" family activity. She displayed her knowledge in a letter she wrote on February 15, 1970, long after she had left the Ranch.

The Eaton family obviously asked Angela some historical questions about Ranch stock and she wrote of one instance in the 1930s when there was a problem about preferred stock. (*Note: The preferred stock was issued to most of the Eaton sisters in exchange for common stock left to them by Willis Eaton.*)

Angela wrote:

> *To the best of my knowledge the only difficulty with the preferred stockholders came back sometime in the thirties, from Arthur S. Cullum, Jr., who was Aunt Lizzie's son* (Note: Aunt Lizzie was an Eaton sister.)*...My memory is dim but evidently he was under the impression that the Cullum family had a good chunk of the Ranch and he'd better come out and help run it. Chances are I'm way off the track on this memory, but it seems to me he was going to turn part of the Ranch into a farm and raise pigs and make a fortune! Anyway, Mr. Fleming was alive then, and he managed in some way to talk him out of it—without any unpleasant results—and the difficulty subsided without incident. However, I know it was not easy to handle the problem.*

Tommy Butler, with John Fleming and Angela Buell, was the third leg of the Eatons' ranch "management stool." Tommy was a "jack of all trades." He could cook, he acted as the postmaster, and he was usually at the forefront when a problem needed a solution. An example was in 1936, when this entry appeared in the *WN*:

> *As January advanced, winter tightened down. There were three weeks in February when Tom Butler didn't crack a ghost of a smile. It's not much fun nursing several thousand feet of pipeline when it's more than thirty degrees below zero. Toward the last of the cold spell, Bill Curtis came up to act as night watchman on the pipeline and Tommy worked only fourteen hours a day instead of twenty-four. Dunc, Emil, and Percy all bundled up in the warmest clothes they owned or could borrow and worked outdoors, hours at a time, when it was close to twenty below zero with a sharp wind blowing. For several weeks, we were only a short jump ahead of heaps of trouble, but everything came out all right.*

In the December 1938 *WN*, Tommy and his wife Anna both received mention:

> *...The postmaster at Wolf (Tom Butler) is preparing for the Christmas rush and vey officially asking everyone to wrap their packages carefully and do their mailing early. He'll also have a job getting these* Wranglin' Notes *headed in the right direction so they'll reach everyone as near as possible on Christmas Day. Anna Butler has taken her skates to town for sharpening, although no one has had the courage to test the skim of ice on the ice pond...*

And *WN* mentioned the rest of the Eaton Ranch workforce often. Some examples are:

1930

...Most everybody has remarked on the fine bunch of corral boys gathered at the Ranch this summer. You see them in the picture...Lee Moore, Jack Boaz (he's the only newcomer, an Arizona cowboy), big Bill Eaton, Reid Kochel, Bobby Espy, Everett Cheetham, Ewin Neely, Alvin Shaffer and George Gentry.

...This overheard at the corral one morning early in July as a newcomer (aged 8) was introducing himself to the cowboys:

To George Gentry, the corral boss: "My name's Peter Burbank. Have you a horse that hasn't been ridden?"

George: "Yes, my boy."

Peter: "Well, just bring him out. I've never ridden before either and we ought to get along all right together."

George used his own judgment in that matter, and Peter got along all right and was very happy with a horse that had been ridden before.

1931

Down in the powerhouse, up the water line, here, there and everywhere Tom Butler can be seen. Anna Butler is found at the house. Angela Buell finds plenty to occupy her time. Peligan is busy with the horses, riding out early in the morning, coming in after sundown.

Working westward, Bill and Patty Eaton and the children are of course at the Rimrock Ranch in Arizona, welcoming friends who are interested in a Ranch vacation during the winter. John Duncan is there with them, also Chuck and Honora Schlegel. George Gentry wrangles the Rimrock horses and Archie Brammer helps him when he's not busy with the truck and cars. Not far away, up the creek at the Beaver Creek Ranch, are Reid Kochel and Curly Witzel...

1932

If we all shouted at once, "Merry Christmas and Happy New Year" it would make a considerable noise. From Wolf would come the voices of Uncle Alden, Aunt Mame, John Fleming, John Duncan, Tom and Anna Butler, Angela Buell, Aunt Mary, Cousin Josie, Aunt Minnie, Billy Eaton, Buddy Alderson, Dick Baum, Annabel and Thelma, Emil, Percy...

At the Ranch, the weather—with a few brief breaks—continued pleasant. Tom Butler established his hunting camp at Big Bend, and on a beautiful warm summery day, the campers left the Ranch, laden down with seemingly needless overshoes, sheepskins, heavy mittens. Two days later, the snow, accompanied by a heavy fog, came down. All at the Ranch camp were safe, but the storm came so suddenly that many hunters were lost for a time from their camps and several perished...

1933

...we agree with Peligan that it's sure tough luck to snap an ankle right at the beginning of the season, and after spending last summer on crutches too...

...and we're as excited over Dunc getting married as if we were taking the great step ourselves. (Note: John Duncan married Dorothy who, as a teenager, accompanied Howard Eaton on a Glacier Park pack trip in 1916.)

1934

Aunt Mame's "Merry Christmas" is cheerful and brisk and she says it again and again to her friends on every hand. Bill's low deep voice follows with "Merry Christmas Everybody," and Patty calls, "Hello there—Merry Christmas" in a high clear tone that everyone can hear. Nancy says, "Merry Christmas" in

John and Dorothy Duncan.
Courtesy of Eatons' Ranch.

a small voice that befits the youngest member of the family. Billy drawls his "Merry Christmas" in a voice as deep as his father's, and John Fleming says, "Have a Merry Christmas, Everybody." Tom Butler's "Merry Christmas" is a quick and ready as his step. Silent John Duncan just thinks *"Merry Christmas," and Angela Buell...well from this angle we can't describe her "Merry Christmas" at all. Chuck and Honora Schlegel, George Gentry, Curly Witzel, Aunt Minnie Reid, Cousin Josie Gillespie, Emil Jacobs, Reid Kochel, Jens Larsen, Ben Sittler, and many, many more of the home folks add their "Merry Christmas Everyone" in voices high and low, large and small, to make a huge volume that sweeps across the land and into remote corners of the Earth to reach all the friends of Eatons' Ranch...*

...The little stone carpenter shop is warm and the machinery is humming along at full speed. "Cousin Bob" Richardson is busy transforming ordinary apple boxes into attractive pieces of furniture, bits of walnut wood into beautiful inlaid cribbage boards. Dunc and Uncle Alden work beside him, all busy with the lathes, the saws, the drills. Dick Baum is here, challenging his friends to a little six-mile walk or a ten-mile horseback ride, then beating them at cribbage in the evening.

1935

In wintertime, the corral boys scatter even farther than the horses they ride. Several of the boys are at the Rimrock Ranch in Arizona—George Gentry, Reid Kochel and Curly Witzel. Omer Maxwell is somewhere in Arizona, probably working for a cow outfit. Perry Aber is snowed-in for the winter on a ranch over near Yellowstone Park, and Archie Brammer is in Sheridan. "Dad" Baker is in Hollywood (in the movies, no doubt). Leo Thompson is home in Arizona, and Nels Larsen is in northern Montana where it really does get cold. Buck Blackburn is "cowboying" in Pennsylvania for Sam Fry, and he says he likes it. Tex Glover is working for the Dana Cattle outfit up on

The corral crew in 1937.
From left: Reid Kochel, George Gentry, Bill Eaton, Billy Eaton, Buck Blackburn, Clyde Vanderen, Hank Leyendecker, T. P. Edwards, Curly Witzel.

the reservation, and Scorp Neely is homesteading down near the Bar Eleven…

1936

Most of the "regular" boys and girls who help with the work at the Ranch were here again. Many of them have been coming every summer for years. At the corral, George, Curly, Buck, Reid, Omer, Leo, Red were all busy saddling horses, riding with people. ..

The Rimrock Ranch will open officially on December 1 this year…Very much the same group of "workers" will be on hand—Chuck and Honora Schlegel, George Gentry, Reid and Agnes Kochel, Emilia Shassetz and probably one or two other familiar home folks…

1937

We can guess what's happening at the corral. George is doctoring a sick horse, and Reid is putting the saddle rooms in order. Bill is roping horses in the corral and Hank is saddling them. The new cowboy from Texas isn't saying much, but his eyes are wide open and he isn't missing much either as he helps Buck with the gravel hauling job. Curly is out rounding up cattle, and Omer is stretching a rawhide rope. Bill is talking business with some horse buyers, and Donn is painting the barn (and hoping desperately that no dude girls will see him at that job)…

Down at the Lower Ranch, Jens Larsen and Harold Curtis are feeding and watching out for the cattle, the work horses, and some twenty or thirty head of saddle horses that have been held on Wolf Creek for the winter. Nels and Annabel Larsen are living in their house a few miles below us, Ben and Claire Sittler are at the Bar Eleven Ranch, of course, keeping watch over the cavvy on their winter range...Mr. and Mrs. Curly Witzel (it happened in October in case you don't know) are Bar Eleven neighbors, too. They're living this winter some five miles horseback over the divide in the house on "Twenty Mile," while Curly puts the finishing touches on his homestead claim...

(Note: Curly married a dude woman, Annie Laurie Jacques. They were married for many years but eventually divorced. By agreement with Eatons' Ranch, Curly and several other employees took out homesteads in their own names, made the necessary improvements with some Eaton help and then transferred the property to Eatons' Ranch. By this method, Eatons was able to expand the Bar Eleven Ranch.

Nineteen thirty seven was the last year Curly worked for the Eatons during this period but he reappeared on the Eaton payroll many years later in the 1950s. During the 1930s, Curly became an aviator. He took flying lessons from Oliver Wallop of Big Horn, and then obtained further training in Billings, Montana, to obtain his commercial license and an instructor rating, which he put to good use by training naval pilots during the Second World War.)

1938

The entire Eaton Outfit isn't yet assembled at Wolf, but most of them are either here or on the way. Buck Blackburn went home to Texas from Rimrock for a few weeks before joining the corral force at Wolf. Tepee Edwards will probably come up with him around the first of June. Chuck and Honora Schlegel spent a few days at Guaymas, down on the west coast of Mexico after the Rimrock closed, and are now en route to Pittsburgh for a quick visit. Julia will soon be present in the dining room, welcoming dudes and seating them in their usual places there...

1939

...it has been thirty years since John Fleming has taken the trail east. He does it now somewhat under protest, and will make it a brief journey spending a few days visiting with William C. (Bill) Arthur in Meadville, Pennsylvania, and then heading west again...

Since the Eaton Outfit purchased the Bar Eleven Ranch in 1925 to provide good care and winter-feed for the arrowhead horses through the long winters, things have gone along at Echeta in a fairly well set pattern. The horses trotted down in the fall when their work was done on Wolf Creek, had excellent feed and attention through the winter months. Fat and sassy, they were driven back to the Wolf Creek Ranch in the spring. There was a little wild hay stacked in the summer, and we knew the fences were up and that everything down there was all right because Ben and Claire Sittler were at home on the Bar Eleven, looking out for things. We closed our minds to the thought that they might some day leave Echeta, that there might ever be a change in the happy arrangement there, but all along we knew it was inevitable that some day Ben and Claire would move to their own ranch.

Last spring the break came. No need to write how we felt about it—to us "Bar Eleven" has always meant "Ben and Claire." And we think they felt the same way. We're re-reading now a note from them, written late in the winter, and Claire says, "For once, I'm not looking forward to spring. It all seems like a very bad dream. Wish we did not own a hoof of livestock or an acre of land. But we do, and we must plan for our later years, even if it is unbelievably hard to make the break." And Ben writes on the back of the sheet, "You know, I've lived in a country like this for a long time and there are a great many things about the river breaks that I like a lot, and Claire likes them, too. We both wonder if we will ever love any other place—even our own ranch—as much. When we get the last load of our old traps in the truck and start out of here...well, twenty years ago things like that didn't mean much to a wandering cowboy, but at that time I'd never worked for Eaton Brothers. If we didn't own our own ranch and have our stock to worry about, the only way you'd get me off the Bar Eleven would be to stop my wages, and even then I wouldn't leave until I got real hungry."...

So now—Reid and Agnes Kochel have moved down to the Bar Eleven to watch over the horses through the winter months. Agnes has helped at the Ranch since she was a schoolgirl, and Reid has been around the corral for fifteen years. We know that they will have the best interests of the arrowhead brand in mind as they go on with their work for the Eaton Outfit...

A new employee hired on at Eatons' in the summer of 1939. His name was Kelly Howie. Kelly, one of nine children, was born on his parents homestead near White Owl, South Dakota, in about 1913. Kelly grew up under tough circumstances and in the process became a skilled horseman.

In his later years, Kelly wrote his unpublished memoirs, and he described how he and his brother Glenn "made a trip up to Sheridan and the dude ranch areas, to see what was available":

By then it was getting close to the middle of June of 1939, and it was time to trail all of the Eaton dude horses from Bar Eleven Winter Ranch to the Home Ranch there at Wolf, Wyoming. My brother Glenn and I had made a trip earlier and found out about some jobs at Eatons' dude ranch and other dude ranches, but I had missed Bill Eaton.

I was going back to Moorcroft on the train. Glenn hired on at Rapid Creek Ranch. As I got on the train, I ran into Reid Kochel, Eatons' foreman and manager for the Bar Eleven Ranch. He told me when the horses would leave for the Eatons' Ranch. That is how we made connections to help trail the horses to summer range. When I got to Eatons' Dude Ranch, the dude season was just starting.

The Eaton family consisted of Bill and Patty (Bill's wife), Aunt Mame, Bill's mother, Aunt Minnie, Aunt Mame's sister, Cousin Josie, young Billie and his wife, Nan Eaton, their baby Frank Eaton, and Billy's sister, Nancy. A great many were long time help and were like family.

We had been there only a few days when Bill told me to go in the corral and rope this sizeable buckskin horse. I was to go with Tepee Edwards (a Texas cowboy) and take some horse over to Tom Moss's ranch on Jackson Creek, not far from Big Horn. This buckskin reared up when I mounted and came down bucking. He bucked downhill almost to the office, then turned and bucked out by Howard Hall. By then he was tapering off. I looked up and saw Bill and Shorty Enderly holding their stomachs because they were laughing so hard. They knew this was going to happen, but I didn't.

After that, this buckskin was put into the wrangling string, and I usually got him. One morning as we went to wrangle a mountain pasture south, we were going up a steep hill, and this ole buckskin blew up and he headed back downhill. He bucked me off over his head, and I hung onto the bridle reins and I got back on him and went on about our business...

Kelly worked at Eatons' through the fall and then spent the winter in Arizona. He returned the next summer and met the love of his life.

The end of the thirties essentially marked the end of an era. All three Eaton brothers—Howard, Willis and Alden—were gone and Eaton Brothers, Inc., was left in the hands of the next generation. As the decade of the forties began, the stalwart management team of Fleming, Buell and Butler remained in place. However, that management equation was to change soon as Eaton Brothers, Inc. faced yet more challenges, including a world war.

CHAPTER 7
The Forties

The War Years

The first hint in *WN* that there was a world war in progress was in the Christmas issue right after the Japanese attack on Pearl Harbor on December 7, 1941:

> *Here at the Ranch we've taken our belts up another notch since December 7, and are looking around to see where we can save a gallon of gas and a forkful of hay. And each individual is trying to economize on those little luxuries we all permit*

> *ourselves. Aunt Minnie is wearing the Red Cross Service Medal that was presented to her by the local chapter this fall, and she's continuing to knit away on garments for War Relief. Nan has long been Ranch Leader of the Bundles for Britain Movement, and she welcomes bits of tinfoil for the "tinfoil box." Scraps of metal and pieces of iron are being hoarded for ultimate shipment to the places where they are needed. Quarters and halves and dollars are coming into Wolf Post Office for Defense Loans. Sheridan County boys are saying, "So long—see you again when we've settled this thing," as they leave for training camp. The Sheridan paper has published a long, long list of local boys who are in Hawaii, the Philippines, and on battleships in the Far East. In many ways, Wyoming citizens are close to the centre of action, really.*

Life went on at Eatons' during the War, but Angela Buell noted the changes in the April 1942 *WN*:

> *War has changed the activities and the thoughts of everyone who lives even in the remote Ranch country, but at the same time it's possible to amble up to the Ranch corral, to step aboard a cowpony and in five minutes be out of sound and contact with anything that might divert pleasure in the immediate surroundings...*

The Eatons economized wherever they could. One change was that the Ranch suspended the publication of the annual Ranch booklet that had been published every year since 1903 (and some before that.) The booklet always contained the "cut and dried" information about the Ranch and was supplemented by the "more frequent and informal publication," *Wranglin' Notes*. The Ranch announced that for the time being Eatons' guests would have to depend on only *WN* for news of the ranch.

The Ranch also ceased the annual trip that Bill and Patty took to the "eastern country" to drum up business:

...but thoughts of a 1942 journey were relinquished many months ago. Bill Eaton has always shunned anything that might border on high-pressure salesmanship, and this year particularly, with memories freshened of his service at home and abroad in World War I, he'd be the last person in the world to suggest casting aside important war work for a Ranch vacation...

The April 1942 *WN* also provided news about Eaton employees and their role in the War:

Tepee, Buck, Rusty, Buddy, Johnny, and last summer's truck driver, Don, either are in uniform or expect to be very soon...

...Don King is still under age for military service and may be back to help us this summer.

...of the office group, Jim Robinson left last fall for Naval Training School and will be an Ensign on the seas by the time dudes start coming west. Bob Stuart is married and practicing law in Springfield, Illinois, with expectations of military service soon. Marie is doing her part in a government job in Washington. Of the dining room group—Glada left early in the autumn to take up hostess work at Jefferson Barracks and Carrie Lee is working in Washington. Leo, of the kitchen department, will receive Wranglin' Notes *in Camp Wolters. The laundry will miss Al, who will be decked out in a new uniform by the time this is printed and on the way to him.*

In June of 1942, *WN* again emphasized Eatons' awareness of the War:

Surrounded by a beautiful and a bountiful Nature we're apt to forget momentarily what's going on in the world at large. Not for long however, for at this point let it be known that the Ranch is most conscientious about War Restrictions. Many of our boys have gone. We adhere rigidly to regulations as they appear, and we hope when it's all over we can say that we have been good citizens and have done everything required, and more, to help along...

And in December, Angela told the readers where all the "boys" were:

We hope to reach all the Ranch boys with this issue of Wranglin' Notes. *George Gentry left home recently for Tucson and hasn't sent his "settling down" address yet. Tepee Edwards is at Camp Roberts in California. Leo Brozek is reached through Seattle, and Wilbur Jester is at Fort Warren near Cheyenne. Al Novicki at Camp Barkeley, Texas...Don Alley is home in Dayton on furlough from Camp Luis Obispo in California. Percy Dickinson is in or near Honolulu, Rusty Holler at Burbank, California. Shorty Enderle's address is Fort Rock, Arizona. Buck Blackburn spent a recent furlough at the Ranch but is now back at Camp Carson in Colorado, where he's with the Veterinary Corps. Lieutenant Buddy Alderson, fresh from officers' training school in Virginia, dropped in for a visit just before Thanksgiving en route to Fort Bliss, Texas. We haven't caught up with Johnny Belish but hope to have his address soon...*

The next year, 1943, there was more news about the Ranch during wartime:

Life goes on at the Ranch. More attention is given to the expanding beef herd. Trips to town on precious rubber tires are less frequent, and the cook studies the menu for the day with greater concentration and care...

The Eatons took great care to make sure everyone knew that the Ranch was open for business, in spite of the War:

...Now, after a year and a half of war, those left at home are largely in the upper age bracket. Right here and now we'll have to admit that few of us will ever see forty again! However, the

Ranch is still Home and the older group is not inclined to lock their doors (doors that haven't been locked in sixty-one years), even though their young people may be busy elsewhere. So here's one of the important messages...Eatons' Ranch goes on, open to guests in 1943...

The Sheridan Press further described the Eatons contribution to the war effort and the effect of the war on the Ranch. The article that appeared in the newspaper on August 15, 1943 was captioned:

Revitalizing War-Weary Business Men and Boosting Beef Supply Job of Eatons' Ranch.

The article was accompanied by a photo of four generations of Eatons: Aunt Mame; her son, Bill Eaton; his son, Billy Eaton; and his son, William Francis, aged three and a half. The write up included the following passage:

With the second summer of war, Big Bill, Tommy Butler and Angela decided they could definitely contribute to the war effort by expanding the cattle production program, and by providing rugged outdoor life for busy men, fagged out by the demands of war. This far they've succeeded.

It is notable that the newspaper article did not mention the most stalwart employee of Eatons' Ranch—John Fleming. That was because he died on April 22, 1943.

John Fleming's death was not expected but probably no one was surprised. John's health had been in slight decline for some time. Two years earlier, he wrote a letter to Robert Dalzell, the son of Aunt Allie, an Eaton sister. In the letter, he mentioned not only his health but also his fondness for Uncle Alden:

...Way in the background these passing years has been a feeling that I am pretty much alone with Alden gone and that he meant much more to me than I realized. True, I kept all burdens

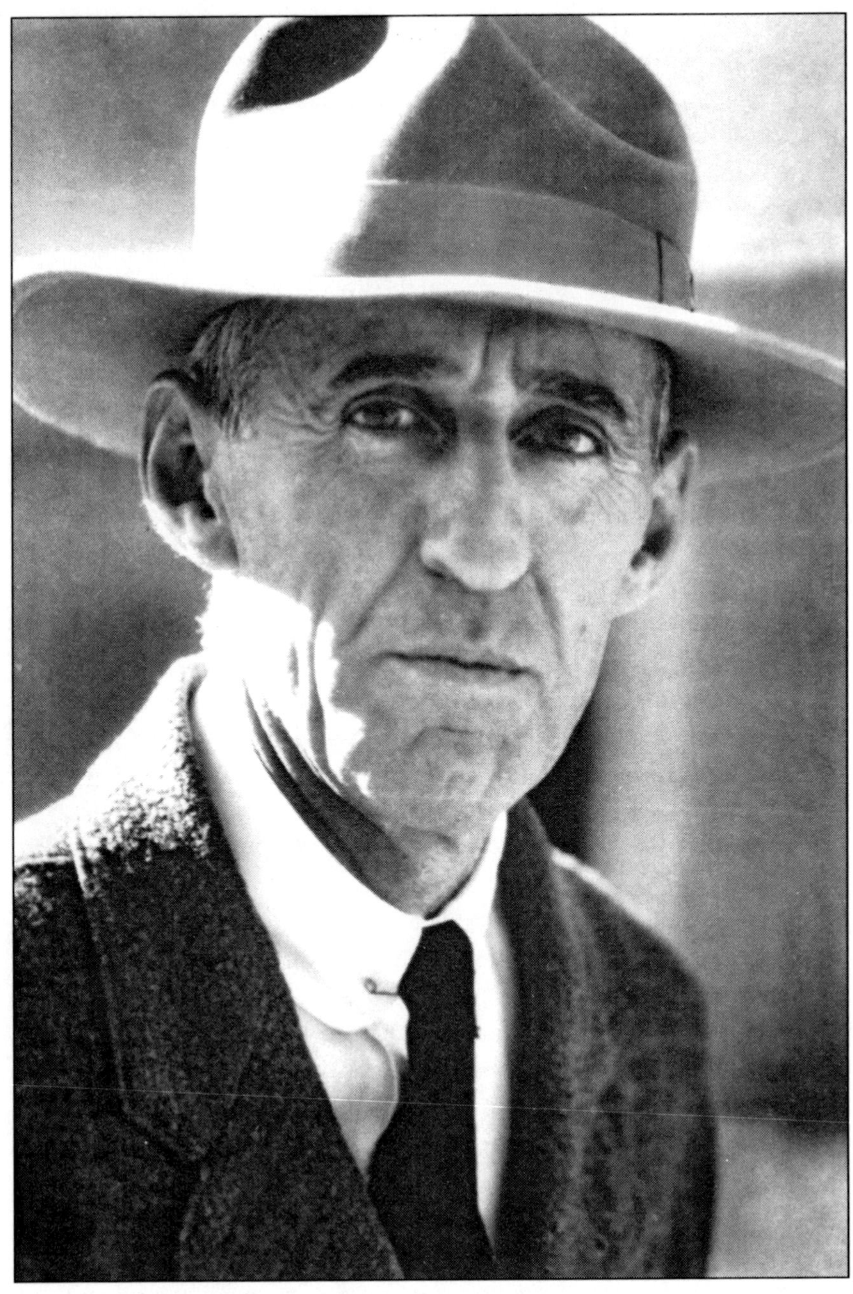

John Fleming in his later years. Photo by Arthur Dailey.
Courtesy of Eatons' Ranch.

off his shoulders, but in turn, he gave me an example of the kind of a man I would like to be and so I kept foiling the medicos more or less by a fair to middlin' record. But last winter was not so good and I knew it. I went to Arizona in April, struck bad weather, and returned without any pickup. Then the steady grind of the summer. Upshot: Dr. Denison persuaded me to get an extra checkup, and I did and now maybe with this and that I can do a little better. Not one thing specially—just a general letdown after so many years pressing against the grindstone. My inheritance—health wise—was not too good and some early childhood ills set the signals against me so if I am careful...it's an old story...

John's health finally caught up with him. He died, not surprisingly, at work in the Eaton Ranch office on the morning of April 23. John was sixty-five years old.

The Sheridan Press reported the story the same day and *t*he story caption read:

John L. Fleming Called By Death
Eaton Bros. Ranch President Dies Suddenly At Wolf

The newspaper also advised the readers that the "Big Goose-Wolf Bond Rally is Postponed" because of John's death.

When John died, the April *WN* had already been written and distributed and so it wasn't until the June issue that Eatons could pay proper tribute. And they did, with a special attachment that included a photo of John, and the following message:

With deep sorrow and a sense of great personal loss, we tell friends of the sudden death of the president of our organization, John Fleming. For forty years, he had been devoted to the welfare and progress of Eatons' Ranch. A man of great kindliness and almost unbelievable modesty, he wished no personal recognition, no personal reward, for his many years of intensive and unselfish service. His only desire was that the

> *Ranch should go ever forward along the lines prescribed by his earlier associates, Howard, Willis and Alden Eaton.*
>
> *As with the passing, one by one, of the three Eaton brothers, we feel a part of the Ranch has gone with John Fleming, that another chapter of our long history is finished. Now, as we start on a new era, we are conscious of the traditions that lie behind us, of the trust we bear, and we will ever be guided by the worthy example of those four remarkable men of a passing generation...Howard Eaton, Willis Eaton, Alden Eaton, and John Fleming.*

Following John Fleming's death, Angela Buell wrote a letter to the Eaton sisters, who were also preferred stockholders, to reassure them their interests were protected and the Ranch was in good hands. One of the letters to Elsie Pelissier read as follows:

> *No need to remind you of the great loss the Ranch has just suffered—you* know. *It was Mr. Fleming's wish that Bill, Tom, and I should carry on, and that is what we will make effort to do, and do well. It is an inauspicious period for dude ranches, and only time will tell a lot of things—but we start out determined to do the best we can.*
>
> *You probably realize that of late years Mr. Fleming was gradually withdrawing as much as possible from the responsibility of decisions, passing them around to the three of us. So we are not suddenly burdened with that new experience—although we shall certainly miss the knowledge that his wisdom was at hand to be drawn on at any time. For a good many years, I have known the office end of the Ranch inside out, and Mr. Fleming and I have often discussed your interest and Aunt Allie's interest and Aunt Lizzie's interest in the Ranch. I know only too well the responsibility he felt toward you and how careful he was to keep you and the others informed of the business in general.*
>
> *So, I'll endeavor to take Mr. Fleming's place to some extent in that respect, and will start by sending you a copy of his Will*

so you will know how he felt about the Ranch in general. His estate was very small—for you know as well as I that it was his practice to give rather than to take, and he took very, very little for his forty years of service and devotion to the Ranch.

Anyway, Elsie, I do want you to know that I have an eye on your note and as long as I'm around, I'll be aware of the obligations of the Ranch and your interest in it.

In keeping with his loyalty to Eatons' Ranch, John Fleming left his common stock in the Ranch to those whom he believed would be the best stewards, namely Bill Eaton, Angela Buell and Tommy Butler. He left the remainder of his estate to a niece, Alice Jeffords, and a nephew William Fleming. Bill Eaton was the executor of John's estate.

In July, Bill Eaton, vice president of the Eaton Brothers Corporation, called a special meeting to "fill the place made vacant by the death of Mr. John L. Fleming." The officers elected unanimously were William A. Eaton, president; Thomas B. Butler, vice president; Angela Buell, treasurer; and William A. Eaton, Jr. secretary.

The torch was passed.

As the war continued, Angela Buell mingled the effect of the war on Eatons' with regular news about the Ranch. In the Christmas 1943 Edition of *WN*, she looked back on 1943 and wrote:

We were pleasantly surprised, which often happens when nothing is expected. Though many friends said that the Ranch went on just the same as ever, in spite of war conditions and difficulties, we know that wasn't true. The grounds weren't as clean and trim as we'd like. There were no thick tender beefsteaks on all-day picnics, meatless days were frequent, the office closed at 5:00 p.m. instead of 9:00 p.m., a limited number of maids couldn't always make goodness only knows how many beds before the lunch hour, some of the horses needed shoes before they got them. The fix-it-quick department didn't always "fix it quick."

Throughout the rest of the Second World War, which ended in 1945, it wasn't discussed much until the Christmas 1946 *WN*, when Angela described a post-war surge of dude business in 1945:

> *We've finished an extraordinarily busy season, but we take no special credit for the tremendous demand for places at the Ranch last summer. It was just a general condition for dude ranches everywhere. Probably will be a decade or maybe two—maybe a lifetime—before we again turn away almost as many guests as we can accommodate. There are several small cabins on the Ranch that have been used only occasionally in recent years as they need repairs and are in line for replacement as soon as possible, but they were pressed into service last summer and gratefully accepted by good friends who had their hearts set on a vacation at the Ranch. Some visitors at the Ranch may have put up with lumpy pillows, worn rugs on the floor, and baths not attached to their cabins, but we were careful to see that they received full value in other ways...*

Ranch Operations

During the 1940s, the Eaton Ranch operation was frequently challenged by the weather. In 1943, the Ranch was hit particularly hard when, according to *WN*:

> *...the weather was so tough the big wooden pipeline at the Ranch froze for the first time in its twenty years of service. And we mean it froze solid its entire 1825 feet. Not the underground pipeline that provides water for drinking and domestic use, but*

the feeder to the hydroelectric light plant. That happened on January 21. The box of candles kept for emergency use came down from the storeroom. Domo's cabin was raided for its kerosene lamps, and camp lanterns appeared on living room tables. Neighbors kindly loaned their extra supply of lamps, radios were silent, the laundry machinery ceased to function, electric razors and hot pads and coffee percolators and vacuum cleaners had a rest, and for almost a month we went back to ranch life as it was in the early days. Then Tommy Butler, whose middle name is "Ingenuity," went scouting.

It was obviously impossible to build fires under a wooden pipeline, but there are two big stationary steam boilers on the Ranch that were ready for action, and to augment them Tommy found at a local coal mine, an old Aultman-Taylor steam boiler on wheels which must have left its plant at Mansfield, Ohio, many years ago—long before our high wheel Avery tractor, now part of Uncle Sam's scrap-pile, was built.

Tom and Bill, Emil, Billy and Ralph Weaver loaded it on a truck and within twenty-four hours, the old steam boiler was alive again on the flat above Rotten Row, belching black smoke and furnishing steam through steel pipe and hose to thaw an opening through the innards of the wooden pipe. It was an effort for the old thing—it quivered and shook and threatened to burst its seams, but day and night the boys kept up steam, inching the pipe and hose forward through openings made in the big pipe.

On February 16, water trickled through again from the dam in Wolf Canyon to the turbine in the little stone building near the dining room. At first, it was a stream just pencil-thick but slowly and surely, with the help of a Chinook that arrived just then, the solid wall of ice gave way. The wheels went round again, we laid away our flashlights, electric lights and gadgets went back into service.

Weather was also a problem in 1948 and Angela Buell elaborated on the general situation at great length in the February 1949 *WN*:

Here at the Ranch on Wolf Creek in Northern Wyoming, and a hundred miles away at the Eatons' Bar Eleven Ranch at Echeta where the main bunch of horses are on winter pastures, we've had plenty of troubles, although it is fitting that we should complain in only a mild way. We've also had plenty of food and plenty of fuel, and have been able to obtain sufficient feed for the cattle and horses—by contrast with many ranchers, who have suffered not only personal privations, but will find when spring comes, if not before, that they're practically wiped out and will have to start over again if they're young enough and strong enough to do that.

Throughout our lifetimes here in the West we've heard stories from the old-timers about the "hard winter of 1886," and when a winter in this modern age of telephones, radios, trucks, tractors, bulldozers and hay by airlift can compared with pioneer days of 1886, then you may be sure it is pretty tough.

For humans in 1948, the suffering must have been less than it was in 1886, for most of them had food and shelter and the possibility of attracting planes with distress signals, but many of the animals, the sheep, the cattle, the horses, hadn't a chance as the wind-driven snow, accompanied by temperatures down to thirty and forty below zero, closed in around them, burying the feed on the range and slowly but surely sapping their strength as it continued day after day and week after week. You've read all that in the newspapers, heard it on the radio, so for the benefit of friends interested in the horses, the cattle, and the folks at Eatons' Ranch, we'll limit this report to our own troubles, which are small by comparison with the West as a whole, but plenty big enough for us.

And then Angela gave her report on the situation at the Bar Eleven and the main Ranch at Wolf:

The first terrible blizzard didn't reach us here except as a bad winter storm with low temperatures. The second wasn't too bad, either, although the situation began to look ominous at the

Bar Eleven. But the third blizzard, with thermometers here registering thirty-eight degrees below zero, we had all hands working to keep warm and save the water pipes, while at Echeta matters were becoming really serious.

Bill and Billy and Newt managed to get in to the Bar Eleven before the third storm struck, then were marooned there in the ranch house, unable to help the horses in to feed from the big snowbound and windswept Twenty Mile Pasture, as the thermometer dropped to forty below and the whirling snow revealed only a blank white wall ten feet ahead. At that point, Agnes came down with the chickenpox, and that didn't add to the happiness of the Bar Eleven household. However, when the storm lifted, Reid and Guy and Newt gathered some of the horses—about two thirds of them. Some were mighty thin and needed care, others had withstood the storms and low temperatures and short feed remarkably well.

As this is written, we're pulling out of the fourth storm—or is it the fifth or sixth?—we've lost count. Word comes from Echeta that more of the horses have been located and brought in, although some are still missing. It's pretty hard to find horses in that rough country in good weather, and it's really tough in bitter weather when tremendous drifts require five miles of riding to advance two. Also, the boys have been able to ride only every other day for the number of grain-fed horses is limited and mounts, as well as men, are exhausted after a day spent fighting drifts. Several carloads of hay are on the way to Echeta by rail and probably by this time, the rest of the horses have been found and brought in near the corrals where they can be fed.

Here at the home Ranch, Tommy Butler is directing frozen pipe operations, and he and his crew are reaching the exhaustion stage, too. We felt a little panicky one day when the main water line down the canyon froze solid, but in no time Tommy had a fire hose rigged to the power waterline to supply water to the main building unit and keep the furnaces and big boiler going, while the truck was hauling loads of manure to cover the hose to keep IT from freezing. We were happy to see our faithful coal-contractor, square-dance-caller, road-maintainer and general trouble shooter, Ralph Weaver, show up just then, and he manned the tractor, which dragged a stone boat loaded with drums of hot water up the Canyon Trail, while others hauled wood and built fires along the line.

It worked...and during the night, the main line loosened and water came through again. The thawing job isn't finished by any means, for there's work going on night and day to free subsidiary lines...fifteen hundred feet of water pipe to Tommy Ferguson's abandoned house is one of the projects. Other lines freeze without warning as the frost goes deeper and deeper into the ground...but we have our eye on the thermometer and barometer and our ears open to weather reports, and hope the next storm will hold off until we're in better shape to weather it.

Angela then topped off her account of the grim situation with:

...This morning a flock of robins, looking a little chilly in the ten-degree-below temperature, landed in one of the apple trees and had a wonderful time picking away at the frozen fruit still hanging on the branches. The opinion seemed to be that they had come in from the north, and that their arrival was not necessarily a harbinger of spring...

A major part of the Eaton Ranch operation was the continuing effort to improve the facilities. They had to throttle down their efforts during the war, of course, but by Christmas of 1944, *WN* elaborated on improvement efforts:

...The office has a new floor and is being remodeled generally and painted inside to make it a cleaner, more convenient place for handling the great volume of detail that flows in and out of that small building twelve months in the year. The general paint campaign isn't finished but we'll complete the big barn, the garage and cow barn, and a few more places

that haven't been reached as yet. Down on Butler Boulevard, a couple of cabins are getting new brick chimneys to make them more comfortable for winter use. The Hennery porch has a new floor...

And the accounts of Ranch improvements, which were of great interest to the Eaton Ranch dude clientele, were included in subsequent editions of *WN* with regularity. For example, the spring 1945 issue of *WN* contained the following:

Working against odds, we hope to have a few more private baths installed by the time summer comes. The fixtures have been purchased second-hand as we could find them, and Lew Crews has just returned with his tool chest and skill at converting cabins built many years ago to models that are more modern. It's slow work but little by little, we progress. We'll probably be concentrating on more and more baths for several years to come, and until that job is out of the way, there's nothing we can do about meeting the increasing demand for private living rooms. We must continue to explain that private living rooms are limited almost entirely to the few large cottages, which are occupied naturally, by the larger parties and family groups...

In 1946, *WN* described the project to increase the hydroelectric capacity of the Ranch:

...Twenty-three years ago Uncle Alden Eaton and Mr. Frank Kennedy superintended the installation of a hydro-electric plant at the Ranch which has run along wonderfully well, with a minimum of trouble and expense, providing light and power. Now the log and rock dam up the canyon needs replacing, and Tom Butler has taken over the job of picking a site farther upstream for a new dam, and extending the big pipeline, so we may have a little more power to meet the growing needs of the Ranch. When finished, we will not have unlimited power by any

means, but it should relieve some of the big load on the plant.

Tom and Emil have made many trips up the canyon figuring how it is to be accomplished, and with the help of George, Al, Leroy, Ralph Weaver, and several others, have dug up, cut, and transported some big pipe from an abandoned power line in Little Goose Canyon some thirty or forty miles away. Next will come the construction of the new dam and the laying of the pipe to connect with the present pipeline. It's a big job, and for a time we'll be without electricity at all, but the kerosene lamps and candles should be back in hiding before many friends arrive in the early spring.

And then, the May 1948 issue contained the following:

There's plenty of activity at the Ranch right now. The cement driveway in the vicinity of the porte cochere *and the kitchen door has been replaced. The Hennery (where the dining room girls live) and adjoining bathhouse has a new furnace. Anna Butler, Elizabeth Hull, and Dorothy Shipley have formed the Butler Boulevard Garden Club and come summer there will be stretches of lawn that were only rock piles in former years…There's a handsome rock wall under construction along the ditch between the Ranch house and Butler Boulevard...Another Rotton Row cabin has been moved to Pig Alley for the use of employees. The guest laundry on The Pike was destroyed by fire a month or so ago, and is now being rebuilt into a more efficient and fireproof building…The kitchen has also been reshingled and has a fresh coat of white paint inside; there's an improved and almost-soundproof telephone booth in the office for the convenience of guests having long distance calls…A new log cabin—a small one—is going up at the end of Butler Boulevard…*

Eatons' Ranch never stopped making improvements, and Angela Buell never stopped reporting them.

Angela also made sure that she reported on other aspects of Ranch operations that she thought might interest readers of *WN*. In 1945, she described the ice-making operation that took place every winter at the Ranch. The ice on the pond at the lower place was:

> *...sawed by Dwight Daniels and Tommy Butler and machine, escaladed to the loading platform by George Gentry and machine, loaded and hauled three miles up the Ranch road by Ralph Weaver, Billy Eaton and machines, escaladed from the receiving platform near the Wolves Club into the icehouse by John Leahy and machine, packed in neat layers in the icehouse by Emil Jacobs and Bill Eaton via hard, ignorant labor (as Patty says)...that in a nutshell is the history of the 1945 ice crop at Eatons' Ranch...*

Family

In the forties, the Eaton family was in transition from the second to the third generation. Bill and Patty naturally assumed the place that Alden and Aunt Mame had occupied as the functional head of the family, but Mame remained a vibrant and respected part of the Eaton family and the Ranch operation. In this time, the family experienced joyous expansion through marriage and births, but also suffered an untimely tragedy.

Except during the war years, Bill and Patty did their duty to market the ranch by visiting Ranch friends all over the United States. In 1940, for instance, *WN* announced that:

> *...They'll be leaving the Ranch on Monday, April the 8th, just about the time these* Wranglin' Notes *are mailed, and*

they're going south to Denver and then on through Texas, expecting to spend the April 15 and 16 at the St. Charles Hotel in New Orleans. Then north to Louisville where they'll be at the Brown Hotel on the 20th and 21st. Their schedule calls for....

And the rest of the itinerary was listed in equal detail and had them returning to the Ranch in early May. The schedule was typical of their journeys. The announcement of Billy and Patty's travels gave interested dudes along the way time to organize receptions, dinners and parties for Bill and Patty and other Eatons' devotees so they could tell stories about the Ranch.

Angela Buell also reported the results of the trips:

Bill and Patty Eaton had a splendid trip, as outlined in the last issue of Wranglin' Notes. *They told us all about the many friends they saw, how kind everyone was to them, and Patty is still talking about the blue bonnets in Texas, the lovely foliage and roses and the redbud in Louisiana and Tennessee, the beautiful dogwood in Kentucky. For more details of their trip, just get Patty in a corner sometime this summer and she will tell you all about it.*

Unfortunately, Bill Eaton carried his profligate gambling and spending habits into the 1940s. In a January 15, 1940 note to Josephine Gillespie, Fleming complained:

Bill's overdraft almost $5,000. I see nothing to do but to take up some of his stock—that is the stock he and his mother own. I think I will just have to take your approval for granted—but there is no way he can refund the money he has overdrawn.

In reply, Josephine wrote:

I am wondering if you can't have a plain talk with BOTH Bill and Patty, and tell them Bill is about wrecking the Ranch, to say nothing of his mother.

Well, couldn't you tell him hereafter he is to draw ONLY up to the weekly income, in any one week, and you will not advance any more nor pay any bills?

I think half his income should be kept back, toward paying Nancy's Dr. bills but maybe that wouldn't do, since Nancy is in school, and has to have some money. I think if half Bill's pay went to Patty she would have something to show for it, and maybe wouldn't be everlastingly complaining of "not having a cent" and "never buying any clothes" and all that.

You must long to throttle Bill!

We do not know exactly how Bill's entire chronic financial situation was resolved, or, indeed, if it ever was, totally. It is common knowledge that Aunt Mame once bailed Bill and the Ranch out by selling a valuable Charles Russell painting, but whether that ended the problem is uncertain. Frank Eaton, Bill's grandson, believes that sometime during the 1940s Bill probably mended his ways somewhat. If there was a continuing problem in later years, it was not documented. After all, John Fleming was not around to write about it after his death in 1943. But Bill and Patty's financial situation did improve in later years as evidenced by the fact that in 1967 they were able to make a temporary loan of $25,000 to the Ranch for "routine conduct of the business."

Billy and Nan Eaton continued to live and work at the Ranch and raise Beaton, the apple of everyone's eye. *WN* often displayed photos of him. The June 1940 *WN* had two photos of him. One was captioned "The baby is growing fast," and the other was "Beaton and his great-grandmother Aunt Mame."

When Beaton was almost two, *WN* gave a status report on the baby: "...Beaton Eaton is talking a blue streak as his second birthday approaches..."

There was other reporting as well. For instance, in the June 1942 *WN*, Angela Buell wrote a passage about how everyone at Eatons' Ranch was willing to buckle down for the war effort and said:

...We may be asked to do more, and if so we sorta think we'll be equal to it, one and all right down to two-and-a-half

Patty Eaton at head of Soldier Creek Trail on all day ride in 1941.
Photo by Thomas McGrath.
Courtesy of Eatons' Ranch.

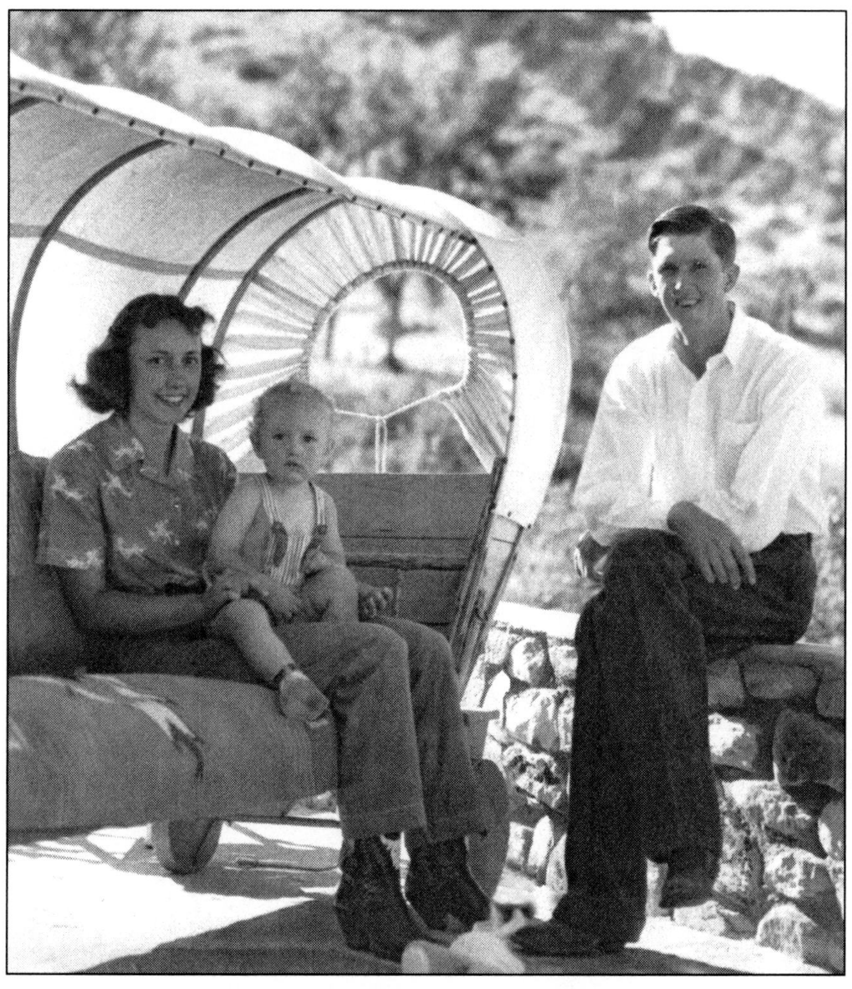

Billy and Nan Eaton with baby Frank.
Photo by W. Thomas McGrath, Sheridan, Wyoming.
Courtesy of Eatons' Ranch.

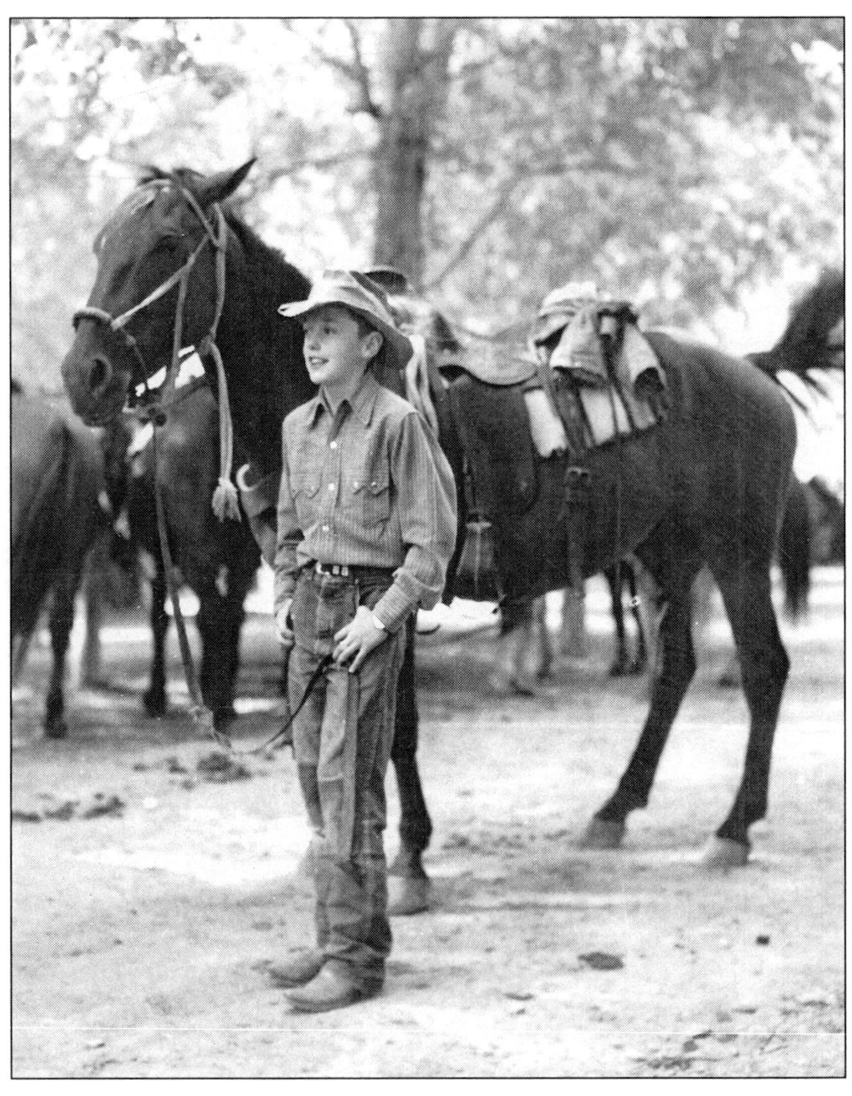

Frank Eaton helped at the corral when he was young and later became the corral boss.
Courtesy of Eatons' Ranch.

year old Beaton (who now says, "Call me Frank"). As we see him, toddling around the Ranch interested in anything that looks like a horse (one of his favorite games now is playing with the horse napkin rings in the office)...

In 1944, a new baby sister joined Beaton in the limelight. His sister Jacqueline Patricia Eaton was born in the Sheridan Hospital just before Christmas on December 6. *WN* made special note of her birth and noted "Jackie Eaton will see her first Christmas tree." (*Note: Jacqueline's shortened name was spelled several ways in* WN*: Jackie, and Jacquie. Nan Eaton eventually decreed that her daughter's shortened name would henceforth be "Jaci," pronounced Jackie, and it still is today.*)

Jaci missed out on the annual trip that her mother took to see her family in Pennsylvania in the spring of 1945:

Nan Eaton and five-year old Beaton are also leaving soon on their annual trip east to visit Nan's parents in Philadelphia, Mr. and Mrs. Frank E. Baker. Small Jacquie, aged four months, must stay at home, but we're hoping the Bakers will return with Nan in late May to enjoy a lovely time of year in the western country and to make the acquaintance of their fine new grandchild, the youngest member of the Ranch household, Miss Jacqueline Patricia Eaton.

That same year, 1945, Beaton Eaton started school noted by *WN*:

It has been a long time since Billy and Nancy Eaton learned to read and write, and do arithmetic at the little white country school house six miles down the road. The years have rolled along and the Eatons are once again very personally interested in what goes on down there. Every morning Frank is in the dining room well before 8 o'clock for his breakfast. Julia brings his lunchbox to him, and he's off. (By the way, now that he's grown up and attending school he's "Frank" not "Beaton." Frank admits liking recess better than anything else he does at school, but he's getting along fine.

Nothing went unnoticed about Beaton and Jaci, and most everything they did was reported in *WN*. Angela Buell even reported on their illnesses, like in 1948 when she wrote, "…Jaci Eaton celebrated Christmas Day with the mumps, but that didn't slow her down very much and they spread no further…"

Billy and Nan were mentioned often as well as the children. In 1943, *WN* reported that Billy applied to join the Border Patrol.

> *…Billy went to Cheyenne for an examination for the Border Patrol, an effort, which we are sorry to say, was not rewarded for he was rejected physically—not enough weight for his height. He came back to the Ranch, oiled his rifle, saddled his horse, and set out for some more coyote pelts, which may see service as part of some soldier's parka in the North Country…*

WN discussed many things, but one of the things not discussed was Billy's frustration about his situation at the Ranch. According to his wife, Nan, Billy was a hard worker. The problem was that he was given "lots to do but never allowed to make himself heard." He had plenty of responsibility, but no authority. Billy came up against a glass ceiling in the Ranch management. With an authoritative father in place, who certainly wasn't going anywhere, and plenty of other "old time" Eaton standbys—like George Gentry, Tommy Butler, Dunc, and others—there wasn't really any place for Billy. This was a source of great frustration for him.

According to Nan, Billy never really voiced his frustration to her, but she knew it was there. Nan also believes that this frustration exacerbated another problem.

Just as his father, Bill Eaton, had an addictive personality that manifested itself in gambling, so, too, did Billy have an addiction. But his was to alcohol. Billy was a hard drinker and it led to his death.

Bill Eaton, Jr. (Billy) died on July 22, 1949. He had developed a bleeding ulcer and his drinking only made it worse. The ulcer flared up when Billy, Nan and the children were visiting Nan's parents in Philadelphia. Billy's condition was so serious that the doctors prescribed surgery. Unfortunately, an infection set in and Billy died.

A special edition of *WN* in August announced Billy's death:

William Alden Eaton Jr.
1917-1949

With deep sorrow and a feeling of great loss
we must tell Ranch friends of Billy Eaton's death
in Philadelphia on
Friday, July twenty-second, nineteen hundred and forty-nine

The tribute read in part:

Last issue of Wranglin' Notes *only a few short months ago, mentioned the absence of Billy and Nan and the children from the Ranch as they visited with the Bakers in Philadelphia prior to a busy summer in Wyoming. And now, years ahead of the time when such an announcement might have been expected,* Wranglin' Notes *goes to friends with the sad message of Billy's untimely death on July 22.*

Sorrow has plowed a deep furrow in the lives of the home folks on Eatons' Ranch this summer. Though everyone knew that furrow was there, it was screened so well by the Eaton family and their long-standing associates, and by the efforts of the understanding dudes, that the children on the place hardly knew anything was amiss and the life of the Ranch went right along. Let us say—that we have appreciated this understanding more than we can express. Of course, the furrow is still there—and it will take many springs and summers and winters and falls—more than we can foresee now—to soften its harshness.

Nan and the children, Billy and Patty, Nancy, Aunt Mame, and the numerous other close relatives and long-time associates who live at the Ranch, are grateful for the expressions of sympathy that have been received from friends and well wishers all over the land. We consider each and every one of them not only a tribute to Bill Eaton, Jr., but a tribute to that stalwart family of which he was a part, and of which, in time, like his father and grandfather before him, he would have been the head and his the guiding hand.

After Billy's death, Nan had to decide where she and the children wanted to live. Nan remembers that her mother's friends in Philadelphia could not imagine that she would not return to Philadelphia: "Why would she want to live in that place out west?" But Nan knew exactly what she wanted to do. She loved the Ranch and knew that was where she should raise her children. It was their home and that was where they were going to stay.

WN explained her decision in the 1949 Christmas edition:

Because so many friends have asked whether Nan and the children would stay on at the Ranch since Billy's death last July, we want to say here that Nan considers the Ranch as "home," and she plans for Frank and Jaci to grow up there, just as their father and grandfather did. Of course, there will be journeys to Philadelphia to visit their Grandfather and Grandmother Baker, but when they return to the Ranch, they'll be coming "home."...

Sixty years later, they would all live on or near Eatons' Ranch.

In the meantime, Nancy Eaton's life took its own course. When she returned from her winter in Philadelphia in 1940, she worked at the Ranch but also did some traveling with her grandmother, Aunt Mame. The March 1941 *WN* described the event:

...A few weeks ago, Aunt Mame Eaton stepped into the car with her chauffeur (Nancy Eaton) at the wheel and waved goodbye to the group gathered at the Ranch door as she started on another of the motor trips she loves through the West. Old story that it is to her, Aunt Mame will motor through ranch country day after day, explore Carlsbad Caverns down in New Mexico, see the bucking broncs at the Tucson Rodeo, drive across the desert, watch the waves break on the beach, dine at El Paseo, sightsee along Hollywood Boulevard, and roll up and down California highways, with more thrills and enthusiasm than many a young person seeing it all for the first time. That's why she's seventy years young. When Aunt Mame and Nancy left the Ranch, they figured their funds would run out around the first of April, so we'll be looking for them home about that time.

And after they got back, the June *WN* had another report on Nancy, but this time it was not about her travels, but rather her as a person:

One more Eaton to mention specially—Nancy, born to Ranch life as were her mother and father before her, with grandparents on both sides pioneer ranch men and ranch women (and that's saying something for a country as young as Wyoming). She has a normal, young healthy interest in things apart from the Ranch but you couldn't pry her loose from home in the summer time, which is at this date, as we mentioned above, the BEST of all the seasons. Nancy has ridden horses constantly from the time she was two years old, sat proudly, and unafraid on a pillow over the saddle horn in from of Uncle Will Eaton. Right now she's just waiting to lead a group of young people her age over the hills and home by way of Domo's for a glass of lemonade before heading for the Ranch and a bountiful lunch.

In the fall of 1941, Nancy was off traveling again, but this time she went east:

As this is written, Nancy Eaton is still traveling about, too. She went east with Gee and Motz Wright in early September, expecting to stay a month or so—and here it is December. Although she does promise to be home by Christmas and that's not far off now. If young people from the East come to Wyoming and the Ranch in the summer time and proceed to "go west," then we can say that Nancy Eaton has evened the score by "going east" in a big way this winter. Norris and Fleta Wright seem to have adopted her and Nancy has had a wonderful time, thanks to them. The Ranch Reunion in New York at rodeo time, with the Wrights organizing and throwing a gay party for all the Eatonites they could gather, was a fine tribute to the Eatons and their friends, and we all wish we could have been there....

The next time Nancy is mentioned in *WN* is when she married Thomas J. (Tommy) Ferguson on September 5, 1942.

Tommy Ferguson was a native of Kirby, Montana, just a few miles from the Wyoming line. His family was an old time Montana family as was Nancy's on her mother Patty's side. In fact, Tommy's uncle was shot and killed by the Indians in the early days, and a posse led by Nancy's grandfather later found his body.

For a time, Tommy wrangled dudes in Arizona in the winter and at the Bob Woods Rapid Creek Ranch, not far from Eatons'. Tommy and

Nancy met each other in the summer of 1941. There was an age difference. In 1941, Nancy was twenty years old, nine years younger than Tommy. But that didn't matter to them. They were smitten with each other, a romance ensued and the following year they were married. Of course, *WN* carried a photo of the newlyweds and described the event in the December issue:

> *The most important picture of all in this issue of* Wranglin' Notes *is the one of Mr. and Mrs. Thomas Ferguson standing outside the office door. Mrs. Ferguson is Nancy Eaton of course, and we must say a few words about their wedding at the Ranch in early September.*
>
> *Large as the living room is for most occasions, it overflowed with friends that September afternoon. Everyone helped in the preparations for the simple home wedding at the Ranch and we can't hope to mention and thank everyone here. Joe Smith sent over an automobile load of his beautiful prize-winning gladioli, dudes helped with the decorating, willing hands shifted dining room tables immediately after lunch to rearrange for the buffet supper to follow the ceremony, Jim Parkinson drove to town on a special trip for the rector, Bill Eaton laid aside his cowboy hat and put on his town clothes for the occasion. Patty wore blue to match her eyes—and when Nancy came down the staircase at four o'clock, she was indeed a lovely bride.*

Of course, the local newspaper, *The Sheridan Press,* covered the event and informed the reader, among other things, that:

> *...Merle Bonham Woods, pianist, played a medley of wedding music before the ceremony and the "Wedding March" from Lohengrin as the bridal party approached the alter...*
>
> *...The Rev. Rex Simms of Buffalo performed the Episcopal service in front of the fireplace...*
>
> *...The bride, escorted by her father, was beautiful in a princess style gown of white duchess satin brocade fashioned with a sweetheart neckline and long sleeves falling to a point at the wrist...*

Newlyweds Tommy and Nancy Ferguson at Eatons' Ranch in 1942.
Courtesy of Eatons' Ranch.

The bride and groom, Nancy and Tommy Ferguson,
with Nancy's parents, Bill and Patty Eaton.
Courtesy of Eatons' Ranch.

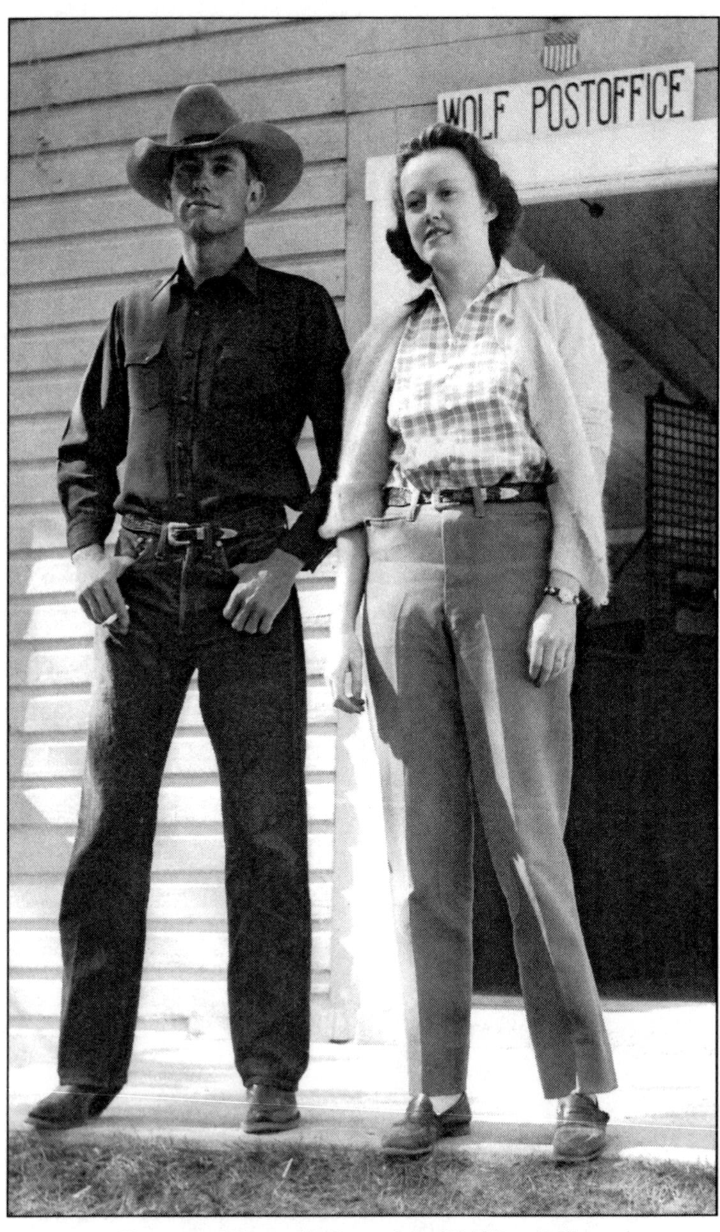

Tommy and Nancy in front of the Wolf Post Office.
Tommy was the Postmaster, among other things,
and Nancy took care of guest reservations.
Courtesy of Eatons' Ranch.

...Miss Nancy Adair Brown, the bride's only attendant, was charming in a velvet and chiffon gown of autumn gold made Basque style with a full skirt...

...Mr. Holliwell Duell was best man for Mr. Ferguson... (Note: Holliwell Duell was a good friend of Billy Eaton and Tommy Ferguson. A cowboy, he worked at Eatons' Ranch and owned ranches himself, but eventually became an Episcopal minister and would marry other members of the Eaton and Ferguson families.)

...Assisting at the reception were Mrs. William Eaton, Jr., and Miss Dorothy Clapp of Fargo, N. D...

Tommy was in the Army when he and Nancy were married and stationed at Florence, Arizona. In order to be near him, Nancy moved to Arizona and found work at Davis Monthan Air Force Base.

WN carried further news about the couple in the April 1943 edition, which reported that:

Nancy Eaton Ferguson is still in Tucson, doing good work on the graveyard shift at Davis-Monthan Airport, and settled down in a little apartment next door to her friend Nancy Brown Hayes, where Tommy stops in on weekend leaves from Camp Coolidge, Arizona. Nancy writes that she is learning to cook, and we'll add that if she turns out to be half as good as her mother in that respect she will be a whiz.

In 1943, Tommy was discharged from the Army and he and Nancy returned to the home ranch in Kirby, Montana, where Tommy went into the cattle business with his brother Dwight. Not long after, in 1944, Tommy and Nancy had their first child, a daughter named Susan Eaton Ferguson. Angela Buell wrote of the occasion:

...Sue happens to live in Montana, some eighty miles from Eatons' Ranch, where she sleeps away the days in the two-room cabin of her ranch home. The bright lights don't bother her for there's no electricity, and the telephone doesn't waken her

for the nearest line is some twenty miles away. When her parents, Tom and Nancy, want to go to a schoolhouse dance as a relaxation from the work of the ranch, they just bundle her up, take her along, and park her with the other babies in the cloakroom while they have a good time. It is all most agreeable to Miss Sue—and we can foresee it will not be many years until she will be bowing to her partner and doing the allemande left, too—and mounting her own horse, and riding after cattle as her parents and grandparents and great-grandparents on both sides of her family tree have done before her.

In 1945, Tommy and Nancy had a second daughter, Judith Alden Ferguson. Sadly, she died when she was only five months old.

Tommy and Nancy ranched on the family place for about three years until it became apparent that the place was not big enough to support two families. They looked for a place of their own, and found it adjacent to the Ferguson ranch. It was the ranch previously owned by Ben and Claire Sittler, who used to work for the Eatons at Echeta. Tommy and Nancy made an offer and it was accepted, but the very day that the closing was scheduled, the deal fell through for unknown reasons. (*Note: Years later, the Kirby branch of the Ferguson family was able to purchase the place that Tommy and Nancy had tried to buy.*)

When Bill Eaton heard the news, he made a beeline for Tommy and implored him, over the course of two hours, to move to Eatons' and become part of the operation. Tommy later told his son, Billy Ferguson, that that was the only time he heard Bill Eaton talk so fast and so long.

Initially, Tommy resisted the idea. He feared that if he went to work for Eatons' Ranch, people would think he married Nancy for the Ranch. He took great pains to tell Bill, "I married your daughter and not the ranch."

In the end, Bill convinced Tommy that he should give Eatons' a try and Tommy agreed to work for Eatons' on a trial basis on November 1, 1946. It is not entirely clear why Bill was so anxious for Tommy to work for Eatons'. Possibly Bill wanted to have Nancy on the Ranch, and Tommy went along with the deal. Or possibly, Bill was looking for someone to step into a management role and he was not confident that Billy Eaton was up to the task. In any event, Tommy did step up to the plate and became a central figure in the management of Eatons'. Tommy's "trial" at Eatons' lasted for thirty-seven years.

The 1946 Christmas edition of *WN* reported the arrival of the Ferguson family at Eatons' Ranch:

> *Nancy and Tommy Ferguson and small Susan have moved to the Ranch from their former home in Montana. Tommy is in the office learning about figures and typewriters, post offices, phone calls, etc. etc. etc., and helping dispatch this issue of* Wranglin' Notes. *Nancy keeps busy with cooking and housework in their home, the Fleming house, just below the main buildings. The house had been unoccupied for many years and it took a couple of months to get it in order for them. We'd stolen the plumbing fixtures, everything needed paint, the furnace had to be rebuilt, the water and power lines checked, etc., but the Fergusons are settled there comfortably, now. It's not only pleasant to come up the road on a winter night and see lights and warmth in that long-deserted dwelling, but fine to have Nancy Eaton with her husband and family home again!*

Tommy was a quick study and soon became a pillar in the Eaton Ranch operation. Three years later, after Billy Eaton died, the board of directors elected Tommy to take Billy's place as secretary for the Eaton Brothers Corporation.

In the meantime, Tommy and Nancy had their third child, a daughter, Patty Barton Ferguson, born on January 6, 1947. *WN* first mentioned Patty in February 1948 with this announcement: "The Ferguson household has been a temporary contagion ward with Nancy and Patty B. down with the chickenpox."

While the third and fourth generation of the Eaton family expanded through marriage and birth and took their places in the Eaton family and the Ranch operation, two members of the first generation—Bill's mother, Aunt Mame and Patty's mother, Domo—were still very much in evidence.

Aunt Mame traveled extensively and always made herself useful. In

1942, *WN* described her as someone who "…runs a mean sewing machine down in the Ranch house, making curtains and mending napkins and blankets…"

In spite of her traveling and activity around the Ranch, Aunt Mame began to show her age and occasionally took ill. Once, in 1943, Angela Buell described one of her "turns":

> *After many years of excellent health, Aunt Mame was reminded one day that she had a heart, which set her back for a short period. She is feeling fine once again, but is carrying a memorandum that perhaps she can't do all the things she used to do when younger. When she was staying in her room those few days, Bill thought she should have a call-bell, and you can guess what he provided…not the tinkling silver gadget used in many sick rooms, but a good old cowbell well coated with rust which came down from the storeroom where the packsaddle and camp equipment spend the winter. Trouble was, if Aunt Mame had used it during the night, we'd probably have thought drowsily that we were back in a tepee up at Big Bend or somewhere on the shores of Lake Geneva or Solitude, and would have cussed out the horses for wandering in so close to camp and turned right over for another snooze until the sun shone in the open door of the tepee and we could hear the cook rattling his frying pan and coffee pot.*

Aunt Mame was by now one of the real "old-timers" and the Sheridan Women's Club asked her to read a paper she wrote entitled *My Life*. The story, which is also a valuable reference for this book, was a huge hit with the audience.

The last mention of Aunt Mame in the *WN*'s of the 1940s was in February, 1948 when it was noted that:

> *…Aunt Mame has gotten an early start and is already superintending the making of needed slipcovers for some of the furniture…" Ever useful, Aunt Mame was eighty years old at the end of the decade and still going strong.*

Domo was the other grande dame of Eatons'. She was frequently mentioned in *WN* with entries like:

> *...Domo has just moved down to the cabin and is getting ready to bake chocolate cakes and make delicious lemonade for weary riders who drop by to see her...Domo Alderson will leave after the holidays for her annual visit in Atchison, Kansas...*

Domo celebrated her eightieth birthday in 1940, and Buddie Irish, an Eaton guest, threw her a party, which *WN* noted in November:

> *...Buddie Irish's party honoring Domo's eightieth birthday. The hand-hewn beams of the historic Sheridan Inn looked down on a scene that must have reminded them of frontier days when the Inn was new and Buffalo Bill its famous host...*

In March 1941, *WN* announced that Domo was collaborating on a book about her life:

> *...Domo started on her annual visiting trip to Atchison, Kansas, where Cousin Effie Symms and her many friends will welcome her in true Western style. A little later than usual, her trip was delayed this year so she and her "ghostwriter" could collaborate on the story of her (Domo's) life. It was Helena Pringle's suggestion, and she came all the way from New York to spend part of January and February at the Ranch and take notes, while Domo looked back sixty years and talked of the days when, as a young bride, she came west from Virginia to live in a sod-roofed cabin in a country, where white women were few and far between, and hostile Indians roamed everywhere. The book,* A Bride Goes West, *by Helena Huntington Smith, will probably be published in the fall, and we'll try to tell more about it later on, as Domo's story takes shape under the capable pen of Helena (Huntington Smith) Pringle when final plans for its publication have been made.*

Nannie Alderson (Domo) on her 80th birthday party at the Sheridan Inn in 1940.
Courtesy of Eatons' Ranch

Angela Buell and John Fleming
at Nannie Alderson's 80th birthday party at the Sheridan Inn.
Courtesy of Eatons' Ranch

Nanny Alderson and three of her children
at her 80th birthday party at the Sheridan Inn in 1940.
From left are Patty Eaton, Fay Alderson and Bud Alderson.
Courtesy of Eatons' Ranch

In April 1942, *WN* announced that Farrar & Rinehart in New York would publish the book on June 4. Then Stanley Rinehart Jr., the son of Dr. Stanley and Mary Roberts Rinehart, wrote a letter to the "Ranch Family" and the letter was included with the June 1942 edition of *WN*:

June, 1942
Dear Ranch Family:

When Domo gave me my first glass of lemonade back in '16, I hadn't the slightest idea that some day I would become her publisher. But that's just happened, for we published her book, A Bride Goes West, on the Fourth of June. I have always thought that her life would make a fascinating book, for she used to tell us parts of it when we rode down to her cabin. However, it took Helena Huntington Smith finally to get it all from her. Now that it is down in black and white, I am more than ever amazed that a young and gently raised girl from Virginia could face the hardships of the West with such courage and gaiety.

Domo was a little shy about my telling you of the book, but I'm not, for I feel sure you will want to read it. It is available through the source you generally use for your book purchases, or from the Ranch store, or from the publishers. We sent a few copies out for Domo to autograph, and if you want one of those, you might write directly to the Ranch.

And here's to Domo herself

Yours sincerely,
Stanley M. Rinehart, Jr.

Domo's seemingly inexhaustible energy was a subject of interest at Christmas, 1942:

Although she has passed her eighty-second birthday, Domo hasn't slowed down a bit and she was just as busy as ever last summer cooking good things to serve riders who stopped in at her little log cabin down the road. Then, often as not, she wound up the day writing by the light of the kerosene lamp in some of the hundreds of copies of A Bride Goes West *that she has autographed for the many friends who wanted that interesting story of her life in the early days. Now that winter has come she has moved from the cabin into the Ranch house, but she expects to leave, after the holidays, for her annual visit to "Cousin Effie" in Kansas. Cousin Effie may not know Domo when she steps off the train in Atchison for she's gotten a little portly this winter. When she moved up from the cabin in October, she weighed all of seventy-seven pounds…and now she weighs eighty!*

Domo lived until September 1947, and Angela Buell wistfully noted her passing:

> *We find that time goes fast, too. Only we note, often with sadness, the changes as they come along. We miss the older generation as they slip away one by one, and this winter we think often of Domo, Patty Eaton's mother, who left us in September. We can't calculate the number of people who enjoyed Domo's hospitality at her little cabin on the Ranch, or how many strangers have known her through her book,* A Bride Goes West. *In the eighty-seven years of her lifetime, Nanny Tiffany Alderson must have inspired a great many people by her example of hard work, her kindly interest in others, and her quiet fortitude in time of trouble. We know that her countless friends will agree with us that Domo will be remembered far into the future with deep admiration and great respect.*

Indeed, she is still remembered. Her book is considered a Western literature classic and remains in print sixty-nine years after it was first published. And the cabin, which was old when she moved into it, and in which she lived for twenty-seven years at Eatons' Ranch, still stands.

Willis E. Pelissier, Hattie's son and Elsie and Mary's brother, died on February 19, 1942. When he died, he was still working at the Sheridan Commercial Company and living with his wife and sons at 231 W. Loucks.

Willis' wife and two sons continued to live in Sheridan and the sons both graduated from Sheridan High School. The oldest son, George, moved to Casper, Wyoming, and for many years worked for the American Red Cross and KTWO-Radio. He married Dorothy Hemmett in 1963. He eventually retired to Mesa, Arizona. He died at age seventy-six on March 12, 1991 at Westview Health Care Center in Sheridan after a long illness. One daughter survived him.

The youngest son, Willis, served in the United States Air Force during World War II. When he returned from the war be began work in the livestock industry and was engaged in it for the rest of his life. He was a brand inspector in Sheridan, Campbell and Goshen counties and worked for the American Breeders Service. He was also affiliated with ranches in Wyoming, Canada, and Arizona including the Padlock, NX Bar and Bar 13 ranches in the Sheridan area. Willis was also a member of the Sheridan WYO Rodeo board of directors.

Willis married Patricia Kelly with whom he had two children: a son, Willis E. Pelissier (who still lives in Sheridan) and a daughter Kelly C. Pelissier. Patricia died in 1973 and Willis married Barbara Harris in 1975. Willis died on October 24, 1989 in Sheridan.

Elsie Pelissier continued to serve as Deputy Clerk of Court in Denver, Colorado through the 1940s. Her son, Jack, continued his career with the FBI. After his initial assignment in New York, Jack served in Philadelphia, Detroit, Phoenix and Denver.

Jack and his wife Helen had two more children. Suzanne was born in 1940 and Jim in 1947. In 1948, Jack and Helen divorced and Jack maintained custody of the children. At the time, Jack was assigned to Denver and he cared for the children and performed his duties with the FBI.

Jack's oldest son, Jack, was twelve years old in 1949 when Billy Eaton died. Nan Eaton and Jack decided it would be helpful if young Jack went to Eatons' Ranch to be a companion for Frank Eaton after the death of his father. Jack spent the month of August at Eatons' and was hooked on the place. He thought it was the most splendid place he had ever been. It was the beginning of a long association with Eatons' Ranch.

Little else is known about Hattie's third child, Mary. After her husband Roy Haywood died, Mary married Al Covington in 1946. When he died three years later, Mary is believed to have relocated to Colorado and her further association with Sheridan and Eatons' Ranch are dim, although she did occasionally visit. In 1967, Mary wrote an unpublished manuscript about her life in Medora in the early years. It is a valuable research resource on the Eaton and Pelissier families. Mary's brief obituary indicates that she had three children, two daughters and one son, and died on June 11, 1976 in Greeley, Colorado.

Dudes

In the Forties, *WN* (aka Angela Buell) kept up the constant drumbeat of "dude news." After all, Eatons' published *WN* primarily for the dudes and they were eager to read of themselves and their friends—and, of course, all things "Eaton."

1940

...Mr. and Mrs. Botsford Young of Chicago (many of the Eaton Outfit remember Bots when he first visited the Ranch with his parents in 1909) will be here soon with their two small boys...

...Fred and Betty Lou Leisch will be here before this issue (June) of Wranglin' *Notes is with the printers. Fred Leisch seems to run into the Eatons whenever they stir off the home range. Billy and Nan boarded the Streamliner at Cheyenne bound for a visit with the Bakers in Philadelphia—and there was Fred. Bill Eaton stepped into the dining room of a Cincinnati hotel for breakfast—and there was Fred. We think we have him corralled for June, however, so if you come to Eatons' Ranch at that time—HERE will be Fred...*

...Mrs. Edward Manigault, Mary and Peter, will be here again. Bud Clapp has a vacation from West Point, and is spending it at the Ranch with his mother, and "Dippy," perhaps more of their family group...

In the November *WN*, Angela looked back on the 1940 season and categorized the dudes:

We look back on a spring, summer and autumn season that brought a group of dudes from coast to coast, many of them old, some of them new to the West, to whom we give much credit for the feeling of full satisfaction that comes to us now. There have always been a satisfying number of old-timers on our lists, but this year there were more than usual. (Some of them said Wranglin' Notes *brought them back.) Our statistical department also noted a rise in automobile travel to the Ranch, which probably was to be expected in a year when regular European visitors started out in the family automobile to see America for a change. New York State and Pennsylvania kept their places as first and second in numbers at the Ranch, but Illinois stole Michigan's place as third. Then came Ohio, California and Michigan.*

Then, as usual, Angela tried to inject a little humor in the article and slip in some more information she thought might interest the readers:

...That's about all the Statistics Expert at Wolf has to offer in the way of news—unless we include the item of 125,000 Douglas Fir trees planted this year by the U. S. Forest Service on the slope above Red Canyon that burned off in 1919, and as against 30,000 planted last year on the old 1909 burn, and the 68,000 fingerling trout put into Wolf Creek in 1940, and against 12,000 in 1939. We don't have a count on the wild plums and chokecherries this year, but estimate several million more than normal...

And then there was more commentary on the dude scene:

Most of the old-timers and many more not mentioned in June Wranglin' Notes *came ranching again. Mr. and Mrs. Henry B. Spelman renewed their acquaintance with the Eaton Outfit for the first time since 1916, and they brought their children—Carolyn, Dorothy, Noyes, Mary and James. Jim Wellman made his first visit since 1909, and one of the things that seemed especially to strike him was the number of trees and patches of green grass that cover the bare ground and rocks that marked the Ranch site as he remembered it in the earlier days... Garneau Weld (with his wife and three children) saw the Ranch for the first time since 1911. Mrs. Philip Wyman (Francis Perin, 1913) brought her son Rufus Smith, and Mrs. E. B. Buck (Constance Tyler, 1916) was here with Nancy. Mrs. Van Sant Alvord (Virginia Van Sant, 1920) came with her son, John. Mr. and Mrs. George Dudley (Betty Fry, 1929) stopped in for the night, went on to Glacier and came back for a couple of weeks...*

1941
October

Pete Dailey was out in September, taking pictures and offering a few friendly suggestions along the line of his special work (he's assistant advertising manager for the Santa Fe), and he thought it would be well if we'd "box in" an item of special importance now and then in Wranglin' Notes. *So we'll give it a trial, and here's the item:*

On August 22nd in mid-morning, a large plane circled over the Ranch, and at that moment we had a telephone call from the radio operator at the Sheridan Airport, relaying a message from the plane as follows:

"This in General Marshall speaking. Please telephone my friends the Eatons and give them my greetings. tell them that at this moment I am looking down on the ranch and wishing that I could see them all. However, it is impossible for me to stop at this time as I am heading for Cut Bank, Montana, but I do wish to send my greetings to all at the Ranch."

...Ed Shaul saw Dippy Clapp in Tucson where she was about to enter the university (sort of a quick decision on her part we understand).

Dippy's appearance in Tucson heralded the beginning of a "dude ranch romance." A dude ranch romance occurs when a dude ranch employee, usually a cowboy, and a female dude fall in love and marry.

This opposed to just "regular" summer romances result in nothing more than broken hearts and jangled emotions. A cowboy could have two or three of those in a summer. Eatons' Ranch has seen plenty of the romances that end in marriage, and there are probably enough to fill a book or two. But the romance of Dippy Clapp from Fargo, North Dakota, and Don King, from everywhere, is one for the ages and deserves special mention here.

Dippy Clapp, who, with other members of her family, had been a guest at Eatons' since 1933, completed her course work at a two-year junior college for girls in New York State. After her spring graduation in 1941, Dippy headed for Eatons' and a summer vacation. It was a fateful summer for her—she met Donald Lee King.

Don King was the son of Arch King. Arch and Don's mother divorced when Don was only five years old and Arch received custody of Don. Don accompanied his father from ranch job to ranch job all over the western United States and Don had to grow up fast. Timothy Evans, in his book, *King of the Western Saddle* described part of Don's early life:

> *Don's life with his father consisted of brief stays on ranches and constant moves. "A lot of people think, well, how could you be that many places, but you've got to realize that in two months here, two months there, you can cover a lot of country." Don attended schools mostly in Arizona and California, often making lengthy trips on horseback to very small schools. He lived with his father in bunkhouses and line camps...He worked as much as he could during the school year and full-time during the summer...At the age of seven, Don had his own string of five horses at a line camp on a large ranch near Tucson...By the age of twelve, he was shoeing and breaking horses, as well as riding steeplechasers and polo ponies...*
>
> *Don dropped out of school halfway through ninth grade, at age fourteen. By that time, he had attended fourteen schools. For approximately the next four years, he travelled the West doing seasonal work with his father or on his own. "I'd worked*

before but I'd just kind of followed him. But when I was fourteen, I took off. Sometimes we would still travel together, work for the same outfit. But I bought my own clothes. I paid my share of the gas."

At the age of fifteen, when he was working for a riding stable in Phoenix, Don began to go in to the famous Porter's Saddlery on a regular basis.

Porter's gave Don the opportunity to learn leatherwork. Don learned and honed his natural skill as a leather craftsman and eventually become one of the best in the world. Evans continued the story after Don got his start in leather carving.

By the time he was in his late teens, Don had established a pattern of managing the corrals at the Tanque Verde Dude Ranch in Tucson during the winter, working at Rudy Mudra's Saddlery in Sheridan in the spring, "wrangling dudes" at Eatons' Dude Ranch near Sheridan during the summer, heading to Porter's Saddlery in the fall, and then returning to Tanque Verde.

And so it was that Don and Dippy met at Eatons' in the summer of 1941, and they were interested in each other. Don planned to return to Tucson in the fall and work at Porter's once again. *WN* commented on that: "…Don King is on his way to Arizona where he'll settle down to finish about six weeks work on leather orders received from his friends here."

Dippy had to make a decision. Since she had finished her two-year college in New York, she had two choices: go home, or go to school somewhere else. Since Don was going to Tucson, Dippy decided to follow him and enroll at the University of Arizona. When she called her family in Fargo, North Dakota, and told them she was either going to come home or go to the school in Arizona, they told her, "Well, you're not coming home!" So, Arizona it was.

Dippy matriculated at the University of Arizona and attended school for two years. She graduated in 1943.

In the meantime, Don had enlisted in the United States Coast Guard. He made this choice because the Coast Guard trained horses at Fort Robinson, Nebraska. Since Don was a talented horseman, he thought Fort Robinson would be an ideal assignment. Don got his wish and received an assignment to Fort Robinson, but not to the equestrian division. Instead, he was assigned to the dog patrol.

When Dippy graduated, she decided to stay in Tucson and got a job at the Marana Army Air Base, near Tucson. It was a fun time for her because her old friend Nancy Eaton Ferguson was also in Tucson and Tommy Ferguson was stationed nearby. On weekends, Dippy recalled, "We tore the place up."

By 1944, Don was stationed in Florida. He sent Dippy a cable (she remembers that it was collect and cost more than eleven dollars) telling her that he was coming on leave and asked her to meet him at the train station at six o'clock in the morning. Dippy showed up to meet a very filthy Don. He wore his white uniform and the train trip across the southwest with the windows open had coated him with dirt.

Don and Dippy went to the boarding house where he used to live so Don could clean up, and then they went to where Dippy lived. When they arrived, Dippy's roommate was just getting out of the shower, and shouted out, "When are you two going to get married?" Don shouted back, "It'd better be pretty soon because I've only got thirty days leave." Don and Dippy got married that very afternoon on February 10, 1944. And they remained married for sixty-three years.

Dippy then sent her parents (her father had never even met Don) a cable and told them what she had done. She received a loving return cable with all the family's blessings.

Don returned to Florida when his leave was up and Dippy accompanied her mother on a trip to New York before she joined Don in Florida. When Don was discharged in 1946, he told Dippy he had job offers in Los Angeles and Phoenix. "Where do you want to go," he asked. Dippy replied that she wanted to go to Sheridan, because she knew he could get work there as well and that's where she thought they should live.

The rest is history. Don and Dippy moved to Sheridan where Don served an eleven-month apprenticeship as a saddlemaker with Rudy Mudra and then eventually founded his own saddle shop that is known today as Kings Saddlery. In his lifetime, (Don died in 2007) Don received worldwide acclaim for his artistry in leather. Don and Dippy had four sons, all of whom became talented leather craftsman and some of them — at one time or another—worked at Eatons' Ranch.

The December *WN* featured a section called "A Representative Ranch Family" which carried a photo of the Nimick family and the accompanying caption:

Mr. and Mrs. T. Howe Nimick of Pittsburgh are both second generation Eatonites: and their daughter "Kassie," with her brothers, Tom and George, have long been eligible for the mythical "Eaton Third-Generation Club."

Mr. Frank Nimick with his boys (of whom one was Howe) first visited the Ranch in 1911. Mr. and Mrs. John A. Murtland and their three children (one of whom is now Mrs. Nimick) came to the Ranch a few years later, and since those early days first, second and third-generation Eatons have highly valued the friendship of the Nimick-Murtland families. Burr Murtland has been a frequent Ranch visitor through the years, and for the past nine seasons, the Howe Nimicks have spent two months, and sometimes more, of every summer at the Ranch. …

1942

The Christmas edition of *WN* contained more news:

Again, we have Pete Dailey to thank for the good pictures in this issue, and for others we're holding back for later release. Pete came out again in September, bringing along not only his faithful camera, which he uses so well, but his nice daughter Mary, too. And here we're reminded of the day he came wandering into the office carrying a pair of boots that obviously hadn't just come from the cleaners. He sniffed loudly two or three times, and then said, "I wonder—do you realize that this office definitely has a smell of horse?" Well, we weren't insulted. After all, we do ride horseback now and then, and we write about horses, and besides with Ranch folks there's no stigma attached to a little good horse odor—so we were very polite and only murmured, "Really, that's interesting," without even glancing at that pair of boots. We know some boys who would give a lot right now for one good whiff of the Eaton corral, and if we could arrange for this issue of Wranglin' Notes *to carry "a smell of horse" plus a little pine and sagebrush fragrance, then Pete would be convinced he was right and we'd be more than happy, too.*

1943
April

We mentioned Harry McCormick. He has spent the winter at the Sheridan Inn, getting out to the Ranch a few times for some horseback riding. The Wilson Lowes still have their house in Sheridan, the Stevens Woodruff family has also enjoyed the winter in town. Young Steve joined the Marines recently and has arrived in San Diego for some training. Big Steve left a short time ago for a little vacation with the Schlegels at the Eatons' old Rimrock Ranch in Arizona...

1943
June

Already this season, some friends have come and gone. Helen and Pat Oiker caught the best weather we had to offer in May (which wasn't very good at that), rode every day, picnicked on Soldier Creek and returned with Wyoming tans to their home in Chicago. Ruby English was here in late April. Aline Halstead (her mother and father met at the Ranch many years ago) bravely dove into the chilly swimming pool in May and will be on her way back to summer session of school by the time this issue of Wranglin' Notes *is mailed.*

Mr. and Mrs. Howard Butcher, Jr., of Philadelphia have returned after many years absence...

...Andrew and Elizabeth Hull, of Newport News, are here, Andrew catching up on some rest after many months of intensive work building battleships and other ocean craft for Uncle Sam...

1943
December

There were people at the Ranch this summer who'd had a shot of it back in the "teens" and were here to get a fresh dose. There were others rather gingerly taking a first inoculation. Mr. Torrence Miller made his first visit since 1907. Dr. Lloyd De Puy remembered the Ranch and his friends the Eatons from his trip way back in 1909. Some friends had not been here since the twenties—Mr. and Mrs. Howard Butcher Jr., Philadelphia, Mrs. Oscar L. Buhr (at that time Frances Depew), Detroit. And John Curtis' interest went back to 1919 when he rode at the Ranch a few weeks before going on to Glacier Park with Uncle Howard Eaton, and when he signed Erie, Pennsylvania, to the Ranch register instead of Chicago. Which proves that the potency of a dose of Ranch medicine does often last for years...

1944
December

We haven't mentioned by name the scores of good friends who were with us the past season because space is so short in this issue, but we are enclosing a special list. (Note: The list contained names of 282 people.) *The asterisk means they're old-timers, and some of them have spent so much time at the Ranch they've become residents of Wolf, Wyoming. For many weeks last summer every cabin on the Ranch was occupied, and here's an interesting point—of the group listed here fifty-two friends stayed two months or longer, a number of them three and four months, and a few even longer than that.*

1945
December

...Boots Labrot, another Eatonite turned cattleman. A few months ago, he purchased the Nicholas ranch on Little Tongue below Buck Blackburn, and his new manager is Lee Moore, a member of the Wolves Club at Eatons' Ranch...

1946

Nineteen forty six was a banner year for the dude business and the December issue contained a separate and exhaustive list of Eaton guests and some discussion about some of them:

...Young Louis Ruckgaber has visited the Ranch only twice, but Howe Nimick came first with his father and brothers way back in 1911. Russell Kettell has missed few seasons since his first visit in 1919. And some, if not every, member of the Leisch family has been here each season since 1935. Practically every state in the Union, and even a few spots outside the country, contributed citizens to the guest list at the Ranch this summer. The Goslings came from Bermuda. Aymar, Richard and Pierre Lechaux came all the way from Le Havre, France. Perhaps the Corkrans from Manchester, Vermont, and the McKenna family from Hanover, New Hampshire, came the longest distance within the country...

1947

We were delighted to greet old-timers, and as usual, they represented just under half the total number of guests. Also as usual, we became reacquainted with friends who hadn't been here in years. Mr. Larz F. Anderson of Easton, Maryland, returned after an absence of thirty-one years. Mrs. Eleanor

Sterret Smith, Towanda, Pennsylvania, hadn't been at the Ranch since 1914. Mrs. Elsie Elkins Russell of Honolulu remembered us from her last visit in 1916. Others returned for their first visit since the twenties: Mr. and Mrs. T. A. Mellon, Pittsburgh, Mrs. Patsy Mellon Schmidt, Pittsburgh, with her husband and children, Charlie and Betty Silverson and their three children, Minneapolis. An even greater number of friends came who hadn't been here since the thirties: Lyman and Isabelle Ayres and their small son from Indianapolis, Mr. Nathaniel Hill of Carlisle, Massachusetts, Peg Young Buckley and her husband of Worcester, Massachusetts. Also Marjorie Lowe of Forest Hills, Bob and Jeanne Hoover from Kansas City, Anne Ayres Taylor and her husband from Indianapolis, Mr. and Mrs. J. J. Walton, Pawtucket, Jimmy McNutt of Indianapolis, the Cecil Fergusons and their two sons from Greene, Rhode Island...

1948

The Christmas *WN* contained another enclosed, lengthy guest list, in small print, of all the people who visited Eatons'. As usual, Angela Buell reflected on those who returned repeatedly and those who returned after many years away from the Ranch. It was on oft-repeated theme, but the Eatonites were perennially interested:

Over the years a great many people have visited the Ranch, and a remarkable percentage of them return. Some come year after year without a break, others return after long absences. Mr. L. A. Osborne, Jr., Litchfield, Connecticut, and Mr. Melvin Spencer, New York, met here again in August and had fun reminiscing about the Ranch in 1912 when they were last here. Mrs. L. T. Vance, Oak Park, was here in 1921, Bill Desolge, St. Louis, in 1929. The "thirties" list is longer—Mrs. Frederic M. Ayres, Indianapolis, 1936, Mr. and Mrs. Wm. D. Gaillard, New York, 1930, Leonard Graham, Jr., Camden, S. C., 1936,

Mrs. Edmond Guerin, Woonsocket, R. I., 1937, Dr. and Mrs. Emil Hauser and Mrs. Mary Thomas, Winnetka, Ill., returned for their first visit since 1938…

1949

Often, Angela wrote about the experiences of particular dudes to illustrate the attractiveness of the Ranch. For instance, in May, Angela wrote that:

> *Dorothy Shipley has been here since early March and when she isn't riding she finds pleasure in raking and cutting and taking care of the fast-growing lawn around her cabin—and right now it's the best-groomed place on the Ranch. Eatons' perennial dudes, Andrew and Elizabeth Hull, complain because the time goes too fast for them. While Elizabeth is out riding, Andrew slips over to the creek and brings in a mess of trout for lunch. Anyone who has tasted trout fresh-cooked out of Wolf Creek lives for the time when he can repeat that experience—or better yet, catch a few himself. Shirley Sammon, John, Ginger and Miss Love, with Shirley's friend Phyllis Rhinelander, have been amazed by the brand of spring weather we turn out in Wyoming (it's been better than usual), and Ernest Thum has paid us a great compliment by bringing his bride to enjoy his old stomping ground at Wolf in early spring. John Leahy, who makes a point of being on hand early in the season to help with the horse and cattle work—rounding up, vaccinating, de-horning, branding—has been here for weeks. Harry McCormick, who reminded us the other day that he had passed his eightieth birthday and has missed few seasons at the Ranch since 1909, takes a horseback ride every morning that many new dudes a third his age couldn't begin to negotiate without eating off the mantel for the next two weeks…*

Angela then paid particular attention to Pete Dailey:

...When we came to Arthur (Pete) Dailey we went all to pieces and put down a question mark. Pete first came here as a college boy in 1912, and for the next ten or twelve years he helped here and there around the Ranch. (Bill Eaton says we might just as well drop a question mark after that word "helped," too.)

Anyway, for a good many years past, Pete and his daughter Mary have spent their vacations at the Ranch, and Pete has tried to even up the score with Bill by taking most of the pictures that have appeared in Wranglin' Notes *and Ranch folders. He usually arrives with a camera that doesn't work to his satisfaction, has some unkind remark about the weather, or complains that the clouds in the sky aren't distributed properly to add the right artistic touch, but we think his pictures are extra fine....*

Most of Pete's pictures are un-posed. Everyone who has been on the Ranch has seen the horses driven out to pasture in the late afternoon a dozen, fifty, hundreds of times. Pete just happened to be hanging around with his camera when Jack Kelly (on the frontispiece) headed a little bunch of horses out of the corral, down the slope on the far side of Howard Hall to the ford below the Ranch house and out to pasture for the night..

Angela included in *WN* a photo that Pete Daily took of all the Eaton grandchildren and used it to talk about the coming generation of Eaton children:

Pete had a great time rounding up the children in the picture on the last page—the 4 children whose lives are bound up in the Ranch just as much as were those of their forebears, the first generation of Eatons. If you've ever tried to make a snapshot of four children on four horses, and have all of them looking their best, you know it isn't easy. Frank's shirttail was out of course and his beloved crew cut wasn't particularly photogenic. Most of the time, Susan was forgetful of herself, and had an eye on her little sister, to make sure she was posing properly. Jaci was not especially enthusiastic about the deal and her eyes were closed against the sun and wind in most of the pictures, while the youngest of the foursome, Patty B., hadn't any idea what the delay at the corral was about—she was on her horse and impatient to go ahead and take a ride. But there they are, the children of Nan and the late Bill Eaton Jr.—Frank aged nine and Jaci four, and the children of Tom and Nancy Eaton Ferguson—Susan aged five and Patty B. aged two. They are as pleasant and pretty and happy and healthy a group of youngsters as anyone could wish. The four of them are Aunt Mame's great-grandchildren, Bill and Patty's grandchildren, and they're growing up so fast we can no more than keep pace with them. Every day Frank goes down to the little country school on Wolf Creek where he learns and plays with the other ranch children of the community. Next year Susan will be there with him, and the following autumn Jaci will be of school age...

It is fitting to note here, that the thousands of pictures that Pete Daily took at Eatons' Ranch over several decades provide a remarkable pictorial chronicle of life at the Ranch. Today, his daughter Mary lives in Sheridan, Wyoming, and is the capable steward of her father's remarkable photographic legacy.

Employees

When John Fleming died in 1943, Tommy Butler and Angela Buell insured that Eatons' management didn't skip a beat because of John's absence. John would have been proud of them, but not surprised, as he had mentored them in preparation for the day when he would be gone. Before he died, John acknowledged their value and dedication to the Eaton family and the Ranch, by proposing a retirement scheme for both of them.

The "Retirement Agreement" for each of them was approved by the Eaton Brothers Corporation on March 3, 1942 for their continuous periods of service—thirty years for Tommy and twenty years for Angela—because they had been "...in positions of considerable responsibility, and in the course of those years, the association has been enduringly pleasant.." The agreement provided for a cash payment based on an average of their wages for the five years prior to their retirement. Angela collected hers fifteen years later when she retired in 1957, and Tommy collected his when he retired twenty-three years later in 1965.

At the beginning of the decade, Tommy Butler and Angela Buell were officers of the Eaton Brothers Corporation—Tommy was secretary and Angela was treasurer. When Billy Eaton died in 1949, Tommy Butler was elected to fill Billy's place as vice president. He served in this office until he retired in 1965 but continued to serve as a director for some years afterward. Likewise, Angela served as treasurer until 1957 when she retired from work at Eatons' Ranch, but she, too, continued to serve as a director in retirement.

There were many other valued employees at Eatons', of course, and *WN* continued to describe their activities over the years:

1940
April

...It's a Sunday afternoon and the corral boys are putting on a home rodeo. No grandstand seats, just the soft grass for spectators. It's fun because the audience knows and has a personal interest in every rider who comes out of the chute. And perched on the bucking chute watching Tepee (Edwards) mount his bronc are a lot of the youngsters—George Nimick, Dippy Clap, Muffet Brown, Mac Talley, Charlie Brown. Bill Arthur has a solid seat on top the biggest post but it looks like Patsy Rinehart is about to lose her balance on the rail. Donn Davies and Everett Cheetham are ready to open the gate, and George Arrowsmith had better move for he'll be right in the way of the bronc when he comes out of the chute, twisting and bucking and trying to get Tepee off his back.

1940
November

The cowboys have scattered. George is on his way to Rancho de la Osa in Arizona where he starts his fourth winter as corral boss. Tepee will be there again this winter to help him. Buck is with Chuck and Honora Schlegel at the Rimrock Ranch in Arizona. Nels is getting established as a rancher on the old Harris place down Wolf Creek and all good luck to him...Stormy, Weldon and Rusty all have winter jobs on Wyoming and Montana ranches. Emil and Hank are leaving soon for California, Hank to visit his mother, Emil to get the frost of several Wyoming winters out of his bones. Woody is en route to Arizona...

Kelly is married and about to start out in the ranch business...

And here we must digress, and talk about another dude ranch romance. Kelly Howie, if the reader will remember, was the young man from White Owl, South Dakota who worked at Eatons' the summer of 1939 and spent the winter in Arizona and Hollywood. In the spring of 1940, Kelly returned to work at Eatons' and met the love of his life. Her name was Elizabeth Merriman.

Kelly wrote about their first meeting:

> *On July 5, 1940, we had to saddle all of the dude horses and send the dudes riding. Reid Kochel, the head fitter, introduced me to Elizabeth Merriman and her two children, Sally and John. As soon as their saddles were fitted, George Gentry, the corral boss, had me take them for a ride. We went down to Domo's and back.*
>
> *It was quite a ride for the two kids. Elizabeth wanted to leave the children and go out for a gallop. My impression is she wanted to feel the breeze in her face. I was designated to ride with her that evening and twice a day for several days until she got to know someone or group to ride with.*
>
> *Elizabeth came to Eatons' very disturbed and upset, as her eleven year marriage had not worked out. Most of the time when a new person or new group came to Eatons', a wrangler would take them on their first ride, and then the next time they went riding, a different wrangler may be assigned to that person or group. Not so, in Elizabeth's case. I was the only wrangler to take her riding. As it turned out, she got to know me better than anyone else at Eatons' Ranch.*
>
> *She needed someone to talk to and that turned out to be me. Over time, she really came to trust me. She ended up telling me her problems, which were her husband. She said she'd never go back to him. I listened with an open mind, and didn't have any real advice for her, because I had no experience in that line.*

Things developed slowly, and, as Kelly wrote:

Toward the end of July, I was asked to join Bill Arthur's group on a pack trip. Members of the trip were Bill Arthur, his bride to be, and her sixteen year old daughter, young Bill and Jim Arthur, Tommy and George Nimick, Dorothy Douglas, Al Green as packer and guide, Kelly Howie packer, and the cook Red Bentley. While on this trip, the sixteen year old daughter said several times, "Kelly, what is the matter with you? You were so much fun last year." I realized I was in love with Elizabeth.

On our last day out, we were coming down the east fork of the Big Goose Creek and ran across Roe Storm. He was out with a family for overnight. I asked him what was going on at the ranch. He answered that everyone had gone to Tepee Lodge for the softball game between Tepee and Eatons'. Just one more worry for me—whether Elizabeth had stayed at Eatons while I was away for ten days, or if she may have left, or if she may have gone to the ballgame.

When we pulled into Eatons' Ranch with the pack string, Fleta and Marion Wright said to Elizabeth, "Let's go see the pack string come in." Of course, Fleta and Marion stepped forward to give me a kiss. Elizabeth was in back of them, and I said, "This is the lady I want to kiss," (of course meaning Elizabeth).

As soon as all of the horses were unpacked and everything put away, I had a shower, shave, changed clothes, and went down to see Elizabeth. We spent the rest of the day talking.

One incident happened ahead of the Bill Arthur pack trip. Elizabeth had come in from the evening ride, and she waited for me to finish at the barn. I walked her down in front of her cabin. I asked her if I could have a good night kiss. The next afternoon we were riding together, and she asked me if the kiss was part of my job. I was rather hurt by her question, but she said she had to know. I imagine if it had been a part of my job, our romance would have ended right there.

Elizabeth had only made reservations at the dude ranch for three weeks, but since she was so unhappy in her marriage, she stayed on. She did send the children back to her husband.

Kelly and Elizabeth's romance blossomed, and Kelly related that when Elizabeth had been at the Ranch for about two months:

> *...Bill Eaton said to Elizabeth in private, "Elizabeth, you know you can get a divorce here in Wyoming in six weeks." That changed her perspective, because I think she may have planned to go through the divorce procedure in California, which took about a year at that time.*

Then Kelly described what happened next:

> *...On a Sunday, I said to Big Bill that I would like the day off to drive Elizabeth up through the Wolf Mountains. His answer: "Does Elizabeth want to buy a ranch?" I finally said, "We haven't got that far along yet." After that, things developed much faster.*

They looked at several ranches and decided the most suitable one was the Hat Ranch south of Buffalo, Wyoming. It is interesting that when Kelly met Elizabeth he was just a cowboy working for wages. Elizabeth, on the other hand—and in the words of Patty Eaton in a recorded interview— "...was one of the richest people in the country." Elizabeth was an heir to the Sunkist Company, which at that time was one of the biggest lemon growers in the world.

Kelly and Elizabeth decided to get married after her divorce was finalized on October 1. Just after she was divorced, Elizabeth wrote a letter to her Aunt Sarah about the big step she was taking:

> *As you know, there has been so much for me to decide. My own feelings trying to see the years ahead for myself and especially the children's future and welfare, as well as considering Kelly's future as regards to the chance he will be taking with me in relation to the big change in my life.*
>
> *Since the first ten days I have been here, Kelly and I have been together constantly, as it was best we should. From a close friendship and understanding has grown mutual love and*

understanding that means the world to us both. My first admiration began with his handling of Sarah and John, and of me when I was in such an emotional and upset time. He was so good for me that you would hardly know me to be the same person. He expects me to keep my chin up, and I do. He wants to help me whenever it is in his power to do so. But when I can help myself, he expects that of me, and Aunt Sarah, that is something I need in my life, badly.

I can't tell you what a fine person he is. So full of gentleness and strength at the same time. He is the hardest most conscientious worker I have ever seen, so full of ambition for life and wanting to learn the things in life he hasn't had the opportunity or chance to learn. Everyone admires him. We both feel that Bill Eaton has thoroughly approved our friendship, as well as our love....Of all the men and women I have ever known, I admire him the most for his courageous outlook and innate kindness and gentleness. He's the sort who never says can't, will try to do anything and do it better than most other kind can do.

Kelly and Elizabeth were married on November 1, and were married and devoted to each other for as, Kelly wrote, "fifty-seven beautiful wonderful years together." During that time, they owned several ranches, raised Elizabeth's two children, Sally and John, and had one daughter, Mary, of their own. Kelly also became an aviator and polo player. Patty Eaton said that after Kelly had money he "was just as nice as he was when he was poor."

1941
June

Among the boys and girls and faithful helpers who return to the Ranch every summer season there will be few new faces this year, and to us that continues to be a remarkable thing. But they all seem to plan their yearly work and schedules so they can be at the Ranch in the summertime—and chances are two to one the same girl will wait on your table in the dining room, the same maid will sweep and dust in your cabin every morning, and the same boys will rope and saddle your horse at the corral. George has been busy planting flowers and vines around his cabin before the horse work claims all his time. Tepee and Buck are home, and Reid will be up from the Bar Eleven before this Wranglin' Notes *reaches you, Rusty came in early from a winter in Arizona, Emil is back from several months in California...*

1941
December

The old log cabins of The Pike, still the favorite summer home of many Ranch visitors and a landmark we would hate to have disappeared, have new and colorful roofs that will make them good for many years to come. Lew Crews, Emil, Dunc and Tommy have been working there for weeks, and Don is now hauling the red shale that completes the job. Tommy Butler arrived at the ranch thirty years ago, and he says the big logs are still as sound as they were on November 20, 1911, when he first saw them...

1942
April

George Gentry has been home for some time and so occupied we catch only a glimpse of him now and then. When he isn't behind the power lawnmower getting Gentry Estates on the terrace in beautiful shape, he's inspecting the morning glories that Patty planted for him early in the spring, or gentling the half dozen good-looking colts we notice tied in the barn every day. He's been breaking a couple of handsome Belgian colts to harness and after lunch when dudes are having their afternoon naps and everything's quiet, he takes a hazardous ride on the stone boat behind them...

1943
April

George Gentry has been in Tucson all winter working as a guard at the Consolidated Aircraft headquarters, and we'd feel mighty sorry for anybody who tried to sabotage anything that was under his surveillance. George had one bitter complaint—he wasn't permitted to wear his cowboy boots on duty. For an old cowboy who has known nothing else in the way of footgear for years and years that was a real tragedy. If you see him wearing shoes around the corral next summer you'll know he's learned to wear and like 'em. George will be headed home soon, right around the first of May. When Reid comes up from the Bar Eleven, he and George and Bill—those three musketeers of Eatons' Ranch who all saw army service twenty-five years ago—will be back again in their places as top-horsemen at the corral

1944
March

Practically all the home folks have been away at some time during the winter, if it was only a change to town, eighteen miles away. Bill and Patty were in Denver for the Stock Show and had a grand time with Wyoming, New Mexico and Arizona friends gathered there...Tommy Butler journeyed to California with Hank Leyendecker in December. Hank is visiting at the Rimrock right now but will be back on the job at Wolf in time for the summer's work, we are sure. Emil tried the hot springs over the mountains at Thermopolis in late winter after the ice work was finished, and now he's home again feeling as frisky as a two year old. George Gentry has been with Consolidated in Tucson since the first of the year, but we know without asking that now he's counting the days until he'll be home again in Wyoming bossing the corral and roping horses for dudes. Rusty has been feeding cattle for Buck Blackburn this winter and we haven't seen much of him for cattle happen to be just as hungry on Sundays as they are on weekdays. Cal finished his school term and is now in Texas temporarily. We catch a glimpse of Julia in town now and then. Reid and Agnes stick pretty close to the Bar Eleven...

1945
December

Some of the corral boys and Ranch family have scattered. Tom Cornish went back to Omaha early in the fall to join his father in the saddle shop. We don't see curly Kelly often but he's in the vicinity. Shorty and Hank left for the Rimrock Ranch in Arizona about the middle of November and no doubt Hank is now in California. Emil is in Texas looking after some property he has down there. Dorothy and Dunc are en route to Washington State for an indefinite visit with relatives. Lee Moore and his bride are setting up housekeeping on the new Labrot ranch. Julia is back in Sheridan after remaining at the Ranch longer than usual this season. Anna Butler is visiting out on the Coast, Mae left a few days ago for a well-earned rest, and Edna is also away for a month or thereabouts. Aunt Minnie has been in Ohio since last spring and we're wondering if she's EVER coming home!

1946
March

Bill and George, Al and Leroy, Jack and Buss, have carried on the routine winter work with the cattle and horses. The horses on pasture require little attention—those kept up at the barn for the winter use must be fed, and watered, and cared for...Most of the cavvy is at the Bar Eleven Ranch on winter range, and the Kochels report all is well down there. Guy Wootten has returned to the Bar Eleven after an absence of almost two years, which will lighten Reid's duties and give him a chance to leave the place once in a while.

Dunc is home, finding innumerable small jobs about the shop. He's been cutting out napkin rings on the jigsaw, using some inferior material, which makes the work harder than usual and the job not as satisfactory when finished. That is only the first step. Next, they must be sandpapered, then painted and marked before they'll be ready to appear on the tables in the dining room next summer. The past few days Dunc has been working up and down on The Pike fixing screen doors, putting in a screw here, a nail there, and soon he'll be making rounds of all the cabins looking for small repairs...

Tommy expects most of the nice Sheridan girls will be back in the dining room when summer comes. Julia will be here of course, to show you to your table in the dining room—her thirtieth consecutive summer at the Ranch. Mac will be back soon to help with the household work, and Agnes will be here with Reid next summer. In the office—Jane left with Rusty (Note: Jane married Rusty Holler—another dude ranch romance that resulted in a lifetime marriage.) *during the holidays and Phyllis Mothersead has taken her place. Shirley will be back soon to help...*

1947
December

Like the horses, the cowboys are scattered now. Glen Howie is in Arizona wrangling dudes. Tom Cornish is trying to convince the University of Nebraska that he's smart enough to graduate next year, and Bots Young is praying he can do the same with the professors at Dartmouth. Johnny Bean got all the saddles and bridles fixed, and he and Bill Skiles are down in Texas. Bill Skiles hopes he won't find any horses that need shoeing in his stocking on Christmas Day. Al Green is taking a vacation in California and Arizona. Cal Davis is an old married man now. Billy Willy and Clayton Conrad are at their homes near Sheridan. Reid Kochel is looking after the horses at the Bar Eleven. He has an eye on Grey Bar, One Spot and Strawberry Jam and all the others, and if the going gets rough, he'll see they have some extra feed now and then. Billy Eaton, George Gentry and LeRoy Wertman are the only cowboys here at the Ranch and they keep plenty busy doing things around the shop and corral that we don't have time to do when you all are here in the summertime...

1948
February

...Shirley Kelly left just before Thanksgiving for a visit at home in Iowa, then went on to Arizona for the holidays at the V Bar V Ranch with the Brocketts and Bill Sullivan. Phyllis Mothersead was bookkeeper for Tommy and office and mail clerk for Shirley during their absences, and now she has gone into Sheridan for a vacation period with her family. Anna Butler drove Buddie Jenkins to Detroit in the late fall, and returned to the Ranch just long enough to pack her bag for Washington State where she's now visiting her family. Dorothy Duncan is also in Washington for a family visit. Tommy Butler has just departed with Harry McCormick for a tour of Mexico. We don't like to mention the ice crop again, but when that chore is disposed of, George Gentry is taking off for the southwest and California...

1948
December

Along in October, after the big game hunting season, Donn Davies stepped in his jeep and headed for California. Charlie Holler got the Texas urge, and Glenn and LeRoy left for winter employment at Camelback Inn near Phoenix. In late November, Shorty figured he'd better be reporting for his winter job at Tanque Verde Ranch near Tucson, and he loaded his car and headed south...

Julia left the Ranch a few weeks ago for home in Sheridan and her regular winter job at Penney's—we'll be seeing her off and on—and when we move back to the big dining room in the spring, we bet she'll be there. Lota is turning out wonderful home-cooked meals these winter days. Emil keeps an eye on the boilers, the light plant and the plumbing...

There's been a turnover in the office, for Phyllis left end of October, and Shirley was married to Angela Buell's nephew, Bill Sullivan...

1949
May

You've guessed it by this time—the Ranch Staff is busy getting ready for summer. Early spring dudes have everything at their disposal: their horses are saddled and waiting for them at the corral when they want to ride, Lota turns out three wonderful meals for them every day, Anne and Betty and Brownie see that their cabins are cleaned and put in order every morning while they're at breakfast. But they have to take care of their own entertainment more or less...

1949
December

...Angela Buell and Jerry Burton took a longer trip down the coast and over to Arizona, and after the hunting season closed, Tom and Anna Butler took a quickie to California with Harry McCormick, and Emil Jacobs left for the coast more recently to spend the whole winter... The corral boys have scattered, practically en masse *to Arizona and winter work. Most dude ranch operators in the Southwest are pleased to have an Eaton-trained corral boy on their staffs, and the boys have little trouble finding winter jobs if they want them. Shorty is back at Tanque Verde Ranch near Tucson, Roy headed for his old job at Camelback Inn at Phoenix. Newt and Clay returned to their home ranches in Arizona, and Ralph is helping his father on the ranch near Buffalo. Glen went south to Arizona, too, but we haven't heard as yet where he is settled for the winter. Jack left for home ranges in Texas, and now is at the Lazy K Bar Ranch at Cortaro, Arizona. Laddie and Larry are back in school. "Old Faithful" George Gentry is right here at Wolf for the present and keeping plenty busy, too.*

The end of the "forties" marked the end of forty-five years of the Eaton operation at Wolf, Wyoming. In spite of the World War, the Eaton operation maintained its place as one of the premier dude ranches in the nation. The key to its success was continuity—continuity brought about by a corps of dedicated staff and dudes, and a resilient family who never lost sight of the Eaton brothers' concept of simple hospitality, a formula that both the old and new guard would carry over into the second half of the century.

CHAPTER 8
The Fifties

Corporate Matters

The officers of the Eaton Brothers Corporation didn't change much during the 1950s. In 1950, the corporation officers were: Bill Eaton, president; Tommy Butler, vice president; Tommy Ferguson, secretary; and Angela Buell, treasurer. The officer line up remained the same until July 15, 1957 when Angela Buell resigned as a director and treasurer of Eaton Brothers. The board accepted her resignation as treasurer with regret, but asked her to remain as a member of the board, which she did until 1968.

When Angela retired as treasurer, Tommy Ferguson was elected to replace her and his wife, Nancy Eaton Ferguson, was elected as secretary.

That slate of officers would remain the same until 1966 when, for the first time in the history of the corporation, all officers were Eaton family members.

In the normal course of business, the corporation occasionally had to borrow money to operate and the loans came from a variety of sources. For instance in 1955, it borrowed $60,000 from the First National Bank of Sheridan and used Ranch property as collateral. Again, in 1959, the Ranch needed a cash infusion, but in this instance, they borrowed $5,000 from Angela Buell for six months. This was not the only time an employee with a long association with Eatons' Ranch would step up to the plate to provide short-term financial help.

The Ranch also signed a series of leases with mineral companies. For instance, in 1952, it signed a five year lease with Shell Oil Company for mineral exploration in the vicinity of Wolf Creek and in 1955, a five year oil and gas lease signed with the Carter Oil Company of Tulsa, Oklahoma, for the Echeta property. The results of the exploration agreements are not really known. What is known is that the Eatons didn't strike it rich but did derive some income from the transactions.

In 1955, Eaton Brothers made its last land purchase in Wolf. For twenty-seven years, Eatons had leased an adjacent 276 acre parcel of property from a Mr. Dickson. When Mr. Dickson finally decided to sell, the Eatons snapped it up at a cost of ten dollars per acre. The purchase of this property increased the total acreage of Eatons' Ranch at Wolf to approximately 7,200 acres, its present size (2010).

Operations and Improvements

The winter of 1950 was not as severe as the previous year, but it was still challenging. It definitely affected the Ranch operation, which Angela described in the February *WN*:

...it has been cold in northern Wyoming this winter. Not many storms—to date not as much snow as we'd like to have, for winter snows bring summer moisture—but the mercury has spent many days around the zero mark and made dozens of excursions far below that point. With little snow to serve as cover, the frost has been driven deep into the ground, way down among some of our water pipes. We haven't had as many difficulties as last year, but it has been annoying, just the same. Tommy Butler and George Gentry will substitute something much, much stronger for that word "annoying." It's tough having to get out in sub-zero weather to dig rock-hard earth and connect steam lines to frozen pipes, but it has been done quickly and efficiently with only a few "annoyances"...Next summer's ice was harvested in the old fashioned way on January days that were ten to twenty degrees below zero, and the cakes thickened so fast they weighed almost four hundred pounds before the last one was cut on the pond at the Lower Ranch, pulled up the chute out of the water, loaded on the trucks, hauled three miles, and packed away in the stone icehouse between the office and Wolves Club. It was all one man could do to handle the thick cakes, and more often than not, two men hooked their tongs into each cake, braced themselves, and slid them around into position.

Frequently, Angela took it upon herself to impress upon *WN* readers just how much work went into the Ranch operation. In February 1951, she offered up this litany:

Now, instead of relaxing and having a vacation ourselves when there are no dudes around, here we (that's a collective "we") are writing Wranglin' Notes, *feeding cattle, cooking three bountiful meals a day, serving them, cleaning up afterwards, making beds, sweeping floors, dusting furniture, tearing rags, weaving rugs, operating on outmoded bedsteads, hauling ashes and trash, sanding napkin rings, delivering coal and kindling, stoking furnaces and boilers, cutting and hauling fireplace wood, making out income tax reports, watching the light plant, keeping accounts, sorting mail, washing and ironing clothes, taking the children to school and hauling them home again, writing letters, fixing, patching and repairing all sorts of equipment, hauling hay, graining colts, going to town for supplies, figuring whether we have enough money and credit to put on some more shingles come spring, and maybe make a few needed improvements, and at the moment getting ready to tackle that all-important-winter-job, putting up ice for the summer. Phew! There's always plenty to do on Eatons' Ranch for anyone who's inclined to look around a bit, dudes or no dudes.*

While the annual routine with the horses was to take them to Echeta in the fall, sometime Eatons had to change the plans, like in 1955 when *WN* explained that:

Since the February storms arrived, Bill Eaton has checked carefully on the Ranch cavvy. There are 300 head on the CX Ranch just over the Montana line (feed was short on our own Bar Eleven Ranch this winter we're sorry to say), about 50 head here on the home ranch and 60 head at the Bar Eleven...

Eatons' Ranch was diligent about making improvements to Ranch facilities. Eatons' dudes didn't expect anything fancy, but the Ranch was conscientious about making any improvement that added to the appearance of the accommodations, and the comfort of guests. Angela Buell made sure, in her own way, that the dudes knew Eatons' Ranch was on the job. In June 1950, she dished up this kind of fare:

...Tommy Butler was flying around at the Ranch getting the annual repair and replacement programs under way...A garage was attached to Nan Eaton's house. The pack shed and one or two other buildings were re-shingled. The corral bathhouse

Eaton Ranch horses make their annual trip through Sheridan past the Sheridan Inn. Circa 1950s.
Courtesy of Eatons' Ranch.

needed attention and now it has a new cement floor, another shower, and a freshly shingled roof. The two large cabins at the upper end of the Ranch have had their faces lifted. The roofs were torn off, lowered and shaled, which not only took care of the leaks developing there and provided better insulation, but also improved their appearance tremendously. Before the extra workmen leave, several more roofs will have had a dressing applied. We seem to have concentrated on roofs this year, but they've been neglected and roofs take a beating in this country where the winter storms are rough, and the summer sun is hot...

In May 1954, more improvements were reported:

...Harry and Clarence have been here for some time, busy with their hammers and saws and trying desperately to accomplish before summertime all the work that's been laid

out for them. Up in the Wolves Club, the old coal stove has disappeared, and in its place are some shiny, modern radiators, designed for comfort rather than atmosphere, in that old log building. In most of the guest cabins dudes still wonder how to start a fire on an occasional chilly evening and how to operate the drafts in their old-fashioned coal stoves, but the cowboys have gone modern (by Ranch standards). We'd better explain that it's true...dudes have equally comfortable quarters when it's winter on the Ranch, and in the Wolves Club it hasn't been too pleasant in recent years with snow drifting through the cracked chinking between the logs and under the beds when the wind was right.

And then, for a bit of historical contrast, Angela made this pitch:

We're inclined to glance back to earlier days in this seventy-fifth Anniversary year of Eatons' Ranch and the faded old time pictures of the ranch house and rough cabins (if you had more than a canvas roof over your head in 1904 you were ritzy), the snapshots of the scrubby Indian ponies that served as mounts, of the stagecoach as it bumped over rough roads with four broncs in front, present quite a contrast to the neat cabins with private baths, swift motor transportation, sleek horses and the personal services offered today.

Later in the decade, there were more reports on improvements, such as in December 1956 when *WN* reported on the state of the first cabins built at Wolf in 1904:

...As we have reported in recent issues of Wranglin' Notes *the old Pike cabins, built in 1904, are gradually giving way to similar but modernized accommodations and there's now a gap where the boys' wrecking bars have demolished four more rooms...to be rebuilt in the spring. Believe it or not, the old sagging cabins are still in demand for they have an atmosphere that's not to be duplicated in modern log cabins. We had a*

struggle talking Jack Quinn and his daughter Amy into more comfortable accommodations this fall. There remains one room on The Pike without a private bath and we're about to refurnish it, as a point of interest, as it was in 1904 when an early dude (perhaps the grandfather of some of those on the 1956 list) was proudly ushered into his then-modern cabin. Patty Eaton has scouted around the place and found an iron bedstead which dates from that time, also an old washstand and bureau, and no doubt there are other furnishings of the era, including a kerosene lamp, tucked away somewhere around here.

Wranglin' Notes reached a milestone in the 1950s. The Ranch published the one hundredth issue in February 1953. "NUMBER ONE HUNDRED!!" was boldly stamped across the page in bright red ink. Of course, Angela made a short comment on the history of *WN*:

One hundred issues and several hundred pictures, at least a half million horseback rides, and exactly thirty winters ago (if we make it inclusive) the first number of Wranglin' Notes *appeared under the heading* Minutes of the Wolves Club. *A few months later—in September of 1924 to be exact—*The Minutes *became* Wranglin' Notes, *and has so remained to this day.* Wranglin' Notes *has recorded many things in those three decades—births, deaths, marriages in the Eaton Family, fires and Depression and other setbacks in plans for the Ranch. But in far greater proportion through the years, the record is of*

> *laughs and fun and the pleasures not only of the Eatons, but also of the uncounted friends who have been with them for a few weeks or many months of comradeship in their ranch home...*

With the exception of the first few issues, Angela Buell served as the editor and singlehandedly produced hundreds of pages of commentary and photographs to provide a detailed chronicle of life at Eatons' Ranch. This remarkable achievement was due to her devotion to an interest in Eatons' Ranch and the Eaton family. *Wranglin' Notes* is her legacy to Eatons' Ranch—and it still endures.

But even Angela could not go on forever. The Christmas 1957 issue of *WN*, number 114, ended with this:

> *And very special Good Wishes at this time from Angela Buell, editor of* Wranglin' Notes *who is about to pull the cover over a typewriter that's a little worn in spots after well over a hundred issues of* Wranglin' Notes. *This doesn't mean that Wranglin' Notes is folding...no indeed. Number 115 will be along with up-to-date news of the folks at Eatons' Ranch well before 1958 is under way.*

Number 115 did come along and the new editor was Jean Davies, from Chicago, who introduced the issue this way:

> *Angela Buell had a knack for making the guests feel welcome at Eatons' Ranch and at home before they arrived, and she took great care and pleasure in making certain that everyone's accommodations were to their liking. After many years of pleasant association, Angela is leaving us for a much-deserved permanent vacation. No. 5 on The Pike will be very lonely without her. Not only has she been a big part of our organization, but also she has been one of the family and part of all the wonderful memories we all have of life at Eatons' Ranch. We are glad she is going to live in her home in Sheridan where we can see and visit with her often. How happy we are, not having to say, "Goodbye."*

Angela's retirement marked thirty-eight years of faithful service to Eatons' Ranch. Although she retired from work, she continued to serve on the board of directors of Eaton Brothers, Inc. and from time to time provided "corporate memory" to the board of directors when they asked for it. She also penned a few special editions of *WN* as a "guest editor."

Family

Aunt Mame survived her husband Alden by twenty years. Though she remained active after Alden's death, her age caught up with her and she died of a heart attack on August 30, 1957, age eighty-eight. Eatons' Ranch prepared a fitting memorial that consisted of a picture of her in her favorite place, the garden, holding a bunch of flowers. The tribute read:

Aunt Mame

Others have lived longer though not by many years. Others may have left deeper footprints in the sand, but not in the affectionate memories of their families and friends. And some may have been happier and more content as they went along, though we doubt that very much.

It was a rugged life with much hard work for a woman on a pioneer ranch in North Dakota in the early 1890s. Mrs. Alden Eaton ("Aunt Mame" to the thousands of Ranch guests and friends who knew her throughout the years) probably had as much pleasure and fun out of life as it was possible for anyone to have in those frontier days, for it was her nature to speak lightly of the hardships and disappointments and privations that were the common lot. Except for brief vacation periods, she was an active dude rancher twelve months in the year from the time she married Alden Eaton and moved west in 1892 until she left us with little warning a few months ago. That is a record...to have been a dude rancher for sixty-five years.

As we record here the passing of Aunt Mame, we salute a courageous pioneer ranch woman whose great love of this western country lives on through her son, Bill Eaton, and through her grandchildren and great-grandchildren. Her graciousness and kindly hospitality long will be remembered by the countless friends with whom she shared the shelter of her home through those many years.

In 1950, Bill Eaton, who arrived at Wolf when he was only fourteen years old in 1904, was now sixty years old and a grandfather. Wolf had been his home since 1904, with the exception of a stint in the Army in the First World War. His wife, Patty, fifty-nine years old, had lived at Eatons' for thirty-six years since her marriage to Bill in 1914.

Bill and Patty were both active and remained so throughout the decade. In 1950, Bill still ran the corral with George Gentry and still team roped steers and gave the occasional roping exhibition with the big loop. Bill had not stopped doing the things he liked to do, and had not started doing things he didn't like to do—like acting as a pitchman for the Ranch. The February 1950 *WN* reiterated Bill's reticence:

Professionals have told ...Bill Eaton that he should set out for Chicago, Cleveland, New York, and all the big cities of the East, with a collection of pictures under his arm and maybe a movie reel in his bag and "sell" the Ranch. The fellows who ventured that advice didn't know Bill Eaton. Even though bronc riding is now a number of years behind him, he'd take his chances on the wildest bronc in the country before he'd march up to a stranger and give him a sales talk. Bill will just stand pat on the reputation of Eatons' Ranch after seventy years, although quietly he'll put a lot of effort into planning and helping make everyone's visit here a pleasant one after they've taken a chance on it. That's the Western way...

Bill and Patty kept up their schedule of winter trips to see friends and just get away from it all like in the winter of 1951:

> *...Bill and Patty are leaving right now for a vacation trip and their idea of the best vacation is to get away from the home ranch for a change, but still to stay within the bounds of ranch country. So they'll follow a straight line south for a thousand miles to Texas, and then swing over into New Mexico and Arizona for the sunshine and visits with old friends living there and wintering there...Bill attended to the horse buying last fall and that is off his mind, but Patty has a commission to look over the Navajo rug situation (and probably it will be just LOOK, for wool and rugs have gone up in price beyond our reach), and to pick up some things for the gift department at the Ranch store...*

Bill also remained camera shy and photos of him were rare. But in 1955, George Grunkemeyer, a Sheridan photographer and filmmaker, happened along and caught George Gentry and Bill Eaton conferring in front of the saddle barn. The caption in *WN* said:

> *Here's a photograph of the Management of the Corral at Eatons' Ranch, which is a truly rare one for they have a reputation of being camera-shy. In spite of the years that have gone by in their long association, it's hard to find a gray hair in Bill Eaton's head, and George Gentry is as hard-muscled and lean as he was back in the early twenties when the flappers' hearts went pit-a-pat as he rode by. In those happy days, the gentlemen above did not carry specs in their shirt pockets, but aside from that, the wear and tear of many long years of dude ranching doesn't appear to have been too devastating. The horses they ride these days may not be quite as "salty," but the ropes they throw are just as accurate. We doubt if there's anyone in the land who has had more experience than these two Western men have when it comes to fitting riders to horses (or horses to riders), one of the most important jobs on a dude ranch.*

Bill Eaton and George Gentry in front of the Eaton barn.
Photo by George Grunkenmeyer.
Courtesy of Eatons' Ranch.

Even in his sixties Bill Eaton did things that provide fodder for stories that are still told today. One who was witness to many of the events is Bob Gaskell. Bob was from Laramie and met Jack Pelissier while they were both students at the University of Wyoming. Bob first worked at Eatons' in 1957 and worked there off and on for the next seven years.

Bob remembers very well the time he and the boys were at Echeta getting ready to bring the horses back to Wolf. Glenn Johnson, one of the wranglers, was mounted on a horse that blew up with him and bucked him off. The horse then stumbled and fell. Bob rushed to grab the horse's reins as the horse got up, and then the horse just fell over and died. Glenn, a bit shaken, asked Bill what happened. In his deadpan way, Bill replied, "He just fell over and died. He never bucked anyone off before."

Several times Bob fell victim to Bill's propensity to drop people off in the middle of nowhere without warning or direction. Bill once took Bob to Echeta and just left him to help get some horses ready for a sale. Bob, who had nothing with him but his saddle, had to call Patty and ask her send him some clean clothes so he could go to the sale.

Often, Bob was called upon to be Bill's designated driver and drove him to horse sales or wherever Bill wanted to go. Once he drove Bill and his friends Bob Tate and Buck Blackburn and several others to a horse sale in Gillette. They all bought horses there and Bill almost bought one by snoozing. Bill fell asleep during the sale and his head kept nodding. The auctioneer thought he was bidding and with each nod of his head, the price went up. They managed to wake Bill up before he bought the horse. On the way home in the car, the boys got to trading the horses they had bought with each other, and by the time they got home there was some confusion as to who owned what.

Bill always had to stop at the Elks Club in Sheridan on his way home to have a drink or two and play cards. Often, he stayed late into the night, and Bob, as his driver, had to wait for him. It was the practice in those days for ranch families to stop by the Elks and leave their kids to wait in the lobby while their parents socialized in the bar. Bob had to wait there so often for Bill that he believed he had more waiting time chalked up than any of the kids. Once in a while the bartender would take pity on him and let him sneak into the bar for a beer even though he was still under age.

Bob also marveled at Bill's skill with a rope. Even though he was in his sixties, Bill was still big and had powerful arms. One day he and Bob were walking across the corral after they had been castrating some colts. Bill carried a long length of "foot rope" which is a heavy cotton rope used to tie up the hind foot of a horse when the horse needs to be controlled. Bill saw a horse about thirty feet away and said to Bob, "I'll bet you two dollars I can rope that horse with this rope." Bob made the bet.

Bill tied a honda in one end of the heavy rope, built a loop, and then roped the horse on the first try. Bob paid up. He still marvels that Bill could throw that heavy rope that far and catch something on the other end.

In 1958, Bill was honored for his long service to the Sheridan-Wyo-Rodeo that he helped found in 1931. *WN* described the occasion in the December 1958 issue:

The Cowboys' Friend

After thirty-seven years service as arena director of the Sheridan-Wyo-Rodeo held in July of each year, Big Bill Eaton retired to the grandstand. The show announcer duly recognized him each day, but that was not enough insofar as all the cowboys were concerned. They felt more should be done for Bill, for his untiring efforts in their behalf.

Each year the Sheridan Elks present a Gymkhana at the rodeo grounds, and the proceeds are donated to the Crippled Children's' Foundation. This year September 14 was advertised everywhere as "Big Bill Eaton Day."

At the conclusion of the gymkhana, George Gentry, the Eaton Ranch corral boss, who has worked for Bill and the Eaton Brothers for thirty-seven years, made the presentation of a bronze plaque of Bill on his favorite horse, Judd. (Note: It was actually thirty-nine years.)

It was a great day! All the guests of the Ranch, along with people from all over Sheridan and vicinity were on hand to honor Big Bill. For those of you who know Bill and George, you will know they are men of the West, and men of few words, and you will be able to mentally picture George handing Bill the plaque with nary a word, and the familiar grunt from Bill saying he appreciated all that was done for him. Of course, we all know big lumps were in their throats, and at that particular moment, a silver-tongued orator couldn't improve on their speeches.

A photo of Big Bill accepting the plaque surrounded by his friends accompanied the article.

The plaque was taken to Eatons' Ranch and attached to the fireplace in the main ranch house, and it is still there today. The only problem with the plaque, at least from a historical accuracy standpoint, is that it is in error. The plaque states that Bill Eaton was the arena director for the Sheridan-Wyo-Rodeo from 1920 to 1957. In fact, the Rodeo did not exist

Bill Eaton receiving plaque for his service to the Sheridan-Wyo-Rodeo in 1958.
From left; Bob Larrimore, Stanley Bohnsack, Reid Kochel, George Gentry, Bill Eaton, Buck Blackburn, Curley Witzel, Stanley Kuzara.
Photo by Vacationland Studio, Sheridan, Wyoming.
Courtesy of Eatons' Ranch.

in 1920. It was established in 1931. So Bill Eaton was not arena director for thirty-seven years. He was actually arena director for twenty-six years because Harry Fulmer was the arena director at the first Sheridan-Wyo-Rodeo. Regardless, even though the details are wrong, Bill Eaton deserved credit for his long and outstanding service to the Sheridan-Wyo-Rodeo.

Patty Eaton continued to be a wife, mother, grandmother and gracious hostess and was at her perch by the saddle barn each morning to call out the horses that needed to be saddled for the dudes.

Patty also insisted that arriving guests should be greeted with fresh flowers. She once wrote about why she kept up that tradition:

> *...Well, changes that are unavoidable come on fast enough, many of them not to our liking, and it is sometimes a hard struggle to hang on to the traditions that we've found worthwhile. It's like the custom of having fresh flowers to greet every arriving guest. People often tell me I'm foolish to keep that up, "they don't do it anyplace else," but I think it's worthwhile. It is the kind of traditional, warm touch that makes Eatons' what it is, and I'll continue it as long as I'm able...*

Patty did have an unfortunate accident in July 1957, which was duly reported in the Christmas issue of *WN*:

> *...Patty Eaton had a nasty fall in her cabin and spent the rest of the summer in the hospital nursing a broken leg. She has been back at the Ranch since September and is getting along fine, though still handicapped in walking and getting around.*

Nan Eaton raised her children, Frank and Jaci, on the Ranch, but she and the children took frequent trips to Philadelphia to visit her parents. She remarried in 1951 and of course, the event received comment in *WN*:

> Wranglin' Notes *cannot close without a romance, and justifying this issue is the marriage of Nan Eaton and LeRoy Wertman. Nan has lived at the Ranch since becoming Billy Eaton's*

Roy and Nan Wertman with their daughter Wendy and Nan's children, Jaci and Frank. The family dog is Peggy. *Courtesy of Eatons' Ranch.*

bride in 1938, and except for a couple of winters at Camelback Inn near Phoenix, Roy has been with us since first joining the corral group in 1943, so neither of them need any introduction to Ranch visitors. They will continue to be Eaton Ranch "home folks," and if you're coming our way this season, you'll find them at home on the Ranch carrying on with the rest of the Eaton Family and their associates.

Two years later, the October 1953 *WN* made an announcement:

...Three year old Billy Ferguson has yielded his place as youngest of the Ranch Family to Miss Wendy Hunter Wertman, the daughter of Roy and Nan Wertman, who arrived on August 27 to join the home folks...

Tommy and Nancy Ferguson, in addition to raising their family and being an integral part of the Eaton Ranch management, often took a break from the Ranch during the winter and, of course, it was a subject for *WN*:

> *The three older members of the Ferguson family—Nancy, Tommy and Susan—have just returned from a pleasant trip through the Southwest. They stopped in Tucson to say "hello" to all the Ranch people gathered there at this time of year, went on to Phoenix for the wedding of Leonard Graham and Gretchen Swindle, spent a few days at the Rimrock Ranch and the V Bar V Ranch nearby, looked into the Grand Canyon, visited Boulder Dam and sampled the bright lights of Las Vegas.*

WN reported another one of their trips in December 1958:

> *An Eaton Visits Homestead*
> *First Time Since 1904*
>
> *...Tommy and Nancy Eaton Ferguson on their trip to the Black Hills this Fall, drove to Medora and were the first members of the Eaton family to return to the spot where the Eaton Brothers started a new industry, that of the dude ranch. And now, in 1958, the fourth generation of Eatons are still "wranglin' dudes."*

Tommy and Nancy Ferguson added the last two members of the fourth generation of the Eaton family. Billy Ferguson, their first son, was born and the birth was heralded in *WN*, Issue 91, in June 1950:

> *We're quick at passing the buck so we'll blame this tardy issue of* Wranglin' Notes *on William Thomas Ferguson, who is only a few days old and hardly able to defend himself. It seemed only right to hold* Wranglin' Notes Number 91 *for the arrival of another great-grandchild for Aunt Mame, one more grandchild for Bill and Patty, and a first son in the household of Tom and*

Nancy Ferguson. Six-year old Susan was well pleased with her small brother but Patty B. insisted that he be exchanged at once for a baby sister. Nevertheless, there was rejoicing among relatives, friends, Eaton Ranch residents and dudes upon the arrival May 15 of the new member of the Eaton Family. William Thomas (hereafter he'll be "Billy") has the good wishes of all for a long, happy, and useful life at the home ranch on Wolf Creek.

The last of the fourth generation was born to Tommy and Nancy Ferguson in 1955 but the event was also coupled with a death in the family. The February 1955 *WN* made this announcement:

One by one, Wranglin' Notes *has recorded the loss of the older generation of the Ranch Family and with sorrow, we now note the passing on January 3 of Miss Josephine Gillespie, who had resided with the Eatons for sixty-two years. She was a familiar figure around the Ranch house in particular, where she chose to keep the many books in order and to help in countless little ways when a willing hand was needed.*

And one by one, Wranglin' Notes *has recorded the births of the now-flourishing fourth generation of the Eaton Family. It's an anomaly that on the very day "Cousin Josie" left us, Thomas James Ferguson, Jr. arrived. He will not take Cousin Josie's place exactly, but in the years ahead, he'll be busy carving his own niche at the Ranch. By the way, his parents, brother and sisters call him "T. J." but he's Jimmy to Grandma Patty Eaton.*

The fourth generation of Eaton children consisted of seven children born during the period from 1939 to 1955. Billy and Nan Eaton had two—Frank and Jaci. Tommy and Nancy Ferguson had four—Susan, Patty B., Billy and T. J. And Roy and Nan Wertman had one—Wendy. During the 1950s, *WN* followed their progress closely. (*Note: Frank, the oldest, was included as both a family member and member of the Ranch staff.*) Here are a few examples of the coverage:

1951
December

...Three of the children are school age now, and Frank, Susan and Jaci show up every weekday morning with their lunchboxes to be driven six miles down the road to the little white schoolhouse where Billy and Nancy learned to read and write many years ago....

1957
February

...The Ranch Family is flourishing, from the 89er down to the two year old. Frank Eaton is in his senior year at high school, is also Private William Frances Eaton now in limited service with Uncle Sam. He drives back and forth to Sheridan every school day with his sister, Jaci, a student at Highland Park school in town, as a passenger. The three older Ferguson children attend the same little country grade school six miles down Wolf Creek road where their mother went many years ago, and the youngest Ferguson who is now past two, and Miss Wendy Wertman who is approaching four, will soon have their lunchboxes in hand, bound in the same direction.

1958
February

Nan, Roy and Wendy Wertman have wintered in with the rest of us. Wendy's faithful companion, her boxer "Peggy," leaves her briefly each morning to greet the ranch family as they arrive at the dining hall for breakfast.

Jaci Eaton is spending each week in Sheridan, living with a friend while attending school, and in this way is able to participate in more of the school activities. However, she joins the ranch family every weekend, and is enjoying the winter weather along with the Ferguson children.

Patty B (Tom and Nancy Ferguson's daughter) had an ice-skating party last week, with a nice warm fire beside the pond. And, what good is a fire without hot dogs and marshmallows? A little water formed around the edge, and of course "T. J." Ferguson, the youngest, was the first to slip and fall in the water. We found Nancy at the fire drying out both "T.J." and his shoes.

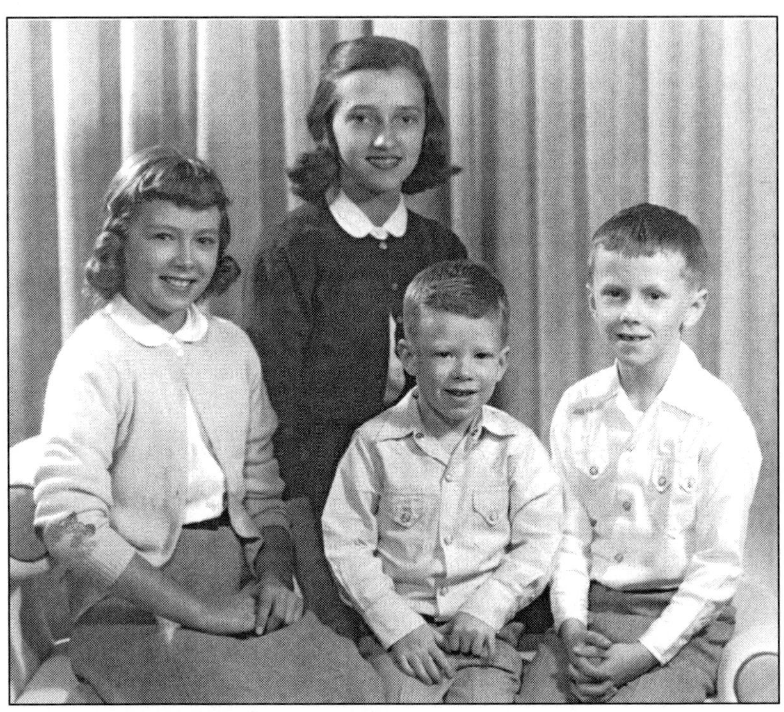

Tommy and Nancy Ferguson had five children.
Four are pictured here, from left: Patty, Susan, T. J. and Bill. Judith.
Their fifth child died as an infant.

1958
December

Frank Eaton left his corral job this fall, and along with Peter Donston is attending the Sheridan Community College. Jaci Eaton is finishing her last year of junior high school in Sheridan, and is only with us on weekends. Susan Ferguson is staying in town for the first time, as now she is a freshman at Sheridan High School. Patty B. and Billy are still heading down the road each day to the Wolf Creek School house, and little "T. J." and Wendy are lost without their pals. However, it won't be much longer before they, too, will join the children at the little white schoolhouse.

1959
May

School days are almost over, which will bring Jaci and Susan back from town to join the family. Frank Eaton commuted every day to the Sheridan Community College and on his days off, would be at the Ranch, pitching in wherever he was needed.

Billy and Patty Ferguson are counting the days off on the calendar until the end of school. Wendy Wertman and T.J. Ferguson, our dear pre-school children, braved the winter here at the ranch, and made life very interesting for all of us.

1959
December

...Frank Eaton, after a summer of typewriters and airline schedules in the office, has returned to the corral to help with the winter work in that department...

The November snows, which blanketed the immediate vicinity of the Ranch, did not prevent Susan Ferguson and Jaci Eaton from attending their classes at Sheridan High School as they are staying in town this winter. The snow did, however, close the Wolf School for a couple of days and provide an unscheduled vacation for Patty B. and Billy Ferguson and Wendy Wertman. "T. J." Ferguson will not start to school for two years, so he spends his time up at the corral, asking George and the boys the millions of questions which occur to a small boy, and in the office, making sure that his father is kept busy in one way or another...

Jack Pelissier moved to Big Horn, Wyoming, in 1951 to be the FBI Special Agent for Northern Wyoming and Southern Montana. He remained in that position until 1963 when he retired and became associated with the Bank of Commerce in Sheridan. Jack also married Rachel Bowman and raised his three children Jack, Suzanne and Jim.

His son, Jack, who first went to Eatons' in 1949 to be a companion for Frank Eaton, worked in the corral at Eatons' every summer from 1951 to 1959, and was often mentioned in *WN*. His sister, Suzanne, also worked some summers at Eatons'.

Dudes

Information about the dude "doings" at Eatons' Ranch continued, in the 1950s, to be grist for the *WN* mill. Examples are as follows:

1951
June

...The Butcher children, whose great-grandfather enjoyed the Ranch in its earlier days, also Anne and Jay McMillan, whose great-grandparents were here in 1908, are here riding horseback. Howard Butcher Jr. and Harry McCormick are swapping tales about the Ranch when they first came in 1909. Alex and Sarah Houk Hammer are about to celebrate the day—June 24, 1913—when they met at the Ranch, and also their wedding anniversary and honeymoon here two years later...

1954
December

...As always, we are impressed by the number who chose to return to the Ranch, though they might have gone to the ends of the earth in search of greener fields and new experiences. Some of them passed pleasant weeks or months at the Ranch and returned for another visit the same season. Mr. and Mrs. E. J. Brach of Winnetka had their customary spring and fall visits with us, as did Harry McCormick, who calls Wolf home although he spends more months in California. Mrs. Charles F. White, Winnetka, and Jack Quinn, New York, were here during the midsummer season and returned for fall visits.

There was something else that pleased us because it

seemed to show that though friends might be away from the Ranch for many years, it didn't mean they had forgotten Western ranch life experiences and the home folks. Mrs. Joseph F. Porter (Miss Julia Shellabarger), Kansas City, who was last here in 1927, returned with her husband and son Jeff. Edward Meanor (1929) of Bryn Mawr returned with his wife and daughter Jane. Next, Chronologically—Mrs. Harry N. Cootes, Washington, D. C., last here in 1931, Miss Dorothy Todtleben, Chicago, 1932, Russell Fortune, Indianapolis, 1933 and Mrs. Peter Belin (Miss Mary Cootes), 1935, who introduced her three small sons, Harry, Alan and Peter, to the Ranch this year...

Sometimes, when she was reciting the dude news, Angela threw in a little something different for amusement, like the following:

Eatons' Guest-Animal Ranch did pretty well last summer, too. We've lost track of the number of guest dogs, but we remember that there were two guest cats, one traveling by rail from New York, the other by car from Key West, and each accompanied by a guest dog. As far as we know, they fully enjoyed the freedom of the West and if one of the strange guest dogs questioned their rights on the Ranch, there were plenty of friendly trees to climb. On the other hand, the field mice practically left the country and we now have a tidy surplus in our 1955 budget for mousetraps.

1956
December

...Harry McCormick has spent forty-four seasons at the Ranch and in his eighty-seventh year is still calling for his horse at the corral and taking a good ride. Along with Mr. Howard Butcher, Jr., he first visited the Eaton Family in their ranch home in 1909.

In December 1958, *WN* paid special and deserved homage to one of the real old-timers at Eatons' Ranch:

Dude Sets Record at Eatons' Ranch

It was 1918 when Dorothy Douglas arrived at Eatons' Ranch for the first time to join Uncle Howard Eaton on his famous pack trip to Glacier Park. It must have been a successful selling trip, as every year thereafter, Dorothy has been back to spend her summer vacation at Eatons'.

Dorothy, a former schoolteacher, is retired now. She arrives early in the spring, staying on until late fall. There is doubt in our minds, that back in 1918 when Dorothy stepped down from the Burlington Railroad at Ranchester, Wyoming, to be met by Uncle Howard, she had any idea she would set a record at the Ranch...and in 1958 own two horses, Jet and Eggnog...and not miss a day in the saddle, except possibly her town day, to get her hair twisted.

Dorothy knows this country...knows every trail and trail gate, and can tell you more stories about her experiences out West than the pioneers of the West. While her other love is a good card game, she'll often be found sitting with a new dude telling them, "way back in such and such a date, I can remember," and then go on from there.

The year 1959 will be her forty-first visit, and we hope to see her back. If she hasn't tired of us in forty years, very likely we'll see her next year, and hope, now that she has set a record, she'll work on her fiftieth anniversary.

Employees

1950
December

Angela Buell gave a rundown on the dudes that were visiting at Christmastime, and then listed the family and employees that remained at the home ranch:

> *...That's a fair number of dudes for this season of the year, and of course, the home folks far outnumber them. Bill and Patty Eaton, Nan and her children Frank and Jaci, Tommy and Nancy with their three—Billy, Patty B. and Susan—Aunt Mame, Cousin Josie, Aunt Minnie and Mary Pelissier Covington of the immediate Eaton Family are all at home. Then there are Tommy and Anna Butler, Angela Buell, George Gentry, John and Dorothy Duncan, Emil Jacobs, Bud Ewoldsen and Helen Jasperson in the office. Lota Barker and her five or six kitchen and dining room helpers, Bessie Kilpatrick to look out for the cabins, Art Steil to check on cabin fires and help in the laundry, Gordon Dau to assist Emil in watching the boilers, light plant and mechanical end of this big place. Roy Wertman and Charlie Cook and Wes Overland at the corral, Jack and Vi Munro at the Lower Ranch, and Bus Janney helping with the outside work, wherever needed. A hundred miles away at the Eatons' Bar Eleven Ranch at Echeta the Kochels—Reid, Agnes and Raymond—with Guy Wootten to help, are all set for the winter, keeping an eye on several hundred saddle horses and a small portion of the cattle herd...*
>
> *George, Reid, Shorty, Roy Eddie and Ralph were the old-timers at the corral last summer, plus the apprentices Laddie and Larry. There were new boys to fill in—Frosty, Bo, Charlie, Wes, Doug and Don. Julia was in her accustomed place*

Julia Siegoski with the Eaton dinner bell.
Courtesy of Eatons' Ranch.

directing the girls in the dining room, keeping a sharp eye on the clock when it approached closing time at 8:45 a.m., 1 p.m. and 7 p.m. We don't know the inside story on this—it sounds like a Bill Eaton Project—but it's a fact that the Western Union office in Sheridan reversed the procedure one day last summer and called Julia to ask her for the correct time. Soon the whole country may abandon Greenwich and operate as we do on J. S. T. (Julia's Standard Time). Julia left recently to spend the winter in Sheridan as usual, but we're sure she'll be back no later than branding time next spring.

The February 1952 issue of *WN* featured a photo of George Gentry and fifteen year old Jack Pelissier standing on a hillside with their horses as George pointed something out to Jack. The accompanying write up explained the photo:

We weren't on the spot when the picture on this page was taken, but, along with some other people, we were loafing on the dining room terrace after dinner, and we could see George and Jack and Grunk on the ridge above Stanley Camp setting up a tripod, getting off their horses, getting on again, making motions that were meaningless to their distant audience sitting comfortably in terrace chairs watching the sunlight slowly climbing to the tip of Chocolate Drop as the sun sank behind the mountains. This is strictly our own version of what Gentry was saying, but knowing that the first shot was thrown out because Jack broke into an irrepressible grin, we're guessing it was something like this: "Now son, I's a busy man in a hurry. I got to get back down this hill and over to the corral to rope a hundred dude horses pretty quick. We're here to help Grunk because he's a swell fellow and if you crack a cockeyed smile while he's grinding away on this sequence I'll sure enough ground you tomorrow, maybe the next day, too, and you can walk instead of ride. So look real attentive because I'm saying something that's important...important to Grunk anyway. You can giggle when it's over and not before. Savvy?"

Evidently Jack did savvy, for the sequence came out wonderfully well in the movie Land of Our Fathers, *which was photographed by George Grunkemeyer, written and largely directed by Mr. F. H. Sinclair, both of Sheridan, for the American National Cattlemen's Association. It's a non-commercial movie and is being shown across the country to promote a better understanding of the lives, the pleasures and the problems of cattlemen, the cattle ranchers of the West in particular. If you run across it anywhere, and you may, don't*

George Gentry and fifteen year old Jack Pelissier.
Photo by George Grunkemeyer.
Courtesy of Eatons' Ranch.

miss the opportunity to see it. We hope to show Land of our Fathers *in Howard Hall next summer if we can assemble the proper equipment.*

1953
February

...George Gentry, Roy Wertman, Bob Masterson and Bill Thompson at the corral find the usual midwinter work of a Wyoming cow ranch quickly done in this good weather, but there are dozens of odd jobs waiting for them...And yet...the boys find time on Sunday afternoons to trail their horses to the new indoor arena on the Sage Ranch over on Rapid Creek where they rope calves and have fun competing with other cowboys of the neighborhood...

...In December we sent the big truck loaded with a special tank, Ralph Weaver at the wheel, to Boulder, Colorado, to pick up several thousand three and four inch rainbows which we purchased with a thought to giving Ranch fishermen something special to work for next summer. There was a storm brewing so Ralph drove through the night on the five hundred mile homeward trip, and in spite of tough traveling, delivered his load here at the ponds in extra good shape...

1954
May

The corral crew is expanding from day to day with Western boys who don't have much to say because dude ranching is different from everyday cow business and they're just trying to catch on as they follow the old-timers George, Roy and Don through the maze of spring work. There's Billy Brown from Texas and Newt Bundy's brother Orvel from Arizona, Lyle Lich from just over the line in Montana—to be joined soon by good old

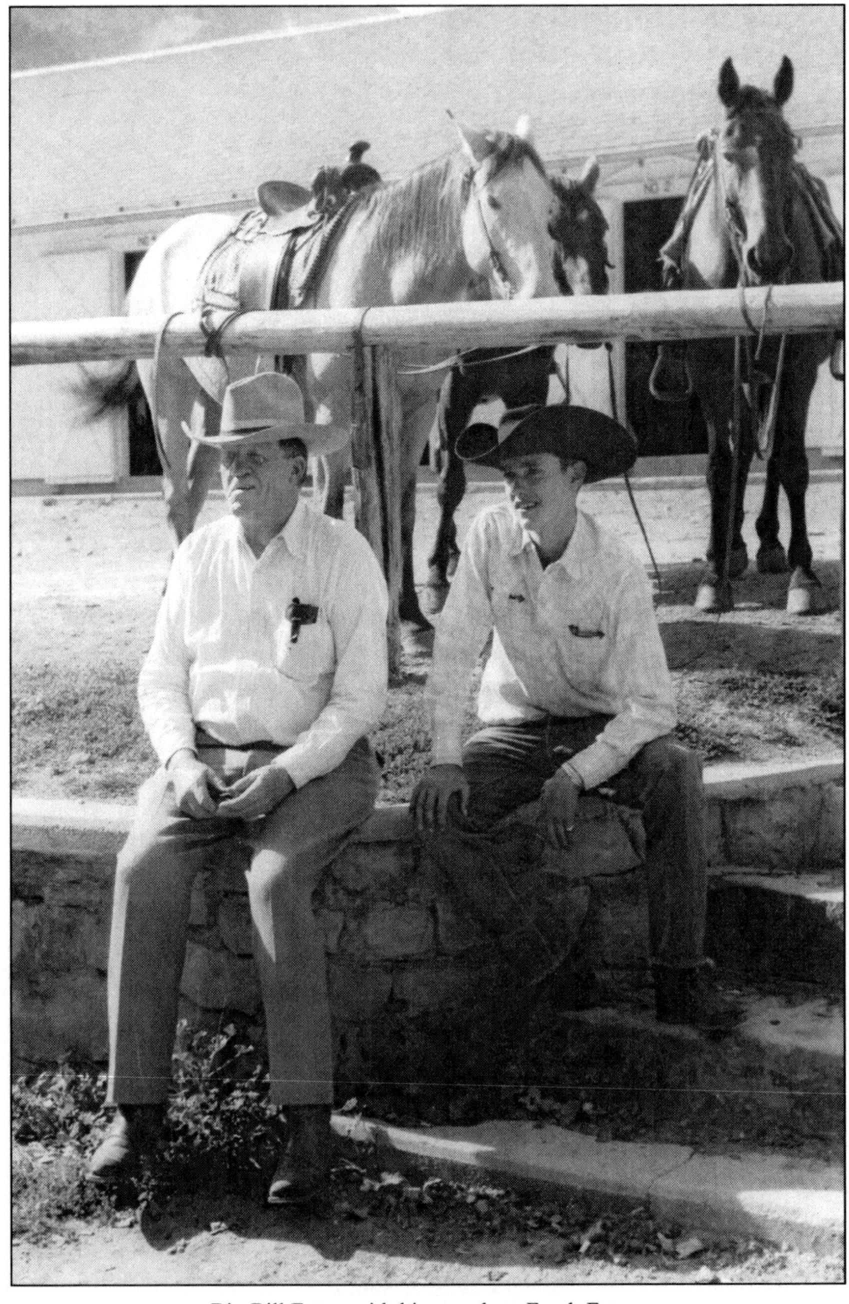

Big Bill Eaton with his grandson Frank Eaton.
Courtesy of Eatons' Ranch.

Shorty, who doesn't spend much time listening to anybody, and by deadeye Reid Kochel soon as the spring work's done down at the Bar Eleven, and by Jack Pelissier, Jay McMillan and Frank Eaton when school is out. Bill Lafferty has been here for some time working with the young horses, getting them used to a bridle and the pressure of the reins, accustomed to the weight of a saddle and following the directions of a rider.

...Julia is back in the dining room starting, starting her thirty-eighth summer at the Ranch...

1955
February

Angela wrote at length about the horse cavvy, which she did every year, and then followed it up by describing what happened at the main Ranch when the horses came back from Echeta:

The boys will be there to saddle them, too. Bill, George, and Roy, with the occasional help of young Frank, will be riding in and out of the big corral with their ropes in hand. Shorty should be here fairly early, and Reid will be up from the Bar Eleven. Rogers will be back in the blacksmith shop to keep the cavvy well shod for their hard trips up and down the mountain...Orvel Bundy has been here all winter and he'll be lending a hand at the corral. The boys have almost finished halter breaking the sixteen frisky colts at the barn, and soon they'll be turned over to Bill Lafferty, who will continue their education. There will probably be more of last season's boys at the corral, and Bill's waiting right now for the fellows to drop him a line about their summer jobs. There will be new boys, too, and Ike Fordyce, whose parents own and operate Tepee Lodge, will be one of them...

1955
June

It's early June now and most of the corral boys are here. Bill Eaton is over-all head of the corral and George Gentry has been his trusted lieutenant for more years than he'd probably care for us to mention. (Note: Sometimes Angela described Bill Eaton as the corral boss, and sometimes she gave the job to George Gentry. In fact, they worked together and it was a joint operation.) *Roy Wertman lives here the year round and knows the corral end of the Ranch thoroughly. Reid Kochel manages the Eaton Bar Eleven Ranch at Echeta where the horses spend their winter vacations, but he's always at the corral in the summertime to lend his years of experience to the job at hand. Shorty Enderle is another old-timer who takes charge on occasion and keeps the ball rolling around the corral and on the mountain trips. Then there are the younger fellows—Orvel Bundy, a ranch boy from Arizona who's been here steady for more than a year now, young Jack Pelissier who is starting his fourth summer at the corral, Bill Lafferty has returned from the ranch country of western Canada for his third summer here, and a new boy, Marty Lund came with him. Frank Eaton will again make a hand at the corral, like his father, grandfather and great-grandfather before him. Ike Fordyce, a ranch-raised boy from this locality, will be here, also Ward Hoblit from down Gillette way, and there will be one or two more fellows to complete the corral crew...*

1955
December

Reid Kochel is watching over the cavvy at the Bar Eleven Ranch with the help of Guy Wootten who has been there almost as many years as we have owned the Bar Eleven. Agnes Kochel has an apartment in Gillette where Raymond is going to school.

Shorty Enderle is back at this winter job at the Smith Ranch but he'll be home for Christmas Day. Orvel Bundy is in his native Arizona, and Marty Lund is home in Canada. Don DeJarnette is back home in Big Horn attending high school. Frank Eaton is going to school in Philadelphia, this winter, but he'll be home for the holidays. Ward Hoblit and Jack Pelissier are roommates at the University of Wyoming, and Ike Fordyce is at Colorado A. & M. Lyle Lich is married and established on a ranch down Gillette way...

1956
December

Here at the home ranch George, Shorty, Roy, and Curly will have an eye on the stock. Bill will drive occasionally to the Bar Eleven to make sure everything's going along all right down there, as Reid Kochel had some hard luck last spring and has been obliged to take it easy. To say than an old bronc rider like Reid went off a gentle horse sounds ridiculous, but unfortunately, it's true. His broken arm mended quickly, but his back has been a slower process although he's about to be dismissed by the doctors...

1957
February

In this issue, Angela wrote about the passing of John Duncan, a perennial Eaton employee:

Most everyone is staying at home, except Dorothy Duncan who has been in Washington State since last October visiting relatives. John Duncan, whose knowledge of hunting and fishing and packing and outdoor life contributed to the pleasure of many Eaton dudes through the many years he lived at the Ranch, left us last July. Like so many old-timers whose pioneering instinct contributed in great measure to the development of a new country and to the pleasure of those who discovered the West as a vacation spot in later years, his life was that of the individual. "Dunc" is being missed at the Ranch, and by his many friends.

A corral crew in the 1950s.
Top row, from left: Ward Hoblit, Pete DuBois, Bryan Sheedy, Bob Gaskell, Shorty Enderle, Jack Pelissier.
Bottom row, from left: George Gentry, Glen Johnson, Frank Eaton, Jim Niner, Donn Davies, Chuck Larson, Johnny Milne, Don Thibault, Roy Wertman, Bill Eaton.
Courtesy of Eatons' Ranch.

1957
May

Overall Boss at the corral this season of 1957, as for many years past, is George Gentry. He has some veteran assistants: Shorty Enderle and Roy Wertman have been on the job all winter. Bob Gaskell and Glenn Johnson started work several weeks ago, and just as soon as school is out young Frank Eaton, Jack Pelissier and Don DeJarnett will be helping, too. Jim Niner, who is a newcomer, will be along soon, and there will be several more boys to complete the corral group…

1957
December

It happens to be early winter now and most of the folks who helped us last summer are scattered. We can't go down the long list but we'll try to cover the corral crew. The seniors, George Gentry, Roy Wertman, Shorty Enderle, are right here—as are Glenn Johnson and Bob Gaskell. Reid Kochel is back at the Bar Eleven, managing that important branch of the Eaton Ranch. Rogers Harwood has returned to his winter job at the Rimrock Ranch in Arizona. And we're really impressed with reports on the younger group who are outdoor boys and would rather be on the back of a horse than hunching over a schoolbook, but there they are using their heads and plugging away with a thought to the future. Jack Pelissier, Ward Hoblit, and Bry Sheedy are at the University of Wyoming, where Bob Gaskell will join them second semester. Don DeJarnett is in junior college in Sheridan. Bill McKinney, Ed Marston, Pete DuBois and Jim Niner are all in schools scattered from the east coast to Montana to New Mexico to Arizona.

…Frank Eaton and Bob Hall chose to put army service behind them and they're at Fort Leonard Wood in Missouri

taking basic training. We figure on seeing them at Christmastime when they are granted leave, and we understand they'll be free for next summer.

1958
May

In the May 1958 issue of *WN*, Angela wrote at length about the "help" that would work at the Ranch that dude season. She always believed that the dudes were interested in who would be "present for duty," and she was correct. They were.

> *Seeing all the horses, and the boys, Don Thibault, Bob Gaskell, Roy Wertman, Jack Pelissier, Jim Niner, Pete DuBois, Ward Hoblit and to have Frank Eaton back home with us again, means happy times and lively times. And, as we pass beside the blacksmith shop, we hear the merry anvil ring. Rogers Harwood is not inside, as he has taken on a year round job in Arizona. But, there's another smiling face. It is Chuck Larsen, our new blacksmith, and he's humming a tune...* Who's going to shoe your pretty little feet?
>
> *...In the corral, Bill McKinney is breaking horses and will be working them all summer. Jimmie Parkinson is polishing the ranch wagon, getting it ready to meet the first guests arriving by train or plane. We know now, for sure, that dude season is upon us...*
>
> *...Our summer hostess in the dining room, Julia Siegoski, will not be with us again this summer after some forty odd years. Another well deserved vacation, but a tremendous loss to Eatons' Ranch.*
>
> *...And speaking of cooks, Frank Emmerling is our new chef. He arrived several weeks ago and the meals have been* "si bon." *Our so-called diets have been forgotten, and the favorite expression is* "Mañana."

And "speaking of cooks" again, it is worth repeating what Patty Eaton had to say about cooks in a manuscript she wrote in 1976 when she was eighty-five years old. What she said could probably apply to any decade at Eatons' Ranch:

> *...one year the chef demanded that Tommy Butler fire four or five of the girls, but he wouldn't give good reason, and Tommy said he couldn't do it unless he knew more about it, and so the cook just walked out and took the second cook and the fry cook with him. Tommy had to take over as chef for several days that time. Of course, Tommy was a good cook, and had to cook more than once. They say, though, that he dirties every pot and pan in the kitchen when he gets out a meal.*
>
> *There was one time that I think is amusin: we had these darky* [sic] *cooks and Bill came in one morning to discover they were using slabs of bacon to start the fires with in those big coal and wood ranges we had. Imagine, a whole slab of bacon!*
>
> *So many cooks are alcoholics. A person could do an article just on cooks. I can see how it would be a problem, cooking could get awfully monotonous, day in and day out. We've had some terrific cooks, but we've just had to let them go because they drank so much they were unreliable. We had an awfully nice boy one year, and he was just wonderful, he could do anything, and he loved to work, a big, tall good-looking fellow, he was just a dandy, but they had to let him go. Well, he went back to Kansas City and went on the wagon, and he wrote to Tommy that he hadn't had a drink for a year and he'd like to come back. He was such a likeable person Tommy thought he should have another chance, but it didn't last. He commenced to drink, and we had to let him go. Once in a while Tommy has heard from him, but we've never had him again because he just can't stay off the booze. It seems to happen to so many good cooks...*

And then Patty proceeded to tell about some of the other "kitchen" problems that had occurred over the years:

...Once, before Bill and I were married, they had a group of professional waitresses and they all walked out at once. I helped, and Bill's mother helped, and practically everybody on the ranch had to help until they got some others in to wait tables...

...Of course, Tommy Butler tells some good tales of some of the troubles he's had. One time the woman in the pantry went berserk and chased the cook out the door with a butcher knife. Tommy talked to her for two hours before he got the butcher knife away from her, but he never did find out what it was all about, she just was off in the head...

...And then one time Bonnie Shedell threw a tray down and jumped up and down on it. She kept doing that until she got it out of her system and she was all right and never did anything like that again...

What Patty did not mention is when Tommy Butler tried to save the Ranch some money. According to reports, Tommy Butler was always thrifty when it came to spending Ranch money. That, for the Ranch, was an admirable trait for an employee to have, but sometimes Tommy's "economies" had unintended consequences.

Once, Tommy made a deal with some German cooks. The deal was that he would pay them a set price to run the kitchen, and if they could operate for less than that, then they could have any money they saved. The consequences were disastrous. The Germans bought the worst and cheapest food they could find, and the quality of food at Eatons' Ranch declined to an unprecedented low. People even got sick. It was a bad time at Eatons' Ranch and the deal was eventually terminated but not, in the minds of many, soon enough.

In February 1959, Jean Davis, then the editor of *WN*, marked another employee milestone at Eatons' Ranch:

Wolf Postmaster Retires

A small, unpretentious, white frame building, housing several desks for the ranch office staff, includes in one corner, the Wolf, Wyoming United States Post Office.

The office staff are also appointed postal clerks by the Wolf Postmaster. They take their post every morning when the mail arrives via a "lady Uncle Sam." Billie Parkinson handles the outgoing mail, bundling it for east, west, or air mail, as the case may be. Two others sort the incoming mail, placing it in its proper slots, labeled for each ranch along the Star Route. This mail is tied and our "mail lady" is then on her way with each bundle for delivery to mailboxes along the route to Ranchester, Wyoming. Here the outgoing mailbags are loaded on the train for their destinations—with each letter bearing the postmark, "Wolf, Wyoming."

Eatons' Ranch has served as U. S. Post Office for the Wolf Community Star Route since 1904. (Note: This is incorrect. Eatons did not take over the Wolf Post Office until 1909 when they purchased the property and Uncle Willis was appointed postmaster.) *For thirty-one years of that time, Tommy Butler has been the Wolf Postmaster... This does not alter Tommy's position at the ranch, that is, our jack of all trades, but all the same, losing the long time postmaster as a sad day.*

1959
December

Tommy and Nancy Ferguson and George Gentry drove to Sun Valley, Idaho, the first week in October on a "busman's holiday" to the annual Dude Ranchers' Convention...

Dorothy Duncan departed on the first lap of her European tour in mid-September and continued to travel until her return to the Ranch in December...

Where are the home folks now? They're all on the Ranch for Christmas. The Bill Eatons, Aunt Minnie Reid, the Fergusons, Butlers, Wertmans, Frank and Jaci Eaton, Dorothy Duncan, Fay

Alderson, George Gentry, Emil Jacobs, the Parkinsons, Minnie Lloyd, Art Steil, Ed Neville, Cal Kelham, Shorty Enderle, Bob Gaskell, Jack Pelissier, and the Needens, plus a few additional helpers who are new this winter, are all right here. The "year round" home folks now include Ed Cattrell who has taken Jean Davies place in the office, as Jean chose to return to Chicago to join her family. (Note: Ed also took over as editor of *WN.*)

...The corral boys, basing their hunting activities from here at the Ranch, hunted early in the morning and at other assorted times when the work schedule was slack, adding four more fine bulls to the total kill. Frank Eaton got a five pointer and Jack Pelissier a yearling spike bull in the box canyon below the second drift fence about three miles up Wolf Canyon. Bob Gaskell and Jim Niner scored early in the season with a pair of six point bulls from the aspen pocket above the cave in upper South Red Canyon.

As the Fifties ended the people—the family, the dudes and the employees—ebbed and flowed. Old ones lingered and then passed on and new ones stepped in to take their place. But through it all, Eatons' Ranch remained essentially the same. It was larger than the sum of its parts.

CHAPTER 9

The Sixties

Operations and Improvements

Just like with previous generations, Eaton dudes continued to thirst for information about "what's going on at the Ranch." Old-timers, some of whom knew every inch of the place and every nook and cranny, were intensely interested in every detail. Angela Buell had never failed to disappoint *WN* readers on this score, and neither did the new editor, Ed Cattrell, as the decade of the 1960s began. It was a time-honored formula. Why change?

In the February 1960 issue, he provided the following:

In the big summer dining room, all is quiet. Back during January, however, the sounds of activity were ever present for the dining room rattled with the thump of hammers and the rasp of saws from morning 'til night as Harry and Clarence put in its new acoustical-tile ceiling. Tommy Butler then spent four days, up-and-down a stepladder, making sure all of the new light fixtures were hung in exactly the right places. Next, the whisper of Jimmy Parkinson's and Art Steil's brushes told that the dining room was receiving a new coat of paint. It is a light airy shade of green that brightens up the walls and compliments the deep warm tones of the dark natural woodwork. Patty Eaton, Anna Butler, and Nancy Ferguson were engrossed many long hours over drapery samples before coming up with just the right one, which provides a finishing touch for the new color scheme. Eaton dudes will now be greeted and served by the "girls in yellow" in a brighter, quieter, and more restful dining room when summer returns to the Ranch country.

As trivial as some of the reports are, they collectively provide a continuous chronicle of life at Eatons' Ranch. There was more to come in the next ten years, some of which is illustrated here:

1961
November

Early in October, the yearlings that had summered on the Big Horn Mountain permit, and the heifers that summer at Munson's, were shipped. George, Jerry, Bob, Billy and T. J. Ferguson drove the cattle to Ranchester, where they were loaded on the train for Illinois. Roy, Nan and Wendy cooked a picnic lunch for the riders and the ones who joined the party for lunch on Tongue River. Of course, Bill and Patty were there, as well as the Fergusons. Angela Buell came out from Sheridan for lunch and to see the cattle weighed...

...Bill and Patty Eaton, who have lived in the Antler cabin

on The Pike since 1929, are just about ready to move into their new quarters on the north corner of the first floor in the main ranch house. Aunt Mame's rooms, which Honora Schlegel has occupied since she has been at the ranch, and the nurse's room adjoining it, are being remodeled into an attractive and modern apartment for the senior Eatons.

1962
March

Among the other jobs around the Ranch, the boys are cutting out napkin rings in the shop on days it's too cold or stormy to work outside. These will be painted, and then decorated by Nan Wertman before the dudes start arriving this summer. The decorating job will have to wait until Nan and Roy return from Florida the end of this month.

Although it is only March, everyone is thinking about the coming summer and all the jobs that must be done before its arrival. Jane is busy mending, making new curtains and slipcovers, trying to catch up with all the sewing chores that cannot be done in the summer. Dorothy Duncan has already ordered seeds for the garden...

John Shreve, who took Ike Needen's place at the Lower Ranch, is busy feeding cattle every day, and it won't be long before the baby calves start arriving. Then George and Bob will be riding the creek pasture every day to check on the new arrivals....

1963
November

Early in September, the main bunch of horses went to Echeta to winter pasture. Nan and Roy were the cooks, and Shorty, Chip, Billy, Bob Ewan, Chuck Silveson and Adair

Jameson drove the horses...

The cattle were shipped late in October, driven to Ranchester where they were weighed and loaded on the cars for feeders in Illinois. This year we had more riders than usual with the cattle—Shorty, Bob, Wilbur Pallesen, Frank and Kathy, Billy and T. J., Colin and B. G. Jameson, S. J. Wright and Dr. Charlie Hansberger all rode and Jimmer Krewatch had to make two trips with the truck to haul the horses back to the Ranch. Jimmer was here last August with the Keen Butchers, and returned in September to work at the corral for a while and then went to the Hosford Ranch at Birney, Montana, to help with the fall cattle work. Nan and Roy cooked for the riders...

In November 1963, Nancy Ferguson became the editor of *WN* and, without skipping a beat, kept to the traditional mold of *WN*.

1964
April

...Wilbur rides every day to count the new calves and John Shreve and his helper are still feeding the cows and yearlings every morning. Frank and George have a bunch of horses out in Chocolate Drop pasture that they are feeding, and Roy is busy in the shop finishing some tables and benches to put in the cabins next summer. During the winter, Frank and S. J. and Wilbur have been repairing and repainting what white gates they could bring into the shop, and Kathy has been stenciling the numbers on them, so this summer most of the gates will be easier to find and are numbered to match the numbers on the trail maps we have in the office. Roy sanded the living room floors in the ranch house before he and Nan left for Florida, and Jimmie Parkinson came out to finish them, making the living rooms look much brighter...

1964
November

Early in September, Wilbur, Monty, Bill and Ed Neville trailed the main bunch of horses to Echeta, with Roy and Nan driving the jeeps and doing the cooking. Shorty started with them but his horse fell with him the first morning and broke his ankle. He's getting along fine now—the cast came off the other day—and is keeping his eye on the horses at Echeta with Clint's help. Clint is also breaking colts down there.

1965
May

Here at the Ranch, everyone is busy getting ready for the summer season. Anna Butler is supervising the household and laundry departments, while the girls are busy cleaning cabins and washing curtains and rugs. Roy and Clarence are putting in some new showers and doing general repair work, while Tommy Butler is busy every minute with the lights and the plumbing. ...George and the boys have been fixing fence, repairing reservoirs, and hauling away the winter's accumulation of leaves and branches. Jim Dawson is back, and has the horses we are using now all fitted with new shoes, and he'll be ready for a steady job when the main cavvy comes up from Echeta early in June.

1966
March

The water in Wolf Creek has been so low this winter that we've had trouble keeping our light plant going, so now the big project is putting in a new power line from Fay's Cabin to the Ranch and switching over to AC current. Roy and Frank have been busy taking out old motors and getting everything ready for the new motors when the power line is finished. The linemen have found the digging slow as the rocks grow big and plentiful in the foothill country of the Big Horns, but we hope to have the power in by the first of May.

(Note: For the first time, Eatons' Ranch had commercial power provided by Montana Dakota Utilities. The old system, the wooden pipe that brought water from Wolf Creek to the power plant had served the Ranch well since about 1923. Today, long segments of the wooden pipe and the stone house that housed the power plant remain as a monument to past days.)

1966
November

Early in September, the main bunch of horses was driven to Echeta, and Shorty has moved back to the Bar Eleven to take care of them this winter. This year's crop of colts has been trucked to the Ranch, and the boys are busy halter breaking them. The first week of October, the beef cattle were driven to Leonard Graham's ranch on Little Tongue, where they were weighed and loaded on trucks to go to market...

1967

Winter is a quiet time at Eatons' Ranch, but everyone manages to keep busy, with thoughts of the summer to come. One of the biggest chores is getting the ice up for use next summer, and Roy and Frank keep a close watch on the ice pond near the Lower Ranch for weeks ahead. After the water is turned into the pond in the late fall and it freezes over, all the first ice has to be floated off, along with the leaves and twigs that have collected in it. Then after it freezes over again, the snow has to be scraped off after each snowfall, and each Chinook postpones the icing time a little more. When, at last, it is thick enough to cut, a crew has to be found to help put it up. This year, we were lucky and finished the job in two days, just in time for Frank and Kathy and Dick to take off for the Denver Stock Show and a little vacation.

After the icing was finished, there were still plenty of other chores to be done. Besides feeding the horses that have been wintering here, Frank and Bob, along with Roy and Ken, have been building new gates for the corrals and also cutting out napkin rings for next year. Nan and Kathy have already decorated four hundred for use next summer, and still have another hundred to do...

1968
May

Jane retired last winter, so Vyrlee will be running the laundry this summer. However, since the laundry equipment is getting old, and parts are practically impossible to get, we have made arrangements with the laundry in Sheridan to have them do all the guest laundry. It will be sent to town and they will deliver it to the Ranch twice a week, and we are also getting some new coin-operated machines in the guest laundry so after June 15, there will be no guest laundry done at the Ranch. We are sorry about this, but with the old equipment and the problem of getting laundry help, we will only be able to do the Ranch laundry from now on.

1969
December

...For the first time in many years, the main waterline and even the wooden pipeline froze solid, and this meant that Frank

and Dale spent many hours hauling water in barrels from the lower ranch until we were able to put a pump in the creek and pump water to the main boiler hoses. When the pipeline did get thawed out, Roy found broken pipes everywhere, and it was a rush to get the pipes repaired and the cabins opened for the first dudes.

It was a busy summer for everyone, particularly in August, when the Ranch was practically overflowing with dudes. A Western Airlines strike at the end of July made things most confusing on the Ranch, but with charter flights, rented cars and Don Singer making trips to Billings and Casper, everyone got in and out of the Ranch practically on schedule...

There was no question about it. There were always challenges at Eatons' Ranch. Often, the place was definitely not for the faint hearted.

Family

At the beginning of the sixties, Bill and Patty Eaton were the last of the "old guard" of the Eaton family left at Eatons' Ranch. By the end of the decade, only Patty remained.

In 1960, Bill was seventy years old. He was still a presence at the corral but had begun to slow down when medical problems caught up with him. In 1963, he had a minor stroke. As Patty described it, "He pretty well recovered from it. He had gotten along pretty well until he broke his hip (in August 1966). They pinned the hip, and he was getting along on crutches."

The combination of the stroke and broken hip pretty much made Bill a partial invalid. Patty said that:

... His mind was perfectly all right and it didn't affect his speech like it does so many. He did have more or less paralysis on one side. He went over to the Gottsche Rehabilitation center twice and it helped him an awful lot...

Nancy Ferguson, Bill's daughter, made little mention of Bill's condition in *WN*, except in March 1967, when she noted:

Big Bill and Patty Eaton are fine, though Big Bill doesn't get out much. They enjoyed having all the grandchildren and the great-grandchildren home for the holidays, and are looking forward to seeing them again during Easter vacation.

During that time, Patty devoted herself to Bill's care. When she died, many years later, her tribute noted several of her outstanding qualities including, "...Patty lavishing tender devoted care that has become legendary on her husband Big Bill in his last years..."

Bill died on December 20, 1968, and Patty described his final days:

...He didn't have another stroke until shortly before he died. He had a massive stroke and became unconscious. He lived from Tuesday until Friday when he died, but he never opened his eyes...

Big Bill was gone. He was seventy-eight years old. According to Patty, Bill's ashes were scattered over the Ranch from an airplane flown by Kelly Howie and Curly Witzel, both aviators and former Eaton employees. When Kelly and Curly were at altitude, Curly opened the window to empty Bill's ashes out of the urn, but the ashes blew back in and all over Curly. Apparently, Curly, who had been the victim of so many of Bill's pranks, said words to the effect, "That damn Bill Eaton. He got the last laugh."

Angela Buell came out of retirement to compose a special *WN* to honor Bill Eaton. It was issued in March 1969, and said, in part:

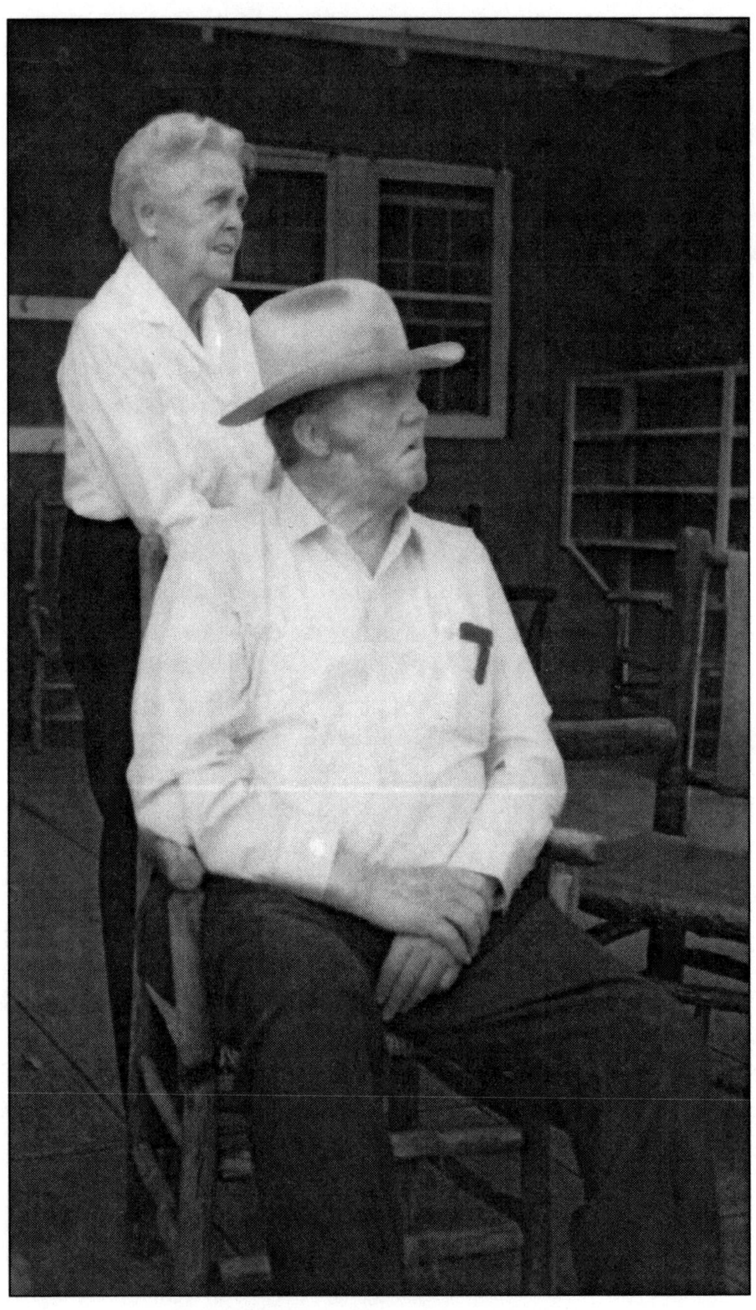

Bill and Patty Eaton the month before Bill died.
Courtesy of Eatons' Ranch.

His father, affectionately known as "Uncle Alden" to generations of Eatonites, always called him "William," occasionally, his mother (Aunt Mame) did so, as well. His grandchildren and great-grandchildren and many others, including the small fry on the Ranch, addressed him as "Big Bill," while to his old friends and contemporaries he was simply "Bill" or "Bill Eaton" whose father and uncles many years ago established and made famous the Ranch where he lived throughout practically his entire lifetime.

And Bill Eaton was well known in his own right, not only in his home community but also throughout Wyoming and the West. He was not a show-off but in his younger days, when sufficiently urged, he would get out his ninety-foot rope (approximately thirty-five feet is standard for ranch work) and lasso seven or eight cowboys riding abreast as they galloped past him as fast as their spurred horses could go. That required a strength, which was embodied in a powerful outdoor man better than six feet tall and possessing great skill with the cowboy's tool, a throw rope.

In the earlier days, when jobs were scarce, many a cowboy rode into Eatons' Ranch broke and hungry and they were never turned away by the three brothers who founded the Ranch or by those who succeeded them. There were always shelter and supper for a driftin' cowboy and feed for his weary horse. Likely as not, if Bill couldn't give him a job (times were often hard and cash scarce on Eatons' Ranch) he slipped the price of a bed and a meal into the cowboy's pocket after breakfast next morning when he mounted his horse to ride on. So throughout the country the Western ranch boys spoke of Bill Eaton as "The Cowboy's Friend," and over the mantel in the Ranch living room hangs today a bronze plaque presented to him a number of years ago which embodies those words.

Thousands of dudes have sought the famed hospitality of Eatons' Ranch since 1879, and during his lifetime everyone, of course, knew Bill Eaton. Practically all guests at the Ranch came from the East and Bill was not always at ease with them, but he relaxed in the company of Western people and particularly the cowboys with whom he talked HORSE for hours in the Wolves Club when the day's work was done. There they roped, blindfolded, saddled, mounted, spurred, fanned, rode and re-rode old Kangaroo and Banjo and Funeral Wagon, and in retrospect some of the tales grew a bit tall with the telling. Many a little field mouse has paused in the warmth of the Wolves Club on a cold winter evening to listen. Then, shaking with laughter, has scampered back through the hole in the chinking (whence he came) when one of the boys spied him and threw a boot in his direction. Sure Shot and Kite and Soapsuds and Maybe So and many others lived far beyond their brief careers as bucking horses in the tales told around the coal stove in the Wolves Club.

Bill left us on December 20, but not without warning. He had passed his seventy-eighth birthday due, in great part, to the devotion and care of his wife Patty when he became a partial invalid several years ago. But we do not think of him in that role. We remember him as a big powerful man, typical of his time and the songs and stories of the West, a man who loved cattle and horses, his outdoor life, and his friends the cowboys. Though he was reticent with strangers, Bill Eaton was not a man anyone met and forgot.

We have written of other remarkable individuals connected with Eatons' Ranch whose combined efforts the past ninety years have produced this outstanding organization. And we say of Bill Eaton—as we have said of others—his personal niche will not be filled. However, in the ten short years which now remain until the centennial of the Ranch can be celebrated, succeeding generations will have developed further, and for many years to come there are sure to be Eatons and their friends riding their horses over the beautiful hills and valley and mountains of Wolf Creek in Wyoming, that country along the Big Horns beloved by many, many people and particularly Bill Eaton.

Patty Eaton survived her husband, by another fourteen years.

Throughout the decade, *WN* continued to inform the readers about the "comings and goings and doings" of the Eaton extended family:

1960
February

...Frank has returned to Sheridan College for the second semester of the school year, and Jack Pelissier is Marine Corps bound in the near future....

1960
November

Early in October, George Shorty, Bob, Patty B., Billy and T. J. drove the yearlings to Ranchester to be weighed and loaded on the train for the feedlots. Patty B. and Billy had made the trip before, but it was the first time for T. J., and, in spite of the long ride, he insisted that he did not get tired.

The late Fall finds most of the Ranch family at home—The Eatons, the Butlers, Roy, Nan and Wendy Wertman, the Fergusons, Aunt Minnie Reid, Fay Alderson, Frank Eaton, George Gentry, Shorty Enderlie, Art Steil, Emma Trouchon, Cal Kelham, Ed Neville, Bob Gaskell, Barbara Saunders, Minnie Lloyd and Dorothy Duncan. Susan Ferguson and Jaci Eaton are living in Sheridan while going to high school, but they do come home on weekends...

1961
May

...The marriage of Miss Kathleen Henry (our last summer's Ranch nurse) to Frank Eaton was the highlight of social activity at the Ranch last winter. The wedding took place

in Sheridan on December 28. The Eatons are back at Wolf and are now living in Pike No. 5…

Last December 3, Aunt Minnie Reid (Note: Aunt Mame's sister who followed her to Wolf Creek from North Dakota.) *passed away at the age of ninety-two. She was well known and well loved by many, many Ranch friends, and the living rooms of the Ranch house are not quite the same without her presence.*

"Bill Eaton Day" has been made an annual affair at the August steer and calf roping contests held on the rodeo grounds of the Kelly Howie ranch at Big Horn, Wyoming. (Note: The first event was held in 1960 and continued for many years. It was a great honor for Bill Eaton and a generous gesture from Kelly Howie, a former Eaton employee.) *A beautiful hand-tooled saddle is presented to the winner of the steer roping. Patty B. Ferguson won the girl's barrel race again this year. The gate receipts are for the benefit of the Wyoming Crippled Children Organization.*

1963
January

The Ranch family is all home now, except for Susan Ferguson, who is at Monticello College, and Jaci Eaton and Patty B. Ferguson, who are staying in Sheridan while going to high school. Early in September, Tommy and Nancy

Ferguson drove Susan to college, and took a roundabout way home to stop off in Rochester, Minnesota, for a few days to visit the Schusters and Harwiks. In early November, Frank and Kathy Eaton, Dick Bacon, Bob and Linda Gaskell and Patty B. Ferguson went to St. Louis for Jack Pelissier's and Sophie Shepley's wedding. It was sort of like old home week there, with all the Ranch friends in St. Louis, and others who came for the wedding, besides several carloads from the Sheridan community.

Fay Alderson stayed in her cabin by the creek until almost New Years, due to the mild winter we've had so far. She has now moved to Sheridan where she'll stay until spring and not have to chop holes in the ice on the creek to get her water every morning.

(Note: Auntie Fay Alderson, Patty Eaton's sister, lived at Wolf for many more years until she eventually entered a nursing home in Sheridan and died at the age of ninety-one in December 1977. Her cabin, which later generations called "Auntie Fay's cabin" was known in earlier years, when Auntie Fays mother, Domo Alderson, lived there as "Domo's cabin." It still stands.)

1963
November

...Jaci and Susan are in Laramie at the University of Wyoming and Patty B. is in Sheridan in high school. Billy, J. T., and Wendy go to Wolf School, about five miles down the creek... and Robbie Gaskell is lonely until they get home in the afternoon. Bob and Lynda have moved up to the Ranch for the winter...

...Frank and Kathy Eaton, Tommy and Nancy Ferguson... will be leaving soon for Laramie and the Dude Rancher's convention...

...Nan and Roy will be at the Ranch until early March, when they will go to Florida to visit Nan's father for a month...

1964
November

Most of the Ranch family is still at home. Dorothy Duncan has moved to Sheridan for the winter and plans a trip to South America early next year. Susan is back at the University of Wyoming, Jaci is in Sheridan going to Sheridan Junior College, Billy is staying in Sheridan during the week going to Sheridan High School and Wendy and T. J. go to Wolf School every morning...

...Big Bill and Patty Eaton have a great-granddaughter, Juli Alderson Way, who lives in Laramie with her parents, Patty B. and Gary...

...Before Thanksgiving, Tom and Nancy Ferguson, Frank and Kathy Eaton and S. J. Wright will go to Helena, Montana, for the Dude Ranchers' Convention, leaving Dick Bacon to run the office and drive the school bus to Wolf School while they are gone.

1965
November

The Ranch family is pretty small now. Big Bill and Patty Eaton are in Thermopolis for three weeks, but will be home in time for Thanksgiving. Dorothy Duncan has gone to visit her family in Montana and Washington, and is planning a trip to Arizona in the late winter... The Butlers have no definite plans for the winter as yet, but will probably be taking a trip after the first of the year...The Wertmans, Fergusons, and Frank Eatons will probably be at the Ranch all winter. Frank and Kathy, Tom and Nancy and S. J. Wright will take a few days off before Thanksgiving to attend the Dude Ranchers' Convention in Cody...

...The Eaton grandchildren are well represented at the University of Wyoming this year—Susan Ferguson is a senior, Jaci Eaton a junior, and Patty B. Way is just starting her college career, and with taking care of Juli, the great-granddaughter, she is plenty busy...

Frank and Kathy Eaton confer during the morning saddling.
Photo by Arthur A. Dailey, Wolf, Wyoming.
Courtesy of Eatons' Ranch.

1966
March

...Bill and Patty Eaton took a short trip to Denver for a change of scenery and to give Jimmy Parkinson time to paint their apartment...

...Frank and Kathy took a short vacation in Billings last month, and the Fergusons plan to take a little time off in early June to go to Laramie for Susan's graduation from the university...

1966
November

Wendy and T. J. are back at school at Wolf School house. Bill Ferguson is in high school in Sheridan, but is commuting when the weather permits so he can help with the young horses after school and on weekends...

...Jaci Eaton was married to Doyl Fritz in late August, and they are living in Laramie, where Doyl is attending the university...

...Patty and Gary and Juli Way are back in Laramie, and Patty and Gary are both going to college again...

...Susan Ferguson is teaching high school in Fountain, Colorado, this year...

...Big Bill is home from the hospital after breaking his hip last August and he and Patty are both glad to be back at the Ranch

1967
November

Roy and Nan and Wendy Wertman and several friends spent the first part of the hunting season at the cow camp on Bear Creek, but the weather was too nice and warm for very good hunting this year, and not many elk or deer were killed here at the Ranch. Wendy had to miss a few days of school to go hunting, as she is a freshman in high school this year and spends the week in Sheridan, but is home every weekend. Bill Ferguson, a senior this year, drives back and forth to school in Sheridan unless the road gets too bad. T. J. is still going to Wolf School, about five miles down the creek from the Ranch. Jaci and Doyl Fritz and Patty and Gary, Juli and Jeff Way are back in Laramie, where Doyl and Gary are finishing their last year at the university. Susan Van Allen is teaching again in Fountain, Colorado, as John is in the Navy and won't be back in this country until next June.

1968
November

The Ranch family is pretty small this time of year. Of course, Big Bill and Patty Eaton, Frank and Kathy Eaton, Nan and Roy Wertman and Tommy and Nancy and T. J. Ferguson are here. Wendy Wertman goes to Sheridan High School, but spends her weekends at the Ranch. ...Sheri Fritz is also back at Laramie, working on her master's degree. Jaci and Doyl Fritz are at Tempe, Arizona, where Doyl is teaching and working on his Masters and Jaci is working in the university bookstore. Patty B. and Gary, Juli and Jeff Way and Allan Taggert are in Denver. Gary and Allan are going to the University of Colorado School of Medicine and Patty B. is doing secretarial work at one of the clinics at the school. Bill Ferguson decided he likes horses better than college, and is training racehorses at a ranch near Pueblo, Colorado. John and Susan Van Allen were here for a short visit and are now in Clinton, Iowa. John is out of the Navy and they plan to go back to Laramie second semester for some extra credits...

1969
November

Jaci and Doyl Fritz came back to the Ranch the first of August after Doyl got his Masters degree at Arizona State University, and aren't sure just where they will be living now. Patty and Gary Way were here with the children in June, and have been back for two weekends, but are still living in Denver where Gary is in his second year of medical school, along with Don Singer. Susan Van Allen taught at Wolf School for the last three months last spring, and then helped in the office until John finished school in Laramie, and they are now in Casper. John is working for Pacific Power and Light and Susan teaching school again...

...Bill Ferguson has gone back to Stewart's near Pueblo

and this year he took Sam Skiles with him and they are both breaking racehorses. They get to Denver every few weeks to visit the Ways and get their laundry done. Wendy Wertman and T. J. Ferguson are in high school in Sheridan this winter, Wendy a Junior and T. J. a Freshman...

By the end of the sixties, the fourth generation of the Eaton and Ferguson families had come of age and many of them were poised to take their respective places on the Eatons' Ranch management team.

Dudes

In the 1960s, "dude news" in *WN* was not near as exhaustive as when Angela Buell was the editor. Nevertheless, when Nancy Ferguson took over as editor she still made sure that the activities of certain dudes were included in *WN* and she kept up the tradition of recognizing the old-timers and their families who had a long history with Eatons' Ranch:

1960
February

At this point, we wish to thank A. A. "Pete" Dailey, whose fine photographs again add greatly to the pages of this Wranglin' Notes. *Pete's pictures have been dressing up this little publication for more years than he probably cares to remember and we are always happy to include them.*

1960
November

This season of the year...finds Eatons' with only a few guests. Those who arrived late in the summer and during the first weeks of autumn, and who stayed on to enjoy the pleasant riding of late September and October, included: Dr. And Mrs. Louie Martin, Mrs. E. G. Clapp, Mr. and Mrs. Peter Rosengarten, Commander and Mrs. Richard Knight, Mr. and Mrs. Walter Stamy, Mr. and Mrs. Oliver Rutledge, A. A. "Pete" Dailey and Mary Dailey, Mrs. Frank Gilbreth, Mrs. Ab Lampson, Mrs. Caroline Gade, Mr. and Mrs. Earl Thompson, and Dr. Charles Harnsberger. The arrival of October also found John Leahy, Dorothy Douglas, Katie Schiller, Dorothy Shipley, Buddie Jenkins, Dora Woodruff, Dorothy Bryan, Marian Hosford, and Elizabeth and Andrew Hull here at the Ranch.

1961
May

Spring rolled in through the main gate a few weeks ago. That means, of course, that the Big Doin's, the summer dude season, is dead ahead and will be here in just a few short weeks. We're happy to say that the 1961 season's early arrivals have begun to return to the valley of Wolf Creek already. Dorothy Bryan and Marian Hosford arrived at the Ranch in mid-April, and Katie Schiller, the 22nd of the month. Buddie Jenkins is due to arrive just before this issue of Wranglin' Notes *is mailed. May will bring Andrew and Elizabeth Hull, Dorothy Douglas, Dora Woodruff, and John Leahy back to the Ranch. Ed and Hazel Brach are arriving in late May or early June...*

1961
November

Speaking of poker, (and we were a few paragraphs back), May Kohler of St. Louis, Missouri, entertained Dottie Burns (Note: Former Eaton dude) *of Mead Creek Ranch and several of her friends with a lively poker party in the main ranch house while May was vacationing here during September…*

Fred Schuster of Rochester, Minnesota, Earl Thompson and Ed Guerin took advantage of the fine weather after the equinox storm to fish the Tongue River near Dayton and Ranchester. They caught some nice ones…

Believe it or not, Buddie Jenkins, Dora Woodruff and Dorothy Douglas, all residents of Wolf, have started to play Gin. Anyone looking for pigeons?...

Caroline Gade of Concord, Massachusetts. arrived in mid-September to be with us for a couple of months and look after her horses…

Katie Schiller of Palm Springs, California—and Wolf—took her annual post-season ride up Soldier Creek, around Walker Prairie to Big Bend, and down Wolf Canyon to the ranch early in September—a trip of a good twenty mountain-trail miles. Christine Smyth of Boston, Mass., Dorothy Duncan and Ed Guerin went along to keep her company.

Dorothy Douglas, who has been making her headquarters at the ranch from May to November the past few years, left during October for her winter home in Brooklyn, New York. Dorothy has been coming to the ranch nearly every year since 1918…

1963
April

Last summer we had our first fifth-generation dudes, when Stan and Fay Rinehart brought their grandchildren to the

Ranch, Jeff and Nora Huvelle and Debbie and Rickie Rinehart. We've had several fourth-generation families on the Ranch, but this is the first time we have had the fifth generation and we're very proud of this record.

1963
November

Pete and Mary Dailey were back again in September, and Pete took a lot of pictures that we'll use in future issues of Wranglin' Notes...

Chuck and Betty Silverson arrived in time for Chuck to get a few rides in before he started the one hundred mile trip to Echeta with the horses. Frances and Ollie Rutledge were back again, and Ollie helped bring the cattle off the mountain from summer pasture in September. Jack Quinn came back for a couple of weeks to deliver his cattle that he had been running during the summer on a ranch near Banner. Charlie Crowley was here for ten days...his last visit was in 1941.

1964
April

It won't be long before some of the old-timers start arriving. Dr. S. J. Wright has been here all winter, so we really can't count him as an early arrival, but Katie Schiller will be along the middle of this month, and in early May, Dora Woodruff and Elizabeth and Andrew Hull will be back, followed by Buddie Jenkins and Dorothy Douglas a little later in the month...

1966
November

...We are planning for the usual number of congenial dudes this summer, old-timers, newcomers, single guests, couples, larger groups. There will be many families, some of them mothers and fathers, who remember the Ranch when they themselves were teenagers and are now introducing their children to the Eaton Family. One couple, Alex and Jim Hammer, who spent their honeymoon here, plan to return this June to celebrate their fiftieth anniversary...

1966
November

...Once again we were visited by some fifth generation guests when Alan Rinehart brought two of his grandchildren to the Ranch...

...The dudes who stayed on and the ones who came out for the nice weather had lots of good days for riding. The Silversons and Rutledges were back again in September, along with Christine Smyth and Bill and Ray Hoagland from Boston. Mary Dailey stayed until the end of September this year, and the Schusters and Kingsburys came from Rochester, Minnesota, late in the month. Fred and Put enjoyed the fishing as well as the riding while they were here. George Webster came back for a couple of weeks, and spent most of his time fishing, bringing in some good catches as usual, in spite of the low water in Wolf Creek...

1967
November

...Pete Dailey, who takes all the pictures for the Wranglin' Notes *and our postcards, took some beautiful colored photographs this year on the Ranch and in the mountains. Our first big snowfall of the year didn't come until the first of November, so the colors stayed a long time. The snowstorm did give Pete an opportunity to get some winter scenes around the Ranch for us to use on our Christmas cards.*

...Other old-timers were Mr. and Mrs. E. V. Thompson who were here for two weeks in late September—they first came to the Ranch in 1912...

1968
November

... Dorothy Douglas stayed three weeks longer than she had planned—her horse fell with her the day before she was to leave and broke her hand. However, the cast didn't keep her from playing cards any chance she had.

...Mary Dailey also came back for a week to visit Pete and to see the Rutledges and Silversons while they were here this fall.

...Other regular fall visitors were Fred and Marge Schuster, Bill and Ray Hoagland, Colin and Adair Jameson, Margaret Lewis and Frances Ferguson. Fred and Bill did a lot of fishing while they were here this fall, and report that there are still plenty of fish in Wolf Creek. Jim and Alex Hammer were here again this year, and Dr. Charlie Harnesberger paid us a visit after an absence of several years. Neil and Jo McKearnan were back—they hadn't been to the Ranch since 1951.

Employees

The decade of the 1960s was truly a time of transition in the employee ranks. Some old guard employees, who had been the mainstay of the Eaton operation for decades, moved on. And as they faded into the past, a new generation of employees appeared. Many of them were members of the fourth Eaton generation, who took their places in the Eaton family enterprise. Like everything else at Eatons' Ranch, it was reported in *WN*:

1960
February

Bob is at the Bar Eleven, helping Reid and Guy and riding a few colts on the side...

January thirty-first saw Tommy and Anna Butler off on the first lap of their trip, which, after an extensive month of motoring through the East, includes a two month tour of the Continent. The Butlers are flying to Shannon from New York late this month and are spending two weeks in Ireland visiting Tommy's relatives. Next, a peek at Scotland is on the agenda, before they travel south to London where they will meet Dora Woodruff, who is accompanying them on the remainder of their tour around Europe. Tommy and Anna are due back to the Ranch by mid-May, and Dora is planning to return to Wolf around June 15...

1960
Spring

Permanent members of the cast include, of course, the Ranch Family and staff. George Gentry is corral boss and in his department the usual number of corral boys will be on hand to help out. This year's corral crew will include several new faces. The new boys are Jack Laurie from Miles City, Montana, Kendy Schiffer from Buffalo, Wyoming, Rob Johnson from over Kirby, Montana way and Dennis Hall and Bud Roberts, two Colorado boys. Wranglers from previous years who will be back at the corral this year are Frank Eaton (who decided that horses and saddles fit his nature much better than the adding machines and typewriters of the office), Pete DuBois, Bry Sheedy, Bob Gaskell and Ed Kelly. Jerry Meyer is again riding colts and Roy Wertman and Shorty Enderle are taking care of pack and all-day trips. Rogers Harwood will soon be setting up shop and getting the forge hot up in the blacksmith shop. In an operation involving 350 head of horses—that all need to be shod every five weeks or so—a good blacksmith is a mighty handy person to have around. Rogers was the Ranch blacksmith during the summers of 1954 through 1957, and we are glad to have him back at the Ranch again this year.

1960
November

...The horses were trucked to the Bosler Ranch near Laramie (about three hundred and twenty miles south of here) this fall. Due to last summer's drought conditions at Echeta, there was just not enough grass to keep the entire cavvy of three hundred and fifty head in top condition. Next spring, the horses will be trailed back to the Ranch, as in the past. This trip will be more than triple the usual distance, however, so we seriously doubt that Big Bill will receive the usual number of requests from ambitious dudes to help bring the cavvy back to the Ranch.

Bob Gaskell will be "babysitting" the cavvy through the winter months and we are confident that he will do his very best to see that all of the horses will come through the winter and will again be waiting at the picket-line to carry their riders over the trails when summer returns to the Ranch country. (*Note: The horses were trucked back to Wolf in the spring because Bob and Bill Eaton were unable to find enough grass for the horses to eat along the proposed route.*) Also, Reid Kochel and Pat Ryan will be keeping a watchful eye on the comparatively few horses that will winter at the Bar Eleven Ranch at Echeta…

1961
November

A change in the Ranch organization has…taken place down at our twenty thousand-acre Bar Eleven Ranch at Echeta, Wyoming, where Eaton horses are accustomed to spend the winter. Reid Kochel, who has been on Bill Eaton's staff since 1925 and the winter manager of the Echeta ranch since 1938, decided to take it easy and retired in October. Shorty Enderle, who has worked with Bill Eaton and George Gentry at the Wolf ranch for over twenty years, has succeeded him. Bob Gaskell will be helping Shorty at Echeta…

(*Note: When Bob was at Echeta, Bill Eaton wanted him to come back to Wolf and train a racehorse that he wanted to enter in the Futurity at the Fairgrounds. Bill kept calling him at Echeta, but the boys were always out riding and didn't answer the telephone. Finally, Bob got a letter from Bill that simply said, "I think you'd better get up here."*)

1963
January

Shortly after Thanksgiving, George Gentry left for California to spend the holidays with his sisters. He planned his trip so he would be in Los Angeles in time to attend the National Rodeo Finals, which he says were wonderful and spoiled him for any other rodeos. He hurried home right after New Years, and is now anxiously watching the thickness of the ice on the ice pond, hoping we can put up the yearly ice crop. Dorothy Duncan moved to Sheridan in October, visited a sister in Montana then went on to Washington to spend Christmas with other relatives...

1963
November

Early in September, the main bunch of horses went to Echeta to winter pasture. Nan and Roy were the cooks, and Shorty, Chip, Billy, Bow Ewan, Chuck Silverson and Adair Jameson drove the horses...

...Bob and Lynda (Gaskell) have moved up to the Ranch for the winter... (Note: Bob married Lynda and became one of the first corral boys to be married.)...

...George is thinking about going to California again for the holidays to visit his sisters, though the Gentry clan did have a reunion at the Ranch this fall when his three sisters and his brother, Bill, all came to visit him...

1964
April

Dorothy Duncan will be moving out from Sheridan soon, where she has been spending the winter with a short vacation in Arizona and Colorado. She is anxious to get her garden started, but will have to wait for some more sunshine before she can start planting...

1964
November

George and the boys who are still here have been busy with the cattle work, fixing fence, and the many other chores that must be done every fall. Soon this year's colts will be brought up from Echeta for the winter, and the boys will be busy halter breaking them in the corral in back of the barn...

1965
May

Shorty and Clint report that the horses have wintered well at Echeta, and are now fattening up on the green grass. At the Lower Ranch, John Shreve and his men have been working from daylight 'til dark trying to finish the spring farming that the snow and rainstorms delayed...

About once a week during the summer, Howard Hall is the gathering place for all ages for dancing. Roy Wertman called the square dances and "Oh Johnny's" and there are also round dances....

1965
November

Early in September, the main bunch of horses were trailed to Echeta for the winter, with Shorty, Cal, Bill and Bruce King and Joan Laverty and Judy Thum driving them, and Roy drove the pickup and did the cooking...

1966
March

After over fifty years at the Ranch, Tommy and Anna Butler retired on the first of January this year. Tommy first came to the Ranch in 1910 and Anna came in 1914, so after all those years of service, we realize they need a rest, but they both will be greatly missed by all the Ranch family, as well as by their many friends who have been dudes here. We are happy that they have decided to retire in Sheridan, where they will still be part of the family, and will be nearby if we have to call on them for advice at any time. Their cabin will be waiting for them anytime this summer that they might want to come out to the Ranch and spend a few days visiting with their old friends...

Tommy left several legacies at Eatons' Ranch. Frank Eaton still laughs when he talks about Tommy and the showers. It seems that when the Ranch first began to install showers in some of the bathrooms, Tommy, as usual, took on the task. He certainly got the job done. However, Tommy was a very small man, and he installed the showerheads at a height that suited his stature. For a normal size person, taking a shower in a "Butler shower" required some creative movements. Most people had to bend down double to wash their hair. One rather tall dude once complained that he couldn't get wet above his belly button.

1966
November

...The Ranch saw several changes this year since Tommy and Anna Butler retired and moved to Sheridan, though they came out frequently to visit us. George Gentry was in California all summer, but returned in September to help with the fall work.

(Note: This was the first summer that George was not present in the corral since he joined Eatons' Ranch in 1919.)

Tommy and Anna Butler after over fifty years service to Eatons' Ranch.
Courtesy of Eatons' Ranch.

Times were changing, and George believed he could no longer command the respect of the corral crew. All the old-timers were gone, and Big Bill was no longer active. Frank Eaton was now the corral boss and other family members, like Billy and T. J. Ferguson, were beginning their careers at the Ranch. In fact, Bob Gaskell, who worked at Eatons' for seven years, remembers that George told him at one point he should probably look for other work because "there's too many family members here now." George went to California to live with his sisters for a while and then returned to Eatons' periodically for a couple of years to help with winter work but never worked in the corral again. Eventually, he moved Sheridan where he took up residence in the Western Hotel and then was later admitted to the Veterans Hospital (VA) in Sheridan, where he spent his last days. His situation was sad and so Doyl and Jaci Eaton Fritz often picked George up at the VA and took him on little road trips just to brighten his day. Bob Gaskell once picked George up because he wanted to get George's opinion about a horse. Unfortunately, George had become almost blind. George stroked the horse and rubbed its head, but told Bob, "I just can't see it well enough to give you an opinion."

> *...Dorothy Duncan also retired this fall, and has moved to the house she bought in Sheridan, but she has promised to come out in the spring to help plant the garden. We will surely miss her touch with the flowers next summer, as well as the picnics she took to the mountains and her fishing trips. We're sure she will be out for visits next summer, however.*

(Note: Frank Eaton has humorous memories of Dorothy Duncan as well. Dorothy was very proud and very protective of her flower garden. One morning she accosted Frank:"Your corral boys have been dumping beer on my flowers!" Frank replied, "My boys would never dump beer. They drink it." "I mean used beer," Dorothy retorted.)

George Gentry surveys the scene from the barn.
Courtesy of Eatons' Ranch.

1967
November

About the middle of September, Shorty, Bill Ferguson, Bobby King and Tommy Alderson took the main bunch of horses to Echeta. Chuck Silverson and Tom Riddick rode with them the first day, and George Gentry went along in the pickup to do the cooking for them. On the last day, Jack and T. J. and Bill Skiles and his son went to Echeta to help pull the shoes on all the horses before they were turned out for the winter.

1968
May

Now that school is nearly out, more employees will be arriving and there will be a lot of new faces this year. Doyl and Big John will be back at the corral again, and along with Frank, Billy, and Jack will be the only old ones there. Fauntella and Kathy will be back again as maids, and Diana King, Patty Clay, Gayla Yester and Kathy Lepper will be back in the dining room. Frank Eggers is back again this year as chef, after a couple of year's absence. Jaci will be in the coffee shop again this year and Shari in the office. Patty and Gary Way will both be working at the Ranch this summer—Gary at the corral and Patty helping Kathy...

Life went on at Eatons' Ranch, same as ever, for the Eaton family, dudes and employees.

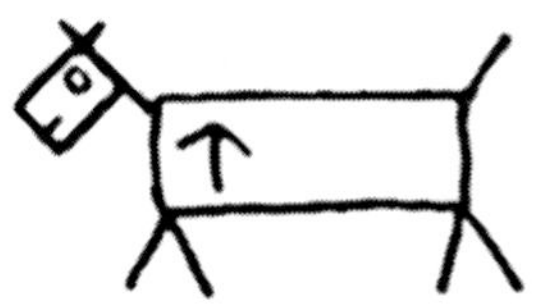

Corporate Matters

When Tommy Butler retired in 1966, he was vice president of the Eaton Brothers Corporation, a position he had held since 1943. Tommy stepped down as vice president, though he remained a director. Twenty-three years later, the position was vacant again. Frank Eaton, aged thirty, the last male heir with the Eaton name, assumed his place on the board. At the same time, Tommy Ferguson was elected as secretary and his wife, Nancy, treasurer. The slate of officers of the Eaton Brothers, Inc., board of directors was now truly a family affair.

When Bill Eaton died in 1968, more changes on the board were in order. Nancy Ferguson was elected vice president, Tommy Ferguson treasurer, and Frank's wife, Kathy, secretary. Frank Eaton, age thirty-three, was elected president of the corporation.

This line up of officers remained unchanged until 1983. After that, there were some slight shifts in officer positions, but Frank Eaton remained as president. Forty years later, in 2010, Frank Eaton still serves as president.

CHAPTER 10

Eatons'—Forty Years Later (2010)

Eatons' is still Eatons'.
It's remarkable how it remains the same.

The Place

Today, anyone who revisits Eatons' Ranch after a long absence will be relieved to arrive at the main gate and find that it's just as they remembered it. And as the visitor drives up the road to the main Ranch, memories will sweep back in waves. They will remember the long meandering road to the main ranch and the middle place along the way where the old fish hatchery used to be, where Billy and Karen Ferguson live now. And as they drive farther, they will remember the wooded areas interspersed by clearings of pastureland, and they will remember the gurgle of Wolf Creek when they drive over the bridge.

As they drive farther, they will recognize the big house on the right, where the Fleming and Ferguson families used to live and where Jeff Way and his family now reside. And they will remember Gentry Field off to the right. As they approach the internal gate—the stone pillars—they will recognize that as well, and perhaps stop to drink in the once familiar scene ahead. It's all the same as ever.

The main stone Ranch house, with its imposing lawn, is straight ahead. And nearby is the Birdcage—what used to be the platform on which passengers would disembark from the Eaton stagecoach. Off to the right is Howard Hall that has been there since 1911. The road winds between them up to the Ranch office and beyond that are the big white saddle barn with the wooden horse painted over the door, and the corrals and the blacksmith shop and the garages and other outbuildings. And across from the saddle barn is the Wolves Club. It hasn't changed.

A meander down through the cabins is equally reassuring. Nothing seems different. True, some of the cabins have been remodeled, others expanded with additional rooms and decks and there is a new one to replace the last one to burn down (Little Antlers in 2006), but that is the only new cabin built since 1954. Eatons' is careful to insure that all work on the cabins blends in with the traditional Eatons' look. The sense and feel of the place is unchanged.

Equally familiar is the way the place operates. Three meals a day in the dining room at specified hours. If you're late, you don't eat. And the food is good, but not fancy, just as always. And people do not dress for dinner. They never have, and they still don't. It is simple and informal. Still.

Friendly hospitality permeates the place—the waitresses, the cabin girls, the corral boys, the office staff, the other guests. It's an Eatons' hallmark.

And you still sign up at the Wolves Club to ride, and if it's your first day, you will have your saddle fitted on Big Brownie and assigned a horse that is best suited to your ability. As always, the corral staff will have your safety in mind. Then Billy Ferguson or T.J. Ferguson or Will Ferguson will go to the corral behind the saddle barn and rope your horse just as Bill Eaton and George Gentry and Frank Eaton did for so many years before. If you already have an assigned horse, it will be called out to the ropers, just as Patty Eaton and Kathy Eaton did.

The corral boys will saddle your horse and you will go riding with a wrangler or with a group or if you know your way around, by yourself. Eatons' is one of the very few places left that allow this. As you ride along the trails, you will remember them, and the beauty through which they wander in the foothills of the Big Horn Mountains and along Wolf Creek. Nothing has changed. The trails and the beauty are the same. The sound of Wolf Creek tumbling out of the mountains is the same. The fresh outdoor smell is the same. It all seems most amazing. After their first day at Eatons', after a long absence, most people can't believe they've ever been away, no matter how long it's been. It's just the same.

Eatons' Ranch is timeless.

Family

At Eatons' Ranch today, there are four family members missing. They passed away in the intervening years. In tribute, their absence must be noted. Those missing are Patty Eaton, Tommy Ferguson, Roy Wertman and Nancy Ferguson.

Patty passed away on February 17, 1982, aged eighty-nine, fourteen years after her husband Bill died. In her memory, the Ranch published a tribute, which included a photo of Patty with her ageless beauty, and the following words:

On February 17 Patty Eaton slipped away quietly in her sleep, ending her life as gracefully as she had lived it. Although she had been bedridden for several months and was not as actively involved in Ranch life as she had been formerly, so great was her presence that her going has left an empty silence that is almost tangible.

Dear little Patty. What a wave of warmth her memory brings to what a vast number of people! Patty: as a young girl, living her life full tilt in her self-proclaimed tomboy fashion; Patty as a young matron, slim and poised, always impeccably groomed, always the charming hostess, taking every irritation in her stride, finding it almost impossible to be anything but gracious; Patty lavishing tender devoted care that has become legendary on her husband Big Bill in his last years; Patty grown elderly but still spry as a wren, still twinkling at people with those intense blue eyes, still presiding with queenly hospitality over her guests, still in command of a remarkable memory for every person she met, and every detail she had ever learned about them. Sweet but feisty right up to the last she was, deeply loved and respected by more people than most of us even meet. You had to admire her even if she was calling you to task, and she could do that if she felt it was called for. Right through her eighty-ninth year she was up with the dawn, tending her flowers, writing those highly individualistic notes with all their under linings, still doing the family ironing, still participating actively in the lives of the far-flung Ranch family, still commenting on the world with positive but loving interest in everything that was around her—from rodeo to the first buttercup of spring.

Even during this last difficult year, when Patty had a visitor she would rally herself and ask about the visitor's family, perhaps a special niece, and a grandchild, even a favorite dog, for that was the essence of Patty. She knew about you, she remembered who you were and what you told her, even if you only talked to her for five minutes. And in that five minutes she could make a new acquaintance feel like an old and valued friend, which they usually became. She was so modest about herself that it was impossible to convince her that she was as dearly loved as any of her predecessors in the extensive Ranch family. She could go on at length about the wonderful talents of everyone else, but never grant her own considerable gifts. Yet everyone who met her took note of her unfailing graciousness and warmth. She had that quality that people associate with the British frontiersman—the kind of social self-discipline that keeps things in their proper place, no matter what. Patty took care of what needed taking care of with no whining or procrastinating or excuses. If you knew her at all, you couldn't avoid being impressed by Patty. Whether you were a guest of the Ranch for many years or a newly hired college student from far away, Patty left her imprint on everyone.

She may have left us physically, but she will not be forgotten.

And she is not forgotten. Twenty-eight years later people still tell stories about her unfailing graciousness. One story involves a character named Art Stiles.

For many, many years—no one today really knows how many—Art was the Ranch deliveryman. He drove an old Model A pickup around the Ranch to deliver things—ice, laundry, coal and anything else that needed delivering.

Art's work uniform was an old set of coveralls that were ingrained with coal dust and any other manner of dirt he picked up from his delivery duties. He wore them all the time, even when Patty, in her egalitarian way, occasionally invited Art to her house for a cocktail. Patty was very fastidious. Her house was always immaculate and she took special pride in two very special chairs. And it never failed that when Art showed up in his dirty coveralls, he invariably sat—coal dust and all—in one of her special chairs. But Patty never asked him to sit anywhere else. She just smiled gracefully and engaged him in polite conversation. She considered Art to be a valued member of the Eaton family and she wouldn't dream of offending him.

She was equally gracious with her great grandchildren. When they were brought to see her, she often had treats for them. And children being children, they were sometimes wont to be unruly, and do childlike things like run around with olives stuck on their little fingers, touching all of Patty's immaculate things. And when their chagrined parents attempted to calm them down, Patty would wave them off with the words, "Oh, don't worry about it."

That was Patty Eaton.

Tommy Ferguson died on March 1, 1983, age seventy. He was married to Nancy for forty-one years and had been treasurer at Eatons' Ranch for thirty-seven years. Tommy was also the general manager of the Ranch, in the tradition of John Fleming, and was the Wolf Postmaster.

Tommy was also active in community affairs. He served on the Sheridan College board of directors for six years, from 1956 to 1962. He also served for twenty years on the board of directors of the Dude Ranchers Association, including four terms as secretary-treasurer, four terms as vice president and two years as president.

Perhaps Tommy's most lasting civic accomplishment was that he was instrumental in the establishment of the Dodd and Dorothy Bryan Foundation. The Bryans, from Philadelphia, were long time guests at Eatons' Ranch, and when Dodd retired they sometimes stayed in the Sheridan area for six or seven months at a time. They had no family, so when Dodd died, Dorothy wanted to use her estate for a worthwhile cause. A friend, Leonard Graham, put her in contact with a local attorney, Bill Redle, and together they established the Dodd and Dorothy Bryan Foundation. The Foundation makes educational loans to students for three Montana counties and three Wyoming counties, including Sheridan County.

Tommy believed very deeply in the Bryan Foundation and served as secretary of the organization for many years. Today, the Bryan Foundation still provides loans to students and Tommy's daughter, Susan Van Allen, is a member of the board.

After Tommy died, the Eaton Ranch would not have another general manager until another family member, Jeff Way, assumed the position thirteen years later in 1996.

E. L. "Roy" Wertman, Nan Wertman's husband died on February 17, 2007, at age eighty-four. After Roy and Nan were married in 1951, they made their home at Eatons' Ranch until 1974 when they moved to the adjacent Flying W Ranch. Roy continued to work at Eatons' until he retired in 1998. His memorial in *WN* stated in part that:

> *...He did just about everything imaginable on the Ranch—cowboying, wrangling, taking pack trips, cooking for barbeques, overseeing maintenance and building furniture for the cabins. The Ranch has lost a person who devoted his life to Eatons' and worked to carry on the tradition that started over one hundred years ago. More importantly, his family has lost a loving husband, father and grandfather. Roy certainly made a lasting impression on everyone who knew him, and he will not soon be forgotten...*

One person who has not forgotten Roy is his son-in-law, Doyl Fritz. Doyl still marvels at Roy's "toughness" and loves to tell "Roy stories." The number of stories is boundless, but two are especially illustrative.

One involves a pack trip. Roy, Doyl and two others took an extended pack trip into the mountains on the Solitude Loop. Roy, who was a drinker, had a few drinks at the first night's camp and then polished off the wine that was to be used for dinner each night. The next day, much worse for wear, on the way up, and on a series of steep switchbacks above Lake Geneva, Roy fell backwards off his horse, rolled down the hill and landed on the trail below.

The only apparent damage was that his arm was quite seriously injured. After Doyl and others had gathered him up and rigged up a sling for his arm, they were prepared to take him back to the Ranch. But, Roy would have none of that. He insisted that they continue with the six-day fishing trip and Roy nursed his arm, except, that is, when he was fishing.

Doyl claims that Roy taught him not to whine. One bitter cold, rainy and snowy winter day, Doyl and Roy were out riding on another pack trip. Doyl's feet felt frozen and he asked Roy, "Aren't your feet freezing?" There was silence for a moment until Roy replied, "I don't know. I can't feel them!"

That was Roy.

Nancy Eaton Ferguson died on July 21, 2009, age eighty-eight, twenty-six years after her husband, Tommy. Nancy had remained at Eatons' Ranch after Tommy's death. In addition to working in the office, she published *Wranglin' Notes* for many years. Like Tommy, Nancy was active in community affairs and during her life served for many years on the Wolf Creek School board, the Hospital Auxiliary board, and was a member of the National Society of Colonial Dames of America in Wyoming, the Book Review Club, and was lady president of the Dude Ranchers Association.

Nancy's memorial service was held at the Ranch, and printed tribute from the family said in part:

> *...Nancy worked in the office handling reservations and Ranch correspondence until 1996. After retiring, although her mobility decreased and was eventually lost, her mind remained sharp. Nancy never lost her passion for the Ranch and her family, and she certainly never lost that quick-witted sense of humor that we all remember and loved so much. There are far too many memoires and stories to capture here, but I am sure, when many of you think of Eatons' Ranch, you think of Nancy and your own memories and stories of her. We are all so thankful that we had the opportunity to know and love our mother, grandmother, and aunt for so many years.*

Nancy died at home in the main Ranch house, in the same room where her mother, Patty, and her grandmother Domo died. At the time of her death, Nancy was survived by her children, Susan Van Allen, Patty Kaufmann, William Ferguson and Thomas J. Ferguson, Jr., ten grandchildren and six great grandchildren.

As the memorial tribute said, Nancy was also the source for some great stories that people tell with glee. Nancy, like her father Bill, was not a great talker and could on occasion be rather blunt, as when Kevin Costner, the well-known movie star, called up and asked if he could make a reservation. Nancy simply told him words to the effect of, "No. We don't have any room." End of story.

Bobby Cagnina, a long time Eaton dude, also relishes another "Nancy" occasion. Bobby and his family usually drove to the Ranch from the east coast, but one year they flew into Billings and arranged with Nancy for a Ranch vehicle to pick them up at the airport. Later, when Bobby got the bill, he noted that the pick-up charge was $250. He called Nancy to ask her about the charge. "You didn't tell me," he said, "that it would cost that much." Nancy replied, "You didn't ask."

End of conversation. That was Nancy.

While the Eaton operation has not changed, there are some differences from long ago. Today, more family members are involved in the management of Eatons' Ranch than before, simply because there are more family members and they choose to be involved.

Nancy Eaton Ferguson with her children and their wives.
Top, from left: John Van Allen, Karen Ferguson, Billy Ferguson, T. J. Ferguson, Kim Ferguson, C. B. Kaufmann. Bottom, from left; Susan Van Allen, Nancy, Patty Kaufmann.
Courtesy of Eatons' Ranch.

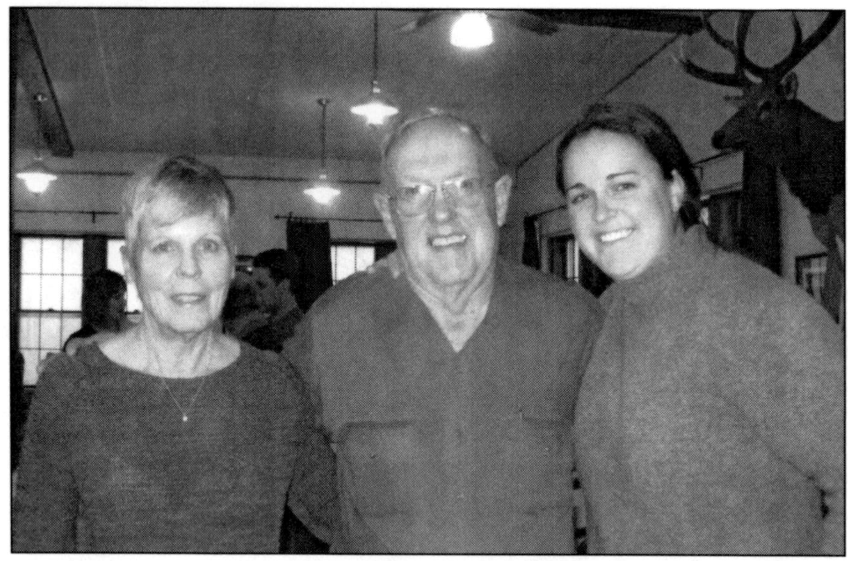

Frank and Kathy Eaton with their daughter Mary.
Courtesy of Frank and Kathy Eaton.

Frank and Kathy Eaton with their daughter Laura.
Courtesy of Frank and Kathy Eaton.

The family has come a long way since the time when Bill Eaton, the only son of Alden Eaton, was the sole heir. In those days, in addition to Bill and Patty Eaton, the ranch management was in the hands of devoted employees like John Fleming, Angela Buell, Tommy Butler, and George Gentry. Today, family does the jobs performed by others in the past, but the things they do haven't changed.

Frank and Kathy Eaton still live at the Ranch, in the house in which Frank was raised. Although Frank and Kathy retired in 2007, they still help around the Ranch on a regular basis and regularly serve up Eaton hospitality to Ranch guests.

Frank still serves as president of the Eaton Brothers Corporation, but Kathy, who was the board secretary for thirty-eight years, no longer serves on the board. During their forty-nine years of married life at Eatons' Ranch, Kathy always turned her hand to whatever needed doing, whether it was supervising the housekeeping department, the dining room, or raking leaves or making the annual supply of napkin rings or calling out the horses at the corral. In addition, she was an ever gracious hostess.

Amongst all this activity, she took care of their two daughters, Laura and Mary Eaton. Today, Laura lives and works in Portland, Oregon. Mary lives in Dayton and works at the Ranch. She manages housekeeping and the dining room during the dude season and works with Jeff Way, the general manager, in the off season.

For most of his career, Frank managed the corral but switched his efforts to Ranch maintenance in 1995 when Roy Wertman had health problems. Like his grandfather, Frank was a member of the Sheridan-Wyo-Rodeo board of directors for many years and served as its vice president and arena director.

Billy Ferguson, the oldest son of Tommy and Nancy Ferguson, manages the corral and the farming and takes care of the cattle during the winter. He is also a vice president of the corporation. Billy married Karen Reeder, from Haynesville, Louisiana, on June 5, 1971. Karen worked at the Ranch for two summers before she married Billy. After they were married, Karen worked in the dining room and the office. She began a new career as a stockbroker in 1995. Karen and Billy live at the Lower Place, down the road.

Tommy and Nancy Ferguson's first son, Bill, started early at the corral.
Bill grew up to be the corral boss.
Courtesy of Eatons' Ranch.

Billy and Karen Ferguson with their two children Will and Amanda.
Courtesy of Eatons' Ranch..

Billy and Karen have two children. Their son Will teaches school at Tongue River High School in Dayton and works in the corral in the summer. Amanda, their daughter, is an attorney and works in Cheyenne.

T. J. Ferguson, Billy's brother, runs the corral with Billy during the summer and is responsible for the operation at Echeta during the rest of the year. T. J. is also a vice president of the corporation. His wife, Kim, is the granddaughter of Martin Koether, who first visited Eatons' Ranch as a boy in 1923 and continues to be an Eaton guest to this day. Kim is a consultant with the Wyoming State Department of Education. Their three children, Alden, Katie and James attend school in Dayton and Ranchester.

Susan Ferguson Van Allen, the oldest daughter of Tommy and Nancy Ferguson, is a member of the Eaton Brothers Corporation board of directors. She and her husband John own and operate Way Oil in Sheridan. Their son David works for John and Susan. He is married to Melissa and

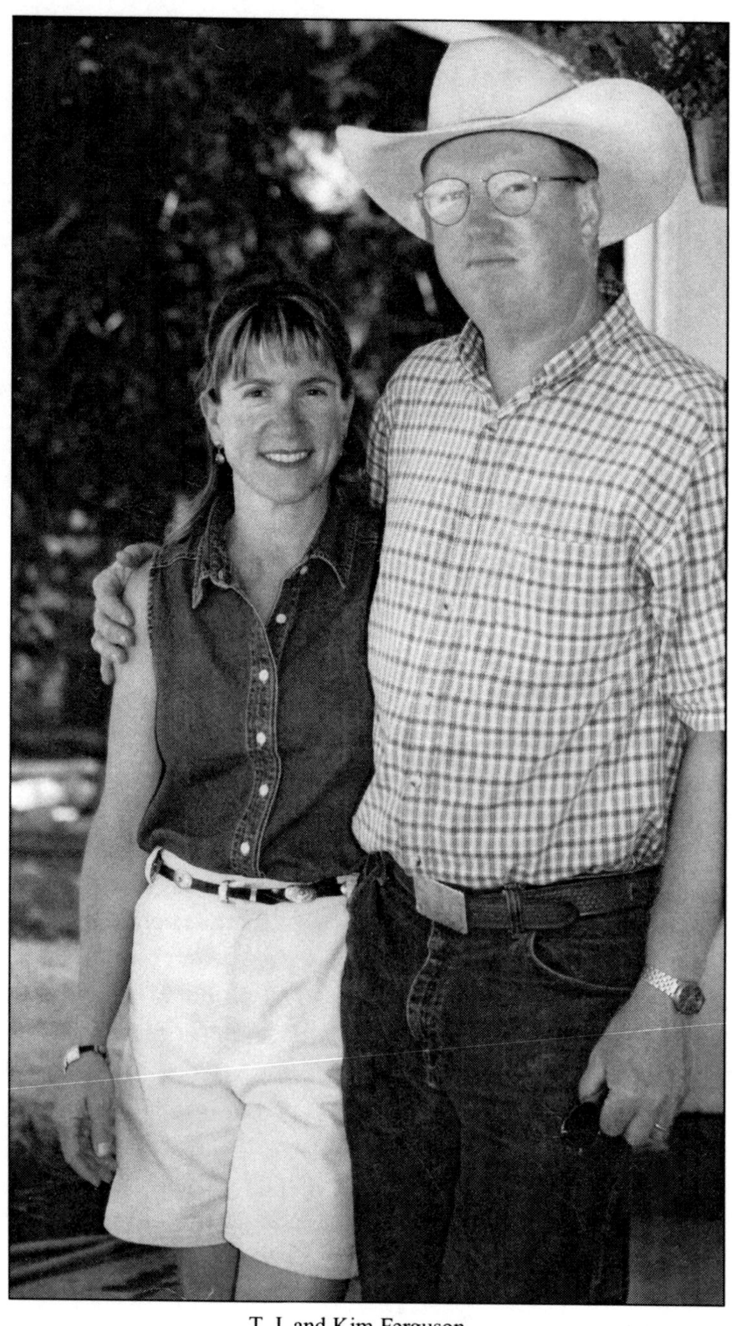

T. J. and Kim Ferguson.
Courtesy of Eatons' Ranch.

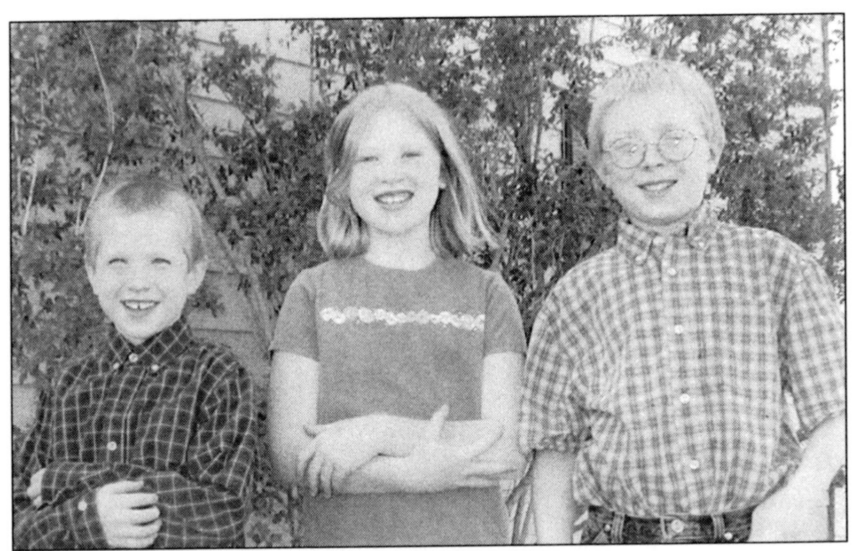

T. J. and Kim Ferguson's three children.
From left, James, Katie and Alden.
Courtesy of Eatons' Ranch.

Susan and John Van Allen with their two sons, J. B., left, and David.
Courtesy of Eatons' Ranch.

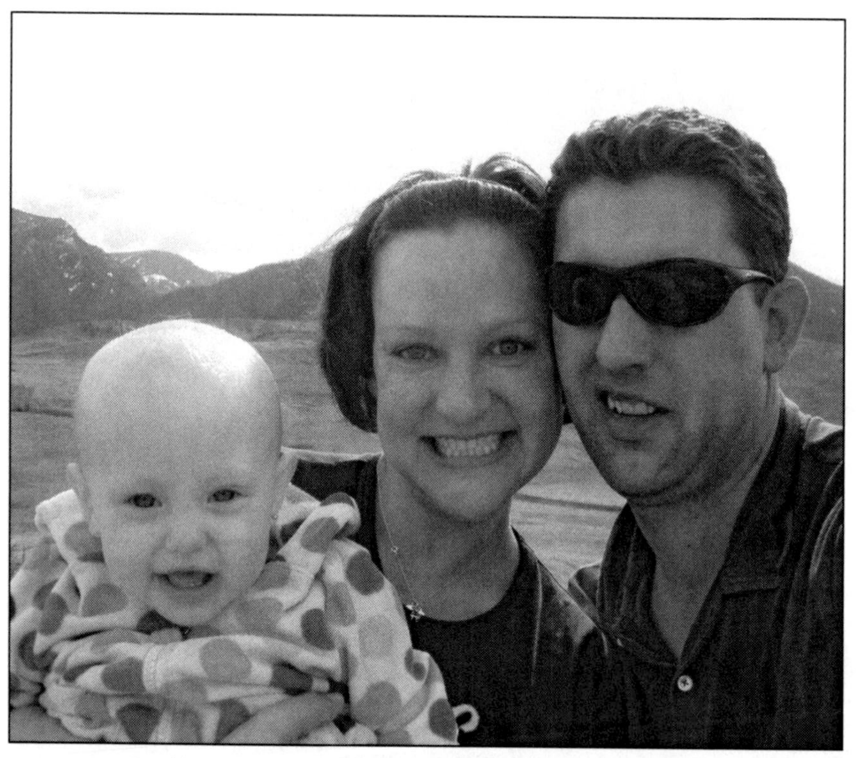

David and Melissa Van Allen and their daughter Ava Elizabeth.
Courtesy of David Van Allen.

they have one child, Ava Elizabeth. Their other son, J. B., works at Eatons' Ranch during the summer and off season.

Patty Ferguson Kaufmann lives with her husband, C. B. Kaufman, in Riverside, Connecticut. C. B. manages his law firm's office in Greenwich. C. B. was a long time guest at Eatons' before he married Patty after her husband, Gary, died in 1980. C. B. serves as a member of the Eaton Brothers Corporation board of directors.

Patty is in her twenty-fifth year at Eastern Middle School in Riverside. Her three children are Juli, Jeffrey and Jami. Juli was married to Barkley Kern and has two children, Hannah and August. Jami is married to Gajus Worthington and they have two sons, Luke and Mykolas.

Patty married Gary Way.
Here they are pictured with Wally Duell at the wedding of John and Susan Van Allen.
Photo by Vacationland Studio, Sheridan, Wyoming.
Courtesy of Eatons' Ranch.

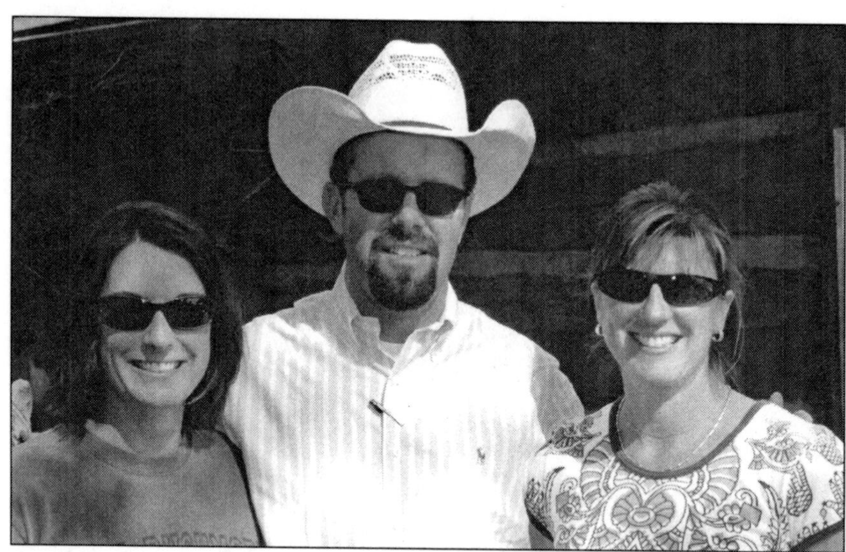

Patty Ferguson Kaufmann's children.
From left, Jami Way Kern, Jeff Way and Juli Way Worthington.
Courtesy of Eatons' Ranch.

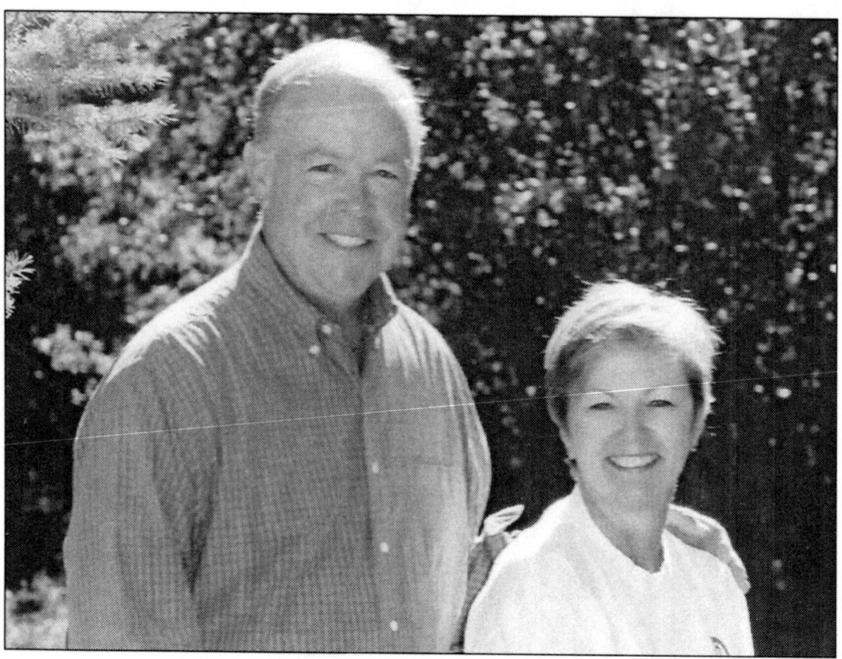

Patty and C. B. Kaufmann.
Courtesy of Eatons' Ranch.

Jami and Gajus Worthington.
Courtesy of Eatons' Ranch.

Juli Way Kern with her two children Hannah and August.
Courtesy of Juli Way Kern.

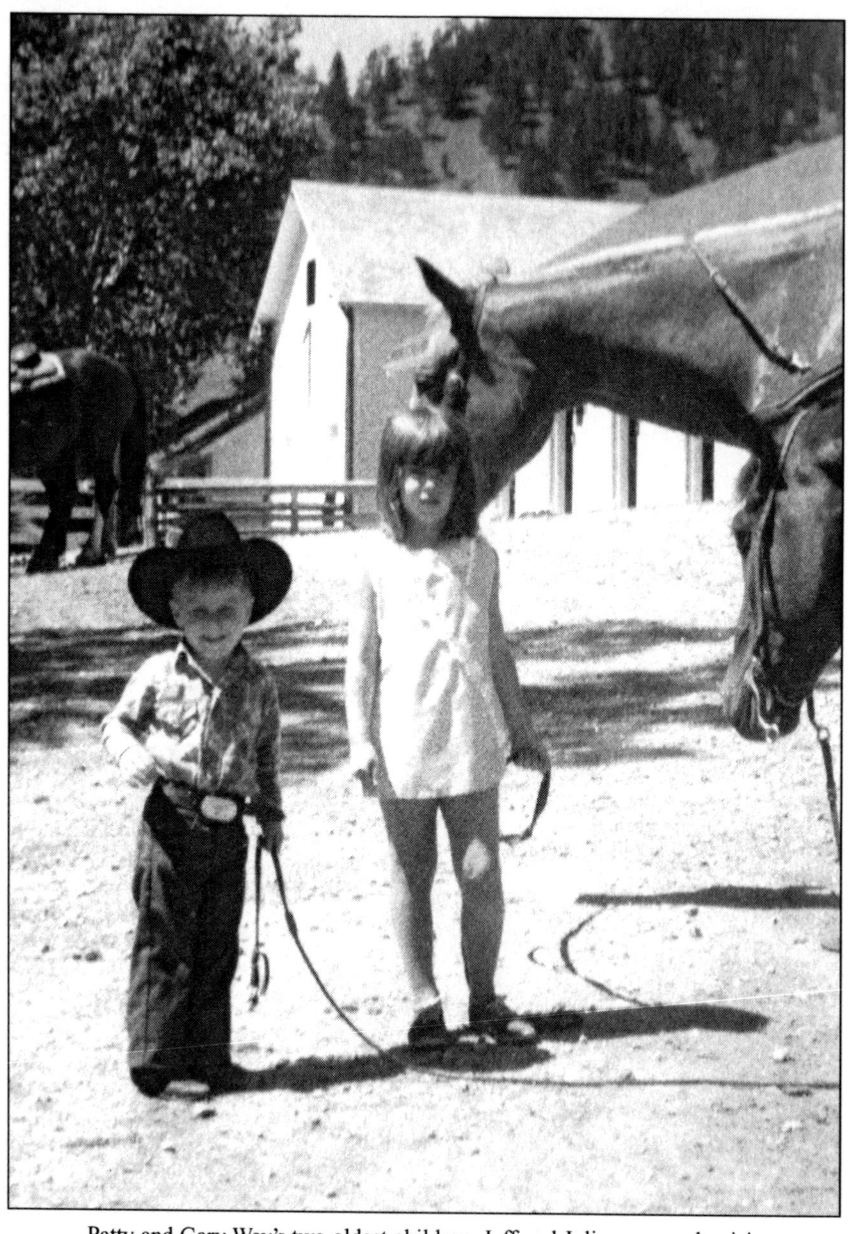

Patty and Gary Way's two oldest children, Jeff and Juli, on an early visit to Eatons' Ranch. Jeff grew up to be the general manager of the Ranch.
Courtesy of Eatons' Ranch.

Jeffrey (Jeff) Way, Patty's son, is the general manager of Eatons' Ranch. In his youth, Jeff was never able to work at the Ranch during the summers because of his athletic activities, but he visited often with his parents and always loved the place. After he graduated from college, Jeff held a very good position with an international company, but always yearned to be associated with the Ranch in some capacity.

The lure was so strong that he quit his corporate job, and went to Eatons' to work as a hired hand for his uncle Billy Ferguson in 1993 to learn the Ranch business. To increase his knowledge even more, Jeff matriculated to graduate school at the University of Denver and earned his MBA. When he returned to the Ranch in 1995, the board of directors held a special meeting and agreed that Jeff would be a vice president of Eaton Brothers Corporation and act as general manager. He assumed those duties in March of 1996 and eventually was elected as secretary-treasurer of the corporation.

Jeff follows in the tradition of John Fleming and Tommy Ferguson, not only in that he has followed in their footsteps as general manager, but he and his family also live in the same house. Jeff married Jennifer (Jennie) Diggins, who worked at the Ranch and edited and updated *Eatons' Ranch,* 125th Anniversary Edition in 2004. Jeff and Jennie have two children: a son, Garrett and daughter, Vivian Rachel.

Jaci Eaton Fritz was elected to the board of directors in 1988, but relinquished her position to her husband Doyl in 1995. Jaci spends time with her grandchildren and volunteers for various local organizations. Doyl has owned and operated his own engineering firm, Western Water Consultants, in Sheridan since 1978. Doyl and Jaci built a house on the Flying W Ranch and live right next door to Jaci's mother, Nan.

Jaci and Doyl have a son and a daughter, Jack and Jennifer. Jack works with his father in the family firm and is married to Michele. They live in Ranchester and have two children, Maya and Isaac. Jennifer is married to Jerry Gulley and they live in Sheridan with their daughter Nan.

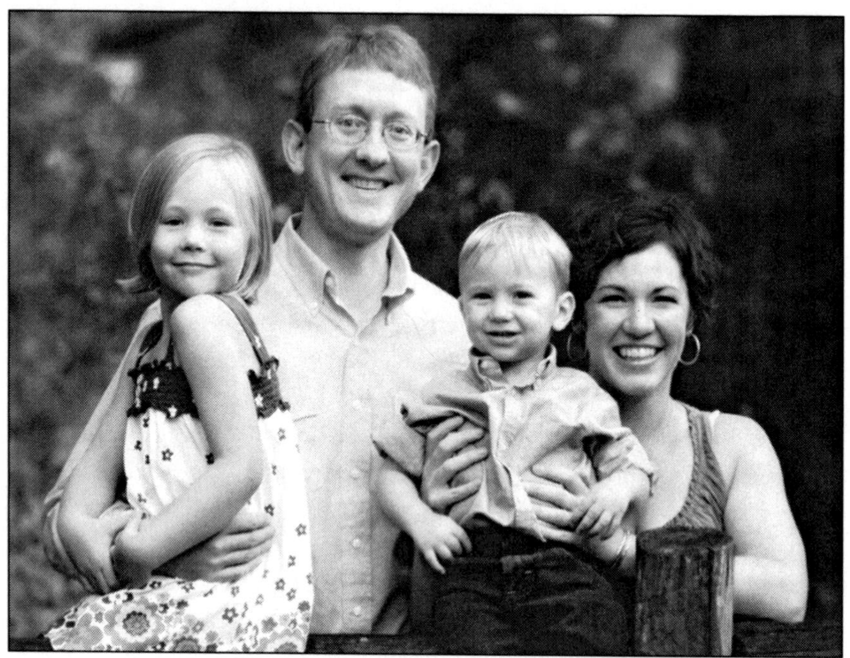

Jack and Michele Fritz with their children Maya and Issac.
Courtesy of Jack Fritz.

The Doyl and Jaci Eaton Fritz family.
From left: Jack Fritz with his wife Michelle and their daughter Maya, Doyl and Jaci and their granddaughter Nan, Nan's mother Jennifer and her husband Jerry Gulley.
Courtesy of Eatons' Ranch.

Wendy Wertman Martin, Nan and Roy Wertman's daughter, is married to Jim Martin. They live in Buffalo, Wyoming, where Wendy is a trust officer with First National Bank. Jim works with Doyl at Western Water Consultants. Their daughter Amy is married to Nick Pierson and they live in Buffalo where Amy teaches at the local elementary school.

Jim and Wendy Martin.
Courtesy of Wendy Martin.

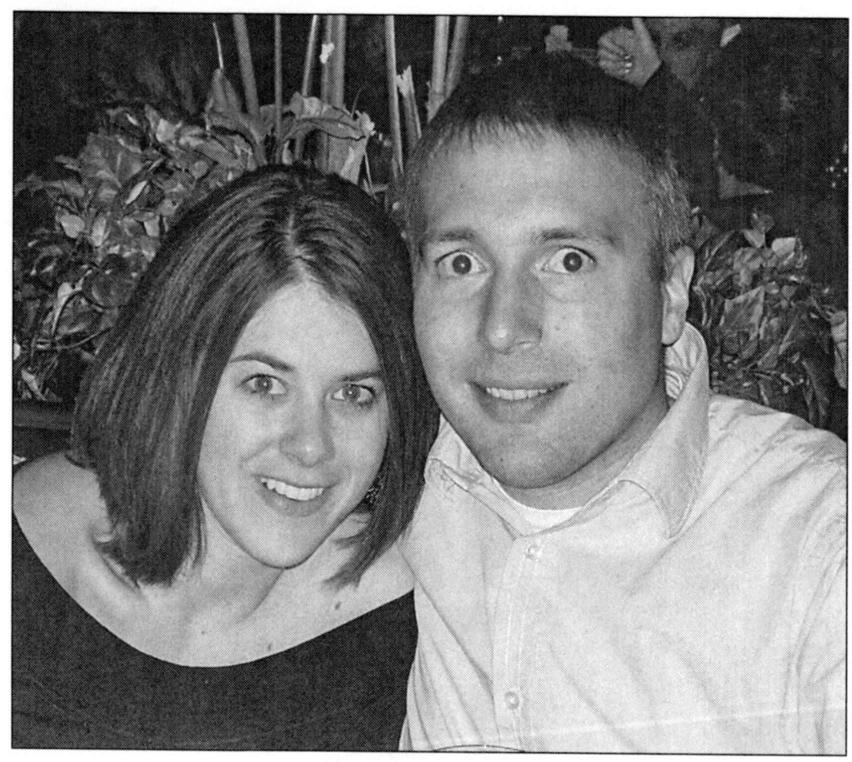

Amy and Nick Pierson.
Courtesy of Wendy Martin.

Nan Baker Wertman is the sole survivor of the third generation of Eatons. She is a sprightly ninety-four year old woman with a quick mind and winning smile. She is a delight.

Many typical "ranch stories" begin when a family ranch is established but, over time, the family becomes less involved and drifts off and the ranch eventually falls into other hands. With the Eatons, it's been just the opposite. In this case, a small family became a larger one, and as it increased in size, so did the involvement with the Ranch. Today, all board members, officers and key managers are Eaton family members. You might say the Eaton family grew into the Ranch.

Eatons' Ranch is truly a family endeavor.

The Eaton/Wertman side of the family.
Top, left to right: Laura Eaton, Frank Eaton, Kathy Eaton, Mary Eaton, Jim Martin, Wendy Wertman Martin, Jaci Eaton Fritz, Doyl Fritz.
Bottom, left to right: Jack Fritz, Amy Martin, Nan Wertman, Little Nan (Jennifer's daughter), Roy Wertman, Jennifer Fritz Gulley.
Courtesy of Eatons' Ranch.

Dudes

Eatons' Ranch still publishes *WN*, but only once a year, and it still reports "dude news." The information is not as extensive or detailed as in previous years, but it still recognizes many dude families who have a long history with Eatons' Ranch. Some of the entries for the last three years are as follows:

2007

...A number of families chose Eatons' as the site for their annual reunions this year. In June, Keen Butcher, who first came to Eatons' with his parents in 1926, gathered his family of twenty-six here for the seventh year in a row. Bill and Bobbie Croft first brought their family here in 1962, and the two have not missed a visit in the last twenty-three seasons. Their group this June included fifteen children and grandchildren...

...Some of those who have been fall guests for years and joined us again were Pete and Peggy Nelson, Mary Dailey, Joe and Betty Lou Girardi, David and Linda Green, Helen Callison and John and Annette Shotwell...

...We received sad news in October when we learned that Tom Nimick had passed away. Tom first came to Eatons' as a child with his parents in 1933. He continued to make Eatons' a part of his and his family's lives for fifty seasons. Beginning in 1986, he visited the Ranch for twenty consecutive years. Tom loved Eatons', and he was one of our biggest supporters.

People like Tom have helped make Eatons' Ranch what it is today. Even though he resided in Pittsburgh, the Ranch was never far from his thoughts. He would call every few months to check in and see how the family was doing and how the weather was. He was always glad to hear if we had had rain or snow because he knew we would have better grass and hay when spring and summer rolled around.

Tom leaves behind his wife Teresa, son Locky, daughters Kit and Vicki, and stepson George Whiteside, along with seven grandchildren. Tom will be missed dearly by all who knew him. Our thoughts are with his entire family.

2008

...We missed seeing two of our regulars this year—Joe and Betty Lou Girardi were unable to join us in the fall for the first time in forty-two years...

...2008 was a year when we lost a number of Ranch friends who shared a part of their lives with us...We received the sad news in April that Chuck Nimick had passed away. Chuck made his first visit to the Ranch in 1934 and even worked here in 1953 and 1954. In all, he joined us during thirty-six different summers.

... We were sorry to hear that E. K. Wallace passed away in November. E.K.'s wife Jean first came to the Ranch in 1935 with her family.

... We would also like to mention the passing of Patsy Mellon Schmidt in 2007. She was first at the ranch as an infant in 1914.

2009

...A number of large family groups joined us once again throughout the summer. Martin and Nancy Koether were joined by Nancy's as well as Martin's children and grandchildren in June. Also in June, W. W. K. Butcher hosted his family of thirty-four at the Ranch for a week...

...The month of March was a sad month for us as well. M. L. "Monty" Young, Bots' brother, passed away on March 19.

Monty and Bots first came to the Ranch as children with their parents, and Monty later worked here for a season in 1943. We were also saddened to hear that W. C. "Bill" Croft passed away on March 21. He was ninety-one years old. Bill and his wife Bobbie started bringing their family here in 1962. They last stayed at the Ranch in 2007, making that visit their 46 over a forty-seven year period... We also sadly lost Marylouise Cowan on March 28. She first came to Eatons' in 1971 and last visited us in 2006 with her children A. R. Tandy and Carol Wright and her grandchildren. Over those thirty-six years, Marylouise visited us during thirty-two seasons...

There were others. But these examples illustrate yet again, how people become so attached to Eatons' Ranch and how it becomes ingrained in their lives. It also serves to illustrate, how Eatons' Ranch values its extended family of dudes and how it expresses its appreciation for their friendship and memorializes them when they are gone. It's all part of the Eaton philosophy that Jeff Way stated in the December 2008 issue of *WN*:

Remember, once you are a guest here, you are always a part of Eatons' Ranch.

Employees

While there are no longer employees at Eatons' Ranch who have worked there for as long as some of the old-timers—like John Fleming, Angela Buell, Tommy Butler, George Gentry—there are still several who have become permanent fixtures at the Ranch. Some of them are:

Marie Vaccaro. Marie is the Ranch driver in the summer and does odd jobs for room and board after the season until April. Marie has been at Eatons' Ranch since 1988.

Lonny and Carol Gibson. Carol, whose father, Frank Ash, did the farming at the Lower Place for several years, first worked at Eatons' when she babysat Laura Eaton in 1977. Lonny first worked at the Ranch in 1979. They left for a few years and returned in 1985. Carol worked at the Ranch until 2008 when she changed careers, but Lonny is still present for duty.

Nate Schmeiser. Nate began work in 2003 during the summer season and fall until 2008, when he started working at the Bar Eleven from November to May and then at the Ranch for the summer season.

Steve Gage. He first worked at Eatons' when he left high school in 1984 and has worked for the Ranch on and off for twenty years. He and his wife Jenn live in Sheridan and have a two year old boy.

Many previous employees live in the local area and, because the Ranch seems to be in their blood, take every opportunity to return to the Ranch for visits.

One example is Dan Alsup. Dan worked at the Ranch one summer, fell in love with the place, and worked every season for the next thirteen years. He even proposed to his wife, Tobie, during one trip with the horses to Echeta. He and Toby currently live in Sheridan with their two children.

Another is Franklin "Sudsy" Miller. Sudsy went to work at Eatons' in 1964 soon after he left high school in Sheridan and worked there for over thirty-five years. Sudsy first worked as a dishwasher (hence the name Sudsy) and in the laundry. In time, he became the Ranch delivery person and delivered ice and linens and anything else that needed to be delivered to dudes. In the off season, he did Ranch laundry and cleaned. Sudsy also was a fixture at cocktail parties where he performed as a bartender. After he retired in 1999, Sudsy found he couldn't stay away and now returns each summer as a dude.

It is difficult to explain why so many employees have become so strongly attached to Eatons' Ranch over the years. What is the draw? Jeff Way, the general manager, probably has the best answer:

> *I have often thought of Eatons' as a sort of way station. They come to work here during a transition in their lives. It might be the transition from college to the "real world", which can be a very long one for some. For some, they started a new chapter in their lives by moving to Wyoming and working here. Many of those people have stayed in Sheridan or eventually moved back here. I have often wondered why these people return to the Ranch for so many years. Do they love their job, is it some sort of loyalty to the Ranch, or is it a place to fall back on if other options don't work out? I really think it is all of those things. If they didn't enjoy what they do, they wouldn't come back. There is a sense of loyalty in that we have developed lifelong relationships with these people. We are a fallback for many of them because we have been a constant, stable, and welcoming part of their lives.*

After 131 years, the chronicle of Eatons' Ranch continues. It is a work in progress. What does the future hold? It's very difficult to predict. But the best view of the future might well have been provided in *Eatons' Ranch, 125th Anniversary Edition.* Though it was written in 2004, it is equally applicable today:

The Next 125 Years

> *Much has changed in the world since Howard, Alden and Willis Eaton* (Note: We now know it was probably Howard, Alden and Charlie.) *started the dude ranching business in North Dakota all those years ago. Life moves at a breakneck pace sometimes, pushing us into the future before we realize what has happened.*
>
> *That just might be the special thing about Eatons'. The pace is as fast as your horse can take you, as quick as Wolf*

Creek runs from the mountains, as breakneck as wildflowers growing in the meadow. Times change in Wolf just as they do anywhere else, but the echo of history is a bit stronger at the Ranch. When you ride up into the Big Horns, it could be 2004 or 1904—the land and its heart-stirring beauty do not change.

So if you find yourself listening for a stagecoach to rumble up to the Bird Cage, or if you suddenly picture Big Bill strolling down from the barn, don't be surprised. It simply means that you have become a part of Eatons' Ranch and its history and its family. One day someone will picture you there and smile in just the same way.

About the Author

Author Tom Ringley was mostly raised in Sheridan, Wyoming. He holds degrees from Sheridan College, George Washington University and Auburn University at Montgomery. He served as a career officer in the United States Air Force for twenty-seven years. Tom and his wife Georgina live in Big Horn, Wyoming.

Tom's first book, *Rodeo Time in Sheridan Wyo* brought us a comprehensive history of one of the country's oldest rodeos. He followed that with *Saddlestring, A History of the HF Bar Ranch* in which Tom told the story of an historic dude ranch where he, himself, had spent a great deal of time. Then Tom went a little farther afield and tackled the story of Turk Greenough, a rodeo cowboy from Red Lodge, Montana, with a checkered history that included a fascinating career and a marriage to the famous "Bubble Dancer" Sally Rand. That book was *When the Whistle Blows.*

And then Tom turned his attention back to the fascinating story and 131 year history of Eatons' Ranch and the generations of "Ranch Family" guests and employees who have claimed it as their own special piece of Heaven.

CPSIA information can be obtained at www.ICGtesting.com
262984BV00005B/3/P
9 781932 636673